MIRROR AND MEMORY

Mirror and Memory

Reflections on Early Methodism

Richard P. Heitzenrater

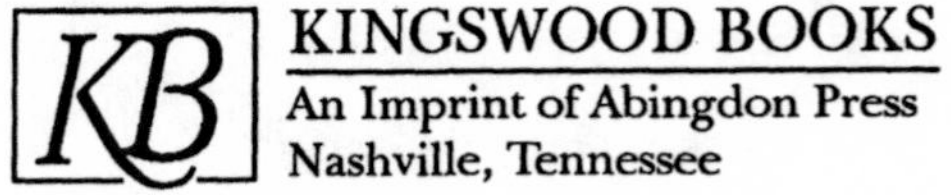

MIRROR AND MEMORY:
REFLECTIONS ON EARLY METHODISM

Library of Congress Cataloging-in-Publication Data

Heitzenrater, Richard P., 1939–
Mirror and memory: reflections on early Methodism / Richard P. Heitzenrater
p. cm.
Bibliography: p.
Includes index.
ISBN 0-637-27069-3 (alk. paper)
Methodism—History. 2. Wesley, John, 1703–1791. I. Title.
BX8231.H45 1989 287'.09'033—dc19 89–6494

ISBN 0-687-27069-3

Printed in the United States of America
on acid-free paper

To
Frank Baker
and
Albert C. Outler,
who have provided brilliant models
of researcher and interpreter
in the Wesleyan heritage

Contents

Preface

Discovery and reflection together are the lifeblood of the historian. *Discovery* is the compulsion that drives every researcher. To discover means literally to remove the covering, to expose to view, to reveal or make known. Discovery is the first task of the historical researcher. *Reflection* is the impulse that sustains the interpreter. To reflect means literally to bend back, to go back in thought, to remind oneself or consider. Reflection is the first task of the historical interpreter.

Discovery may at times seem accidental. But if the method of research is to leave no stone unturned, the researcher will be constantly uncovering new and interesting things. Not all discoveries will be significant in themselves. The basic method of historical interpretation is to see the relationships among literally hundreds or thousands of seemingly small facts—to discern meaningful constellations of factors, perceivable dynamics of change, and significant patterns of development.

To fulfill most adequately the historian's task, one must also work within a meaningful understanding of the goal of that task. Several typical uses of history or definitions of heritage are prevalent today but are highly inadequate for the purpose of fully understanding a living tradition:

> Heritage as *nostalgia*—relying on sentimentality and a detached recollection of "the good old days" that are marked by martyr-heroes and folktales;
>
> Heritage as *antiquarian display*—focusing on the quaint trivia and beloved relics of another age, preserved and passed on with "proper" reverence and awe;
>
> Heritage as *proof-text*—picking out portions of the past to support one's own particular opinions or prejudices and to prove that they represent the "real truth" or authentic "orthodoxy";

> Heritage as *panacea*—assuming that if one could just transport the ideas and/or institutions of the past into the present, the problems of the contemporary age would disappear.

These perspectives, though certainly common, are not fully helpful in any attempt to develop an adequate understanding of the past. The first two are narrow and provincial, and the latter two are shallow and simplistic.

The prevalence and pitfalls of these approaches should not discourage us from carefully examining our past on the basis of a more adequate, though often more difficult, perspective. Just as the historian's task entails *discovery* and *reflection*, we might also say that a heritage can be understood as *mirror* and *memory*. In reflecting upon who we *are* and where we are going, we are helped by discovering who we *were* and from whence we came. In this process, we need a good mirror and a clear memory. The mirror should clearly reflect the image of the past in order to provide a sound basis of accurate knowledge. The memory should fully comprehend the richness of the past in order to provide an adequate framework for recapturing the plenitude of the heritage. Knowledge of, and reflection upon, our past is an indispensible part of an adequate self-assessment in the present. And in confronting the challenges of the future, practitioners of a living and vital heritage are able to remember the vision that set them on their way as well as to grasp the possibilities that continue to move their tradition forward.

An important part of United Methodism's self-understanding is a fully adequate knowledge of its Wesleyan roots. Acknowledging that American Methodists (and especially United Methodists) are more than simply Wesleyans, we must still recognize that Methodism of any brand cannot be fully understood without a clear view of the Wesleyan heritage. Knowledge and understanding are, therefore, two of the basic goals of Wesley studies, for these goals, if met, will allow for the proper anchoring of the tradition and the potential renewal of the heritage.

The task of the historian is built around the threefold process of research, discovery, and interpretation. The discipline of careful research can sometimes involve years of tedious investigation into literally thousands of source documents. The historian is propelled through the drudgery and tedium of such a task by the anticipation of discovery, the uncovering of new information that will help reveal some new understanding of the past. The fruition of the task entails minute analysis, thoughtful reflection, and careful interpretation of the information uncovered.

The detective-like nature of this work has an attraction all its own. But it has been my privilege also to have made several discoveries that have particular relevance for the historical reinterpretation of the Wesleyan movement. Five discoveries in particular form the basis for much of the material in this book:

(1) Discovering the key to Wesley's diary code in the MS diary of Benjamin Ingham, making possible the decoding of five volumes of unpublished early Wesley diaries, resulting in a reinterpretation of the rise of Methodism at Oxford, its manner of organization, the development of Wesley's thought, and the impact of these developments on the later movement.

(2) Discovering in Charles Wesley's MS sermons shorthand notes indicating that most of his published sermons were actually written by John Wesley (thus adding nine or ten early texts to John's sermon corpus), and finding a set of Charles Wesley's holograph sermons in shorthand (adding five or six early sermons to Charles's prose works).

(3) Discovering an obscure seventeenth-century Latin treatise on justification that attacks a little-known school of thought called by the author *nostri Novae Methodistae* ("our New Methodists"), opening up a new line of investigation into the theological significance of the term "Methodist" as used in that century and as connected with the later Wesleyans.

(4) Discovering an unpublished paragraph in the MS Journal of the 1808 General Conference, allowing for a clearer interpretation of the First Restrictive Rule of Methodism's constitution and the related question of historical doctrinal standards.

(5) Discovering four unpublished sermons preached by John Wesley and recorded in shorthand by one of his preachers, more than doubling the extant manuscript material of this sort that helps us understand Wesley's oral preaching and its relationship to the published sermons.[1]

The essays in this collection contain reflections of various sorts upon the early history of the Wesleyan heritage. Although they all combine primary research and reflective interpretation, some emphasize one more than the other. The different forms of the essays indicate a variety of origins, from dissertation research to journal article, from academic lecture to workshop presentation. Five of the essays represent material that has already appeared in print. Three essays contain some material that has previously been published but is here expanded and revised. Three additional essays appear here for the first time. The essays have some overlap and repetition, given the independent purposes for which they were originally written. In this edition, the footnote citations have been revised for consistency and accuracy. References to Wesley's *Works* are to the new *Bicentennial Edition of the Works of John Wesley* (Abingdon Press) whenever possible. Citations to previous editions are noted with their editor: *Letters* (Telford), *Journal* (Curnock), and *Works* (Jackson).[2]

Most of the essays have been presented, in one form or another, to various audiences from Oxford to Tokyo and have benefitted from the critical comments of many friends. Some of the work has been through several stages of revision over the years; other material stands closer to its original expression. None of it is definitive—the "conclusions" of historical scholarship must always be tentative. The best one can claim or hope is to have furthered the study of a field by discovering new information or providing insightful interpretation that will help correct, clarify, and/or shed new light on a topic. If we have succeeded in any of these endeavors, the effort will have been worthwhile.

My special thanks go to two persons who suggested this book: my assistant, Wanda Smith, and my wife, Karen, both of whom have provided encouragement and help at every stage of the task.

Richard P. Heitzenrater
Southern Methodist University
10 February 1989

Chapter 1

What's in a Name? The Meaning of "Methodist"[1]

"What's in a name?" The Bard of Stratford, you will recall, had Juliet go on to say, "That which we call a rose / by any other name would smell as sweet."[2] This well-known comment reflects the medieval debate between the realists and the nominalists as to the nature and location of reality.[3] How does a name relate to the reality of that which it names? This question of essential meaning was no doubt in the back of Shakespeare's mind when he penned those words, "Romeo, Romeo, wherefore art thou Romeo?"[4] The question posed in this essay has a similar implication in its casting—"Methodist, Methodist, wherefore art thou Methodist?" Methodist, in what sense are you Methodist? What is the relationship of your name to who you are? Does it make any real difference that your name is Methodist?

"What's in a name?" Followers of John Wesley have been called Methodists for over 250 years. From the beginning, some confusion has clouded the source and meaning of the name "Methodist." There are conflicting opinions, even from the Wesleys, as to the origins and significance of the term. And by the time it had become officially attached to an actual denomination in America at the end of the eighteenth century, the name seems simply to have become (with the passing of the generations) an accepted and comfortable tag.[5] It was not always so.

The first printed reference to the Wesleyans as "Methodists" appeared in a written attack upon them in a London newspaper, *Fog's Weekly Journal*, in December 1732. It was, in fact, the first published notice whatsoever of this small group of a half dozen or so university men at Oxford who had taken upon themselves the cloak of piety and scholarship in a conscientious manner untypical of that day. The sharply worded letter to the editor used several epithets in reference to the small society, including "sons of sorrow," "shameless gut-gazers," "madmen and fools." The term that caught on, however, came in a comment that characterized "this sect called Methodist" as pretending to "great refinements" to "the speculative" as well as "the practical part of religion."[6]

The letter proceeded to criticize both the theology and practice of the Oxford men. The dual focus of this criticism bears close examination, since the first half (relating to theology) has always been overshadowed by the second (relating to practice) in the minds of members and observers alike.[7] Although the name "Methodist" certainly fits both their ideas and their actions, it is their ideas that provide a specific rationale for designating them at that time and place as Methodists. Although this fact has not generally been noticed, a close look at both sides of the issue will elucidate the specific relevance of the early Wesleyan theology in the first application of their name.

"What's in a name?" What did the name "Methodist" mean when it was first applied to the budding movement in the eighteenth century? Some of the typical explanations base the title in the early Wesleyans' methodical *practices*; but there are also some intriguing precedents that link the term specifically to their method of *theology*. A careful assessment of the background and original application of the term to the Wesleyan movement has significant implications for Methodist self-understanding today.

Methodists in Practice

The most obvious general meaning of the term "methodist" is quite simply "a person devoted to some method or laying great stress on method."[8] And the first place we tend to look for evidence of method is in the actions of daily life. This particular purview seems appropriate when applied to the Wesleyans in eighteenth-century England. The Wesleyan life-style was, from the beginning, typified by the use of various *methods* to accomplish specific goals. John Wesley's diaries indicate that his years at Oxford were marked by the implementation of a variety of "methods"—a method for studying, a method for visiting the prisons, a method for making acquaintances, a method for reading Scriptures, . . . a method for nearly everything.[9]

Wesley's methodical approach to university life seems to have been shaped in part by his mother's view that there is "nothing like a clear Method" when it comes to getting something done efficiently.[10] Wesley's inclination toward order was reinforced not only by his family but also by a small treatise used regularly by the Oxford

Methodists entitled, *The Way of Living in a Method, and by Rule* (1722).[11] The reading and following of such works gave rise to a definition of the term "methodist" that found its way into Samuel Johnson's *Dictionary* (1755): "One of a new kind of puritans lately arisen, so called from their profession to live by rules and in constant method."[12]

Wesley's small group of friends at Oxford had been designated as "Methodists" by the autumn of 1732, when he wrote a defense of their nature and design, explaining that the group was "doing what good we can; and, in order thereto, communicating as often as we have opportunity; . . . [and] observing the fasts of the Church"—in a word, patterning their life and thought after the disciplined approach of the Early Church. This method of living and study, by that time visibly at variance with the common life-style at the university, brought the group some notoriety along with the title "Methodist."[13]

Wesley was slow to adopt this term of disparagement. Even in his own writings, he most often used it as a name thrust upon them: "I say 'those who are called Methodists.' for let it be well observed that this is not a name which they take upon themselves, but one fixed upon them by way of reproach, without their approbation or consent."[14] As he later explained to a persistent critic,

> By the odious and ridiculous ideas affixed to that name they were condemned in the gross, without ever being heard. So that now any scribbler with a middling share of low wit, not encumbered with good nature or modesty, may raise a laugh on those whom he cannot confute, and run them down whom he dares not look in the face.[15]

His hesitation in accepting the designation Methodist was matched by his confusion in explaining its historical or ideological referent.

In 1742, Wesley recalled that John Bingham, a student (fellow) of Christ Church, had first designated his little group with that title by remarking that "Here is a new set of 'Methodists' sprung up."[16] Wesley gives no date or occasion for that comment, but goes on in that instance to give two possible explanations for the origins of the term: (1) the name refers to an ancient sect of physicians called "methodists"; or (2) the name refers to the "regular method of study and behaviour" of his small group of friends at Oxford.

Wesley elaborated on his first explanation by saying that the term was an allusion to an ancient set of physicians, flourishing about the time of Nero, who taught that "almost all diseases might be cured by a specific method of diet and exercise."[17] There *was* in fact an ancient school of physicians, denominated "Methodists," who in the first century followed their leaders Themison and Thessalos in their understanding of disease and cure. In treating an illness, these physicians observed in particular three standard conditions of the body—its dryness, its fluidity, and a mixed condition of the two, as well as variations of these in the stages of the disease. The task of the physician was to induce the condition opposed to the disease. In this approach, these Methodists differed basically from the Empiricist and Dogmatic schools of physicians.[18]

This set of doctors appears to be the only specific historical precedent that Wesley knew for the term "Methodist." But the strain of making a direct etymological connection between the ancient physicians and the eighteenth-century Wesleyans was recognized even in Wesley's day by such critics as Dr. Free, who reacted to such a link with disbelief:

> The person who gave you this name knew nothing in all probability of any such ancient sect of physicians as you mention. Nor was there any similitude between your profession and theirs that could induce him to distinguish you by that title. Neither did you ever at that time of the day pretend to derive the origin of your name from that occasion yourselves.[19]

When Wesley later repeated his explanation of the source of the Oxford group's name, he tended to make the same improbable connection between their methodical life-style and the prescriptive medical style of Greek doctors, saying that the exact regularity of the students' lives and studies brought upon them the name Methodist, which alluded to the ancient sect of physicians.[20] The distance in time, the obscurity of the group, and the lack of specific rationale for drawing any such lineage between such an ancient set of doctors and the methodical life-style of a group of university students would seem to question the propriety of such an explanation. The obvious connection seems to be found only in the more simple and general use of regular routine in their daily lives, the second of Wesley's explanations.

George Whitefield seems to support Wesley's second explanation, method of living, suggesting (in 1740) that "the world . . . gave them the title of Methodists, I suppose from their custom of regulating their time, and planning the business of the day each morning."[21] Years later, Charles Wesley also recollected that it was their early attempts at Oxford to follow the method of study prescribed by the statutes of the university that brought upon them the name "Methodist."[22]

In addition to the use of method in general, more specific practices or applications of method were also proposed (in hindsight) as pertaining to the Wesleyans. Wesley himself recalled one comment by an Irish gentleman: "Methodists! Ay, they are the people who place all religion in wearing long beards."[23] John Free comes closer to making a viable connection (though fallacious in its particular explanation) between the name and their actions when he claimed that the Methodists were so named for being "so uncommonly *methodical* as to keep a diary of the most trivial actions of their lives."[24] Bishop William Warburton, no friend of the Wesleys, suggested in a published attack on them, that "Methodism signifies only the *manner of preaching*; . . . it is the *manner* in which Mr. Wesley and his followers attempt to propagate the 'plain old religion.'"[25]

Wesley would not have been the first to be called a "Methodist" on account of a particular style of preaching. A sermon published in 1639 contains a passing reference to "plaine pack-staffe methodists, who esteeme of all flowers of rhetoricke in sermons no better than stinking weedes, and of all elegancies of speech no better than prophane spells."[26] Walter J. Ong has gone to great lengths to explain how this plain Puritan preaching style of the seventeenth century was associated with a certain rhetorical school that embodies a Ramist concern for "method" as a means of producing clarity (as opposed to those who relied upon ornateness and flowers of rhetoric to move the listener or reader). He then proposes that this was the precedent upon which the name might be applied to the Methodists of the eighteenth century.[27] This argument fails to be fully convincing, however, as an adequate explanation of the first application of the term to the Wesleyans, since their style of preaching in the early 1730s was neither notable nor especially plain.[28]

The term "methodist" in relation to preaching certainly does agree with Wesley's later sentiments that his sermons consisted of "plain truth for plain people," and his further claim that the reader of his *Sermons on Several Occasions* would find no "show of learning" therein. He had labored "to avoid all words which are not used in common life, and in particular those kinds of technical terms that so frequently occur in Bodies of Divinity."[29] But one brief reference in an obscure sermon published in 1639, such as that cited by Ong, hardly makes for a convincingly obvious precedent for the naming of the Wesleyan group a century later even if the Methodists' preaching style does eventually bear either a professed or retrospective rhetorical resemblance.

Methodists in Theology

Theological methodology was another sense in which the term "methodist" was in evidence during this period. The question of "method" in theology had been part of the heated discussions during the Protestant Reformation of the sixteenth century. On one particular side of the issue, John Calvin disputed with Cardinal Jacopo Sadoleto over the question of which of them was following the ancient and true teachings and which was the innovator. The Roman Catholic cardinal tried to tag the Protestants as the "innovators on things ancient and well-established."[30] But Calvin responded sharply:

> You know, Sadoleto, . . . not only that our agreement with antiquity is far closer than yours, but that all we have attempted has been to renew that ancient form of the church, which, at first sullied and distorted by illiterate men of indifferent character, was afterward flagitiously mangled and almost destroyed by the Roman pontiff and his faction.[31]

He continued the attack by delineating just "how widely [the Roman Catholics] differ from that holy antiquity" that was the true measure of authentic doctrine and discipline. The Protestants claimed that they were following the truly "old" method, grounded in the "oracles of God" and exhibited in the ancient church, and that the Roman views had developed subsequently and separately from the Bible and therefore were the "new" and innovative (i.e., wrong) views.[32]

Specific use of the term "new methodist" with this sense of "innovator" appears in the seventeenth century in both England and on the Continent. In 1634, Jean Daillé, a French Protestant, published an attack against the Roman Catholic Church, reiterating the Calvinist claim that medieval Catholicism was the seedbed of heretical innovations. His work, *La foy fondée sur les Sainte Escritures contre les nouveau Methodistes,* argues that the Catholics have adopted a "new method" of doing theology.[33] "New," again in this case, is a pejorative term. The "old" (i.e., good or orthodox) method, in Daillé's argument, was the scriptural or reformed way, also found in the Early Church. The "New Methodists" (those using the new method) were burdened with erroneous doctrines based upon a faulty methodology that relied upon inadequate authorities. The teachings of the Reformed Church were the old (true and orthodox) doctrines based on the revealed truths of Scripture.

According to Daillé, these "New Methodists" of the Church of Rome used a "brave method" to "gag the ministers and subdue all the enemies of the Church," demanding formal passages of Scripture to prove any controverted point that is claimed by their opponents as "scriptural." They also required adversaries to point to formal passages of Scripture to positively refute the beliefs of the Church of Rome.[34] But Daillé asks how it is "that neither Jesus Christ nor his Apostles, nor the ancient Doctors of the Church have ever taught [this method to] their disciples?"[35] The true method entails using the Old and New Testaments, "determining doubtful things by certain, clearing the obscure by the evident, and persuading those things, which they reject as false, by the connexion and dependence which they have one with the other, that they confess them true." This method, claims Daillé, was used by Augustine as that used by the Lord and his Apostles.[36] The author follows the basic Protestant principle "that all the things which we ought to believe as necessary to our salvation are taught in the Scriptures," but also slightly extends the principle: "that which is concluded evidently and necessarily from the Scriptures is veritable and Divine, and is part of the Scripture."[37]

It is crucial to note that Daillé and some of his Reformed colleagues were willing to concede a great deal of common ground of basic beliefs with the Roman Catholics. A key point of similarity was the manner in which the Reformed teachers were willing to relate justification to sanctification in such a fashion that they could say, "without holiness, no man shall see God."[38] In spite of his irenic tinge, Daillé devotes a whole section of his book to proving that the controverted beliefs of the Church of Rome and its New Methodists are by no means an evident and necessary consequence of scriptural truths.[39]

A century later, the church historian Mosheim characterized those whom Daillé and his friends had branded New Methodists on the Roman Catholic side as fitting into two categories or parties: (1) those disingenuous doctors who would shift the responsibility to the Protestants to make them prove all their beliefs, in which group he would place the Jesuit François Véron, the "apostate" Berthold Nihus or Nihusius, and Cardinal Richelieu; and (2) those eloquent disputants who would attempt to overwhelm the Protestants by the weight of some general principle or presumption comprehending all the contested points, in this group placing the Jansenist Pierre Nicole and the Bishop of Meaux, Jacques Bénigne Bossuet. Mosheim views this whole dispute as a bit of sophistry exercised among scholars with little or no effect on the larger population of the churches involved.[40]

In this debate, however, the "Romish peace-makers" found allies among the Protestants, especially in some Calvinist theologians disposed to "enter into their plan" on the basis that the points of difference in the debate were insufficient to justify their continued separation. Among these, Mosheim mentions Louis LeBlanc and others at Saumur.[41] In retrospect, these irenic French Protestants, from Daillé on, were beginning to be considered as part of the New Methodist party by association. It is interesting to notice the wide spread of seventeenth-century groups containing persons tagged as Methodists, from Jesuits and Jansenists to Huguenots and Puritans.

Half a century after Daillé, the debate had crossed the English Channel. The English scholar William Wake took issue with Jacques Bossuet and John Johnston, the French bishop's English "vindicator." Wake characterized the dispute in the words of the Vindicator, "The true state of the question betwixt us is, 'Whether the Protestants or Papists do *innovate*?'"[42] Not unlike Daillé, Wake held that the Church of England held "the ancient and undoubted foundation of the Christian faith." He also criticized the "weakness and sophistry" of the papists' methods and carried Daillé's critique a step farther by suggesting that "our new *Methodists*" not only had less than adequate authority upon which to base their doctrines, but also (especially the English supporters of the cause) had taken up scurrility, trivial jestings, ridicule, and other mean artifices as additional "new Methods."[43]

The Daillé/Wake line of thinking provides both an etymological basis for a theological use of the term "methodist" and the theological framework within which the term can eventually be applied to the Wesleyans' perspective in the 1730s. Not only is the term "new Methodist" a pejorative term applied to one who uses a new (i.e. bad) method, but the theological position of those "methodists," both Roman Catholics and their Reformed antagonist-compatriots (at Saumur, etc.), is characterized by a particular view of justification. The traditional Reformed view of justification was typically grounded in a view of God's sovereignty that limited the role of human free will (and with it, good works), while at the same time emphasizing the necessity of faith. The more irenic of the Reformers allowed some possibility that both faith *and* good works (as human responses to divine saving grace) have some efficacious role in the process of salvation.[44] It is interesting to note that the term "new methodist," first applied by some French Protestants to their Roman Catholic antagonists, eventually became associated with some of the Reformed theologians as well (perhaps not accidentally, those who, while attacking the Roman Catholic methodology, were willing to agree with much of their doctrine). As might be expected, a sharp controversy developed within Protestantism on certain key issues such as justification, in which the more radical Protestants felt that their more irenic colleagues were jeopardizing the very heart of the Reformation theology.

The classic appearance within Protestantism of the theological tension in the area of justification can be seen in the seventeenth-century dispute between the "orthodox" Calvinists who accepted the decisions of the Synod of Dort (1619) and the minority group who sided more or less with the Arminian party that had been denounced in the Dortian decisions. The debate took several forms, but seemed most often to take its energy from differences of opinion on the relationship of human free will and divine sovereignty (although in its more practical form, it came out as a debate over faith and works). Within the larger Calvinist/Arminian debate, the defense of the old-line orthodox Calvinist position against the Protestant "new methodists" is strongly stated in two publications of the 1670s and 1680s by Theophilus Gale and Johannes Vlak.

Gale's main concern in Part IV of his major work, *The Court of the Gentiles*, was to rescue the Calvinistic doctrine of predeterminism from moral difficulties, particularly to vindicate the Calvinists from "that blasphemous imputation of making God the author of sin," as charged by his main opponents, the Jesuits, the Arminians, and some "new Methodists."[45] The fine point that Gale was defending was the doctrine of "God's efficacious predeterminative concurse to the substrate matter (entitative act) of sin."[46] He notes that immediately after the Synod of Dort there sprang up some divines who, while consenting with the decisions of the Synod, "contrived a new method, especially as to universal grace, reprobation, and God's concurse to the substrate matter of sin, in order to a coalition with the Arminian partie."[47] He quotes Richard Baxter as seeing the hinge of the controversy in the question of "whether man hath truly any free will."[48] The party of the "new method," much to Gale's chagrin, generally agreed with the Arminians and Remonstrants in asserting "a general simultaneous indifferent concurse, such as is determinable by the cooperation of the human will."[49]

One does not have to understand all the finer points of the argument to catch the main point that the "new method" party, the new Methodists, had, in Gale's view, strayed from the "correct" Calvinist line on predestination and come too close to the Arminians and Molinists. The danger from the Calvinist point of view, of course, is that such a view of free will leans heavily in the direction of Pelagianism, apparently giving some value to human initiative (read "good works") in the process of salvation. The New Methodists, Gale claimed, were not wrong on every point, but had "chalked out a middle way,"[50] dividing the battle between the Calvinists and Arminians by agreeing, on the one hand, to particular election and efficacious grace, yet also owning, on the other hand, universal grace, conditional reprobation, and denying predetermination as to the entitative act of sin. Gale saw the name of the party as correctly identifying the character of their position:

> And what term or title to give this new sect of adversaries more proper than New Methodists I know not, this being the softest title, and that which they seem to recreate themselves in; some term them downright Arminians . . . , yet I dare not lode them with this reproachful style, because they generally assert efficacious grace. I think we might term them without injustice "Semi-Arminians" . . . because they assert conditionate reprobation and all the consequences thereof. . . . I give them only this [title] of "new Methodists" because they affect and attempt to give us a "new Method" or scheme of predestination, efficacious grace, divine concurse, etc.[51]

Gale goes on to express his fear that these New Methodists will by and large be drawn wholly into the Arminian camp. Those whom Gale lists as past and present New Methodists include, not surprisingly, some names that we have already seen: Louis LeBlanc (the French theologian), John Cameron, Moses Amyraldus, Josué de LaPlace (all of Saumur), and the Scotsmen John Strang (Strangius) and Peter Baro (Baronius), whom Gale sees as a "rank Arminian."[52] By the last quarter of the seventeenth century, the name Methodist was becoming a more common epithet for those who, in one form or another, proclaimed universal grace, allowed some place for human free will (and/or good works), and challenged double predestination—positions that were commonly related to the Arminian party.[53]

About this same time in the Low Countries, another publication was published to defend the orthodox Calvinist position against the "new methods" of the Arminians. Johannes Vlak's *Dissertationes Trias* points out that the "new method corrupts the doctrine of justification by faith alone."[54] Among "*nostri novi Methodistae*" mentioned by Vlak are (again) Amyrald, LeBlanc, Cameron, and Baro.[55] He also notes that in England the doctrines of free will and universal grace had resulted in a doctrine of justification grounded in "*justitiam propriam operum.*"[56] Among the English authors mentioned who thus misunderstand the covenant of grace are Richard Baxter, John Owen, George Bull, and Alexander Pitcarne, whose *De harmonia Evangelica Apostolorum Pauli & Jacobi in doctrina de Justificatione* (1685) was anathema to the Solifidians.[57]

The main controversy involving the New Methodists in England took place during the decade before John Wesley's birth. The outbreak of the debate was occasioned by the republication of the works of Tobias Crisp, an unflinching Antinomian Nonconformist who had converted from Arminian tendencies in the 1640s.[58] The second appearance of his works in 1690 brought a storm of controversy among the Nonconformists between the Antinomian party and the Neonomian party, as each was called by its opponents. Joining in the attack on Crisp's Antinomian work were Richard Baxter and Daniel Williams, two of the leading nonconformist ministers in London. Isaac Chauncy, a Harvard graduate, provided a typical defense of the Solifidian (if not Antinomian) position in his work *Neonomianism Unmasked, or the Ancient Gospel pleaded against the other, called a New Law or Gospel* (1693).[59]

In the midst of this decade of controversy, a pamphlet appeared under the title *A War Among the Angels of the Churches; wherein is shewed the Principles of the New Methodists in the great Point of Justification*, written by an anonymous "Country Professor of Jesus Christ."[60] The New Methodists are portrayed as a dangerous compound of Arminianism, Socinianism, and Bellarmines, and championed by such writers as John Goodwin and Richard Baxter.[61] The author claims that the correct Reformed view of justification was held until the Arminians raised a new war in the seventeenth century; there was then a long tugging over the principle until John Goodwin went off the stage (1665). He goes on to say that the Protestant "angels" propagating this doctrine were, "till of late," inhabitants of France, but the dispersion of their ideas brought an end to the short silence in England when a new angel of the church (Baxter?) took up the battle again.[62]

This "new method" of divinity, according to the author of this treatise, undercut the basic doctrine of the imputation of Christ's righteousness by asserting that sincere obedience, resulting in inherent righteousness, was essential to justification, pardon, and salvation. A compound of "wood, hay, and stubble," this new method "will be burnt up by the fire of the Word."[63] Nevertheless, the "Country Professor," perhaps with tongue in cheek, gives the New Methodists some benefit of the doubt, saying

> We would believe [they] intend not what others interpret their notion unto; for it's evident to us that their real design is to promote Holiness, and not willing to derogate any Honour from Christ, and take it to Self-Righteousness. We always think that both sides intend the same thing, but yet cannot agree at what door to bring in Works and Holiness.[64]

The tract contains a quotation from William Saller's *The Two Covenants, of Works and of Grace* (1682) that embodies the basic principle of the "new method" and the "sense of the New Methodists." Saller outlined two essential components of the righteousness of the Law of Grace: "(1) The righteousness which consisteth in the forgiveness of sins, and (2) the righteousness of sincere obedience."[65] The Solifidians were particularly upset by this double approach to justification and especially opposed any attempt to ground salvation in the inherence of human sincere obedience. They saw the New Methodists' attempts to talk about "faith as imputed for righteousness" as referring to the *acts* and *fruits* of faith, and therefore saw their position as a challenge to the doctrine of the imputation of the Christ's righteousness *apart from* human effort. For the Calvinist Solifidian, only the perfect obedience of Christ could satisfy the demands of the Covenant, while they saw the "New Methodist" as claiming that personal inherent righteousness (sincere obedience) is necessary to fulfill the requirements of the New Covenant (which, like the Old Covenant, is typified by the language, "Do this and live").[66] Any talk about the necessity of "growing in sanctification" was seen by the Country Professor as implying subsequent justification(s), a challenge to the "true" doctrine of justification.[67]

The author, to highlight the practical dangers of this new method, proposes a prayer that would incorporate their heretical views, including such comments as

> We have repented of our Sins, and obeyed the Gospel commands; and though our Obedience (the fruit of our believing) be imperfect, yet we are sincere in our profession of it, which thy Merit renders to be acceptable for this great end.[68]

The implications of this "new divinity" are clear to the strict Calvinists—the New Methodists had challenged the doctrine of justification by faith at its very heart, giving human action (sincere obedience) an active role in a process that should rely only upon divine grace for its efficacy. The labels thrown upon this position by the Antinomian (Solifidian) party were predictable: Arminian, Jesuit, Socinian, Pelagian. The New Methodists were to them just another manifestation of a long line of heresies that misunderstood the nature of the New Covenant and continued to propagate a doctrine of salvation by works-righteousness.

This "methodist" controversy between the Antinomians and Neonomians came to an inconclusive cessation in 1699/1700 with the publication of Dr. Williams' *Peace with Truth, or an End to Discord*, and Isaac Chauncy's *Alexipharmacon; or, A Fresh Antidote against Neonomian*

Bane and Poyson to the Protestant Religion. Three years later, John Wesley was born in Epworth, son of Samuel and Susanna Wesley, both of whom had been raised in Nonconformist families. Although John Wesley himself seems not to have been familiar with the specific debates over the "New Methodist" theology, he did have some definite Arminian tendencies in his blood.

What was at stake in this long and convoluted controversy was, for the one side, the central reality of divine sovereignty and for the other side, the essential nature of human responsibility. In spite of the fact that many of the combatants in this struggle felt that the fundamental integrity (if not the entire future) of Christianity was in jeopardy depending upon the outcome of the dispute, this particular episode in the longer struggle came and went within a generation in England, and the vitriolic attacks upon the "New Methodists" were by and large forgotten in the excitement generated by the Deists at the turn of the century. As the eighteenth century wore on, the controversial ideas on both sides of the Neonomian debate persisted, but the "war of the angels" and the terminology it generated was remembered for the most part only by church historians and encyclopedists.[69]

From the foregoing survey, we can see that the precedents for the name "Methodist" fall into two main categories. On the one hand, the term might simply indicate a life-style characterized by regular routine—"living by rule and method." If a special type of method is to be seen as the precedent, pertaining to diet, exercise, or style of preaching for instance, there are several candidates for ancestry, including some that seem to have little connection to the Wesleyans, such as the ancient sect of Greek physicians or the plain-style preachers mentioned by Spencer. On the other hand, if theological method is to be seen as the source of the name, there is general precedent for the term in the seventeenth-century French Roman Catholics attacked by Daillé, or their English Recusant counterparts described by Wake, all of whom were at one time or another denominated "Methodists" or "New Methodists." Some of the irenic French Reformed theologians are put into this same category, by association, for their willingness to agree with the "popish methodists" on key issues, such as the nature of justification. And finally there are some other theological parties, with overlapping personnel but some common views on the *ordu salutis*—the Low-Country Arminians described by Vlak, the Semi-Arminians described by Gale, or the Neonomians attacked by "the Country Professor," all called "Methodists" or "New Methodists" by their opponents. In trying to determine what sort of precedent might be most appropriate as a source for the name of the Methodists in the eighteenth century, we must look more closely at the circumstances surrounding the naming of the Wesleyan group to see if any clues might help us ascertain the relevant connections with previous uses of the term.

The People Called Methodists

The first record of the term "Methodist" being applied to the Wesleyan group at Oxford is in 1732, after William Morgan had left Oxford and John Clayton had joined with the Wesleys in their activities. The first actual use of the term in a contemporary document is in a letter from John Clayton to John Wesley on 6 September 1732. Wesley had gone to London for a short time and seems to have left Clayton in charge of the activities of their little society. Clayton's first report to London, listing the status of the various prisoners, the activities of his associates, and the problems in the university, mentions to Wesley, perhaps with a note of irony if not jealousy, "now that you are gone, we have lost the honourable title of 'Methodist.'"[70] The term seems to have been directly associated with John Wesley and particularly appropriate to him at this point in the development of his life and thought. It is crucial for our study, then, to examine the nature of Wesley's activities at this specific time.

A survey of Wesley's diary for 1732 indicates that the general sense of the term "Methodist," in the meaning of living by rule and method, would certainly apply at this point, though not by any means to the same extent as would be appropriate after another year or so. His first talk of "method" with his pupils was noted in December 1731; the first specific manifestation of it in his own routine comes in May and June 1732 when he developed a "method for [visiting the] Castle."[71] Wesley had only just begun to collect together a few rules and resolutions in the back of his diary at this point. The long lists of general and particular rules, however, do not appear until several months later. The same is true for any specific rules regarding diet or regimen of health, certainly noticeable at this time, but by no means as rigid or zealously applied as in the succeeding years. There is justifiable reason for applying the term "Methodist" to Wesley and his friends at this point on account of their methodical life-style, but whether it would have been an *especially* noticeable or the *only* notable rationale is questionable.

There is little to suggest that the term "Methodist" (especially as a term of derision) would spontaneously and naturally come to the mind of an observer of the Wesleyans in the first half of 1732 based simply on the routine of their daily pattern of living, even though in hindsight such a connection certainly seems plausible. And the possible tie to an ancient sect of physicians seems to have even less specific basis or rationale at that point in time. Neither does it follow that other persons in the group (or groups, as were then developing) would lose that name (given either rationale) simply as a result of Wesley being absent for a short period. In fact, Clayton himself seems to have inspired the disciplined life-style that the Wesleyans adopted after his entrance into their fellowship in the spring of 1732, a life-style patterned after the discipline of the early Christians (a special interest of Clayton and his circle of friends, the Manchester nonjurors).[72] Hence, if the term Methodist were directly tied to a style of living, it would have adhered as closely to John Clayton as to John Wesley. Therefore, while there certainly are some grounds for seeing the term Methodist as applying to the Wesleyans' general manner of living, the rationale is less than fully convincing or satisfying as a specific basis of their first being named "Methodist" in 1732.

As for the Wesleyans being the namesake of various other precedent groups, the tie to two groups we have mentioned seems also to be very loose and only appropriate in retrospect. The "plaine packstaffe Methodist preachers" mentioned once a century earlier may in fact come to the mind of a person looking at Wesley's later preaching career or his published sermons (and their intentionally "plain" character), but it is doubtful if his preaching record prior to 1732 would have brought that obscure reference to any contemporary observer's mind, especially as a term of derision. And very few persons at that time would likely have made a direct connection with the French Roman Catholic "New Methodists" mentioned by Daillé and Wake; the tie there would certainly not be based on the specific criticisms of Daillé or any actual comparison with the method of those "papist Methodists." Certainly, a person especially conversant with the theological developments of the previous century might have been aware of the polemical history that tied together the Catholic and Calvinist "New Methodists" but would not really have needed to go back quite so far in order to have a viable precedent for such a perspective in England itself.

As we have seen, the history of the epithet "New Methodists" in the matter of theological method had come to a sharpened focus in the controversies in England at the end of the seventeenth century. The term was derisively applied, by Calvinist critics, to those theologians who seemed to have Pelagian or Socinian tendencies and might generally be categorized as "Arminians"—those who emphasized human freedom and responsibility (assuming universal atonement rather than predestination),[73] sincere obedience (attempting to fulfill the "Law" even under the New Covenant), good works (pressing on to holiness or sanctification), inherent righteousness (resulting in double justification or subsequent works of grace).[74] Wesley's theology at Oxford in 1732 was clearly grounded upon what the Calvinists of his day would have called "Arminianism." The Puritan antagonists of the 1690s would have recognized Wesley's theology rather precisely as the Neonomian approach of the "New Methodists." Specific examples of this connection can be found in Wesley's writings in the early 1730s.

A most striking example of the "New Methodist" perspective, in terms of sincere obedience, can be seen in Wesley's interpolations into his abridgment of Robert Nelson's work on the Sacrament, which Wesley titles, "The Duty of Receiving the Lord's Supper."[75] In describing the necessity of receiving the communion as often as possible, Wesley comments, "And are we not bound to obey every one of God's commands as often as we can? Is not this the very condition on which we hope for salvation: The obeying God as much as we can?" To bolster this point, which he views as being "of more concern than any other in our whole religion," Wesley adds a proof "from the nature of God's covenant with man." Thereupon follows Wesley's description of the two Covenants, Old and New:

> Whereas the first agreement was, "Do this and Live," the second was "Try to do this,* and live" [*"Do what thou canst," erased]. To man in his strength God said, "Do everything which I command"; to man in his weakness God said, "Use thy best endeavours to do everything which I command." Perfect obedience was made the condition of the first covenant; earnest, hearty obedience of the second.[76]

This explanation is Wesley's version of the "sincere obedience" which we saw earlier as one of the basic principles of the "new method" outlined by Saller and criticized by "the Country Professor."

Wesley finished this work on 19 February 1732. In March he transcribed this manuscript, which he referred to as the "Sermon on the Sacrament," and read the fifty-page document to his brother Charles. During the following months, Wesley used this treatise many times with his friends and students. Clayton commented in his report to Wesley in September that "your Sermon [on the Sacrament] is under God the occasion of any good that shall be done this way [concerning] the necessity of being active."[77] The theology of active obedience that permeates this work was receiving some attention throughout the university as the result of Clayton's active proselytizing by using Wesley's writings.

Wesley was openly responsive to the criticisms that came his way in late 1732. At the very time the first attack on the Methodists appeared in *Fog's Weekly Journal*, Wesley was busy preparing a sermon to preach before the university. It was to prove a landmark in his theological development, at one and the same time owning the holy living tradition and yet showing that sanctification was not outward works-righteousness but rather the work of the Holy Spirit in effecting an inward inclination of the soul, the "Circumcision of the Heart," as the title calls it.

It is significant that this sermon that sets forth the heart of Oxford Methodist doctrine starts by recalling a "melancholy remark of an excellent man," that "he who now preaches the most essential duties of Christianity runs the hazard of being esteemed by a great part of his hearers 'a setter forth of new doctrines.'"[78] This phrasing does not necessarily reflect the precise designation of "New Methodist" but indicates that Wesley was feeling a similar pressure from his critics.

The theme of his sermon, from Romans 2:29, is clear: "Circumcision is that of the heart, in the spirit, and not in the letter." He elaborates:

> The distinguishing mark of a true follower of Christ, of one who is in a state of acceptance with God, is not either outward circumcision or baptism, or any other outward form, but a right state of soul—a mind and spirit renewed after the image of him that created it.[79]

This consistently inward focus found throughout the sermon was no doubt a surprise to some of Wesley's contemporaries who had already begun to see him and his friends as disciplined activists who engaged in good works beyond the ordinary expectations of the university community.

Wesley attempts to make the connection between inward and outward religion in this sermon by harkening back to what will become the foundation of his doctrine of Christian Perfection: "love is the fulfilling of the law," "the end of the commandment."[80] But his comments about the "royal law of heaven," the Spirit as being the perfecter "both of our faith and works," love being "the sum of the perfect law," were shibboleths to some of his Solifidian critics and sounded the warning of a pervasive Arminianism.[81] All of Wesley's intentions to ground his holy living perspective in a view of faith working through love, flowing from the divinely instilled virtues, were for nought to the critic who saw here a blatant synergism that was based on necessary obedience and gave human effort some role in the process of salvation.[82]

Other Wesley sermons from the early 1730s also contain many references that illustrate this same theological perspective. His sermon, "The Love of God," defines that love as "obedience to him"[83] and calls upon the active believer to "press on to the high mark of our calling" in terms that would distress the Solifidian quietists: "Do ye act, do ye speak, do ye reason, do ye love? Do all to the glory of God."[84] The call to active obedience reaches new heights in his sermon on the Lord's Prayer, where Wesley exegetes the phrase "Thy will be done" by saying that we are thereby commanded to imitate angelic obedience to the will of God.[85]

A sermon preached at the ordination service in Christ Church Cathedral in the fall of 1731 (and repeated twice more at Oxford in the next half year) contains the injunctions for the clergy to "submit to the law of God," and "to do what in them lies."[86] This view reflects precisely the point of a phrase Wesley found in Thomas à Kempis: *Fac quod in te est*—"Do what in you lies," or, "Do the best you can, and God acknowledges your good intentions."[87]

Wesley's correspondence during this period also reiterates this same theme of the necessity of actively pressing on toward "that degree of holiness which become them whom God thus delights to honour."[88] The motivation for Wesley's own activities can be seen in his comment to Anne Granville toward the end of 1731. What kept him going in the face of failures and adversities was, as he called it, "the hope of our calling: to know that our hope is sincerity not perfection: not to do well, but to do our best."[89]

This goal is clearly portrayed in the preface to his first publication, *A Collection of Forms of Prayer* (1733), in which he attempted to sum up "the whole scheme of our Christian duty." The fifth step in Wesley's outline is, "Christ liveth in me: This is the fulfilling of the Law, the last stage of Christian holiness; this maketh the man of God perfect."[90] This also maketh the Calvinist mad.

It is more than simple coincidence that the *sola fide* message of the sixteenth-century Reformers was directly aimed against this apparent emphasis on human effort that had been emphasized in the late medieval church, and that the Solifidians of the seventeenth century fought against the same sort of "Neonomianism" found in the covenantal theology of some of the Puritans. It is probably no accident that the appearance of this theology in the sermons and teachings of John Wesley at Oxford in 1732 should remind someone of the "New Methodists" of the previous generation.

Of course, only the person who gave the Wesleyans the nickname "Methodist" could tell us for sure what was in his mind when he first applied that term to Wesley and his friends. We do know who that person was, but we know very little about him. Wesley mentions, in the preface to the first edition of his *Character of a Methodist* in 1740, that the term was a term of reproach "first given to three or four young men at Oxford by Mr. John Bingham, then Student of Christ Church." He goes on further, there as well as elsewhere (as we have seen), to point out that the young gentleman of Christ Church had said, "Here is a new set of Methodists sprung up."[91]

It would be sheer speculation, of course, to suggest at this point that Wesley may have heard or recollected the phrase inaccurately, although he frequently misquotes even familiar sources. And yet, if Wesley were not familiar with the New Methodists (which apparently he was not), would he have understood the significance of a slight reordering of the same words?—"Here is a set of *new Methodists* sprung up." Probably not! But history cannot be written in the subjunctive: "What if Mr. Bingham actually said, 'set of new Methodists' . . ."? The theological precedent and rationale for a connection does not rely on mere speculation. The point has been made well enough: the theology of John Wesley at the point he became tagged with the nickname "Methodist" displays the same perspective that Wake, Gale, Vlak, the Country Professor, and others saw fit to call "Methodist" for theological reasons in the previous generation. And it was a term not unfamiliar to some in Wesley's own generation and to observers after the fact as well.[92] The theological precedent deserves at least equal consideration with the other possible explanations, even though Wesley himself never mentions it.

Before leaving the matter of the naming of the Wesleyans, we might make one further observation regarding the perpetuation of the name Methodist into the eighteenth century and beyond. Why, among the various titles, did that one persist? Again I would claim that the matter of timing was important. The first published attack on the Wesleyans at Oxford came in the fall of 1732 at a time when the term Methodist was especially associated with the group. The letter to the editor printed in *Fog's Weekly Journal* had been written on November 6 and included a reference to the Wesleyans as "this sect call'd Methodists." Wesley's diary notes that, upon the appearance in Oxford of that edition of *Fog's*, on 11 December 1732, the talk in the Lincoln common room turned to the subject of "the Methodists"—the first use of that term in Wesley's diary.[93] The very first use of the term in his writings had come six weeks earlier in a letter describing and defending the nature and design of their small society of friends, written to the father of William Morgan, Wesley's former student who had died the previous summer, purportedly as a result of his rigorous fasting. This letter found its way into the hands of an anonymous writer who, in February 1733, produced a pamphlet entitled *The Oxford Methodists,* the first published defense of Wesley and his friends.[94] These two published items seem to have fixed the title in the public consciousness, and the name "Methodist" was associated with the Wesleyan movement from that point on.

Conclusion

"What's in a name?" Methodist, wherefore art thou Methodist? Perhaps more than enough has been said to confuse and not enough to convince that the term Methodist has a solid theological rationale behind it, that it is not just a general reference to doing things methodically. Does (or would) the knowledge of that make a difference in how Methodists perceive themselves? Would the recognition of a theological basis for the name make Methodists any more concerned with theological issues?

Perhaps Methodists, United and others, are encumbered with a name that need have no specific significance other than to distinguish them from other churches and schools in the phone book. Perhaps the significance is a matter of the past knowing itself and the present having a bad memory for names. Perhaps the natural tendency is simply to clutch empty names from the past, names now devoid of meaning or reality. This would bring us to the position of Adso in the conclusion of *The Name of the Rose,* who in despair says, *Stat rosa pristina nomine, nomina nuda tenemus*[95]—"The former rose stands with a name; we hold empty names."

"What's in a name?" Wherefore art thou Methodist? Wesley pointed out to his critics that he would rejoice "if the very name might never be mentioned more, but be buried in eternal oblivion." He goes on to say, however, "But if that cannot be, at least let those who *will* use it, know the meaning of the word they use."[96] Strange, perhaps, that Wesley was not clear on that matter himself. Nevertheless, that should not stop Methodists from looking further at the background and meaning of their name in order to sense the significance of their theological heritage and to come to a clearer understanding of themselves as the people of God.[97]

Chapter 2

THE CHURCH OF ENGLAND AND THE RELIGIOUS SOCIETIES[1]

"We are gradually fallen into that vicious modesty which has in some measure worn out from among us the appearance of Christianity in ordinary life and conversation."[2] Thus spoke *The Spectator* in 1712, depicting what has come to be an often-repeated stereotype of the general tenor of society in early eighteenth-century England. The historian who wants to verify this view has no trouble filling in the details with contemporary illustrations of the depravity of that era. Whether these sordid pictures are adequate representations of the character of the age, however, remains a question. History paints her own picture with small strokes, and only with the passage of years does the observer have the distance and perspective necessary to discern patterns and meaning from the splotchy canvas of time. As historians attempt to understand the history of the eighteenth century, however, they are forced to recognize that much of what they see is a canvas that has been retouched or even recopied. Contemporary observers themselves began the process of interpretation by drawing together in bold strokes certain emphases that were more or less obvious to them, but which may have required a brightening of the colors or a deepening of the dark areas to highlight what they were trying to portray.

The eighteenth century was constantly being informed that it was decadent, corrupt, and mad for pleasure. This message was transmitted in two ways, either by portraying the dark side of the picture even worse than it actually was (but close enough to reality so that everyone would recognize it), or by drawing an ideal picture of the way things ought to be. Both methods are combined in the art of the satirist, who thrives in an age marked by strong contrasts. Satire was the language of the eighteenth century.[3] Although the art of Hogarth or of *The Spectator* may have been a caricature of the period, these commentators by no means invented the types of persons and the sorts of conditions they were portraying.[4] The "wail of lament over the irreligion and immorality" that pervaded the century must certainly have been more than simply a general reflection upon the corruption of human nature.[5] The constancy of the cry, on the one hand, indicates that there was a segment of society that was aware of the problems confronting it, and yet, on the other hand, hints that the attitudes pervading a major portion of the society were such that little was done to alleviate the situation.

In an age of contrasts, the extremes stand out. In early eighteenth-century England, commentators found it is easy to emphasize either end of the spectrum, according to the intentions of the commentator. Nineteenth-century writers tended to use bold dark strokes in portraying the decadence of their predecessors, hoping thereby to emphasize the lustre they saw in their own age. Mark Pattison tried to point out that the historian is compelled to portray the period as "one of decay of religion, licentiousness of morals, public corruption, profaneness of language—a day of 'rebuke and blasphemy.'"[6] In this sentiment, he is merely adding a commonly repeated refrain to many similar comments made during the century itself, such as the observation by Bishop Gibson in 1740 that "the decay of piety and religion, and the increase of sin and vice, are so visible . . . in this corrupt and degenerate age."[7] Hoping to increase the stature of their own hero, biographers of the Reformers of that period often tend to emphasize that it was generally not an age which nurtured the heroic virtues in mankind.[8]

At the same time, a person wanting to judge the faults of his own day against the virtues of the past can find much that was good in the eighteenth century. The revisionist attempt to correct the hypercritical view of the period has led some authors to focus on the redeeming qualities of the century.[9]

As we look back on the early eighteenth century, then, what stands out is the contrast between the extremes—poverty and wealth, Jacobites and Republicans, rationalism and enthusiasm, immorality and virtue.[10] What post-Restoration English society desired, however, was the stability of the golden mean, the "middle way" in every aspect of life. In reaction to the turmoil of the Reformation, the Commonwealth, and the Glorious Revolution, Englishmen were paralyzed by fear of extremism. Much of the activity of both church and state in the age of Walpole appeared to be geared toward the achievement of tranquility and the maintenance of the status quo. In this sense the virtues of the period were the very seeds of its vice. The careful restraint, the willingness to compromise, and the desire for balance in all things resulted in a sense of harmony, quiescence, and equilibrium that might very well have caused the lethargy, stagnation, and comfortable slackness that marks much of English society after the Hanoverian succession.[11] For many persons, the status quo seemed to represent the last word of divine wisdom and goodness.[12] They were therefore willing to accept the world as they found it and to respect the established forms as the embodiment of eternal laws. Those who detracted from the given formulae in an attempt to find a better way were branded as enthusiasts, while at the same time those who accepted the given forms too literally were also seen as dangerous.[13]

The moral and spiritual lethargy of the people was explained by *The Spectator* as being a reaction against "those swarms of sectaries that overran the nation in the time of the great rebellion" who carried hypocrisy so high that "they had converted our whole language into a jargon of enthusiasm." As a result, after the Restoration men felt they "could not recede too far from the behaviour and practice of those persons who had made religion a cloak for so many villanies," and thus every appearance of religious deportment was lost.[14]

There was, according to the bishops' report in 1711, one good consequence of the growth of the infidelity that had infested the country after the "long unnatural rebellion": "that the zeal of devout persons, hath thereby been excited to do every thing, that in them lay, toward resisting and stemming this torrent of impiety." Although most of the endeavors of "publick or private persons" to stop this trend appeared to be "ineffectual," the bishops were quick to point out that such endeavors had not been entirely fruitless.[15]

That the Church of England did not rise as a whole to meet the challenge, however, is not only the verdict of later historians, but the general observation of many contemporary observers. The clergymen in Hogarth's prints illustrate the extent to which the spiritual inertia of the times had permeated every level of society, including the clergy. The bite of the print lies not in the portrayal of some gross act of evil by a man of the cloth, but rather in the picture of his willingly and insensibly participating in a scene that should arouse his moral indignation. He still holds himself slightly above the level of the rest of society but appears to fall far short of the divine work that the artist assumes everyone knows has been entrusted to the good parson. In "A Harlot's Progress," he is more concerned with matters of preferment than the immanent downfall of the young country lass.[16] In "A Midnight Modern Conversation," he is only slightly less drunk than his friends.[17]

The Church may have been in intimate touch with the life of the age but did not generally stand conspicuously above it.[18] The leadership within the Church, which might have been expected to lead the way by example and instruction, was often engaged in an intellectual duel with the forces of Deism, Socinianism, or any one of a number of philosophical threats to the religion and/or politics of the establishment in England. A deft and clever pen handled by a bishop could divert attention from a multitude of inadequacies in his own pastoral leadership.[19]

But if the intellectual weight of the Church was attempting to correct a theological imbalance in the developing ideas of the times, increasing numbers of clergy and laity in the Church were trying to revitalize Christian standards among the people. This concern for Christian *praxis* found explicit expression in the development within the Church of England of the religious societies, which began in the late seventeenth century and continued into the early eighteenth century. The origin of the religious societies in England represents a rather spontaneous fusion of moralism and devotionalism, brought together within a fairly strict adherence to the structure and liturgical patterns of the Church of England.[20]

This outcropping of zeal for the promotion of "real holiness of heart and life" contrasted sharply with the sentiment of the age.[21] If the religious societies were not primarily searching for new formulae and methods, they were indeed taxing the given forms of the system to the fullest in a period when the prevailing lethargy had resulted in a deadening inelasticity within the institutional structure of Church life and thought. In that age when toleration of dissenting bodies was to become the law of the land, but comprehension within the established Church was an ideal still to be pursued by many, the Church of England made a concerted effort to secure such reforming zeal within its own structure through the religious societies.[22]

The religious societies in England began with the work of Anthony Horneck in 1678.[23] Within twenty years, this form of religious organization had established itself within the structure of the Church as a feasible expression of Christian piety and social concern. Around the turn of the eighteenth century, the movement gave rise to the great societies that were in turn to provide the model for (and encouragement of) religious societies throughout the realm. It is no small circumstance that Samuel Wesley, rector of the Epworth parish, became involved in this movement. And the fact that his son John became a member of the Society for Promoting Christian Knowledge had direct consequences in the early development of the people called Methodists.

The religious societies began during the period following the Restoration when English society was in the throes of a reaction to its recent encounter with politicized Puritanism. The effects of the nationwide sigh of relief that accompanied the return of the Stuart monarchy seem to have permeated the life of the nation quite beyond the political level. The return to the principles of the Elizabethan Settlement brought with it a measured abhorrence for the fanaticism, moral as well as political, of the Puritan Commonwealth. Within two decades, the debilitating effect of this sentiment upon the moral fiber of the nation was viewed with alarm by Horneck and certain other Englishmen who saw the growth of immorality and irreligion as a crisis that must be met by a rejuvenation of religious life within the Church. The organization of concerned persons into religious societies in England followed some of the basic patterns evident in certain pietistic and mystical tendencies on the Continent at that time. Such European models as may have been transferred to British soil, however, were also transformed by their adaptation to the life and thought of the Church of England.[24]

The religious societies attacked the problem of immorality on a personal, individualistic basis. Theirs was no social program to reform England in one grand stroke. The approach instead was to work toward the transformation of society by changing one person at a time, by working first with those for whom there seemed to be some hope for moral improvement. Their method in such an endeavor was to encourage the development of a life of personal piety. The movement was not marked by an evangelistic zeal to bring vast numbers of persons into the religious societies. Rather, their approach aimed toward quality more than quantity and was grounded in the process of nurture more than conversion.[25] In some ways the program of the religious societies can be compared to the development of the lay "third orders" within the Roman Catholic Church.[26]

Although the members of the societies were encouraged to use their "utmost endeavor to enlarge the Society with suitable Members," membership was reserved to those who were recommended favorably by a majority of the present members. They measured propects with respect to their "religious purposes and manner of life." The stated purpose of the societies was to promote "real holiness of heart and life."[27] To this end, the meetings provided mutual encouragement in the development of devotional piety based on a study of the Bible and other works of devotion, and assisted in the promotion of a life of personal holiness and morality.[28] The *Orders* of one society furnished a list of particular duties that the members were expected to make "their serious Endeavor" as a guide to holy living:

1. To be just in all their dealings, even to an exemplary strictness: as Matt. 5:16, 20. Matt. 7:12.
2. To pray many times every day, remembering our continual dependence upon God, both for spiritual and temporal things. 1 Thess. 5:17.
3. To partake of the Lord's Supper at least once a month, if not prevented by a reasonable impediment. 1 Cor. 11:26. Luke 22:19.
4. To practise the profoundest meekness and humility. Matt. 11:29.
5. To watch against censuring others. Matt. 7:1.
6. To accustom themselves to holy thoughts in all places. Ps. 2, 3.
7. To be helpful one to another. 1 Cor. 12:26.
8. To exercise tenderness, patience, and compassion, towards all men. Titus 3:2.
9. To make reflections on themselves when they read the Holy Bible, or other good books, and when they hear sermons. 1 Cor. 10:11.
10. To shun all foreseen occasions of evil; as evil company, known temptations, &c. 1 Thess. 5:22.
11. To think often on the different estates of the glorified and the damned, in the unchangeable eternity, to which we are hastening. Luke 16:25.
12. To examine themselves every night, what good or evil they have done in the day past. 2 Cor. 13:5.
13. To keep a private fast once a month, (especially near their approach to the Lord's Table) if at their own disposal; or to fast from some meal when they may conveniently. Matt. 6:16. Luke 5:35.
14. To mortify the flesh with its affections, and lust. Gal. 5:19, 24.
15. To advance in heavenly-mindedness, and in all grace. 1 Pet. 3:8.
16. To shun spiritual pride, and the effects of it; as railing, anger, peevishness, and impatience of contradiction, &c.
17. To pray for the whole Society in their private prayers. James 5:16.
18. To read pious books often for their edification.
19. To be continually mindful of the great obligation of this special profession of religion, and to walk so circumspectly, that none may be offended or discouraged from it by what they see in them, nor occasion be given to any, to speak reproachfully of it.
20. To shun all manner of affectation and moroseness, and to be of a civil and obliging deportment to all men.[29]

The members not only nurtured each other while meeting together, but also monitored each other at other times. Every member was expected to "look as near as he can" after the deportment of each of the others, and if any were found to be walking "disorderly," he was to be privately admonished by one or more of his compatriots, or reproved by the whole society if necessary.[30] The societies thus used both positive and negative methods to promote the advancement of pious living among the members.

Upon this rather exclusivistic base, the societies attempted in some small measure to spread their influence within English society. The rules for the Cripplegate Society hint that their inclination to reprimand immorality extended beyond the limits of their own small gathering and into the public realm. Every member was to be ready to do what might be advisable "towards the punishment of publick prophaneness," the rules carefully explaining that the motivation for such an endeavor should not be "popular applause or malice to any man," but rather should arise out of "pure love to God and charity to men's souls."[31]

In a more positive vein, the societies also encouraged certain charitable causes, for which the members subscribed regularly as their circumstances would allow. Any member of the society could recommend an object of charity to the stewards, who would, with the consent of the majority of members, dispense their funds "as the occasion requires."[32] The society did not promote philanthropy so much in the simple humanitarian sense of the word, but rather dispensed funds to foster the rather explicit goals and purposes of the societies. The orders of one society, for example, state the primary aim of building up a "publick stock" to be for "maintaining a sermon and to defray other necessary charges."[33] The *Orders* published in 1724 also mention that at the death of any member of the society, a funeral sermon would be preached "at the charge of the Society."[34]

The charitable exercises of the societies grew naturally out of the concern the members exhibited for each other. When members of a religious society were sick, the other members were admonished to "take all convenient opportunities of visiting such sick members."[35] The concern for the spiritual and physical needs of fellow members simply could not be confined within the small select groups. At a very early stage in their development, the societies began to demonstrate a special interest in the needs of the poor and disadvantaged. They gave food and money to the needy, visited the sick and the imprisoned, and taught the children of the unfortunate.

Many contemporary observers saw the problems that accompanied the increasing prevalence of illiteracy and poverty in the burgeoning lower classes of England as the major contributing factors to the growth and spread of immorality and vice. The intention of the religious societies in working with the poor was not so much to raise their standard of living in an economic sense but rather to improve their life in a moral sense. The fear in eighteenth-century England that such movements would cause drastic changes in the economic structure of society made it necessary for the religious societies to take an apologetic stance in supporting such programs as the development of charity schools. They pointed out very carefully that these schools were not intended to teach the children of the poor a sense of discontent with their station in life but rather "to instruct them very carefully in the duties of servants, and submission to superiors."[36] The societies also helped to support the establishment of workhouses in the cities as another means of dealing with the problems of the poor. The dual emphasis within these institutions upon work and education was so designed that "the next generation of persons in lower life" would "be made better." In this setting, the children of the poor, "instead of being bred up in irreligion and vice, to an idle, beggarly, and vagabond life," would have "the fear of God before their eyes, get habits of virtue, be inured to labour, and thus become useful to their country."[37]

The great Church societies in and around London at the turn of the eighteenth century embodied in somewhat definitive form the variety of methods used within the religious societies to promote holiness and virtue through both positive encouragement and negative vigilance. What we have seen as a negative approach was institutionalized in the Society for the Reformation of Manners in 1691.[38] This organization arose out of a desire among certain inhabitants in the Tower section of London to suppress open immorality, which seemed to prevail in their suburb. The Society encouraged and assisted the Justices of the Peace to perform their duties in the enforcement of laws regarding moral offenses. This design was accomplished by means of informers who came forward as witnesses against the offenders. Within two years, supporters of the Society were claiming a "visible Reformation as to some scandalous crimes in many parts of the city and suburbs." This improvement had been achieved by about forty or fifty zealous members of the Church of England who had "voluntarily engaged themselves one to another to employ part of their time in observing the manners of others and in accusing and witnessing against such as they [found] breaking the laws against profaneness and debauchery."[39] Several sub-societies arose in and around London to promote the reformation of manners, with subscriptions being solicited from members and other friends who would contribute toward the prosecution of immoral offenders.

Although the association of like-minded persons interested in improving the moral fiber of the populus through the Society for the Reformation of Manners did have the natural consequence of the membership "provoking and encouraging one another in good works,"[40] the generally negative approach of the Society (particularly the use of informers) tended to incur widespread reproach. This reaction contributed to the decreasing influence of the religious societies after the first three decades of the eighteenth century.

A different focus and approach found more lasting success and influence. In 1698, a small group banded together to form the Society for Promoting Christian Knowledge. The impetus for its inception is shown in the preamble to one of their early documents:

> Whereas the growth of vice and immorality is greatly owing to the gross ignorance of the principles of the Christian religion, we whose names are underwritten do agree to meet together, as often as we can conveniently, to consult (under the conduct of the divine providence and assistance) how we may be able by due and lawful methods to promote Christian knowledge.[41]

The Society began as a company of close friends who were already members of other religious societies in and around London. This society (as well as its sister group, the Society for the Propagation of the Gospel in Foreign Parts) differed from the more general religious society movement primarily in its positive outward thrust. Whereas the religious societies generally fulfilled the primary purpose of mutual encouragement in holy living among the membership (or the discouragement of immoral living), the SPCK attacked what it considered to be the root of the problem, ignorance, by developing specific means of educating the public in Christian principles.[42]

The program of the SPCK was fairly straightforward. It furthered the establishment of Charity Schools for teaching the poor, promoted the spread of lending libraries, and encouraged prison visitation to instruct the inmates and provide them with religious services and books. To this end, the Society engaged in an extensive publishing program. The Society fervently advocated dispersing "pious books and catechisms" among the public, particularly the poor, as a means of bringing "the generality of the common people to a true knowledge of God, a sense of the great importance of religion, and a serious concern for their everlasting welfare."[43] Within the first two or three years of the Society's existence, its leaders estimated ("by a moderate computation") that they had given away nearly a million books—Bibles, Common-Prayer Books, Catechisms, Treatises on the Sacrament, and a "multitude" of practical and devotional pieces.[44] This ardor for reforming the English people through the printed word did not abate with the passing of time. By 1734 the Society's catalog of printed books "For the Use of the Poor" listed 140 items. The bound books were available at "prime cost" (the Society defraying the cost of binding), and the stitched treatises were available to members at half the prime cost.[45] The Society gave many books to schools, prisons, and other charitable causes, and in some cases "as presents" to their members.[46] The expense of such a program was underwritten by the regular subscriptions of the "residing members" (later called "subscribing members") of the Society, bolstered by the casual benefactions of friends.

In addition to their publishing enterprise, the SPCK supported the growing missionary movement. Not only were the first members of the Society instrumental in the incorporation of the Society for the Propagation of the Gospel in Foreign Parts (1701), but they continued as a voluntary society to support particular mission projects with money, books, and other forms of assistance.[47] From the beginning the Society supported the mission work in the "plantations" of America. In 1710 they began to assist the Protestant mission to the East Indies and in the next decade helped to send missionaries to Madras. In another major project, undertaken in 1732, the Society came to the support of the persecuted Salzburgers in Germany, providing for their relief and aiding in their transport to the colony of Georgia in America.

The program of the SPCK continued to flourish in spite of the general demise of the religious societies in the second quarter of the eighteenth century. For although the SPCK had grown out of the religious society movement, the outward thrust of its program carried it beyond the introspective and elitist tendencies of the private societies. Its publishing interests and its educational endeavors in the charity schools and the mission field supplied a foundation of service and usefulness to the general public that encouraged further support and development of the Society as an important institution in British life.

The Wesleys were among the many persons who were influenced by the Society for Promoting Christian Knowledge. John's relationship with the Society was significant to the growth and shape of early Methodism.[48] In many ways, however, his own direct connection with the SPCK was anticipated by his father's interest both in the work of that particular group and in the development of the religious societies in general. In 1700 Samuel Wesley undertook to set up a small religious society in Epworth on the model of the societies in London. Samuel ordered books and tracts from the SPCK, of which he had become a corresponding member.[49] Within two years the good rector had established a small society, launched with a few of "the most sensible and well dispos'd persons" from the choir in his parish. He founded the group upon a set of rules and orders "the same in substance with those at London," except where their peculiar circumstances warranted modifications.[50] In many ways, the purposes and structure of his group followed very closely the designs set forth in Woodward's *Account of the Religious Societies,* which Samuel had obtained from the SPCK. He reported in a letter to the London-based Society that the intent of his circle of friends was "First to pray to God; secondly, to read the Holy Scriptures, and discourse upon religious matters for their mutual edification; and thirdly, to deliberate about the edification of our neighbour, and the promoting of it."

Following the generally accepted pattern, the members of the society at Epworth were not hasty to admit new members, especially those "of whose solid piety they [were] not yet sufficiently appris'd." To this end, and to prevent their "religious design" from falling of its own weight, the group was limited to twelve members. However, a procedure was adopted in case God should stir up more persons with a powerful desire for religious edification. A new society could be formed around two members who would separate themselves from the first society. This second group also would be limited to twelve members, with the provision that out of that society could grow another, following the same pattern.[51]

Within this organizational scheme set up at Epworth, the "first society" had priority in matters of policy. Thus any debate that arose regarding any question of "amending or reforming" the Church in point of "manners" or public morality was referred to the first society, while the others were to be content with "their own edification." While Samuel was careful to point out that the first group would "in no wise assume any prerogative to itself," if a member of the other societies came upon something that would tend to the public edification, he was obliged to bring the matter to the first society (or at least to some member of that group), "lest one society should hinder another, and because all are not fit to be counsellors." It appears also from the rector's comments that, with the above precedence in mind, the membership of this first society was to be quite select and only such "as are able to help the Church by their wisdom and good advices" would be admitted.

In his design for the Epworth Society, Samuel attempted to emulate rather closely the outward thrust of the SPCK within his country parish. Five of the fourteen rules of order that he wrote for the society dealt with the charitable activities that he hoped their subscriptions would support, including the following:

> Their first care is to set schools for the poor, wherein children (or if need be, adult persons) may be instructed in the fundamentals of Christianity by men of known and approv'd piety.
>
> Their second design is to procure little practical treatises from Holland, England, and Germany, &c. to translate them into the vulgar tongue, print them, and so to give or lend them to those who are less solicitous of their own and others edification.
>
> The third is to establish a correspondence with such Societies in England, Germany, &c. that so they may mutually edify one another.
>
> The fourth is to take care of the sick and other poor, and to afford them spiritual as well as corporal helps.

To what extent these rather ambitious goals were realized in the Epworth Society is difficult to assess on the basis of available records. The vision of such possibilities, nevertheless, even within the rather remote setting of the Isle of Axholme, was a part of the Wesley family heritage. Samuel was by no means a stranger to the publishing world himself, and his own personal correspondence included many of the ecclesiastical and political leaders in England. Whether or not this personal participation in the scholarly and literary pursuits of his day, exemplified in part by his association with the Athenian Society in London, was effectually transferred to the group at Epworth, Samuel's inclination to attempt these pursuits with his society no doubt had some bearing on the direction his sons would take three decades later at Oxford.

The design of the religious societies of the early eighteenth century "to promote real holiness of heart and life" was characterized by a High Church piety that depended upon an intense study of Scripture and other works of practical divinity, that demanded personal moral discipline, and that expressed itself in charitable acts toward the disadvantaged elements of society. The practice of the societies to meet regularly to encourage each other in "practical holiness" was part of a larger design to retreat from the snares of "the world." In this respect there was more than a passing similarity with the purposes of the medieval monastic orders. As Samuel Wesley noted in his "Letter Concerning the Religious Societies,"

> I know few good men but lament that after the destruction of monasteries, there were not some Societies founded in their stead, but reformed from their errors, and reduced to the primitive standard. None who has but looked into our own church-history, can be ignorant how highly instrumental such bodies of men as these, were to the first planting and propagating Christianity amongst our forefathers. . . . A great part of the good effects of that way of life, may be attained without many of the inconveniences of it, by such Societies as we are now discoursing of.[52]

Such sentiments, combined with certain tendencies of the High Church party, were construed by some critics to indicate a dangerous element of Jacobitism among the supporters of the societies. The stipulation that new members be well-effected toward both Church and state did little to allay the suspicions of some.[53] On the other hand, such inclinations within the societies did not bother the Wesley brothers, who had a tendency to lean toward High Church Jacobitism anyway.

Oxford University in the early eighteenth century reflected many of the problems that characterized English society as a whole. While one contemporary observer felt that Oxford was a "seat of good manners, as well as of learning (the people being 'more civilized than the inhabitants of any other town in Great Britain'),"[54] it must be said that the spiritual and academic endeavors of the university were at a low point in the history of the school.[55] The problems that beset England in general thus confronted John Wesley at Oxford, both in his relationships within the university and in the conditions of the city and surrounding area. When in 1725 the direction of his life began to change toward a more vital expression of practical piety, he began a spiritual and intellectual pilgrimage that led him within the ensuing decade through the pages of hundreds of books, into dozens of country parishes and city prisons, across the paths of a multitude of new acquaintances, and even to the shores of the New World. Wesley found himself not only pursuing the goals expressed by the religious societies in their search for "real holiness" but also adopting some of their methods. In this venture he was perhaps led (if not encouraged) by the earlier experience of his father. Wesley's search during this period for a meaningful understanding of the demands of Christian living led him to tie together the perfectionism of the Pietists, the moralism of the Puritans, and the devotionalism of the Mystics in a pragmatic approach that he felt could operate within the structure and doctrine of the Church of England. The manner in which Wesley and his company of friends at Oxford proceeded in this search and the methods they developed through the years helped determine in some ways the later shape of the Wesleyan movement. This story of the Oxford Methodists is aptly referred to, by Wesley himself, as "the first rise of Methodism."[56]

Chapter 3

The Search for the "Real" John Wesley[1]

"His history, if well written," concludes the writer of Wesley's lengthy obituary in the *Gentleman's Magazine*, "will certainly be important, for in every respect, as the founder of the most numerous sect in the kingdom, as a man, and as a writer, he must be considered as one of the most extraordinary characters this or any age ever produced."[2] This piece of effusive eloquence is perhaps only slightly exaggerated. John Wesley has come to be known as one of the major figures of the eighteenth century, his impact being felt both in Great Britain and in America. He played a major role as one of the leaders of the evangelical revival that swept much of the Protestant world in his day. His literary production was prolific, and writings such as his *Journal* are still seen as models of eighteenth-century style.[3]

But Wesley's importance goes beyond the realm of literature and religion. Concerned with such issues as education, prison conditions, and poverty, he played an important role in the development of early social reforms in an increasingly industrialized society. Trained at Christ Church, Oxford, he was intrigued by the current trends of science and medicine, and he published many popular treatises on diverse subjects ranging from experiments in electricity to home remedies for the gout. He produced a flood of pamphlets on a wide assortment of topics ranging from linguistics to music. As a recognized leader among the people, he entered into the political swirl surrounding the revolutionary movements of his day, offering his services to the king to raise a regiment of troops to fight the French, and giving his advice to the colonial secretary on the explosive matter of the American revolt.[4]

Wesley sensed the spirit of the English people perhaps as well as any person in his day. The true nature of his own mind and spirit, however, appears somewhat more elusive. His own breast felt the heartbeat of a staunchly loyal Tory; yet he could feel well the pulse of a nation that stirred with the rumblings of revolution. He was able to remain an Anglican clergyman to his dying breath and at the same time harness the energies of revival into a new form that was to become a major force in Protestant Christianity, namely, Methodism.

From the very beginning of his public activities, Wesley was a controversial figure. Persons of differing religious and political persuasions did not hesitate to attack him in print as well as in person. His fledgling movement was already being decried in the newspapers in 1732, and his character was publicly slandered and attacked in court as early as 1737.[5] Through all the controversies he was not without supporters; every spirited attack elicited a zealous defense that tended to bolster the developing Wesley legend. At his death, friend and foe alike rushed to produce biographical portraits of the Wesley they knew.[6] From the beginning, the descriptions of Wesley presented to the public have caused no small amount of confusion, as well as controversy, as successive generations have tried to sift through the various accounts of this complex and rather elusive man, looking for the "real" John Wesley.

The problems confronting persons looking for the "real" John Wesley are typified in the attempt to find an "accurate" pictorial representation of the man. Dismissing for the moment the problems faced by nineteenth- and twentieth-century artists who tried to depict Wesley long after his death, we would expect to find some standard, recognizable visage among the eighteenth-century portraits of Wesley. The wide variety of images that confront us, even among portraits done by the best artists of the day (many of whom were looking directly at the man as they painted), is confusing and serves to symbolize and illustrate the larger problem of trying to catch the essence of his life and thought. There is no consensus in either case, visual or interpretive, and the variety of representations can be disconcerting.

In the search for the elusive John Wesley, the question of physical appearance is more than just the passing fancy of an antiquarian historian. It is, among other things, one indication of the limits of factual information that might be retrieved from a given period. For example, we might ask the simple question, What color was Wesley's hair when he was a young man? One eyewitness, who lived under the same roof with him in Georgia in 1737, referred to his "Adonis locks of *auburn* hair which he took infinite pains to have in the most exact order."[7] Just a few years later (1744) another eyewitness, describing Wesley's appearance in the pulpit of St. Mary's, Oxford, mentioned in particular his "*black* hair quite smooth, parted very exactly."[8] The contradiction of these two literary descriptions is further confused by a third impression, portrayed on canvas by John Williams at about the same time (1741). The painting does exhibit the neatness of Wesley's hair, as mentioned by the other observers, but shows the color to be black in general, with a brownish tint where the light reflects off the curls and waves.[9] On the basis of the contemporary sources of evidence, we are left with no definitive answer to the question.

The problem of hair color is difficult in one sense because few descriptions (literary or graphic) were drawn up of Wesley as a young man. The portraits proliferate as he grew older and more famous. The problem of hair color disappears, since his hair turned gray and then white. But another, even more surprising problem arises. Among the dozens of paintings, drawings, busts, and other representations, there is little or no consensus as to Wesley's facial features. The most one can say is that he apparently had a rather prominent, pointed nose. This, combined with the usual portrayal of his hair as long with curls on the end, and the almost universal presence of Geneva bands around his neck, gives a note of uniformity and recognition to a vast array of portraits that otherwise do not much resemble one another. In some cases, on these grounds alone, portraits have occasionally been identified as "possibly" representing John Wesley, even though the general impression would otherwise cause the viewer to be skeptical.[10] The problem was somewhat upsetting to some nineteenth-century British Methodists who, in the face of such confusing evidence, commissioned an artist to create a "standard" portrait of Wesley in the 1820s, a generation after his death. The resulting "synthetic" portrait was conceded by most to be notably unconvincing as a replica of Wesley's visage and was unable to garner lasting support as a standard portrait.[11]

Our inability to specify with any assurance the color of Wesley's hair or the exact nature of his visage is, perhaps, a minor point. Nevertheless, it does suggest the sense of caution with which we should approach our attempt to discover the "facts" on other, perhaps more significant questions, even when we are using firsthand, eyewitness accounts (*about*, or even *by*, Wesley). A simple illustration can be seen in the question of Wesley's name.[12] Contemporary evidence, usually very illuminating and valuable, can also at times be skimpy, inaccurate, misleading, contradictory, and confusing. Although often the best source of information, primary source material must be used critically and carefully.

In trying to sort through the contemporary accounts of Wesley's activities, character, and significance, one must do more than merely differentiate those views that attack him from those that defend him. In some cases, the most virulent attack or vicious satire may, in fact, be built upon some grain of truth that might be overlooked in a more favorable description of the man. Most biographers have either disregarded Wesley's detractors as a source of information or have seen their attacks as simply spurious fabrications, and have been willing to rely almost entirely on the defenders of Wesley for their view of the situation.[13] But what judge would ever assume that the defense, no matter how pious, was by nature or necessity the only reliable source of believable or factual information?

To make the matter more complicated, both Wesley's enemies and friends were attracted to him not only by who or what he *actually* was (if that could in fact ever be known for sure), but by what they (and he) *thought* he was. Observations of contemporaries can, of course, be analyzed on the basis of their known prejudices and purposes. But these same guidelines must also be applied to Wesley's own descriptions of himself; his autobiographical comments need always to be tested against other available evidence.

In some cases, Wesley makes statements that either can be easily misinterpreted or simply exhibit a bad memory. For instance, he mentions in his *Journal* that in 1771 he visited South Leigh, adding that "here it was that I preached my first sermon, six and forty years ago." Based on this reference, biographers have assumed that Wesley must have preached there the first Sunday after his ordination in 1725. A brass plaque on the pulpit of that church still proclaims this to be the case. However, Wesley's own handwritten copy of his first sermon (with his note on the cover, "The first sermon I ever wrote") tells another story. It lists on the back the places and occasions of preaching, with South Leigh listed as the ninth occasion, in 1727. This does in a sense confirm that Wesley "preached his first sermon" in South Leigh, but it was not his first occasion for preaching, nor his first preaching of that first sermon![14]

Biographers have often repeated many such inaccuracies and half-truths and have magnified many of the legends that sprang up in Wesley's own day; then they have often recast all these to fit their own purposes. Many an account of Wesley is but an editorial gloss on the man, an attempt on the part of an author to prove some point about either Wesley's thought or, more likely and less obviously, the author's own. By careful selection and editing, an author can make Wesley appear in a number of guises. Our task is to recognize as many of the guises as possible, then to ferret out the disguises in which he has been placed, and thereby to discover as accurately as possible the full range of thought and activity that characterize this remarkable man.

One of our primary tasks, then, in trying to discover the elusive John Wesley is to recognize that *all* the information that comes to us must be examined critically, no matter whether it was written by Wesley himself, recounted by an eyewitness (friendly or otherwise), or compiled years after the events. No single type of source, in and of itself, is necessarily a sufficient resource for our quest. Firsthand accounts are in many ways, of course, the best, but are not without problems of bias and shortsightedness in that they are in some cases too close to the events they describe. Secondary accounts, while suffering from the problems of historical distance, might at the same time benefit from the more inclusive objectivity that such hindsight makes possible. Taken as a whole, these materials provide a vast amount of information that must be sifted carefully by the observer with an eye toward discovering a full and accurate basis upon which to develop a credible and edifying picture of the man and his times.[15]

Having recognized the problems of personal bias in the sources we are using, we must also then realize that the same problem will exist in the mind of the person examining the materials. We all come at historical data with certain prejudices, sometimes anticipating the results of our investigation, while at other times actually molding the material to fit our own preconceptions. Recognizing these tendencies, and consciously resisting the temptation to impose our own biases onto the historical material, we must realize that the result of our quest might not be what we expect or even desire. Especially when looking at primary documents for the first time, we must expect surprises. Such expectations of the unexpected make the historical enterprise both exciting and rewarding.

Considerations in the Quest for Historical Accuracy

The success of any exploratory journey depends not only on the selection of a potentially fruitful direction of enquiry but also on careful preparation. Wesley's recognized significance as a historical figure and the wide variety of sources available for our study almost guarantee the value of our venture for the person interested in discovering John Wesley. But the confusing variety of images of Wesley portrayed in his own day as well as over the past two centuries gives us some pause as we start on this journey. Part of our preparation must include the anticipation of problems that will confront us in our quest of the elusive John Wesley.

There are several reasons why Wesley was and is a rather elusive figure, as a person, as a leader, as a writer. Some of these are normal considerations that confront almost any attempt to reconstruct the life and thought of a historic person. Other situations are more particular to Wesley's own situation. In every case, a recognition of these considerations will make the search for an accurate and full basis for the portrayal of Wesley, though perhaps no easier, more fruitful.

(1) *Wesley was a legend in his own day*. He had a heroic public image based on a life-style that approached epic proportions. The traditional rehearsal of the statistics of his life speaks for itself: 250,000 miles traveled on horseback, over 40,000 sermons preached during a span of sixty-six years, more than 400 publications on nearly every conceivable topic, all of these activities continuing almost to his dying day in his eighty-eighth year.[16] These are the marks of a man certain to appear larger than life-size, in spite of his small physical stature (five feet three inches, 122 pounds).[17] Never mind that some of those miles in later life were actually covered in a finely appointed chaise or that many of those publications were extracts from other authors or quite brief tracts. These statistics still represent a monumental production for one lifetime, and many of the people of his day, though perhaps not familiar with the precise statistics, were aware of Wesley's reputation as a notoriously busy, seemingly tireless person who was always on the move.[18]

To say that Wesley's reputation may have outstripped his "real" capabilities (an element of any legendary status) is not to say that we must disregard or throw aside any resource that tends toward hyperbole. What people (as well as Wesley) believed to be true about him is an important consideration in his own autobiographical development, in the flow of historical events around him, and in our attempt to understand the whole story. One of the most ticklish tasks that confronts the historian in reconstructing the past is to sort through various perceptions of reality as expressed by contemporary participants and observers, for each of whom, we should remember, reality was based upon whatever they believed to be true.

Wesley himself seems to have adopted a self-perception that was based upon, or at least contributed to, a heroic image. His writings often contain autobiographical recollections that reflect a somewhat magnified, or perhaps idealized, view of his character or personality. This tendency resulted in part from the necessity of defending himself in the forum of public opinion. Part of his apologetic method was quite naturally to put forth his best side whenever possible, even if his editorial management of the truth might result in some distortion of the historical facts.[19]

In spite of his good intentions, Wesley's accounts of himself are occasionally marked by discrepancies and contradictions that at times tend to inflate his good image. A simple example occurs in Wesley's sermon, "Redeeming the Time," in which he promotes the virtues of rising early in the morning. He cites his own experience at Oxford as an example of one practical way to discover just how much (or little) sleep a person needs each night. His solution to the problem of spending more time in bed than was necessary (indicated in part by persistent insomnia) was to procure an alarm that woke him an hour earlier each morning for four or five days until he settled on an hour of rising that suited both his physical and spiritual needs—4:00 a.m.[20] A good story to illustrate a good point. As for the historical facts of the matter, Wesley had recorded in his diary the process of working back toward the 4:00 a.m. rising time as a gradual development that took place over several months. In the sermon illustration, he simply telescoped several months into four days, making a much better story, but at the same time giving a picture of himself that is perhaps more remarkable than the facts warrant.[21] The main point being made in the sermon is no less true, but the illustrative story should not be taken either as a historical episode in its details or as an accurate indication of Wesley's capacity for effecting instant solutions. That the people (and perhaps even Wesley himself) came to believe these stories to be accurate representations of his character is, however, a fact that must be considered in our attempt to recover the perceptions of the eighteenth century.

Wesley's heroic image was built in part upon his own inclination toward seeing himself as a martyr. This self-impression is not often explicit in his own writings. He did, however, frequently express the opinion that persecution was a necessary mark of a true Christian, and his *Journal* is in one sense a lengthy rehearsal of events that display in great detail the confirmation of that truth in his own life.

The underlying tone of these accounts is perhaps as revealing as the actual content. For example, his narrative of the riots at Wednesbury concludes with a comment that indicates Wesley was not at all ruffled by the violent physical struggles that had just occurred. He then goes on to analyze the various ways in which God's providence might be perceived as evident in those events. His brother's journal for that period records an even more telling reflection; there Charles indicates that his brother John understood how the early Christian martyrs could stand in the persecutors' flames and not feel any pain. Wesley's self-perceptions of this sort could not help finding their way into the consciousness of the public, and the biblical allusions and martyr-like experiences were certainly not lost on them.[22]

(2) *Wesley's public image can be distinguished from his private image.* This rather commonplace observation could be made about almost any famous person and is mentioned here simply because it is often overlooked in many studies of Wesley. His own writings display this point rather nicely. The "public" documents, such as his sermons and journal, at times give quite a different picture from that contained in his "private" documents, such as his letters and diaries. To say this is not to imply any devious intent on Wesley's part. Rather, the distinction between the two images is based upon the difference in design and intent of these two types of material. Sermons designed for the propagation of practical divinity, whether preached or published, have quite different perimeters of self-revelation from letters written to one's brother in the depths of despair.[23] To read each with an eye toward discerning the "actual" situation being described, we must have an analytical sensitivity to the circumstances out of which the writing was generated. Such is also the case when we look at the writings of contemporary observers who claim to be able to describe the private, as distinguished from the public, image of a person.[24]

Wesley's public image, nearly legendary in scope and proportion, certainly fed the tendency toward hero worship on the part of many of his followers. But at the same time, the exaggerated picture of piety and perfection inherent in such a perception of the man served to fuel the antagonism expressed by many of his detractors. Many critics inflamed the imagination of the public by contrasting this public, almost unreal image, with a demonic portrait of the "real" nature and intentions of the private person that lurked behind that public image.[25] These attacks, often dismissed by Wesleyan adherents as the work of twisted minds, we should not simply discard out of hand without first recognizing that the sale and popularity of such writings, scurrilous as they may seem, depended upon their having a degree of credibility in the public eye. Just as there was a public image of Wesley that approached sainthood and was undergirded by a repertoire of appropriate anecdotes, there was also a public view of him that resembled a dangerous, ranting enthusiast and resulted in people believing the vilest of epithets. Both were flawed interpretations, yet both gained that degree of credibility because they contained a kernel of truth. The task of the careful historian is to try to discern just what the kernel of truth might be in specific instances that would allow seemingly obvious scurrility (or exaggerated virtue) to pass for a believable representation.

One might note in passing that many of the persons who were quite ready to attack Wesley in the public eye and do almost anything in their power to bring ridicule upon him and his movement found it difficult if not impossible to attack him privately as a person. This may, in part, reflect Wesley's own method of disputation, focusing on principles rather than personalities, but also may demonstrate a recognition of Wesley's personal integrity even by most of his enemies.[26] This tendency to distinguish between the private and the public Mr. Wesley, for better or worse, is only one part of the larger picture of his controversial involvements, which have even wider repercussions in the attempt to discover the elusive John Wesley.

(3) *Wesley was a controversial figure.* This consideration, like the last two points, is by no means a new observation on the life of John Wesley. But likewise, it carries with it certain implications that are often overlooked by persons trying to recapture an accurate picture of the man.

Wesley faced opposition from many quarters on a variety of issues. From the very beginning, the attacks came from both inside and outside the movement. The Oxford Methodists were not "of one mind," in spite of Wesley's oft-repeated comment to that effect; his own diary shows that some members who were "piqued" at him bolted from his group and even, in one case, wrote a theme "against the Methodists."[27] As the movement grew and developed, some of Wesley's preachers challenged his ideas and leadership, especially in the 1750s and 1760s. His brother Charles often disagreed with him on important matters of policy and procedure.[28] The continuing reaction to many of Wesley's controversial actions and ideas during his lifetime set the stage for many of the disputes within the movement after his death.

The external attacks came from several directions, including opposite ends of the theological, political, and social spectra. Wesley was portrayed by different opponents in a mind-boggling variety of garbs; he was seen as a Quaker by some, a Papist by others, a ranting enthusiast by many, and an upper-crust snob by others.[29] To discover the real Wesley simply on the basis of these attacks is of course impossible, even though they might unwittingly tell us something useful about the public's perception of him, as we have seen.

The writings generated by these controversies, however, should not be overlooked as a valuable source of information in our quest. Although they present a confusing picture in many ways, a careful look at this material will tell us quite a bit about the inner character of Wesley's life and thought, and particularly about his intellectual methodology. The writings include not only the attacks by Wesley's opponents and the defense by Wesley, but also the observations of many third parties, some quite obviously friendly to Wesley's cause but others less certain about their affiliation. The problem facing us is not to decide who is friend or foe, or to figure out who is right or wrong. Rather, we must decide what the attacks and the friendly defenses can tell us about Wesley, and what we can discern about Wesley from his writings in his own defense.

Wesley's own writings have caused the most problems for some recent authors who have been quick to point out that his controversial works (which represent a significant proportion) do not seem to maintain or develop any sort of consistent or systematic treatment of the major themes in Christian doctrine.[30] It is difficult at best for a person to find anything approaching a well-developed system of thought, easily defined as "Wesleyan," in the whole of his works. Therefore many conclude that Wesley was not a major thinker of any significance. In the writings that arise from his many controversies, Wesley does appear from time to time to have made statements that even seem to be quite contradictory, in tone or emphasis at least, if not in substance. Some scholars, therefore, treat Wesley as a self-contradicting, confusing intellectual "lightweight" and dismiss him with comments such as that of Ronald Knox, who said that Wesley "is not a good advertisement for reading on horse-back."[31]

We should not be too quick, however, to pass judgment on Wesley based only on someone's evaluation of the "rightness" or "wrongness" of his positions or the consistency or inconsistency of his writings. Wesley was neither a "Mr. Facing-bothways" in the Bunyan tradition nor an indifferent (much less superficial) theologian. At the same time, he had not the luxury of time nor the inclination of mind to spend time in his study developing a thoroughly consistent theological system. He faced issues as they arose, in the midst of an active ministry to the poor. His theology was hammered out on the anvil of controversy. He was, you might say, a man fighting in the trenches, waging his battle for truth (as he saw it) with the enemy wherever it raised its head, countering attacks from left and right as they came. In that context, he often found it necessary to change his stance to face an opponent more effectively, not unlike a swordsman changing his direction and shifting his footing while holding his ground. When defending himself against the left, he appears to be coming from the right; when facing right, he seems to be defending the left. This is an important consideration when we are trying to discover a basic "Wesleyan" theological position; and, when we look at Wesley's controversial writings in this light, we are likely to discover that he was more consistent than many persons have acknowledged. In fact, he was in most cases trying to hold a middle ground, a stance that is characteristic of his theological method.[32]

(4) *Wesley embodied ideals and qualities not always easily held together or reconciled.* Part of the enigma of Wesley is characterized by the frequent portrayal of him in such guises as a "radical conservative," a "romantic realist," or a "quiet revolutionary."[33] While these designations seem to be inherently inconsistent, they do speak to the tension and balance that is a basic element of Wesley's life and thought.

Wesley was an educated upper-class Oxford don who spent most of his life working among the poor and disadvantaged. This paradoxical life-style left its mark on the character of many of his activities. He was a champion of the poor, yet a defender of the political establishment that had caused many of their problems. He was a master of expression in several languages, yet strove to express "plain truth for plain people."[34] In his outlook and activities, he attempted to unite, in his brother Charles's words, "the pair so long disjoined, knowledge and vital piety."[35] He combined in his ministry the preaching of the revivalist and the concerns of the social worker. His religious perspective was at the same time evangelical and sacramental. If we fail to keep in mind this tendency to hold seeming opposites together in unity (though not without some internal tension), we will miss one of the significant keys to understanding his life and thought.

The eclectic methodology that underlies much of Wesley's work, both as a controversial writer and as a mediating theologian in the Anglican tradition, entails the holding together of ideas or emphases that appear to come from opposing sides of the religious spectrum. In a given controversy, Wesley at times found himself having to defend or emphasize one side of such a tandem set, often at the apparent expense of the other side. This combination of eclectic and polemical methodologies on Wesley's part has often confused many observers (past and present), especially if they have not seen a particular selection from his writings, containing only one side of Wesley's view, in the larger context of the whole of his life and writings. So we can find, for example, quotations from Wesley that appear to sound a note of advanced liberalism and to play down the importance of theological differences among professed Christians (e.g., "if your heart is as my heart, give me your hand"), and yet in close proximity we find a call for firmness on fundamental doctrines.[36] If one side of this balance is lost, or one side is overemphasized, the wholeness of the basic Wesleyan position is destroyed (even though Wesley can be cited to support either side in an argument). All this is to say that, in trying to recapture the whole John Wesley, we should look at the context in which his writings were produced. We should pay attention to the nature of controversies that gave rise to certain writings as well as remember that his writings can be best understood when viewed in the light of both the variety of sources that provide the tapestry upon which his developing thought was woven, and the rather massive body of his own works, written over a long lifetime. This observation leads us to a final consideration.

(5) *Wesley's life and thought are marked by growth and change.* The story is told of a professor who once lectured on Wesley to a group of inquisitive youngsters. At the conclusion of his presentation, one of the questions from his young audience was, "How old was Wesley?" The professor thought for a moment before replying, "Well, you see, he was different ages at different times." A silly comment, perhaps, but it points to a truism that is frequently overlooked—Wesley grew and changed and developed.[37] We like to define Wesley's life and thought in categorical and simplistic statements that overlook the obvious fact that Wesley was at one time young, that he matured, that he grew old. His life spanned nearly the whole of the eighteenth century. It is quite natural that he developed and changed in many ways (as did the environment around him). His activities, his outlooks, his habits, his thoughts do certainly exhibit some continuity throughout his life; but historians and biographers have had a tendency to see more continuity than is warranted in some areas while overlooking it in others. Wesley's sermons, especially the forty-four "standard" ones, are often treated as a unified body of doctrine, as though they can somehow define the whole of his thought from beginning to end. They are treated, moreover, as though they can stand apart from any historical context or any other sermons he may have written earlier or later. The underlying assumption seems to be that he had all his worthwhile thoughts between the ages of thirty-five and sixty, and that everything before and after was either consistent with those views or otherwise inconsequential. We must be careful to recognize that Wesley developed many of his lifelong habits and ideas as a young man, and also that many of his finest and most mature reflections are exhibited in his writings from the three decades of his life after age sixty.

The problem of analyzing Wesley's development is not simply confined to distinguishing areas of change that are often overlooked.

Another tendency to be guarded against is that of seeing changes themselves as being more pervasive and definitive than they might in fact have been. In the most radical of changes there are usually significant threads of continuity. In Wesley's case, the traditional division of his life into two time periods—before and after "Aldersgate"—distorts the picture of his spiritual development and in some ways clouds the actual significance of that crucial event in his life. There has been a tendency in some circles to view the early Wesley as being less than fully Christian and not worth studying, while assuming that the transformation of his evangelical experience of 1738 resulted in a totally new person who was thenceforth consistently persuasive and successful in both his proclamation and experience of the gospel (and therefore more important and worthy of study, if not emulation).[38]

We must recognize, then, that there is more *continuity* between the young Wesley and the mature Wesley than is generally recognized. At the same time we must realize that there is also more *difference* between the mature Wesley and the elderly Wesley than has usually been noticed.[39] The early Wesley, often portrayed as "unenlightened" and "unconverted," exhibits a mind and spirit that provided the foundation and framework for many of his later thoughts and activities. A simple indication of this is the fact that many of the works quoted in his later sermons come from his reading list as a student and tutor at Oxford. On the other hand, some of Wesley's best reflective writing came after his sixtieth birthday, after the last of the "standard" sermons had been written. When he finally published a collected edition of his works in the 1770s, he incorporated nine of these later sermons into the earlier group (bringing the total to fifty-three). Some of these new sermons modified or extended the ideas expressed in the earlier writings. A decade later, he produced yet another edition of his sermons, more than doubling the number of his published sermons by including dozens written after his seventy-fifth birthday. These and other writings from Wesley's later years deserve more attention than they usually receive.[40]

One pitfall that must be avoided in the attempt to discern the nature and character of Wesley's development is, again, the temptation to generalize on the basis of Wesley's own comments, taken out of context. He does occasionally express a view of his own growth and development that he himself later challenges. This is most noticeable in his *Journal* comments regarding the state of his soul in the 1730s. These comments were first published in the 1740s, and then later qualified in the 1770s. We must assume that what he believed about himself at any given time is true for him at that time. Later reflections upon his earlier conditions must be accepted for what they are, an indication of his self-awareness at a later time. That is to say, neither one is "right" or "wrong" absolutely, but simply must be understood in the historical context of his own developing self-consciousness. Thus in 1725, he thought he was a Christian; for a while after 1738, he thought he had not truly been a Christian in 1725; by the 1770s, he was willing to admit that perhaps his middle views were wrong, and that he could understand himself as having been in some real sense a Christian in 1725.[41]

Each of these five considerations listed above, then, emphasizes the necessity to view Wesley in the light of the whole of his life and thought. The private man must be considered along with the public; his defense must be placed alongside the attack; his apparent leanings in any given direction must be measured against his penchant for a mediating balance; his views from any given period must stand the test of his own changing mind. We must look for the elusive John Wesley in the context of the many events and controversies that shaped his mind and spirit from beginning to end. And we must look at the sources with a critical eye, noting whether they are early or late, friendly or antagonistic, public or private, exaggerated or simplistic, firsthand or secondary accounts. As a result of this approach, the object of our quest, John Wesley, though still elusive, will in the end be more understandable and believable as a human being.

Twice-Told Tales: Two Centuries of Wesley Studies

Many biographies of Wesley are still repeating favorite, time-worn images of the man that are as inadequate (if not inaccurate) today as they were two hundred years ago. A handful of stock answers have developed over the years to respond to a short list of standard questions that seem to fascinate most authors who join the attempt to portray Wesley for their generation. The questions are usually phrased something like this:

Was Wesley's Aldersgate experience a "conversion"?

Did his influence prevent a revolution in eighteenth-century England?

Did a mother-fixation cause problems in his developing relationships with other women?

Did he intend to start a new denomination?

Was he fascinated more by organizational schemes than theological consistency?

These questions cry for a yes or no answer, and traditional arguments abound to support both sides. If the truth were known, in most cases *both* answers would likely be possible, and *neither* by itself would be fully appropriate.

Part of the problem is that in many cases the wrong questions are being asked, and therefore the answers often do not focus on the most significant issues. It has been said that historians have an uncanny penchant for answering questions that nobody is asking. Many Wesley biographies demonstrate a slight variant of this tendency, answering questions that are being asked, to be sure, but that are off the mark or poorly phrased. As an example, the first question above (about Aldersgate) certainly can be answered yes if one is to believe Wesley's own testimony in the weeks and months immediately following the event. It can also be answered no if one is to believe Wesley's own later alteration of his earlier opinion. A question that would serve us better in trying to understand the significance of this event in Wesley's life would be, What part did Wesley's Aldersgate experience play in his own developing self-perception (at the time and later) and in his lifelong theological and spiritual development?[42] Asking the question this way begins to point us toward areas of investigation that demand no less interpretation but are less prone to invite an immediate division into polemical parties or opposing sides, which in the end would have only limited usefulness in moving us toward a more adequate view of Wesley. It is of little value to continue to ask these same questions and then to pick one or another of the old (or even new) stereotypes that argue a poor answer to a bad question.

One reason that traditional questions about Wesley have been the focus of concern over the last two centuries is that most of the major studies of Wesley have been written by persons who would claim to be in the Wesleyan tradition (though not necessarily with a "Methodist" affiliation). Not that the followers of Wesley are somehow inherently incapable of producing good work—fortunately there are many good books and articles around that disprove such an assumption. There has been a tendency, however, for Wesleyans (including Methodists) of various persuasions to "use" Wesley to prove their own point of view or to substantiate the perspective of their own particular branch of the developing, increasingly fragmented heritage. Any one of several brands of "Wesleyanism" can be identified by its use of a predictable litany of certain answers to the time-worn list of standard questions.

A similar tendency toward interpretive categorization can be seen in writings that come out of other, transdenominational groupings. "Evangelicals" have portrayed a Wesley who looks much like a frontier revivalist; the "social gospel" folk like to see Wesley the philanthropist and social worker; the "holiness" faction stresses the centrality of his doctrine of sanctification; the "ecumenical" types emphasize his catholic spirit; the "fundamentalists" build upon a defined package of his essential doctrines—each of these, and others besides, editing Wesley carefully so as to fit into a mold that is, not surprisingly, identical to their own. Most of these interpretive positions tell us something important about Wesley but fall short of seeing the larger scope of his life and thought.

In the face of all this, many Methodists began to disregard Wesley some time ago, and most non-Methodists have seen little reason to change their long-standing tendency to ignore him. The hagiographical tinfoil that the hero cults put around Wesley's image certainly was not designed to attract serious scholars, and the variety of sectarian claims for a "true Wesleyan" position often discouraged nearly all but the partisans of one side or another. The interpretive writings of specialists provided help only within limited areas of interest.

Writings focused on Wesley by non-Methodists generally decreased in number over the years until very recently. The polemical attacks died out early in the nineteenth century, and subsequent less polemical works were more often than not politely ignored by the majority of readers (for the large part, Methodists) or even treated with a hint of disdain (to think that an "outsider" would presume to understand "their" man!). This trend began to change early in this century as the ecumenical movement began to gain momentum, and the interest in Wesley by non-Methodists has been sustained and promoted by the move toward more interdisciplinary studies in the last twenty years. Students and scholars in many fields are increasingly attracted to the richness and variety of motifs wrapped together in this one fascinating eighteenth-century person.[43]

Unfortunately, in the face of this renewed interest in Wesley's life and thought both from inside and outside the Methodist traditions, we stand in dire need of basic resources such as a fully adequate biographical study and a critical, annotated edition of his works.[44] While not a biography, and certainly short of definitive, *The Elusive Mr. Wesley*[45] is intended to introduce the reader to the problems of and procedures for discovering John Wesley—to introduce the novice to and remind the expert of the many possibilities as well as the pitfalls that await persons trying to understand John Wesley. Through looking at a variety of selections of writings by Wesley himself, by his contemporaries, and by successive generations of historians and biographers, the reader can see the origin of many of the time-worn stereotypes and legends, as well as the places where some revisions need to be made. And through it all, the reader will recognize and be reminded that Wesley is a fascinatingly complex and elusive (though not incomprehensible) eighteenth-century personality.

Chapter 4

THE QUEST OF THE FIRST METHODIST: OXFORD METHODISM RECONSIDERED[1]

Every account of origins is laden with its myths and legends. The story of Methodism is no exception. John Wesley himself is responsible for many of the familiar tales about the beginnings of his movement at Oxford in the late 1720s and early 1730s. The moral or didactic purpose of these anecdotes often led him either to oversimplify or to embellish the facts. Such is the case with his autobiographical recollection of having cured insomnia by setting his alarm an hour earlier every day for four consecutive days until he was rising regularly at 4:00 a.m.[2] He was making a point about "redeeming the time" and simply decided to heighten the impact of the story by telescoping into four days a development that actually occurred over a period of several months. Wesley also had a tendency, in his occasional reflections upon the first Methodists at Oxford, to portray the group with more uniformity of purpose and pattern than was the case. He pictured the young gentlemen, to a man, as being zealous adherents to the doctrine and discipline of the Church of England "to the minutest circumstance" throughout the Oxford period.[3] In fact, however, the Methodists increasingly exhibited a diversity of thought and action that eventually saw many of them discard their Wesleyan principles and even led some of them to leave the Church of England.

These examples from Wesley's own published recollections illustrate two tendencies—to exaggerate and to generalize—that were perpetuated by his early biographers. The resulting view of Oxford Methodism, in both form and substance, has been inadequate and confusing from the outset. To complicate matters further, nineteenth-century historians, eager to emphasize the evangelical roots of the Wesleyan movement, often portrayed Methodism as simply the organizational fruits of Wesley's "heart-warming" experience at Aldersgate Street in 1738. They had no qualms about dismissing the previous decade as a period in which John Wesley and his friends had a very imperfect view of "true" Christianity.[4] They also re-told the old stories and repeated the generalizations but with a view toward portraying the Oxford Methodists as stiff, High Church Ritualists, an important part of their effort to enhance the spiritual brilliance of later stages of the Wesleyan movement.

This approach to early Methodist history has generally prevailed and, combined with a lack of readily accessible information about that period, has resulted in an unfortunate neglect of critical study of what Wesley himself called "the first rise of Methodism" at Oxford. The perpetuation of old stereotypes, assisted by vivid flights of the imagination, has led to the persistent acceptance of some striking though misleading portrayals of the famous Fellow of Lincoln College and his friends, even in our own day. This is the stuff of which many a flourish of the pen and brush is made. Nehemiah Curnock presents a vivid description of the newly ordained Wesley winding his way through the Oxfordshire lanes in 1725 to preach his first sermon amidst the fresco-covered walls of the parish church in South Leigh—a moving scene, but entirely imaginary.[5] In similar fashion, John S. Simon gives us a lively picture of William Law scurrying about Oxford seeking to ferret out information concerning Wesley and his friends in order to write an account of the Methodists.[6] These are only two among many conjectural tales that combine to give a distorted view not only of the events surrounding the early development of Wesley's thinking but also of the growth of Oxford Methodism.

Perhaps the portrait that has done the most to fix the image of the Oxford Methodists in the minds of later generations is the rather fanciful painting by Marshall Claxton of "The Rev. John Wesley and his Friends at Oxford," often reproduced with the simple title, "The Holy Club," and accompanied by the note, "The room is the one in which the meetings were held."[7] This picture is typical of many of the verbal as well as visual misrepresentations of Oxford Methodism—the portrait is not only inaccurate in many of its details but also misleading in its overall characterization of the movement. The artist, like many historians, has shown most of the better-known early Methodists meeting together in Wesley's room to hear their leader expound upon the Scriptures or some book of devotion.

Several misconceptions are evident in this portrayal however. The persons in the picture were never actually together at Oxford at any one time. Contrary to what the picture suggests, they rarely ever met in groups larger than half a dozen in number and did not meet consistently in any one room. They expended more energy in acts of social concern throughout the city than in acts of corporate devotion within the walls of the university. When Wesley's friends did gather together, they did not simply listen to their spiritual tutor but also shared ideas and experiences in a mutual nurturing of Christian growth. These activities gave Oxford Methodism a characteristic shape that was more than simply the lengthened shadow of one man.

However, the general impression which this picture engraves upon the mind, namely, that the Methodists at Oxford were a *club*, is most unfortunate. As early as 1731 Samuel Wesley, Jr., noted with distaste that his brothers' small group, which numbered five or six, was at that time being called in derision the "Godly Club" or the "Holy Club." "I don't like your being called a club," he wrote to John, "that name is really calculated to do mischief."[8] John himself continually resisted the temptation to establish a firm set of rules that would bind his friends and followers—or himself, for that matter, for his own vision of the Christian life was still growing. Consequently the movement experienced flexible and dynamic development through the months and years at Oxford. Several groups began meeting throughout the university and city, more or less following the Wesleyan scheme of holy living (without necessarily being personally led by John Wesley himself). As we shall see, one could be a Methodist without being a member of John Wesley's own personal study-devotion-action group. If the term "club" ever did apply to Wesley's movement, it certainly was no longer appropriate after 1732.

Wesley's own writings indicate that he did not attach particular importance to any single name for his cluster of friends. He used several different terms to designate his group of associates at Oxford. He was not unalterably opposed to using the term "society" in relation to his group, as several references to "our little Society" indicate. His reluctance to cling to such titles, however, arose in part out of his high respect for the religious societies of his day,[9] as well as an apparent avoidance of titles that might have indicated some sort of closed organization with membership requirements. In 1731 the term Holy Club might have been applicable, but a study of the developments within the Wesleyan movement indicates that at least as early as the autumn of 1732 a plural designation such as Oxford Methodists may have been more appropriate. To understand why, let us look closer at both the rise of Methodism during this period and the nature of the movement as it developed.

Diaries and Methodists

The key to a more accurate and careful appraisal of Oxford Methodism has been provided, perhaps unwittingly, by Wesley himself. In his personal diaries, meticulously written in a unique combination of cipher, shorthand, abbreviation, and symbol, Wesley gives an almost hourly account of his life during the crucial decade from his ordination (1725) to his embarkation for Georgia (1735). These documents, intended primarily as a private means of spiritual pulse-taking, have never been fully transcribed or published. For years they were in private hands and physically beyond the reach of most scholars. Luke Tyerman, the most prolific nineteenth-century biographer of Wesley, noted with dismay in 1873 that these materials were not available: "Where are those manuscripts and why are they not given to the public?"[10] Thirty-five years later, Nehemiah Curnock took the first steps necessary to bring those documents before the world, photographing the manuscripts held by the Colman family and beginning the difficult process of deciphering some of the diaries. He included a summary of the first diary (1725–27), along with selected transcriptions, in his introduction to the "Standard Edition" of Wesley's *Journal* published in 1909. As for the other four volumes of Oxford diaries, Curnock remarked, "Those who would ransack the archives of the dead and refuse sanctuary to their most confidential self-communings would print the diaries as they now stand." Perhaps this sentiment arose in part from his own frustration at being unable to see clearly through the increasingly more complicated systems of abbreviation and cipher in these later diaries, as he noted, "Fortunately they are in unknown tongues, and few would care to devote months to the task of decipherment."[11]

Those who have attempted the task, such as Richard Green, V. H. H. Green, and Wesley Swift (late archivist of the Methodist Archives), proceeded little farther than Curnock in the mind-boggling complexities of these little notebooks. But in 1969 I had the good fortune to discover another small volume in the Methodist Archives—the diary of Benjamin Ingham, also an Oxford Methodist. This diary contains a key for the Wesleyan scheme of symbols and abbreviations, which has unlocked vast stores of coded information in the Wesley diaries. Moreover, it has opened a new window into the life of the Oxford Methodists, helping us to understand more fully the intricacies of the movement.[12]

The Wesley diaries add a wealth of detailed information about this crucial decade of 1725–35. But more importantly, they also allow for a re-drawing of the general shape of the movement. A new picture of Oxford Methodism begins to emerge from the hundreds of pages of diary notations. The movement no longer appears as a simple uniform phenomenon. Quite definite stages of development can be discerned. Certain changes of emphasis become evident in the life and thought of the Methodists. The organizational structure of the movement can be seen developing into an increasingly complex system of interlinking groups. And Wesley himself is shown to be bent and torn in several directions by various theological pressures and tensions that he attempts to resolve and adapt to his own developing method of living the Christian life.

The design of Oxford Methodism as it changed and grew during this period is quite naturally bound to the personal story of John Wesley. Wesley was, as John Gambold said, the chief manager of the Methodists, and although he had persuasive powers and "something of authority in his countenance." he nevertheless was always open to the ideas of others.[13] Consequently, many of the characteristic activities of the Methodists originated not with Wesley himself but with his friends. Not every Methodist participated in, or agreed with, all that John Wesley promoted. Wesley did not always appreciate certain aspects of his friends' daily routine. But as a whole, these persons had willingly associated themselves with others who were also seeking, in Wesley's words, "a right state of soul, a mind and spirit renewed after the image that created it."[14] The means used in striving for this goal were not in themselves the measure of who was a Methodist. The common bond was their search for this "one thing needful" and their consequent attempt to have a "single intention" in life—to please God by improving "in holiness, in the love of God and . . . neighbor."[15] To this end they were willing more or less to follow the "method" John Wesley was developing as a means of attaining that goal.

It must be remembered, however, that Wesley himself was also deeply engaged in the search for "a right state of soul." While he had settled upon the need for a basic theology of holy living in 1725, the following decade saw him trying to resolve the tensions and hammer out the practical implications of ideas he found in the Scriptures, the early fathers, the medieval and English pietists, the continental mystics, and the latitudinarians. Consequently his method was not a static, settled scheme but rather an approach to life that continued to develop and change. New friends brought different ideas; fresh challenges resulted in further insights. His acknowledged leadership within the movement came from his ability to fit various ideas and practices together with a sense of purpose that gave direction to the spiritual impulse behind the Methodists' search for salvation.

This present study of the rise of Methodism at Oxford, about which little has been written, focuses on the questions of origins—who? when? where? how? why? Using the diaries and letters of the time to give a more adequate view of the whole Wesleyan phenomenon at Oxford, this reconsideration of early Methodism will also furnish the backdrop for a fuller understanding of subsequent developments in the life and thought of John Wesley and his followers.

The Quest of the First Methodist

The search for the very beginnings of Methodism has been clouded by the confusion of early conflicting accounts, the repetition of inadequate stereotypes, and the zeal of some writers who have been inclined to overemphasize Charles Wesley's role in the foundation of the movement.[16] As early as 1765 John Wesley noticed, "It is not easy to reckon up the various accounts which have been given of the people called Methodists."[17] Wesley himself would seem to be the logical person to clear up any difficulties concerning the origins of the movement, but his own numerous references to the "young gentlemen at Oxford" merely set the pattern and provide the substance for later contradictory accounts. His first written account, in a letter of October, 1732, outlined for Richard Morgan, Sr., the beginnings of their activity three years earlier when "your son, my brother, myself, and one more agreed to spend three or four evenings in a week together."[18] This reference to the *four* young men who came together in 1729 provides the basis for most later allusions to the rise of Oxford Methodism.

But as early as 1742, variations begin to appear in Wesley's own recounting, and in succeeding years the number of "original"[19] Methodists mentioned in his recollections varies anywhere from four down to one. Half a century after the fact, Wesley referred more than once to the origins of Methodism simply in terms of his own spiritual autobiography, beginning in 1725. Having an "earnest desire" to live according to the rules found in the writings of Thomas à Kempis and Jeremy Taylor, Wesley "was constrained to travel alone, having no man either to guide or to help him" until 1729, when he "found one who had the same desire."[20] Or, as he wrote to a recalcitrant preacher shortly after speaking these last words, "It pleased God by me to awaken, first my brother, and then a few others; who severally desired me as a favour that I would direct them in all things."[21]

These different accounts of the beginnings of Oxford Methodism, like many of Wesley's references to other aspects of the movement, must be seen in the context of the various controversies within which he was writing and speaking.[22] He tended to prune and cull as he saw fit, not intending to alter the facts, but often overlooking accuracy of detail in favor of some larger purpose. Seldom does he include enough information in his published accounts to satisfy completely our historical curiosity. The unpublished diaries and other manuscript sources, however, do fill in many of the details and help us to paint a more accurate picture of Wesley and his movement.

The first observation that we can make on the basis of a close study of these contemporary documents is that while a *date of origin* might be the pedagogue's delight, and a list of "charter members" the archivist's dream, neither is immediately apparent in the detailed accounts of Wesley's daily life during this period. It is far too simplistic to say that Methodism began in November 1729 when John Wesley returned to reside in Oxford and took over the direction of the "Holy Club," just as it is stretching a point to call Charles Wesley "the first Methodist." There was no Holy Club as such in 1729, much less an organization that Charles might have started and John then taken over, as most of the current accounts would have it. And the first use of the epithet "Methodist" is still nearly three years in the future when John Wesley resumed his duties at Lincoln College in 1729.

The origins of Methodism, as with many movements, comprise at least two major phases which are related yet quite different. First, there is the gradual appearance of Methodism as a life-style based upon a theology adopted by certain individuals (a "living by rule and method" that became characteristic of the Wesleyan movement). Second, there is the beginnings of Methodism as a corporate manifestation of this distinctive approach to Christian living (recognizable to the participant and/or the outside observer as a more or less structured relationship among persons with a common purpose). In the case of Wesley and his friends, the shift from the former to the latter is not easily discernible, and the subtleties of the transition are usually ignored.

Certainly John Wesley had taken upon himself most of the characteristic marks of living by rule and method as early as 1725. The turning point for him seems to have been the decision to enter holy orders, following his desire to pursue the academic life of a tutor and fellow at Oxford.[23] His approaching ordination had a profound effect upon this Christ Church graduate and resulted in his adoption of a lifestyle increasingly marked by serious study, self-denial, careful use of time (monitored by a diary), attendance upon the Sacrament, and various sets of rules and resolutions—all typical elements of the "method" to be adopted a few years later by his friends.[24]

Charles Wesley had a similar change of attitude during his collegiate years at Christ Church (which began in June 1726), partly as a result of John's influence. The younger Wesley's life-style seemed at first to be more compatible with that of their mutual friend, Bob Kirkham, who matriculated at Merton College in 1727.[25] John's diary for that summer, when the three friends were together at Oxford, is now lost and there is no other extant source to describe their relationship or activities during that period. But during 1728, while John was back home at Epworth acting as curate for his father, Charles's demeanor took on a solemnity and gravity that led his oldest brother Samuel to tell John, "[his] every motion and look made me almost suspect it was you."[26]

Charles and Bob were clearly upset by John's apparent decision to stay in the north country "for life—at least for years."[27] While Bob, still less than a serious student, decided to plague John and the Epworth rectory with his presence during the winter of 1728-29, Charles was content to seek (and receive) by post very specific advice from John to assist him in his "first setting out" in religion: what books he should read, how to keep a diary, how to deal with acquaintances (both friend and foe).[28] The younger brother saw their separation as a trial to be endured, and hoped that he would not fall into his "former state of insensibility" before they could be together again. He did not have long to wait.

John decided to spend the summer of 1729 in Oxford, perhaps in part to bolster his brother's pursuit of holiness, but no doubt also attracted by the battle-lines being drawn at the university to combat the encroachment of deistical thinking.[29] In any case, Charles rejoiced at the prospect of John's return, waxing eloquent in a letter to his brother:

> I earnestly long for and desire the blessing God is about to send me in you. I am sensible this is my day of grace, and that upon my employing the time before our meeting and next parting will in great measure depend my condition for eternity.[30]

Charles's expectations may have been somewhat overstated, but the summer of 1729 did prove to be a crucial stage in the development of a shared approach to holy living among these friends. Kirkham was still "wretchedly lazy" ("you can't imagine how small a share of either learning or piety will content him"), but Charles had brought a fourth person into the small circle of would-be Methodists. William Morgan, also a student of Christ Church, had broken loose from those "vile hands" and the "cursed society" that seemed to prevail in Oxford at the time, and Charles was trying to keep him from falling back into that company.[31] If the definition of "first Methodist" requires sharing the experience with at least one other person in the same location, then perhaps Charles qualifies in May 1729.

For several weeks after his arrival in Oxford on 17 June 1729, John spent many hours with his three comrades, and although no rigid schedule of group activity is evident in the pages of his diary, faint traces of a pattern begin to emerge. Wednesday and Saturday evenings usually saw John going to Charles's or William's room for study and "religious talk," with Bob occasionally joining them (though his demeanor is not in keeping with the others as yet). Sunday evenings also provided the opportunity for Charles and Bob to read some work of divinity with John, such as Saint-Jure's *The Holy Life of Monsieur de Renty*. When John was not preaching on Sunday mornings in some nearby parish church, he and Charles attended the Sacrament at Christ Church Cathedral. On one evening the brothers went to "visit a woman," perhaps an early expression of their concern for the poor.[32]

John Wesley's manner of living during this summer at Oxford is essentially no different from that of the previous four years since his ordination, except that for the first time he had some companions who were also seriously concerned about the practical implications of Christian living. The two brothers and at least one friend (usually Morgan), encouraged by each other's efforts, occasionally meeting together for study, prayer, and religious conversation, attending the Sacrament regularly, keeping track of their lives by daily notations in a diary, represent the earliest manifestations of what will become Oxford Methodism. The gatherings are not regular, not everyone attends every time, the daily routine is not set, the light recreation is still evident now and then, but the marks of the Wesleyan movement are present in the group.[33] The only difference between these summer experiences of 1729 and the developments later in the year (November being the traditional "first rise") is that John Wesley was only visiting and had not yet resumed his position as a resident Fellow at Oxford.

These four friends were separated for most of the autumn of 1729, John and Charles returning to Epworth for the holiday between terms after having accompanied Bob home to Stanton in August. But in November, these three were back at Oxford with the Irishman, William Morgan. John had responded to the call of his college to return to his duties as a fellow and moderator. For the next ten months, the small circle of friends followed the pattern of activity they had begun that summer. There was no formal structure to their group, nor even regular meeting times yet, but the focus of their activity together was unmistakably tied to a "scheme of study," as Wesley would call it. They resembled an informal literary society more than anything else, consciously designed to promote learning and piety. Their evening gatherings are clearly discernable in the mass of abbreviated diary entries by which John carefully noted who had come together and what they were reading.

By the end of February 1730, however, a regular pattern of meetings becomes evident in the diaries, and by the following month the group had entered upon a set schedule: Tuesday evenings at Charles's room, Thursdays at Bob's, Saturdays at John's, and Sundays at William's. This regularity was coincident with (if not inspired by) Bob Kirkham's personal reformation, whereby he began studying diligently, "struck off his drinking acquaintance to a man," and began spending his evenings either alone or with the Wesley brothers and Morgan.[34] If a regular schedule of meeting is a necessary prerequisite for the organization of "Methodism" at Oxford, then perhaps Kirkham should be recognized as having a significant claim upon the title "first" Methodist.

This important step in the evolution of the Wesleyan group as a society (using the term hesitantly, as Wesley did) did not immediately bring public attention from the university community at large. Except for their regular attendance at the Sacrament every Sunday morning at Christ Church, for which they were dubbed "Sacramentarians" by some of the students of the college, their activities went quite unnoticed. However, when the small company of friends began to take their program of piety and Christian concern to the prisoners and poor people of Oxford in August of 1730, their notoriety increased. This crucial step, giving the movement one of its most characteristic features, was a conspicuous if not controversial move and brought the movement out of the college walls into the streets of the city, where it could hardly go unnoticed. This program of social outreach had been Morgan's idea, and since it became one of the identifying characteristics of the Oxford Methodists, perhaps Morgan could lay some claim to the honor of being its first proponent, the first Methodist as such. It seems, however, that although Morgan may have initiated the visiting, and Wesley incorporated it into their schedule, Bob Kirkham was the first to bear the brunt of taunting attacks from his fellow students, being derided in November for belonging to "The Holy Club."[35]

By the end of 1730, then, the "four young gentlemen" had established a pattern of living that was a corporate and public expression of the "method" begun by John Wesley five years earlier. Although they had not yet actually been called "Methodists," they had laid the foundation upon which the movement would develop during the next five years. It had not been a simple process—there is no way we can easily point to one person who is clearly the "first Methodist." John's vision of holy living and the theology it elicited resulted in the initiation and development of a methodical scheme that became basic to the character of the group; Charles was instrumental in implementing this approach at Oxford by convincing Morgan to join with them; Morgan's social concern resulted in much of their program of activity; and Kirkham seems to have inspired the regularity of their association together. One more major influence, John Clayton, would have a lasting impact on the shape of Methodism at Oxford and beyond, as the theology, organization, and mission of the movement continued to grow and develop through an ever widening circle of friends who shared the Wesleyan vision of the Christian life.

The period of the Wesleyan movement at Oxford during the two years beginning late in 1730 presents a picture of Methodism that is familiar to any who have read Wesley's letter to Richard Morgan, Sr. While this small treatise does give a fairly good description of the changes in personnel and the early challenges that the group confronted up to mid-1732, it does not explicitly mention the occasions that gave rise to the name "Methodist" and fixed that title in the public consciousness, including one of Wesley's key sermons at Oxford and a published attack and defense of the Methodists.[36]

By the end of 1730, the group's involvement in the life and problems of the city and university of Oxford had also attracted some small measure of support as well as criticism from within the academic community. The most noticeable indication of support was the addition of two faces to the group, John Boyce and William Hayward. The increased pace of their charitable activities in Oxford caused Wesley virtually to give up his former pattern of preaching frequently in the surrounding country parishes. The horse which he had purchased a year earlier specifically for that purpose, he sold in December 1730. The following year and a half he spent primarily in Oxford developing the scheme of activities that had begun in the late summer of 1730. He also continued to develop and expound his theology in letters, treatises, and sermons, exhibiting a perspective that was almost identical to the "New Methodists" of the previous generation and which may have been instrumental in the first application of that name to the Wesleyan group in 1732.[37]

In the spring of 1732 came the first major shift in personnel among the group. Kirkham and Boyce had left Oxford in February of that year, Hayward and Morgan would be gone by June, the latter returning home to Ireland because of ill health. Three new friends now joined the company of the Wesley brothers: Westley Hall, one of John's students at Lincoln College; Matthew Salmon and John Clayton, both of Brasenose College. Although Hall and Salmon would remain in the Wesleyan group until the Wesleys themselves left Oxford, it was John Clayton who, during the seven months he was to remain at Oxford, would become the most important influence (after Wesley and Morgan) upon the developing character of Methodism. His impact was especially significant in three areas.

(1) Clayton impressed upon Wesley the importance of the Early Church as a source of authority regarding both ideas and practices. In Wesley's own reflections upon this period of his own theological development, he recalled that the Essentialist Nonjurors (Clayton and his friends) helped him sort through the confusing and at times conflicting variety of suggestions provided by the English pietists who had started him on his pilgrimage of holy living. Wesley rediscovered the idea of consensus and felt now that this unifying factor in Christendom was most purely expressed in the apostolic age, in such writings as the Apostolic Canons and Constitutions.[38] During the summer of Clayton's presence, Wesley and his friends were convinced to adopt certain practices of the Early Church as well, such as the regular observance of the Stationary Fasts (the "Stations") every Wednesday and Friday. These very visible forms of self-denial (Wesley felt that all opposition would cease if they gave up fasting) and the Arminian theology that undergirded them may have precipitated the appellation "Methodist," the first contemporary use of which appears in a letter from Clayton to John Wesley.[39]

(2) Besides this very noticeable effect on the Methodists' churchmanship, Clayton seems to have introduced some significant alterations in the organization of the Wesleyan group. Shortly after Clayton began associating with the group, the weekday sessions started to move away from a singular concentration on the ancient classics. Wesley began meeting with two separate groups: reading Caesar with Charles Wesley and Westley Hall, but reading de Renty with John Clayton and brother Charles. Everybody still gathered on Sunday for their usual study of some work in divinity. In addition to this shift in

focus, Clayton himself seems also to have introduced a new element in the organizational scheme. He had what he refers to as "a small flock" at Brasenose College—persons who had previously associated themselves with Clayton for similar purposes and were now learning the Wesleyan methods through Clayton. When Wesley noted in his diary for 30 June 1732 that they "divided men and business, at the Castle, Bocardo, and in town," he seems to have taken into account these new associates.[40] Clayton promoted the idea of spreading their influence, reporting to Wesley later in the summer of 1732 that he hoped they would soon have "at least an advocate for us, if not a brother and fellow labourer" in every college of the university.[41] An expanding organization with a widening circle of cell groups, various levels of commitment, and different combinations of activities (though all more or less under the leadership of John Wesley) becomes more obvious within the following year. Clayton himself was instrumental in expanding the activities of the Methodists in the city of Oxford, opening up St. Thomas's Workhouse to their visitations.

(3) While these developments were taking place in churchmanship, organization, and activities, Clayton opened up another area that was to have a significant and lasting effect on the development of Wesley and Methodism: Clayton introduced Wesley into a new circle of acquaintances in Oxford, Manchester, and London. Besides the Brasenose students who became associated with the movement, these new acquaintances included Richard Clements (bookseller) in Oxford, Thomas Deacon (nonjuror) and John Byrom (inventor of a shorthand system that the Wesleys soon began to use) in Manchester, Sir John Philips (prime mover in the SPCK and other philanthropic ventures), William Law (the pietist/mystic), and Charles Rivington (the publisher) in London. This group of new friends effected the Methodist design from the smallest details to the largest patterns, from the methods of diary-keeping and the sources of reading material to the theological bases and organizational manifestations of the movement. It eventually even contributed to the brief geographical displacement of the Wesleys from Oxford to America.

If "Methodist" implies a certain appreciation of the Early Church, an emphasis on the disciplines of the Christian life, an organization that involves a connection of small groups, and the use of the term "Methodist," then perhaps John Clayton has some claim to priority in the application of that name. The story continues, of course; others continued to come into the fellowship of the Wesleyan groups and in turn influence the shape and direction of their activities. With the appearance in late 1733 of John Whitelamb, who had excellent linguistic abilities, Wesley's own small group turns to a very intense concentration upon studying the Greek New Testament, the first explicit manifestation of what Wesley will later recall as their all being "*homo unius libri.*"[42] If that characteristic is essential to the concept of "Methodist," then perhaps Whitelamb deserves some attention in that regard. And so it is for several of the others, including George Whitefield, who comes into association with the Oxford groups very late, in 1734/35, but who for the first decade of the revival is the one who takes the brunt of most of the published attacks against the "Methodists."[43]

Conclusion

The early documents that best illuminate the rise of Methodism at Oxford portray a picture that is at times ambiguous and at best complex. The quest of the "first" Methodist is a difficult search in terms of chronological priority, partly because it is difficult to know when the phenomenon "Methodism" is actually present. In a sense, the answer to the question, in a chronological sense, depends upon a definition of the term "Methodist" or upon some assumptions regarding the use of the term (e.g., can we see the "first Methodist" before the term "Methodist" was being used?). If the criterion is more conceptual than chronological, the problem gets no simpler; the issue simply shifts to a search for the "essence" of what it meant to be a Methodist. If the question of priority is one of primary and lasting leadership within the movement, then of course the quest becomes simpler, since there is little to challenge John Wesley's primacy of leadership, even in guiding his brother Charles through the first few steps of his activities at Oxford. All things considered, John Wesley is the only one who can be seen as having a central role at nearly every step of the early developments at Oxford. But having come to that almost predictable conclusion, we must remember the complicated journey that brought us there.

It is of crucial importance in trying to understand the dynamics of Oxford Methodism to note that the various activities which characterize its public image (visiting the prisons, helping the sick, teaching the poor, attending the Sacrament) were in most cases not originated by Wesley himself. It must be remembered that Wesley was deeply engaged in the search for "a right state of soul." Consequently, his method was not a static, settled scheme, but rather an approach to life that grew and developed and changed as he confronted different crises, had further insights, and met new friends. As we have seen,

John's leadership within the movement came from an ability to fit these various pursuits together with a sense of purpose that gave direction to the spiritual impulse behind the Methodists' search for salvation. To catch the essence of Methodism at Oxford, then, is to recognize this impulse as well as the developing life-style which it elicited.

Not everyone who became associated with the Wesleyans at Oxford shared every aspect of John's own program. If the criteria for determining who was indeed a Methodist are to take into account the complex circumstances surrounding the growth of the movement and yet catch the essence of what it meant to be so called, they must go beyond a statistical record of academic meetings or charitable activities and try to indicate who those persons were who had willingly associated themselves with others who were also seeking, in Wesley's own words, "a right state of soul, a mind and spirit renewed after the image of him that created it." Having reached this goal is not the criterion. The means used in striving for this goal are not in themselves the measure. Rather, the Methodists were those who were striving for "the one thing needful," and to that end had a "single intention" in life—"to please God" by improving "in holiness, in the love of God and . . . neighbor."

Chapter 5

The Meditative Piety of the Oxford Methodists[1]

Diaries as Mirrors and Windows

The eighteenth century was an age of diarists. Persons of all sorts had a penchant for jotting down personal observations in little notebooks, foot-holds for the memory. The purpose of such an exercise, however, at times went beyond the simple desire for easy recollection of times and events. The diarist often hoped that recording and reflecting upon past activities would prove a means of moral or spiritual improvement.[2] This is especially true of the religious diarist whose explicit intention was to record God's providential activity but whose real hope was to improve in holiness.

The diary was an Oxford Methodist's constant companion and conscience, a ledger of the soul and a mirror for the spirit, recording and reflecting the progress and pitfalls of his struggle to advance along the path of holy living. The diary of an Oxford Methodist was by intention a religious diary even though it records a great deal of information that would seem beyond the scope of such a design.[3] Wesley's own diary provided the model. John Wesley had begun to keep a diary at Oxford in 1725, about the time he decided to enter holy orders, shortly after receiving his bachelor of arts degree. His intent was to follow Jeremy Taylor's first rule of holy living, care of one's time. The diary was to be a means both of promoting and of charting his progress in holy living. The system of notation Wesley developed for his diary soon became a personalized code. Abbreviations, symbols, and a complex cipher were woven together to allow secrecy for many of his entries. It was a complicated but useful system that also saved time and space. When Charles Wesley decided to keep a diary in 1729, it was to his older brother John that he looked for a method.

> What particulars am I to take notice of? Am I to give my thoughts and words as well as deeds a place in it? I'm to mark all the good and ill I do; and what besides? What cipher can I make use of? If you would direct me to the same or a like method with your own, I would gladly follow it for I'm fully convinced of the usefulness of such an undertaking.[4]

Charles was not the only person to look to John for guidance. While a tutor and fellow of Lincoln College, John Wesley gained as many as forty or fifty adherents to his pattern of holy living during the next five or six years. Most were not among the handful of persons who met regularly in a little society with Wesley, and not all of them followed every aspect of Wesley's own scheme of thought and activity. But from references in the extant diaries of three (John Wesley, Benjamin Ingham, and George Whitefield), we know that at least fifteen of the Oxford Methodists learned the coded system of diary keeping that Wesley was developing.[5] The reasons for using this "code" were secrecy and economy; the purpose of everyone's using the same system was to enable them to share and compare diaries.

Ingham noted in his diary that he learned the Wesleyan method of keeping a diary through Charles Wesley rather than John, an intriguing clue to the organizational pattern of Oxford Methodism. Although Charles's diary has not survived, we can surmise that it would match the style of both Ingham's and John Wesley's since the latter two are nearly identical.[6] And a comparison of changes in format in the extant diaries shows how the diary method, as well as many other aspects of Oxford Methodism, was transmitted from John Wesley to those around him. During the last week of January 1733/34, John changed his diary format from a paragraph style to a fuller and more precise ("exacter") columnar style. After using the new system for a few days, John met with Charles on a Friday afternoon in early February and "talked of diaries," no doubt focusing on the new format. Presumably Charles then adopted the new scheme in his own diary. On the first day of March, Charles began teaching this "exacter" diary method to Ingham and Richard Smith, who were meeting regularly to study in Charles's room. Three days later, the new style appears in Ingham's diary. Two weeks after adopting this columnar format, Ingham began talking about it with some friends who were meeting regularly with him at Queen's; within a few days he taught *them* this "exacter" method.

The Ingham notebook, then, contains his first attempts at diary keeping and also reflects some of the major changes in the Wesleyan diary method. Because Ingham was learning the system and teaching it to others at the same time, his diary tends to be more explicit and less complicated than John Wesley's even though both used the same method. As a result, the format and content of the Ingham diary present information that is useful in illuminating many of Wesley's diary entries as well as fascinating in its own right. On the same day that Ingham began the "exacter" diary method, he also transcribed several important lists into his diary. On some blank pages in the front, he began recording many abbreviations, signs, and symbols used in the Wesleyan system, along with their meanings. Inside the front cover Ingham noted more symbols, defining each. Since Wesley left no such key to his coded scheme of signs and symbols, these two lists in Ingham's diary help unlock parts of the Wesley code that would otherwise defy explanation.[7]

Because Wesley also neglected to place headings at the top of each column in the "exacter" format, several vertical rows of cryptic entries on each page of his diary lie mute without a hint of their significance. Fortunately, Ingham identified each column in his diary with a heading, thereby revealing the topics of the corresponding rows in the Wesley entries: temper of devotion, degree of recollection, resolutions broken, resolutions kept, blessings.[8] The coded entries in both diaries now begin to make sense, disclosing an intricate record of self-examination that sheds new light on the spirit of religious contemplation that characterized the early Wesleyans.

Ingham's hourly description of his activities, besides being more explicit, tends to be fuller than Wesley's.[9] For example, Ingham frequently outlines the specific content of conversations, at times recounts the positions held in arguments among his friends, and often records the focus of his meditations or prayers. When Ingham visited Wesley on the morning of 17 March 1734, the latter simply noted in his diary, "Ingham, religious talk," followed by "Robson, tea, religious talk of diary." Ingham, on the other hand, delineated the details of the conference in an expanded version that occupies fourteen lines in his diary. This richness of description, along with the record of pervasive self-analysis and the keys to the Wesleyan method of diary keeping, makes the Ingham diary a most important document for understanding the life and thought of Oxford students and the early Methodists in the 1730s. This amazing little volume, divulging its secrets two and a half centuries later, not only casts new light on one man's pilgrimage of faith, but also opens a new window into the sometimes obscured corners of life and thought in Georgian Oxford. From these materials and with the help of other contemporary documents, we may glean information that helps us understand more clearly the nature and design of Oxford Methodism, the formulation and development of Wesleyan theology, and the manner and style of university life in early eighteenth-century England.

Organization

The picture of Oxford Methodism revealed by Ingham's diary bears little resemblance to the simplistic portrait of the "Holy Club" described in most studies of the Wesleyan movement. The image of a single group of Methodists meeting in John Wesley's room at Lincoln College is an impression that is incomplete and even misleading. Unfortunately, most descriptions of the first rise of Methodism resemble a collection of twice-told tales, and even recent attempts at revision are usually only reinterpretations of inaccurate and inadequate information.[10]

The old stereotyped image of the Holy Club was fixed as an icon in the Methodist memory by Marshall Claxton's painting, *The Institution of Methodism.*[11] His portrayal is based primarily on a letter written by John Wesley in October 1732.[12] The account as given in Wesley's letter is misleading in two ways—in the simplistic version of the origin of the group, supposedly in November 1729, and in the description of its structure, which was even then beginning to change. Wesley's own diary offers a corrective to the first problem, showing the complex early development of the group over a twenty-month period from the summer of 1729 to the fall of 1730.[13] Ingham's diary, together with Wesley's, helps solve the second problem by revealing the complicated network of relationships that was the matrix for Methodist activities after the middle of 1732.

Historians have been confused from the outset in trying to describe Oxford Methodism, especially during the period from 1732 to 1735. John Wesley would seem to be the one best suited to clarify any difficulties in that regard, but in fact his own attempts to do so merely set the pattern for much of the confusion that later prevailed. For instance, on the matter of how many Methodists belonged to the movement at Oxford, Wesley claimed in January 1734 that there were only four members in his little society, whereas his student, Richard Morgan, Jr., told his father that there were seven.[14] Wesley's diary confirms that there were only three people meeting with him at that time, making four in the group. Morgan seems to have included in his reckoning individuals who were associated with the Methodists but did not meet regularly with Wesley's own personal group. That is to say, Morgan answered the question, How many Methodists are at Oxford? whereas Wesley answered the question, How many persons meet with me in my little society? On the other hand, if Wesley's diary is used as the measure of historical accuracy, his later recollection that his little society grew to fourteen or fifteen by 1735 must have been calculated to answer the Morgan-type question, for his diary indicates that the group meeting with him in 1735 is no larger than seven or eight people at the most, although he would have known of at least as many more around the university who were following his methods.

Ingham's diary helps clear up the confusion. Oxford Methodism consisted not of one group but of many. The core society was indeed gathered around John Wesley and by the beginning of 1732 consisted of six persons. But this simple pattern of one group, complicated only by some fluctuation of membership, began to change in mid-1732 when John Clayton joined the Wesleyan movement. Clayton already had a "small flock" meeting with him at Brasenose College for study and devotion, and his joining with the Wesleyan company gave the Methodist movement a two-level structure, the Wesley group and the Clayton subgroup.[15] Another satellite group appeared in town in 1733 led by Miss Potter, to whom Wesley also provided guidance and with whom he occasionally met. Ingham's diary indicates that in 1733 Charles Wesley also had at least one subgroup meeting with him at Christ Church, consisting first of himself and Ingham, and later including Richard Smith, Henry Evans, and Richard Carter, all Christ Church men except Ingham. Ingham, Smith, Evans, and Carter, like the persons in Clayton's subgroup, did not meet with John Wesley's small company but learned the Wesleyan pattern and methods through a member of Wesley's company who was the leader of their subgroup.

It is somewhat startling to discover that Benjamin Ingham, traditionally thought to be a member of the so-called Holy Club did not in fact attend the meetings of Wesley's little society. Equally startling, however, is the revelation in Ingham's diary that, having learned the Methodist pattern of living from Charles Wesley (with occasional consultations with John), Benjamin Ingham himself started several groups at Queen's College, faithfully attempting to duplicate Wesley's scheme in his own college. This spreading activity represents a third level in the organization of Methodist cell groups at Oxford.

Ingham's descriptions of the meetings of these various clusters of persons constituting Oxford Methodism reflect some of the complexity and variety evident in the movement by 1733. For instance, the most common *time* for their meetings was from seven to nine o'clock in the evening, but some of the groups met at other times, such as one o'clock in the afternoon, for their reading and/or religious talk. The *purpose* of the meeting sometimes determined the schedule. Some groups met regularly at three in the afternoon on fast days for breakfast (to break the fast) as well as for study and discussion, and at least one small band prepared for Sundays by meeting late on Saturday evenings to "watch," pray, and read. Other groups met for purposes that did not necessarily determine their schedule: to read logic, to study experimental philosophy, to compare diaries, or to read the Greek Testament. The *frequency* of meeting also varied among the groups, some meeting only once a week, others meeting on a regular schedule as often as three or four times a week. The longevity of the groups varied widely. In some cases, four or five meetings were sufficient for them to accomplish a particular purpose such as reading a book together. In others, such as Ingham's Friday evening group or the Wednesday-Saturday-Sunday group, meetings persisted regularly for months in spite of several changes in focus and/or personnel. The *place* of meeting also differed from one group to the next. Many rotated their meetings among the rooms and colleges of the members, some on a fairly regular schedule, as did John Wesley's group, and others in a more random fashion. Some groups met consistently in the same place—Ingham's meetings with Charles Wesley's little band always took place in Charles's room, never in Ingham's room at Queen's or in the rooms of the two or three other Christ Church men in that group. The Friday night gathering at Queen's met almost exclusively at John Ford's room for five months before switching to Ingham's room in April 1734.

The *composition* of these groups is as varied as their patterns of meetings. The size of the groups generally ranged from three to six persons, although some regular meetings involved only two. Although most were men associated with the university, at least one woman, Miss Potter, was hosting (and perhaps leading) a group in town. Some combinations were mostly undergraduates; others included masters and bachelors, tutors and fellows. Although there was some identification of groups with specific colleges, there was no necessary limitation in this regard. Christ Church, Lincoln, Queen's, and Brasenose were the primary centers, but Merton, Exeter, Pembroke, and Magdalen had their Methodists as well. The diaries also reveal that considerable shifting and overlapping of personnel took place among as well as within the groups. Ingham, as noted, met with Charles Wesley's group at Christ Church, and although two of those Christ Church men (Wesley and Carter) never came to Ingham's groups, two others did begin to attend meetings at Queen's College (Smith and Evans). James Hervey of Lincoln College, often portrayed as a close associate of John Wesley in the Holy Club, appears more often in Ingham's diary than Wesley's, first as a member of a small company centered at Lincoln which included Ingham (but not Wesley!), and then as a new person "admitted" into the group of mostly Queen's College men that met on Wednesday-Saturday-Sunday. John Robson and Thomas Greives, also Lincoln College students and both associated with John Wesley's little society, also shifted their affiliation, at least for a time, to meet with one or another of Ingham's groups. Will Clements, one of John Wesley's students at Lincoln and a regular participant in his Methodist group, became piqued at his tutor early in 1733. Wesley noted in his diary that Clements was talking of "breaking up our society." Within days, he stopped meeting with Wesley and began attending Miss Potter's group.[16] The Ingham and Wesley diaries are sprinkled with notations of "prevailing" upon persons to join their activities or of "convincing" persons to adopt a particular notion or practice; other notations indicate when a friend had "revolted" or "left us," not wanting to meet with them anymore, or had "agreed" to meet with a group only if certain other parties would not be present. In some cases, Wesley himself seems to have instigated changes in the composition of groups in order to further certain individuals' progress in particular aspects of the Methodist design.

Many of the persons trying to live by the Methodist pattern were reluctant to adopt such practices as regular fasting, early rising, or meticulous diary keeping. Even the most active participants were guilty of occasional backsliding. "Membership" might therefore be too definite a category to use in trying to describe the ambiguities and complexities of an individual's relationship to the Methodist movement as seen in the diaries. There was no rite of initiation, no cause for exclusion. One's association was totally voluntary. In spite of their lists of resolutions and questions, the Methodists had no required regulations, no measurable parameters of membership, no single meeting place. Clayton had discouraged Wesley from organizing an avowed society with a set of rules, pointing out that "it would be no additional tie upon yourselves and perhaps [be] a snare for the conscience of those weak brethren that might choose to come among you."[17]

By 1733, the association of Wesley and his friends was no longer called a "club" and certainly had begun to assume a structure that belied such simplistic designations. The term "Methodist," first used the previous year, had appeared coincidentally with a new stage of complexity in the organizational pattern. From that point on, it is difficult to think in terms of "members" or "nonmembers"; it is not merely a matter of affiliation with a particular group or adherence to a particular standard. The primary requisite for being called a Methodist was the desire to work out one's salvation and to engage in the pursuit of perfection. To catch the essence of Methodism at Oxford is to recognize this impulse as well as the developing life-style that it elicited.[18] Accordingly, the diaries of the Oxford Methodists do not report clear-cut designations of who "belonged" to this blossoming movement so much as they display a diverse array of persons whose Methodist inclinations can and must be measured individually by their seriousness of intention and the degree of their participation in a Wesleyan pattern of life and thought.

Activities

The various activities that characterized the life of the Oxford Methodists, such as fasting, visiting the prisons, rising early, attending the Sacrament, helping the poor, and meeting for study and prayer, were not in themselves new or unique to the university scene, even in post-Restoration England. Samuel Wesley, father of John and Charles, had visited the prisons at Oxford when he was a student at Exeter College in the 1680s.[19] George Fothergill reports that he himself had gone frequently to his tutor's room at Queen's College in 1722 with other pupils for prayers at nine in the evening.[20] Tutors as well as preachers were enamored of various "methods" by which to inculcate their programs or ideas.[21] Certainly Methodists were not the only persons to attend the Sacrament at Christ Church and St. Mary's.[22] What made Oxford Methodism distinctive, however, was the peculiar combination of activities and personalities that composed the movement, and even more particularly, the intensity and persistence with which their "methods" permeated (or were intended to permeate) their lives.

The Wesleyans were, in the first instance, a small study group or literary society made up of persons with pietist inclinations. From their first setting out on the path of holy living, the Wesley brothers were doing little more than following diligently the stipulations and expectations of the university statutes with regard to the life and study of Oxford students. Charles's own personal "reformation" late in 1728 was in fact coincident with a resurgence of concern among many of the university officers that the tutors

> discharge their duty by double diligence in informing their respective pupils in their Christian duty, and . . . in recommending to them the frequent and careful reading [of] the Scriptures and such other books as may serve more effectually to promote Christianity, sound principles, and orthodox faith.[23]

Before the autumn of 1730, the two Wesley brothers and their one or two friends can be defined as a group only insofar as they were becoming of one mind in their intention to lead holy lives and, starting in the spring of that year, were meeting together regularly for study and "religious talk." The public did not take any notice of them until they began, toward the end of 1730, to attend regularly the Sacrament at Christ Church and to visit the prisons and the poor folk in town. To these public acts of piety and charity, which brought upon them the name Holy Club (succeeded shortly thereafter by the title Godly Club), they added in 1732 a pattern of disciplined religious practices modeled on the life and thought of the Early Church, most notably the observance of the Stationary fasts on Wednesdays and Fridays. These activities and the theology that lay behind them brought upon the group a new name, "Methodist," which soon found its way onto the printed page and thereby fastened itself on English minds and lips.[24]

By January 1733, then, the basic design of Oxford Methodism had emerged insofar as the main branches of its activities are concerned: study, devotion, charity. During the following two years the pattern was put to the test with several new adherents trying out the Wesleyan methods of pursuing inward and outward holiness. This increase in numbers was accompanied by more variety and intensity in their activities along with a certain amount of tension and conflict, both internal and external. These last two years that the Wesleys spent in residence at the university represent the fullest expression of Oxford Methodism, and it is this period that is described in Ingham's diary.

Scholarship

The scholarly concerns of the Wesleyan movement at this stage are clearly reflected in the pages of Ingham's diary. The range of books read by Ingham and his friends at Queen's is almost identical to the spectrum read by Wesley's group. The classical authors basic to an

Oxford education are clearly evident: Homer, Cicero, Virgil, Juvenal. Other common textbooks in the Oxford curriculum appear regularly, such as those by Aldrich, Sanderson, Gravesande, and Kennet. At the same time, the type of devotion to be expected in a pietist reading bibliography is well represented in the works of Thomas à Kempis, Law, Taylor, Horneck, Goodman, and Francke. The sermons of Norris, Lucas, and Beveridge follow the same line. The meditative perspective is found in works by Hall, Ken, and Gerhard. Scougal, Scupoli, and Rodriguez bring a mystical element into the list. The lives of Bonnell, Bonwicke, and de Renty provide patterns of holy living, and *The Second Spira* (by Richard Sault) gives warning of consequences in the other direction. The writings of the Early Fathers of the church appear frequently, as do works about them by Cave, Deacon, and Reeves. The Greek New Testament and Robert Nelson's *Fasts and Festivals* were staple reading for Ingham and his friends, and the *Country Parson's Advice to his Parishioners* was in many ways the foundation of their whole approach to covenantal holy living.[25]

Only a handful of authors appearing on Ingham's pages are not mentioned by Wesley during these years, including Robert Jenkin on the reasonableness of Christianity, Johannes Leusden's edition of the Greek Testament, Simon Patrick on the Sacrament and on fasting, Thomas Ittig on the Early Fathers, and an apparently anonymous treatise entitled *The Penitential Office for the Sixteenth Day of the Month*.[26] Although works of divinity predominate in the readings at meetings of the Methodists during this period, providing the grist for their religious talk, the popular literature of the day is not completely disregarded by Ingham or, in fact, by Wesley. In the spring of 1734 Wesley had begun to advise some students against reading "secular" writings, including even the classics, but he never made it a general rule. Wesley never completely avoided such literature himself, content to "sanctify" his reading program by including a preponderance of good religious books.[27] And even though Ingham at one point "talked against [the] poets," we find no pervasive antipathy in him toward poets or secular writers.[28] His personal reading included not only the *Tatler*, *Guardian*, and *Spectator*, but also occasional reading from Voltaire, Pope, Vanbrugh, Milton, Herbert, and Young.

Religious writings nevertheless made up the core of the Methodists' reading program. When no published work was available that seemed in Wesley's mind to satisfy their needs, he circulated handwritten copies of material that he himself had composed on important subjects, just as he passed around various lists of rules, resolutions, and questions for his friends to ponder. It is not surprising that we find

Ingham reading Wesley's crucial letter to Richard Morgan, Sr., which gives the rationale for the Methodists' development at Oxford, and Wesley's circular "letter of company." Ingham sometimes would read a Wesley sermon when meeting with his friends, such as the sermon on the Sacrament widely used by the Oxford Methodists.[29] In one instance, Ingham shared with his friends a sermon Wesley had preached that very morning in St. Mary's. Another Wesley composition in manuscript form that received wide circulation, though not universal acceptance, was his essay ("treatise" or *genesis problematica*) on the Stationary fasts, written during the summer of 1733. Wesley eventually resorted to publishing some of the material that was circulating among the Methodists, such as his collection of prayers, which Ingham notes having read at Charles Wesley's in January 1734 only three days after John received the printed copies from London.[30]

Ingham also tried his hand at writing religious treatises. In addition to the exercises for his degree, which included writing *geneses*[31] on the Sacrament and on the Stationary fasts, he also wrote what he called "a short scheme of the reasonableness of our practices of rising, fasting, etc." as well as a "scheme for daily examination." The diary also shows him writing three sermons, beginning to compose the first one, on Matthew 19:17, by writing a *genesis problematica solitaria*. It appears, however, that Ingham did not distribute or use his own writings in his study groups.

The Methodist program often fused academic and devotional interests, as can be seen in their meetings, which consisted primarily of two types of activity: (1) study and discussion of useful books that would help them promote their common design, and (2) religious talk about their progress in holy living, which included praying ("the chief subject of which was charity" or love), reviewing their progress in holiness (which often included comparing diaries), considering their charitable activities, passing out "pious books" for their own and others' use, and determining the duties of the following day or days.[32] It appears that those who were more intensely involved in the Methodist design participated in the religious talk sessions, whereas the reading sessions were at times attended by a wider range of interested persons.[33]

Although the diaries never indicate explicitly that a meeting as such is taking place, this usually can be deduced from the listing of those who are gathering, and the description of what they are doing and when the activity is taking place. We can tell for example that when Ingham is getting together with Watson, Washington, Smyth, and Ford every Friday evening from about seven to nine, reading

William Law's *Serious Call*, and having "religious talk," they are having a Wesleyan-type meeting for scholarly study and discussion. The term "religious talk" in itself is not a clear indicator of a Methodist meeting, since its most common use is to describe the nature of simple conversations between two persons, noted several times each day in the diaries. But when Ingham meets with Robson on Monday nights for "religious talk," we know from earlier diary entries that they are discussing their spiritual progress and their charitable activities at the workhouse. There are many occasions when the time, place, and personnel indicate a Methodist meeting, but the description "religious talk" is not specific enough to determine the precise nature of their discussions.

Devotion

The various clusters of Wesleyans meeting around the university and city of Oxford were, in effect, following the *Country Parson's Advice* to unite in friendly societies, "engaging each other in their several and respective combinations to be helpful and serviceable to one another in all good Christian ways."[34] To that end, their corporate endeavors extended beyond the basic program of study and discussion. Confession was a part of their group experience: not only did they compare diaries at some of their meetings as a means of confessing their own sins, but they did not hesitate to point out the faults of others, howbeit striving to do so "with tenderness." Reprimands among friends for past sins were complemented by methods of encouraging proper conduct in the present—Ingham and his friends developed a series of hand signals to warn each other in public when they saw or heard one of their company saying or doing something that "did not tend to God's glory." The discussion at their meetings often focused on their progress in holy living, noted in Ingham's diary as "religious talk of ourselves and our friends." Ingham's daily entries exhibit a constant concern for friendship and friends, one recurring question in that regard being "how to manage 'em." John Wesley's letter of company, a document now lost, seems to have offered suggestions (a *method*, if you please) to the Methodists on how to promote holy living through the proper management of one's personal associations.[35]

The life of devotional piety encouraged and nurtured by the association of Wesleyans at Oxford was grounded in the personal and private exercises of meditation, self-examination, prayer, and Bible reading. The meditative practices used by the Methodists at this point were part of the mystic, holy living tradition that goes back to the

Early Fathers of the church, but which had been rationalized, regularized, and methodized in Europe during the fifteenth and sixteenth centuries.[36] Joseph Hall helped transmit this tradition to England through his *Art of Divine Meditation*, which Wesley abridged in 1733 and used with his friends.[37] Several other books of meditation (or containing meditations) were also used regularly by Ingham, Wesley, and their companions, including Johann Gerhard's *Meditations*, Thomas Ken's *Meditations*, Anthony Horneck's *Best Exercise*, Simon Patrick's *Christian Sacrifice*, Francis de Sales's *Introduction to a Devout Life*, Jeremy Taylor's *Holy Living* and *Holy Dying*, and Robert Nelson's *Practice of True Devotion*. The subjects of these meditations range from the life and death of Christ, the attributes of God, and the virtues desired by the Christian, to the follies of the world, the faults and infirmities of the sinner, and the impending judgment. At least an hour a day was set aside for meditating, the purpose of which was to help one develop self-knowledge and improve in virtue.[38] Charles Wesley advised Ingham that if he were "irrecollected" for two consecutive hours, he might use a book of meditations for at least a half-hour to recover a state of "recollection" or spiritual composure. The Wesley brothers had learned the importance of meditation from their mother, who also had pointed out to them in March 1734 that their schedule might include even more time for meditation, which she saw as "incomparably the best means to spiritualize our affections, confirm our judgments, and add strength to our pious resolutions of any exercise whatever."[39]

Meditation was at the heart of the spiritual exercises that the Methodists used to develop virtue, the wellspring of the holy life. Self-knowledge was an important goal of meditation, and self-examination was a primary means to that end. One facet of the scheme or method used by Wesley and the Methodists was similar to that outlined by Ignatius of Loyola in his *Spiritual Exercises*. A "general examination" demanded accountability for one's thoughts, words and actions on the basis of a list of questions:

> Did I in the morning plan the business of the day?
> Have I been simple and recollected in everything?
> Have I been or seemed angry?
> Have I used the ejaculations once an hour?

These and similar questions, numbering about fifteen in most of the Wesley brothers' various revisions of the list, were the framework for a daily examination of conscience, measuring how well one was adhering to the habits of holy living outlined therein.[40] Ingham used a general examination of this sort weekly (on Friday evenings) for several months before changing to a daily examination in January 1734. In March he copied the Wesleys' list of "general" questions into his diary and began using it as a basis for hourly examination throughout the day (recorded in the "exacter" diary format), still noting a "daily examination" every afternoon and using the term "General Examination" on Friday evening to designate his review of the previous week.

In addition to the list of General Questions, Wesley's scheme also contained lists of Particular Questions (in the Ignatian manner) that provided the basis for "particular examination."[41] This exercise featured the special virtues assigned for each day of the week, with lists of questions arranged under those virtues:

Sunday	Love of God
Monday	Love of Man
Tuesday	Humility
Wednesday	Mortification and Self-denial
Thursday	Resignation and Meekness
[Friday	Mortification and Self-denial]
Saturday	Thankfulness

The purpose of this endeavor was to ferret out specific sins and to plant in their place the corresponding virtue. These were not rules that demanded obedience; the emphasis was not on the performance of certain good works. Rather, the questions were designed to use the examination of one's performance as a measure of the development of virtue, and thus to gauge the inclination of one's heart and affections, an unfailingly inward focus.[43]

As with most forms of vital Christian spirituality, the Oxford Methodists' life of meditative piety was marked by regular, one could say constant, use of prayer. Ingham's daily activities, as noted in his diary, are bracketed by periods of prayer that become more and more frequent as the year passes. He is careful to differentiate various sorts of prayer. *Private prayer* is distinguished from *public prayers* (the service in the Church) but does not necessarily indicate spontaneous or personal prayers. He frequently notes "private prayer" when in the company of his friends, and even when alone he used many prayers from various books of devotion. *Ejaculatory prayers*, short prayers of praise or petition, were used by many of the Methodists at the start of every hour. Ingham began to use these prayers hourly in March 1734, along with the hourly self-examination that was the basis of the newly begun "exacter" form of diary keeping. The Oxford Methodists also used a set of specific *collects* for nine o'clock, noon, and three o'clock, besides special collects for the beginning of each day of the week. Ingham copied many of these frequently used prayers into the front of his diary. Wesley had also developed a collection of prayers arranged according to the virtues for each day of the week. Thinking this useful for his friends, he published selections from this collection in 1733, incorporating questions for self-examination. The Oxford Methodists also used many other sources for the wide variety of forms of prayer noted in the diary, such as prayers of resignation, preparatory prayers for the Sacrament, and prayers to be used before reading at night. The methodical regularity of their practice of prayer seems to have drawn an occasional friendly protest, such as Anthony Natt's expressed desire at one point that they might pray "indifferent as to the days."

Bible reading was an essential part of the Methodists' devotional life, as well as a fundamental basis for their theological reflection; here again the spiritual and scholarly concerns overlap and fuse. Wesley later reflected that from "the very beginning" at Oxford, the Methodists were, "each of them, *homo unius libri*—a man of one book."[44] In view of the wide-ranging bibliography read by Wesley and his companions, this statement should be understood as corresponding to the definition of a Methodist provided by Wesley's *Complete English Dictionary* of 1753: "One that lives according to the method laid down in the Bible." The practical side of this guiding perspective is evident in Wesley's dictum, passed on to Ingham by John Gambold on the first day of April 1734, that one must "try all human writings [and actions] by the test of scripture."[45] Wesley's diary during this period reveals an increasing amount of time spent reading the Bible (in English, Greek, and Hebrew), the study of Scripture providing the major, almost exclusive, focus of his study group during the fall and winter of 1734/35. Ingham also read and studied the Bible regularly, resolving in mid-November 1734 to read three chapters in the Greek New Testament every day, morning, noon, and night. In some instances, he shared the activity with a colleague. In the course of the one year recorded in his diary, Ingham read the Greek Testament through the Book of Acts twice, read Romans once, and Matthew four times. He abridged Daniel Whitby's *Paraphrase and Commentary on the New Testament* from Matthew through Hebrews, studied the verses marked with an asterisk in Johannes Leusden's edition of the Greek Testament, and read August Hermann Francke's *Manuductio ad lectionem Scripturae Sacrae*.[46] In addition to this, Ingham read the Bible frequently to children and "old people" at the workhouses.

These private aspects of the Methodists' personal life-style (meditation, self-examination, prayer, and Bible reading) were complemented by other activities that were also personal but, by their nature, could not be quite so private. Various acts of self-denial, such as fasting and early rising, were for the Methodists an important means of evoking and exhibiting humility, a necessary corollary to their basic principle of loving God and neighbor. The opening pages of Ingham's diary show him grappling with the question of fasting. Within a week he was persuaded by Wesley that the Stations (Wednesday and Friday fasts) should be observed, but only after subsequent readings in Wesley's treatise on the subject and Robert Nelson's comments on fasting did Ingham actually begin to abstain from eating until three o'clock on the Stationary days. Others at the university might not have noticed whether or not the Methodists were having their breakfast at three in the afternoon instead of eight in the morning since the latter was not a community meal. But the statutes required that students both reside and take their meals in the colleges and any Methodist's absence from the hall at dinnertime on Wednesday or Friday would be noticed.[47] This attempt to follow the discipline practiced by the Early Church was not unique to the Wesleyans by any means. The Church of England in fact prescribed fasting but it was typically promoted and practiced by the High Church, nonjuring pietists whose religious zeal struck many observers as bordering on fastidious fanaticism. Wesley, who began his faithful observance of the Stations under the influence of John Clayton in 1732, was later told by one of his Methodist pupils, "I believe if I would go into the hall on fast days all my other activities would be less taken notice of."[48] Ingham seems to have felt the same pressures; from the very start of his observance of the Stationary fasts in October 1733, he changes the usual noon notation on Wednesdays and Fridays from "dinner" to "Hall."

As might be expected, the Methodists were not of one mind on all aspects of the fasting issue. Ingham's diary is dotted with disputes among his friends on the question, with mixed results. In one case, Robert Watson became convinced that observing the Stations was even more obligatory than observing Sunday. Ingham was not always ready to accept every aspect of fasting promoted by the Wesleys. Although he did adopt Charles's Lenten rule to have only one meal (at three o'clock) on fast days, he was "not fully determined" to accept Charles's suggestion to refrain from eating "flesh" at supper. John Wesley tried to impress upon Ingham both in person and through his writings the necessity of fasting, including even the rather obscure fast on the sixteenth day of the month. Even though Wesley was shortly to begin questioning the unequivocal position he held in 1733/34, he nevertheless encouraged fasting among the Methodists throughout his lifetime.

Among the Methodists, fasting was observed on specific days; temperance, however, was a constant rule. One of their Resolutions for Every Day asked, "Have I been temperate in the desire and in the use of sensual pleasure, and particularly have I been recollected and thankful in eating and drinking?" More specific injunctions were stipulated in the Resolutions for Lent, including the suggestion "to limit the quantity before sitting down" at every meal. Ingham recognized his weakness in this regard, and his diary discloses many occasions when he ate too much, to which he sometimes attributed subsequent headaches or "dullness." "Intemperance" in eating or sleeping is a frequent confession in Ingham's diary as in Wesley's, and "not intemperate" is the occasional note of joy for unexpected conquests over temptation. Ingham tried to follow Wesley's Rules for Eating and even made special lists of general and particular questions. His trials in this regard may be the reason why he suggested to Hervey, in a conversation about drawing up resolutions, "not to insert anything about eating."

If temperance was a trial for Ingham, early rising was a real battle, and the constant skirmishing presents some of the most amusing notations to be found in the diary. The basic principle of this part of one's fight against "the world, the flesh, and the devil" Ingham noted succinctly in shorthand: "From sufficient and sad experience I do consider that it is sinful to lie waking in bed, or to sleep longer than the health and strength of our bodies require." He tried to follow the Wesleyan pattern of rising at 4 a.m. but was frequently unsuccessful. On one occasion he lay in bed from four to five "to warm my shirt," as he confessed in his diary, followed by the warning, "No more such trivial excuses." Three days later one diary note, "I doubted whether I should rise or not," is juxtaposed with another which may explain the first: "Meditate no more on the bed." A stronger note of chagrin appears in the diary during July: "I was waking at 4:30 and would not rise; Oh! Shame!"

Ingham tried several methods to overcome his sloth in this area: sleeping without a mattress or sheets, "sconcing" himself a penny for going back to bed after once rising, doing without dinner or supper, "watching" at night a proportional amount of time, and even having a friend sit "century" (sentry) by his bed during the night. He tried Thomas Broughton's suggestion "to leap out of bed at the first ringing of the larum and, falling on [my] knees, pray for purity." At home in Ossett he arranged to have Molly Harrup (a neighbor or servant?) call him in the mornings. Resolutions, friends, fines, and prayer notwithstanding, he was unable to persevere and just at the point of success, disaster often struck. After boasting to James Walker one night that he never missed hearing his alarm, Ingham overslept the very next morning, which convinced him of his "inability to do anything" of himself. The moral (as he noted in his diary that morning): "Trust not to thine own strength, but be humble."

If Ingham had some problems of consistency with early rising, he certainly made up for it in his attendance at public church services. His attendance at morning and evening chapel service at Queen's was unfailing; the time of these services can be charted daily for nearly ten months from his diary entries.[49] In addition, he attended the 10 a.m. sermon on every saint's day and other festivals of the church. Moreover, Ingham had no difficulty adopting Wesley's suggestion to receive the Sacrament whenever possible.[50] At the beginning of every term (in this diary), Ingham attended the statutory celebration of the Eucharist at St. Mary's, a record better than Wesley's. He also joined other Methodists quite often on Sunday mornings at Christ Church or at the Castle prison to receive the Sacrament. He had read Wesley's sermon on the Sacrament (which admonished "constant communion") and, as time went on, found increasing opportunities to commune. Not all of Ingham's friends shared his enthusiasm in this regard, however. When Ingham heard of a Sacrament to be offered on Maundy Thursday for the servitors at Christ Church and discovered that Wesley and other Methodists would be there, he tried to convince some of his friends to go along. A heated debate ensued, with John Ford arguing that they were not duty-bound to receive the Sacrament "as often as we have opportunity" because they would then be obliged to receive "four or five times a day" (perhaps a bit of a hyperbole). In two weeks' time, however, Ford began to relent and after an intense round of debate, enticement, and prayer on the part of his Methodist companions, he agreed to ask the president of his college for permission to attend the Sunday morning celebrations of the Sacrament at Christ Church cathedral. This story is duplicated many times in both Ingham's and Wesley's diaries as the Methodists gathered their forces for this public expression of their religious commitment. Theirs was more than just a nonchalant decision whether or not to go to a church service. George Whitefield's comment about seeing the Methodists "go through a ridiculing crowd to receive the Holy Eucharist at St. Mary's"[51] is confirmed by Ingham's note after the service at the beginning of

Easter term: "I was very bold, and not at all concerned at the crowds of gazers." Such trials did not deter Ingham, Wesley, and some of the others, who had a touch of Madame Guyon's tendency to think that hardship and persecution were the seal of one's Christian calling.[52] Several Methodists even began participating as often as possible in private administrations of the Sacrament in the city of Oxford. Wesley began taking the Sacrament to sick persons as early as March 1732, and occasionally some of the Methodists would attend as well. Ingham first noted receiving the Sacrament with a sick woman on 8 April 1734 after receiving the celebrant's consent. On at least six occasions during the next two months, he attended such private administrations of the Sacrament in homes and at the workhouses, at times with as many as nine other Methodists present.[53]

Social Outreach

The activities of religious devotion just described were only one manifestation of the Methodists' adherence to the *Country Parson's Advice* "to lay open that piety which they practice in secret and to let the world know, by actions suitable to a good profession, that there are some that own the cause of real holiness."[54] Yet holy living, in the centuries-old tradition the Wesleyans had adopted, also stressed the second half of the Great Commandment, "love thy neighbor," which meant that their personal exercise of piety included a program of charitable activities directed toward their community. The Methodists at Oxford developed a program of social outreach aimed primarily toward the poor and disadvantaged: the prisoners at the Castle prison and Bocardo jail, the inmates at the workhouses, the children of the poor, and other individuals with special needs.

Visiting the prisoners had been suggested to the Wesleys in 1730 by one of their earliest religious companions, William Morgan. John Wesley frequently preached and administered the Sacrament at the Castle prison, and his friends helped read prayers, teach the prisoners to read, and provide some of their financial and legal needs. They also developed, at about the same time, a similar program at the Bocardo jail. After the middle of 1732, their "method" in both places included a rotating schedule of visitation and a system for donating funds for the support of needy prisoners. John Clayton, who joined the Wesleys about the time Morgan left Oxford in 1732, extended this program to include one of the local workhouses in St. Thomas's parish.[55]

Although Ingham and his friends from Queen's College did not become involved in the Methodists' work at the Castle (other than to attend the Sunday morning service and Sacrament frequently) and did not visit the Bocardo at all, they did become active in the program at the workhouses—even more so than Wesley himself. The workhouses presented an ideal opportunity for the Methodists to exercise their beneficent intentions toward disadvantaged people. Ingham first visited St. Thomas's Workhouse, near the southwest corner of Little High Bridge, in January 1734. He immediately resolved to go there two or three times a week to teach and catechize the children, read family prayers, talk with the old people, and read the Bible or some devotional work such as *The Christian Monitor*. In March he and Robson decided to apply to the workhouse the "method" of scheduling used by Wesley at the Castle: everyone would choose a day and go morning and night to perform their mission of teaching, reading, and prayer. Ingham's day was Wednesday, but he often took Ford's turn on Mondays or Smith's on Fridays as well.

In mid-April, Ingham and two Queen's colleagues decided also to begin visiting the paupers at St. Bartholomew's Hospital (Bartlemas House), a medieval foundation near Cowley Road that had become, in effect, a city almshouse. Four visits in one week all proved fruitless as there were no almsmen to be found. Understandably, the group "resolved to go no more." Instead, Ingham began to visit the poor people in the Hamel in St. Thomas's parish, reading to them *The Christian Monitor*.[56] Before another week had passed, Ingham and Hervey decided to try visiting the workhouse at Whitefriars in Gloucester Green. They found many poor folk there also, and a master, James Piggot, who was amenable to their reading family prayers morning and evening. During the six weeks prior to Ingham's receiving his bachelor's degree and his subsequent departure from Oxford, we find him and his friends filling a very busy schedule of charitable activities.

In addition to this general ministry to groups of poor persons, Ingham and the other Methodists also sought out individuals who had special needs, especially among the children and the aged. The sick and infirm were particular objects of their concern; Ingham and Wesley both note frequent visits to such. Some hungry poor folk were at times provided with food. Ingham's giving away his commons (college meal) now and then was more likely the result of his Methodist inclinations than the consequence of an old (and probably disregarded) Queen's College tradition.[57] Children received special attention, particularly in the workhouses, which, unlike the prisons, provided for children as a normal part of their routine. Besides teaching and catechizing at the workhouses and prisons, the Methodists helped to support schools for the poor children. Wesley's financial accounts for this period included notes of gifts to the Grey-Coat School, a charity school in Oxford. Ingham visited two such schools at Oxford with Hervey and shortly afterward convinced some of his friends to give sixpence a month "to maintain some poor children at the school." This may have been the school for which the Methodists had assumed responsibility, a school set up in the first instance by William Morgan and taken over by Wesley after the Irishman's departure.[58] Ingham's interest in the plight of such children and in teaching them, which begins to bud in this period (particularly after he returned to his home in Ossett), came to full blossom later in Georgia and in his subsequent activities in Yorkshire.

The scope of the Methodists' good will seemed to be boundless at times. Many of their colleagues did not understand or appreciate the inward motivation that elicited their visible and public, much less their personal and private, program of activity. The outward manifestations of their religious perspective appeared fanatical to many in that age of spiritual lethargy, overshadowing anything that might have been said by way of theological rationale. Two hundred and fifty years after *Fog's Weekly Journal* published the first vitriolic description of these "sons of sorrow," we are compelled to do more than repeat the old criticisms or the timeworn apologies; to smirk at the Oxford Methodists as well-intentioned Pharisees who had not yet seen the light (or had not yet felt its warmth) is no better than to decry their "enthusiastick madness and superstitious scruples." The activities of the Oxford Methodists were of a piece with their theology, a relationship worth trying to understand since both the life and thought of Oxford Methodism had a positive and basic impact on the development and shape of Wesleyan theology and activity.

Theology

The extant diaries of the Oxford Methodists (Ingham, Wesley, and Whitefield) do not contain many explicitly theological entries. But the pattern of Christian living described in the diaries (including the diary keeping itself) does exhibit a theological perspective that is quite explicable when viewed in the light of the books they were reading. In fact, the life-style described in these diaries cannot be fully understood without a clear grasp of the theological impulses from which these activities sprang.

Part of the legend of the Wesleyans at Oxford is that the name Methodist was given them because of their methodical life-style. Historians have almost universally overlooked the fact that their theology could also be designated by the same term. The theology of holy living that provided the basic structure for Wesleyan theology in the early 1730s was essentially the same as that of the so-called New Methodists of the seventeenth century. The term derived from their opponents point of view. Strict Calvinists of that day saw any tendency toward synergism, freedom of the will, a conditional covenant of grace, or any other concept that detracted from the sovereignty of God as an attack on orthodoxy and as a "new method" of doing theology ("new" being of course a derogatory term in this case). Attacks against the New Methodists could be aimed in a number of directions—against the Pelagianism of the papists, the moralism of the Socinians, the active mysticism of the Bellarmines, or the Arminianism of some Anglicans and Dissenters.[59] The common denominator in the list of charges was that each of these "new methods" incorporated some degree of "works-righteousness" in its soteriology.[60] In England, the targets were persons such as John Goodwin and Richard Baxter whose emphasis on the continuing necessity and possibility of obedience to the "Law" even under the new covenant of grace seemed to challenge the two main pillars of Reformed Protestantism, *sola fide* and *sola gratia*. Such ideas were seen to undermine the derivatives of these pillars most emphasized by the Calvinists' unconditional election, limited atonement, and irresistible grace (in a word, predestination).

The holy living tradition adopted by the Wesleyans at Oxford shared much of the theological heritage represented by the New Methodists and suffered (then and now) under the same common misrepresentation of having a doctrine of salvation by works-righteousness.[61] Although the Wesleyan brand of Methodism was not, strictly speaking, a doctrine of "salvation by faith" in the more radical evangelical Protestant understanding of that term (which to some implied the antinomian dangers inherent in the Solifidian position), it was definitely a doctrine of "salvation by grace" (not "by works"). And although this theological perspective did result in a disciplined life-style characterized by charitable and devotional activities, the emphasis was always on the interior aspects of holiness. Works were not seen as the *means* to any state; they were the manifestations of virtues, which had been carefully cultivated through various meditative practices.[62] Salvation, spiritual health, and freedom involved being restored to the original state of humanity as created—in the image of God.[63] This was the purpose of the redemptive act of God's grace in Jesus Christ, making possible the restoration of human beings to their intended relationship to God, as before the Fall.[64] This restoration is only effected when the believer has faith, a faith that works through love[65] and draws the person closer toward "having the mind of Christ, and walking as he walked."[66] Individuals are thereby enabled to fulfill the expectations of the Law, not through their own activity alone, but through the grace of God acting in them.[67] The concept of a universal atonement that this perspective assumes (theoretical as in Amyraldus, or actual as in Wesley) was protected from a Pelagian works-righteousness by an understanding of prevenient grace: no act that contributes to a person's salvation is self-initiated but is rather the result of God's grace, which "prevenes" (comes before) any human act.[68] Salvation is not a momentary event but involves a process of restoration and becoming holy, of cultivating the love of God in such a way as to draw closer to the goal of "having the mind of Christ." The emphasis of the Christian life then was on sanctification as one pressed on, with the assistance of God's grace, toward perfection in love and final justification.

The personal discipline evinced by such thinking had a dual focus represented by the *imitatio Christi* on the one side and the *pugna spiritualis* on the other. The goal was, in the end, Christian perfection, but this objective was not meant to imply having the ability to conform one's actions to every jot and tittle of the Law (as defined by any particular set of rules or standard of activity). Perfection must be understood in the context of a virtue-oriented ethic. The desired end is not perfect obedience to a standard of conduct; it is perfect conformity to a model of divine-oriented virtue. Being restored in the image of God is basic to the whole process. The goal is not to be able to act perfectly; the goal is to be perfect, to achieve an inward perfection of intentions and attitudes, of will as well as of understanding. Truly good actions are the result of the inward dispositions of the soul (virtues)—thankfulness, meekness, humility, self-denial, mortification, chastity, love of neighbor, and (the ground of them all) love of God. The Christian life involves a life of devotion that will cultivate these virtues (the imitation of Christ) as well as contend with "the world, the flesh, and the devil" (the spiritual combat). The means by which this double-edged form of spirituality could be effected in the life of the believer was the practice of meditation.

Meditation for the Oxford Methodists, as for many of their spiritual forebears, was different from the contemplative mysticism of the Eastern Church.[69] Meditation was inextricably tied to the whole process of self-examination that lay at the heart of the discipline of holy living. By contemplating Christ and the many virtues exemplified in his life and death (his active and passive work respectively), one was made vividly aware of one's own sinful state and of particular faults that precluded achievement of the desired virtues. The one or two hours a day set aside for meditation were as apt to be filled with thoughts of "sins and infirmities" as they were of "God's perfections" or "Christ's sufferings." The list of virtues mentioned as topics for meditation in the diaries follows very closely the topics under which questions for self-examination were arranged.[70] Sin was not so much the commission or omission of a particular action but rather the absence of, or at least the failure to manifest, a particular virtue, thus a falling short of the glory of God as seen in Jesus Christ. Everything was to be done to the glory of God, as seen in one of the questions for general examination by which the Methodists daily tested their conscience: "Have I said or done anything without a present or past perception of its direct or remote tendency to the glory of God?"[71]

The Methodists used many books of meditation, but the method exhibited by most of those works displayed the "modern" form of a centuries-old tradition of meditative piety and "spiritual exercises" seen in Thomas à Kempis, Ignatius of Loyola, Lorenzo Scupoli, Francis de Sales, Joseph Hall, Johann Gerhard, Richard Baxter, Jeremy Taylor, Henry Scougal, Madame Guyon, Anthony Horneck, and William Law—each one having a slightly different perspective, but most of them superimposing a practical Pelagianism upon a mysticism of *sola gratia.*[72] One interesting aspect of this strain of thought is the fascinating combination of people who make up this "family," including French Catholic mystics, Jesuits, English Puritans, nonjuring bishops, continental pietists, and Scottish Divines.[73] They are all, however, theological cousins, and several common features evident in their writings are significant not only for Oxford Methodism but also for the subsequent shape of Wesleyan theology. In the face of theological bickering and divisions, many of these writers stress the need to return to a simple religion based on the love of God. On the basis of this common denominator, they call for an approach that emphasizes unity in the essentials of belief and toleration of differences in the more subtle theological distinctions. In this regard, the Early Church (its unity perhaps idealized by these writers) becomes an important model and source for thought and action.[74] Religion is not seen as a matter for argument but for practice.[75] The Great Commandment is the bedrock of such a theology, the life of Christ its pristine manifestation, and the lives of the saints its further confirmation. Love of God manifests itself in a virtuous life—this theme even provides the organizing principle for the biographies of exemplary Christians.[76] The center of this religion is in the heart. The life of God in the soul of man redirects the affections, purifies the intentions, restores the virtues, and brings about a life of love. This "theology of the heart"[77] was not simply visceral emotionalism but an attempt to understand God's saving activity in ways that were more biblical, apostolic, historical, and personally authentic than the antiseptic intellectualism (and divisiveness) of rationalistic or scholastic theology; more ethically responsible than the Antinomianism of the quietist mystical theology; and more Christ-centered than the humanistic moralism that seemed to challenge biblical theology in every age. It is no surprise that the earliest of Wesley's sermons to ring forth this theme was "The Circumcision of the Heart" (1733), a clarion call to holy living that stressed the necessity of inward holiness ("that habitual disposition of the soul") and outlined its implications in terms of "being cleansed from sin" and "endued with those virtues which were also in Christ Jesus."

One problem that constantly accompanied such a theology was that of assurance. How does one know one is saved? How does one know when one is proceeding in the proper direction in an attempt to press on toward perfection? If the emphasis is more on the *process* of salvation than the *state* of salvation, how does one know he or she is doing the right things? The answer that permeates the perspective of the Oxford Methodists (as well as many of their theological forebears) is that one's hope rests in one's *sincerity*.[78] As long as a person is doing the best one can, one must trust that God will not withhold his grace. In trying to deal with the tension between impatience on the one hand and want of zeal for improvement on the other (or between scrupulosity and self-indulgence), Wesley noted in the front of his diary in 1734 a quotation from Thomas à Kempis: "*Fac quod in te est, et Deus aderit bonae tuae voluntati*," which he translated in his edition of Kempis the following year, "Do what lieth in thy power, and God will assist thy good will."[79] This was entirely in keeping with Wesley's understanding of a theology of grace—while sincerely doing one's best, one must acknowledge that every effort springs from God's grace. Thus a person exercises the prevenient grace given to one by God, responding to the promptings of the Holy Spirit and cooperating with God's grace in the present moment to conform one's will and affections to God's will and intentions. Holy living is thus the exercise of grace[80] in the development of those virtues which make a person fully human (renewed after the image of God, seen in Christ) while at the same time one continually struggles with the contrary vices. Grace is not given in opposition to the exercise of the will, but rather it directs (or redirects) the will. The saints are not those who had a more excellent nature, but rather those who had a more exact care over it, by the grace of God.[81]

But if the emphasis is on the process (tentatively allowing for the possibility of reaching a level of perfection), then the question of assurance persists as a nagging companion in the struggle. And resting one's hope in one's sincerity is little consolation to a person who is also struggling to develop a sense of humility that recognizes that his or her own efforts must be distrusted.[82] The closer and more intricate the process of self-examination becomes, the more evident one's failings become. The practices of meditation and self-examination that are supposed to assist the process of improving in holiness simply serve to point out just how feeble and worthless any efforts are, no matter how sincere. The methods used in this process often lead to the temptation (felt even by predestinarians) of becoming obsessed with good works which, though thought to be a secondary manifestation of an inner condition, are the primary measure of that condition and, therefore, the focus of attention.[83] This problem in part led some theologians to emphasize the necessity of passivity (passive obedience), which can result either in a rejection of any good works (and the sacraments) as means of grace (as in the quietism of Molinos, Molther, and others) or in a preoccupation with suffering as the mark of a true Christian (as in the mysticism of Guyon, Bourignon, and others). Some of the Oxford Methodists, notably Ingham, Gambold, and Wesley, were eventually attracted to Moravian Solifidianism, which helped solve the problem of assurance by a reliance solely on faith but which also bordered on a type of quietism that Wesley soon found necessary to refute. Although Wesley's adoption of an emphasis on *sola fide* finally helped him reorient his understanding of the order of salvation during the years 1736 to 1738 (particularly the nature and place of "justification by grace through faith" preceding sanctification), he never allowed it to supplant the necessity of holy living and pressing on toward perfection. The pervasive synergism of Wesley's mature theology, with its tension between "faith alone" and good works, testifies to the solid grounding he had at Oxford in the synergistic perspective of the holy living tradition.[84]

It might be said that the Oxford Methodist concept of true Christianity in 1734 was not so much patterned after any particular system or systems of theology as it was modeled upon the lives of persons the Methodists considered to have epitomized the Christlike life. The religion of Ingham, Wesley, and the others could not be defined simply by applying terms such as Arminianism, Puritanism, pietism, or mysticism. Rather, it was best described in terms of the holy lives of de Renty and Guyon, the "Christian gnostic" of Clement of Alexandria, August Hermann Francke's *Nicodemus*, and a long series of witnesses to the love of God in the lives of human beings, from Ephraem Syrus and Augustine to Ambrose Bonwicke and James Bonnell.

In summary, the Oxford Methodists shared a view of Christianity with a long-standing heritage in the holy living tradition. Their perspective embraced the simple essentials, which were grounded in the Great Commandment—to love God and to love neighbor—revealed in Scripture and epitomized in the life of Christ, which they hoped to imitate. The focus was upon nurturing the virtues basic to the Christian (Christlike) life and combatting the vices that impede the development of inward holiness. This tradition, while based in Scripture, is confirmed and exemplified in Primitive Christianity; the Bible and the Early Fathers are the sources for the Oxford Methodists' thought and action. Their theology is irenic and ecumenical, with an emphasis on unity (consensus) and toleration and with an aversion to disputation and speculation. Theology was not unimportant in this whole enterprise, but theology was the handmaid of holy living, a practical theology devoted to Christian living.[85] Salvation, "the one thing needful," meant being renewed in the image of God, recovering that purity of love once lost, and nurturing the virtues so constantly as to purify (perfect) the heart of conscious sinful inclinations. The life of the faithful Christian is a grace-full life, one that cultivates the virtues through the practice of meditation, self-examination, and prayer and manifests its inner reorientation in a disciplined life of devotion and charitable activities.

This basic outline describes a perceivable tradition that exists within many Christian bodies, a tradition that cuts across denominational and national lines. It is neither exclusively Catholic nor uniquely Protestant; it cannot be enclosed within simple terms such as puritan, pietist, or mystic.[86] It has authentic representatives within many different Christian traditions, differing perhaps on some points of theology or ecclesiology but sharing a common approach to the Christian life of meditative piety. One can see why Wesley, Ingham, and the other Oxford Methodists did not conceive of themselves as straying from their Church of England roots, even while developing a close kinship to other groups, for example, the Moravians. Most of the ideas found in the "puritan" Catholics, the "pietist" mystics, or the "spiritual" moralists they were reading (and with whom at times they were linked) were repeated and confirmed by many of their favorite

English writers who also shared this perspective (Law, Deacon, Norris, Taylor, Nelson) and who considered themselves no less Church of England men for their interests in reform and renewal.

The eclectic methodology of the Oxford Methodist theology that Wesley continued to exemplify throughout his later theological development is very much in keeping with the tolerant, ecumenical orientation and methodology of the meditative pietists in the holy living tradition. The particular strain of active devotion that is obvious in de Renty, Guyon, Fénelon, Taylor, Law, Francis de Sales, Scupoli, the Country Parson, and Thomas à Kempis helps us understand how Ingham, Wesley, and their friends could combine the emphases on the apostolic Fathers and the Scriptures, acts of charity and devotional contemplation, ethical responsibility and a theology of grace, sincerity and faith to yield a special blend of disciplined devotion, methodical meditation, and practical piety that gave shape to their own pattern of Christian thought and life.

Chapter 6

GREAT EXPECTATIONS: ALDERSGATE AND THE EVIDENCES OF GENUINE CHRISTIANITY[1]

John Wesley's familiar words describing his experience of 24 May 1738 have been for some time the basis of monumental commemorations and the focus of annual celebrations among Methodists: "I felt my heart strangely warmed. I felt I did trust in Christ, Christ alone for salvation, and an assurance was given me that he had taken away *my* sins, even *mine*, and saved *me* from the law of sin and death."[2] For much of this century, a running dispute has been carried on between some who view this event in Wesley's life as a conversion experience with singular significance as a watershed in his life and others who challenge that view for a variety of reasons.

The proponents of the "heart-warming" as a conversion or watershed point to Wesley's own comments at the time, his claim that he was *now* a Christian whereas previously he was not. They support their view of the watershed nature of the event by quoting Wesley's occasional references to a significant shift or beginning point occurring in or around 1738, and by repeating a general perception that the Methodist movement began to spread like wildfire across England in response to Wesley's new-found zeal.[3]

The opponents of the view of "Aldersgate" as a conversion or watershed also use Wesley's own comments to support their views, noting that before 1738 Wesley claimed to be a Christian, that he also claimed several times after 1738 that he was not now a true believer and in at least one instance implied that he never had been. On the basis of Wesley's own comments, they discard the watershed concept and see several important developments occurring in Wesley's life and thought (and Methodist history) from 1725 onward throughout the century, some of which modify or even reject the points of view that he held in 1738.

Proponents of both sides of the controversy, however, must embrace some anomalies that cause disjunctures in their own argument. Although there are a few references in Wesley's writings that can be seen as referring to a significant personal alteration in or about 1738, these comments generally occur within a few years of the event and tend to disappear completely as the century proceeds. Most of the references refer to a shift in his theology and preaching. He does not later harken back to it as his "conversion" experience,[4] much less celebrate the day as a spiritual anniversary, nor does he represent his own personal experience as a model for others to follow. Why, if it were a watershed, would Wesley ignore this event for the last half of his life? Why was it not more determinative of the shape of his autobiographical reflections? And why, in later life, would he go so far as to qualify his own earlier published autobiographical reflections on the event and its significance?[5] On the other hand, if the event was not a watershed, why did its central feature (the experience of assurance, the witness of the Spirit) become a fixture at the heart of his preaching and theology? Why did the perceptible inspiration of the Holy Spirit become a central feature of his soteriology? And why did he continue to insist upon assurance as one of the distinguishing marks of the Methodist movement?

The answers to these questions do not emerge from a simple attempt to solve the problem of whether or not Aldersgate was a conversion experience for Wesley. For the answer to that question, based on Wesley's own testimony, is both "yes" and "no," depending on when he spoke to the question and how he then defined the concept. Moreover, the primary issue in 1738 for Wesley (both in terms of anticipation and experience) was that of *assurance*, and the direct tie between assurance and conversion, assumed by Wesley at the time, he eventually dropped in his mature theology. The more important question, then, is to ask what significance this experience of 24 May 1738 had in the overall span of Wesley's life and thought, and how Wesley viewed this experience—what were his expectations? what were his immediate reactions? what were his subsequent reflections? Wesley's own attempt to resolve questions relating to the experience of assurance, as it turns out, provides a major stimulus for his continuing theological development throughout much of his life.

In looking at these questions, we would also do well to distinguish between Wesley's spiritual pilgrimage and his theological development. We will see that while Aldersgate was a crucial step in his *spiritual* pilgrimage at the time, his expectations were not fully met by the experience, and his subsequent reflections on the event caused him to modify many of the *theological* premises upon which those expectations were based. There is, of course, an obvious and essential connection between the two: his theology quite naturally develops in conjunction with his life experiences. But one soon discovers that Wesley is often more facile at *describing* his experience than at *analyzing* it. The process of theological reflection often takes years to work through a given problem—to integrate scriptural concepts, church teachings, life experiences, spiritual inspiration, and rational reflection. His descriptions at any given time must also be seen in the light of his later reflections. And later reflections need to be understood as incorporating the hindsight that comes with continued maturation.[6]

The problem that confronted Wesley at Aldersgate was the question, How do I *know* I am a Christian? a child of God? How do I *know* that I am justified? forgiven? The issue was essentially that of *assurance*. He had been convinced as a young man that persons should be able clearly to perceive if they were in a state of salvation. His problem was, in one significant aspect, epistemological—how does one know? And given his philosophical tendencies in this matter, his approach was to look for *evidence* upon which to base his knowledge. What he was looking for, then, was the evidence that he was really a Christian.

Several variables immediately enter the problem: (1) How is "Christian" *defined*? The definition entails in part some descriptive model that exhibits such things as necessary traits, minimal qualities, requisite standards. (2) How does one *become* a Christian? An understanding of the process ("what must I do to be saved?") entails crucial definitions and weighing of essentials in the process, such as grace, faith, good works, the work of the Holy Spirit. (3) How does one *know* that he or she is a Christian? What are the grounds of any certainty that a person is a Christian? What is the evidence (internal or external) that can verify one's condition? These questions pertain to both the process of knowing and the content of that knowledge.

In all three of these areas, Wesley's views changed over the years. We cannot fully understand Aldersgate without recognizing where Wesley stood on each of these issues at that time in the light of how he got to that point and where he went from there. His spiritual and theological development up to 1738 (which in part shaped his expectations) depended upon his stance in each of these areas, and his subsequent development (which was affected in part by his evaluation of Aldersgate in the light of those expectations) shows significant modifications in each of these areas. Of particular interest is the increasingly essential role that the Holy Spirit plays in Wesley's understanding of not only how people *become* Christians but also how they *know* they are children of God. It is important to recognize that Aldersgate represents a significant conjunction of pneumatology and epistemology in his life (spiritual pilgrimage) that took many years for him to work out in his thought (theological development). It also represents a testing of his theological methodology, his manner of weighing various criteria as he attempted to use rational processes to explain scriptural truths manifest in the human experience of divine realities. His theology, centered as it is upon soteriology, is an attempt to explain the *via salutis*,[7] based in part upon his observations of that spiritual pilgrimage in his own life and the lives of others, looking for the evidences of genuine Christianity (as he understood it at any particular time).

Our attempt here will be to examine the place of Aldersgate in Wesley's development. It will focus upon *how Wesley himself understood it:* the shape of his expectations in anticipation of such an event, his description of the essential features of his experience of the event, and his retrospective views of these features in the light of his subsequent theological analyses of this step of his spiritual pilgrimage. The plain story of these developments is central to our examination. Since the Moravian influence is crucial to an understanding of events in 1738, we will focus our attention upon the narrative of the chronological development of his thinking and experience through the time of his association with the Moravians up to 1740, then summarize some of the more important developments beyond that time. We will use recently discovered sermons and correspondence from his early years, along with material from his personal diaries, to put together the story in a way that has not previously been told.[8]

The Quest for Certainty

The central issue for Wesley in the spring of 1738 is the question, How do I *know* that I am a Christian? Another way of stating the same question is, What *assurance* (or certain evidence) do I have that I am a child of God? These questions were by no means new to Wesley. He had long felt that one should be able to know the answer to these questions with some certainty by seeing the *evidences* of genuine Christianity in the life of the believer. This approach, of course, fitted nicely into his generally empirical approach to questions of knowledge. He had quite early settled upon a Lockean approach to matters of this sort.[9] A letter to his mother Susanna reveals his inclination to apply an empirical approach to this question as early as 1725. Referring to the Lord's Supper, in the celebration of which "the Holy Ghost confers on us the graces we pray for," Wesley writes:

> Now surely these graces are not of so little force as that we can't perceive whether we have them or not: and if we dwell in Christ and Christ in us, . . . certainly we must be sensible of it. . . . If we can never have any certainty of our being in a state of salvation, good reason it is that every moment should be spent, not in joy, but fear and trembling.[10]

Wesley himself had recently exhibited an "alteration of his temper" that Susanna had noticed. She was hopeful that the change might have proceeded "from the operations of God's Holy Spirit" and that he, in response, would "make religion the business of [his] life" as "the one thing that strictly speaking is necessary." She had pressed him to use self-examination in order to increase self-knowledge, "that you may know whether you have a reasonable hope of salvation, . . . whether you are in a state of faith and repentance or not. . . . If you are, the satisfaction of knowing it will abundantly reward your pains."[11]

John also was fairly clear about the general form of evidence by which one might be assured of being in a state of salvation. As Susanna had written to him, "Our blessed Lord . . . came from heaven to save us from our sins . . . knowing we could not be happy in either world without holiness." Happiness and holiness were constantly linked as visible results of God's saving grace in the life of the believer. The goal, a gift of grace, was Christian perfection: "sincerely endeavouring to plant each virtue in our minds that may through Christ render us pleasing to God." This holiness, centered in the virtues, was directed toward eternal goals, opened to human eyes and ears by the Lord who "opens and extends our views beyond time to eternity."[12]

With all of this John agreed, but his desire for certainty outstripped his parents' understanding of the means to such assurance. John understood faith to be a basic building block of this certainty. At that time he defined faith as "a species of belief," and belief he defined as "assent to a proposition upon rational grounds." His conclusion was that "without rational grounds there is therefore no belief and consequently no faith." This definition of faith was borrowed from Dr. Fiddes and grounded in his own correlation of faith and rational knowledge. Wesley assumed that "no knowledge can be where there is not certain evidence" (a variation of the empirical maxim that "there is nothing in the mind that is not in the senses") and that the divine testimony was "the most reasonable of all evidence whatever."[13] The present and future prospects of certainty with regard to salvation he explained in the following manner, providing both the rationale and the evidence:

> That we can never be so certain of the pardon of our sins as to be assured they will never rise up against us, I firmly believe. . . . But I am persuaded we may know if we are *now* in a state of salvation, since that is expressly promised in the Holy Scriptures to our sincere endeavors, and we are surely able to judge of our own sincerity.[14]

Samuel and Susanna soon disabused John of what they viewed as an inadequate notion of faith. Susanna provided two long discussions on the manner in which "all faith is an assent, but all assent is not faith."[15] Samuel, with typical pungency, pointed out the dangers of John's position in one cryptic sentence and tagged on a word of advice: "He that believes *without* or *against* reason is half a Papist or enthusiast; he that would mete revelation by his own shallow reason is either half a deist or an heretic. O my dear, steer clear between this Scylla and Charybdis."[16]

John capitulated in the matter: "I am therefore at length come over entirely to your opinion, that saving faith (including practice) is an assent to what God has revealed, because he has revealed it, and not because the truth of it may be evinced by reason."[17] The response of his mother/spiritual director was typical: "I am much more pleased and thankful because I have observed sometime that the Holy Jesus (to whom the whole manage of our salvation is committed) seems to have taken the conduct of your soul into his own hand, in that he has given you a true notion of saving faith, and, I hope, an experimental knowledge of repentance. . . . Dear Jacky, I hope you are a good Christian."[18]

Wesley's view of a "good Christian" up to this point had been largely determined by his childhood training in the Epworth rectory. As he later pointed out, he had early learned that the Christian is one who has received the saving grace of God. His early understanding of the means of attaining salvation was typical for the Church of England: a balance of faith and works, following the scriptural injunctions to believe, hope, and love, using the means of grace.[19] During his years at Charterhouse School where, beyond the immediate constraints of his parents his outward sins tended to proliferate, he relied for his hope of salvation upon a threefold approach: not being so bad as others; having a fondness for religion; going to church, saying his prayers, etc.[20] The evidence for such hope and the signs of genuine Christianity therefore depended upon external measures: a Christian is one saved from sin, therefore a Christian avoids sin and does good whenever possible, and upon failure to do so, relies upon repentance.[21]

A New View of Religion—Holiness of Heart

The changes that took place in Wesley's life and thought in 1725 were caused by a shift in his definition of salvation. His view that salvation amounted to freedom from sin (which the Christian exhibited by the grace of God through *outward* goodness and upon failure turned to God's mercy in proper repentance) was enlarged to include the striving for *inward* holiness. Wesley began to view true religion as seated in the heart: "God's law extends to all thoughts as well as words and actions."[22] Wesley found many helpful tutors in this regard in the books he read: from Jeremy Taylor he learned the importance of purity of intention; from William Law and Henry Scougal the necessity of a proper inclination of the soul; from Thomas à Kempis the way of appropriating the mind of Christ; from Robert Nelson a practical method of meditating on the virtues for each day of the week.

He now set upon a new life in earnest, watched against all sin *and* aimed at inward holiness. This development, which his mother had noticed and encouraged as part of his new determination to prepare for holy orders, manifested itself in several ways which Wesley himself began to chart. Meditation became the means of implanting the virtues; lists of rules and resolutions provided some measure of their presence; self-examination was the means of testing their effects. But a reliable measure of inward intentions and virtues was more difficult than spotting the absence of outward sins. A daily diary provided the ledger upon which the hourly dispositions of the mind and soul could be recorded. Sincerity became the measure of one's progress toward perfection, trying to imitate the life of Christ, having his mind and walking as he walked.[23]

The result of Wesley's endeavors in this regard was that he considered himself at the time to be a good Christian, in terms of his definition of what a Christian is, how one becomes a Christian, and how one knows that one is a Christian.[24] It is interesting to note in passing that Wesley in later life will confirm that this is the point at which he resolved to become a *real* Christian.[25] In 1725 he was not hesitant to use the term "servant of God" to describe the Christian, a term which he will eventually come back to and recognize as useful in describing a valid Christian.[26]

Wesley's conviction of the necessity of inward holiness was heightened by his study of William Law's writings in 1728–29, which convinced him even further of the "exceeding height and breadth and depth of the law of God," inward and outward. Wesley describes the impact of this insight: "The light flowed in so mightily upon my soul, that everything appeared in a new view." Wesley felt even more strongly then that he would be accepted by Christ and that he was "even then in a state of salvation."[27] At age twenty-seven, he "strove against all sin," used "all the means of grace at all opportunities," and "omitted no occasion of doing good" (another good summary of his later *General Rules*). He was convinced, however, that all this must be aimed at inward holiness, the restoration of the image of God in the life of the believer.[28]

Faith and Knowledge

The problem was still the question, How does he *know* if he is a Christian? Wesley's fascination with epistemological questions is evident in three writings he produced at the end of 1730—two sermons, and an abridgment of Peter Browne's *The Procedure, Method, and Limits of Human Understanding*. In the first of these sermons (on John 13:7, "What I do thou knowest not now") Wesley points out the possibilities and problems of our attempts to know God, speaking of the Christian's perception of the sovereignty of grace, knowing *that* God works in human lives without being able to explain either *how* God works in a person the life of grace or *why* some attain to such heights of virtue and happiness. At this point, Wesley grants that God reveals enough to undergird our faith *that* God's ways are wise and good and gracious (which allows us to *believe* and give assent to this) but acknowledges that we do not have the sensible perception of God or his truth that would allow us to know these things for *certain*. Likewise, the springs of spiritual life are ultimately unsearchable—*that* the Spirit works in us, "experience, and reason, and Scripture convince every sincere inquirer; but *how* he worketh this in us, who shall tell?"[29] The reason God clouds our vision of him is to lead us to humility ("conscious of how little we can know of him, we may be the more intent upon knowing ourselves") that we might "walk by faith, not by sight."[30]

In the second writing (sermon on Genesis 1:27, "In the Image of God") Wesley contrasts human nature in the perfection of creation and the debilities of the Fall. Created in God's image, Adam could know everything "according to its real nature; truth and evidence went hand in hand; he was a stranger to error and doubt."[31] The first step of sinful humanity toward a recovery of the image of God is humility, self-knowledge; if we cannot know God fully, at least we can know ourselves. A just sense of our condition will result in our understanding being enlightened: we must know that we are all originally foolish and vicious; then we know the necessity and the divine efficacy of our religion.[32]

Wesley's abridgment of Browne the following month broadened his perspective somewhat not only on the matter of "where knowledge ends and faith begins" but also on "where they meet again and inseparably combine for enlarging our understanding vastly beyond its native sphere, for opening to the mind an immense scene of things otherwise imperceptible."[33] Browne reiterates the basic empiricist proposition: our senses are the only source of those ideas upon which all our knowledge is founded. He goes on to describe the various kinds of knowledge and evidence, distinguishing between knowledge and faith and between different types of certainty (illustrated by scientific and moral certainty). While pointing out that sensible evidence is the ground not of faith but of knowledge, Browne goes on to say that "evangelical faith" is an act of the will beyond assent to evidential religious propositions and is based to some extent upon things that are immediately comprehended. Browne uses a definition of evangelical faith that will become central to Wesley's eventual understanding of how knowledge and faith combine in matters of religious certainty: "the 'evidence of things not seen' [Heb. 11:1] or the assent of the understanding to the truth and existence of things inconceivable, upon certain and evident proof of their reality in their symbols and representatives."[34] In his abridgment, Wesley omits this specific reference, but does refer to this "evidence which is peculiar to a quite different sort of knowledge" than knowledge of "matters merely human."[35]

Sincerity as Evidence and Hope

One major question in all this, of course, is, What is this evidence by which one can discern progress toward inward holiness or be assured of a proper status with God? Inward holiness is more difficult to sense with certainty and much harder to measure than outward holiness. In counseling a friend at this time (1731) regarding the interplay of faith and doubt, Wesley stressed one typical Anglican response to the dilemma, a reliance upon sincerity. In the process of explaining, he used a metaphor of sense perception (i.e., sight) that was becoming common to him and would provide a useful image throughout his life: by "faith . . .'the eyes of her understanding can be enlightened to see what is the hope of our calling,' to know that our hope is sincerity, not perfection; not to do well, but to do our best."[36] One's sincerity, then, provided whatever measure of hope or assurance there might be of salvation. The virtue was in the attempt; the assurance was manifest in the sincerity of the attempter.

A few months later, Wesley expanded upon the idea of "doing our best" in a gloss to his abridgment of Robert Nelson's work, *The Great Duty of Frequenting the Christian Sacrifice*.[37] One of Wesley's answers to objections against what he called "constant communion" was that man is bound to obey the commands of God "as often as he can." To explain this point, Wesley argued that since the Fall, man is no longer required to exercise perfect obedience to every command of God (the stipulations of the old covenant), but rather to follow the "new covenant" that was made with fallen man and to "perform it as well as he can." Rather than the original agreement, "Do this and live," mankind is now bound by the second, "Try to do this, and live."[38] The sincere attempt would be recognized by God, who would acknowledge one's good intentions.[39]

The dilemma of assurance was not completely resolved, of course, by this approach. Sincerity might be an appropriate (perhaps even the best) measure of an inward reality, but how could anyone ever be certain, ever rest assured, that they were indeed doing the best they could? In fact, Wesley's own attempts to measure his progress in this regard by keeping track of his spiritual pulse by means of a diary seemed only to frustrate this approach by revealing the opposite—the closer he kept track of himself, the more he became aware of his shortcomings, doubted his sincerity, and feared lest he should fall short of the mark of his calling.

Nevertheless, the conviction that true happiness came from an inward holiness was firmly planted in Wesley by the late 1720s. In 1733 he graphically characterized this inward focus as "the circumcision of the heart" in his first major sermon on Christian perfection. That Wesley and Oxford Methodism were essentially concerned with inward religion (not works-righteousness) and focused on a virtue ethic (more than an obligation ethic) has not been generally recognized by those who would try to see Wesley's life before 1738 as being in dark contrast to the light that follows 1738.[40] In this sermon, which sets the course for a lifelong emphasis on Christian perfection as love of God and neighbor—"having the mind which was in Christ Jesus"[41]— Wesley strikes a note that disarms those who see the Oxford Methodists as trusting in their own works: "the distinguishing mark of a true follower of Christ, of one who is in a state of acceptance with God, is not either outward circumcision or baptism, or any other outward form, but a right state of soul, a mind and spirit renewed after the image of him that created it."[42]

In this context, Wesley speaks of the necessity of faith as "a sure light of them that are in darkness." It must be a *strong* faith, however.[43] Such a view implies variations of faith in degrees and raises (but does not answer) the implicit question, How strong does faith have to be in order for one truly to be a Christian?[44] Faith implies new sight: to the one who thus believes, "the eyes of his understanding being enlightened, he sees what is his calling," including an assent to that important truth, "Jesus Christ came into the world to save sinners; he bore our sins in his own body on the tree; he is the propitiation for our sins; and not for ours only, but also for the sins of the whole world."[45] This proclamation of the belief in *Christus pro nobis* (Christ died for us) is eventually the ground of his experience of *Christus pro me*.[46]

Measuring a right state of soul and testing a renewed spirit, however, presented a challenge. Wesley at this point states that the marks by which one can judge his state of acceptance are the presence of a humility that brings with it a conviction of corruption, an honest attempt to walk by faith in the light of eternity, and the assurance given by "the witness of the Spirit with his spirit that he is a child of God."[47] The rules of the Oxford Methodists served the same purpose as the rules of later Methodism—a means by which one could test the external evidences of an inward inclination of the soul and the active presence of the virtues (especially the central virtue, love), which were the genuine fruits or evidence of real religion.[48]

The One Thing Needful

Wesley's conviction that holiness of heart was the focus of true religion was heightened by his contact with the mystics after 1732, who nearly convinced him that outward works were useless in the pursuit of inward holiness, which they defined as "union of the soul with God." Writings by and about Mmes Bourignon and Guyon, Cardinal Fénelon, Pierre Poiret, and Monsr de Renty, as well as direct contact with William Law (who by 1732 had come under the influence of Böhmist mysticism himself), encouraged his attempts to overcome his growing obsession with rules of holy living.[49] If the goal of the Christian was union with the divine being, the first step toward this goal was "purgation," the expulsion of "the world, the flesh, and the devil" from all thoughts and actions. All temporal concerns were seen as impediments to the process of transcending this world and becoming one with the divine. Rules and disciplines of life thus simply increased the fascination with the world in the attempt to overcome its power. He recognized that the mystics presented yet another "entirely new view of religion," especially in their total rejection of temporal concerns; even the rejection of "the world" should not be used as evidence of progress, lest even in this negative fashion the world become a point of focus.[50]

The mystics advised that "love was all"; this motif is reflected in Wesley's sermon at the time in which he sees the love of God as the "one thing needful" to perfect human happiness. Love is the fulfilling of the law, the end of every commandment of Christ, the first principle of all religion.[51] This "singularity of attention" is Wesley's fascination at this time, though it comes out in a variety of ways. "The one thing needful" in a sermon of the same title the following year is the recovery of the image of God, whereby one is restored to health, liberty, and holiness through redemption, new birth, and sanctification. This desideratum is not just an important concern, the *chief* thing needful; it is the *one* thing needful.[52] Another sermon on "If Thine Eye Be Single" reiterates this same theme: the Christian must have a singular intention, "to please God," or in other words, "to improve in holiness, in the love of God and thy neighbor."[53]

Wesley's Oxford Methodist friend Benjamin Ingham exhibited the same resolve in a diary notation about this time. He balanced his personal intentions with a recognition of the need for grace: "I am resolved, God's grace assisting me, to make the salvation of my soul my chief and only concern, but never to depend upon my own strength because I can do nothing without God's assistance."[54] Wesley himself gave similar advice to George Whitefield just a few weeks later, when asked by George whether weakness of body and spiritual despair should excuse one from the disciplines of Christian living. Wesley advised him to maintain the observance of external practices as much as possible, but "not to depend on them in the least."[55] Wesley was still prone to look for evidence, however, and considered the virtues to be good evidence of that love that was the manifestation of faith.[56]

The tension here between the life of discipline, which Wesley had long since adopted, and the dispensation from all such obligations, which the mystics so strongly advocated, put Wesley in a real quandary. How was he to know if he was pursuing the proper path to God? It did not take him long to discover that he was in a state of confusion in this regard. He found himself fluctuating between obedience and disobedience, continually doubting whether he was right or wrong and never out of perplexities and entanglements.[57] The dilemma presented by the mystics could not be resolved satisfactorily by his usual test of "sincerity," though he did suggest that traditional answer to his own query in his diary:

> Question: How steer between scrupulosity as to particular instances of self-denial, and self-indulgence?
>
> Answer: *Fac quod in te est, et Deus aderit bonae tuae voluntati.*[58]

Resting one's hope in one's sincerity is little consolation to a person who, on the one hand, is pressing on toward perfection and yet, on the other hand, is struggling to develop a sense of humility that recognizes that his or her own efforts must be distrusted.[59] Can sincerity be an adequate measure of certainty when perfection is the goal, "doing your best" is the watchword, humility is a necessity, and good works are taken away as evidence? What sort of certainty could be expected from sincerity under these circumstances?

The mystics had not only taken away good works as an outward measure (a tempting indicator even to predestinarians), but also left Wesley in the predicament of having no reliable form of assurance to fall back upon. Among the options he considered were those of becoming preoccupied with suffering as the mark of a true Christian (Guyon, Bourignon, etc.) and of relying upon a solifidianism that stressed faith alone instead of sincerity as the prerequisite (and the evidence) of inward holiness. At this point, however, Wesley's understanding of faith provided very little if any sensible evidence—"things that are eternal are not seen, but only through a glass darkly." He could quote "we walk by faith, and not by sight," but the faith of which he spoke at this point was a nearly blind faith.[60] And every moment of doubt immediately placed faith in jeopardy. About this time, John's father had, on his deathbed, suggested to him another manner of assurance that would soon supercede the others in John's experience: "the inward witness, son, the inward witness; that is the proof, the strongest proof of Christianity." Wesley later admitted that "at the time, I understood him not."[61]

Faith, Doubt, and Fear

The dilemma of having no solid grounds or evidence for assurance of salvation produced much of the anxiety that Wesley felt upon the eve of his departure for Georgia in 1735. Having been "tossed by various winds of doctrine," he was ready to find a right faith, which would then open the way to a right practice. Confusion had caused uncertainty; doubt had challenged faith. He hoped "to learn the true sense of the gospel of Christ by preaching it to the heathens." In the pristine setting of the New World, he felt the uncorrupted natives would "know of every doctrine I preach, whether it be of God." Wesley's own insecurity at that point was great enough to cause him even to doubt his state of salvation; to John Burton he wrote that his chief motive for embarking to Georgia was the hope of saving his own soul.[62]

The Atlantic crossing, however, added yet another source of anxiety to his quest for assurance. To his *doubt* would be added *fear*, which confirmed the insecurity of his faith. Wesley faced God in the depths of the ocean, and the first storms showed that he had no faith, for he was "unwilling to die."[63] In contrast, the German pietists on board the *Simmonds* exhibited not only humility and meekness, but also fearlessness in the face of death. On 25 January, these German Moravians continued their services without intermission while the sea raged, the mainsail was split, and the water poured over the decks "as if the great deep had already swallowed us up." His fear contrasted sharply with the Moravians' confidence. The hour of trial had given him clear evidence of the difference between those that fear God and those who do not. It was a momentous occasion: "This was the most glorious day which I have hitherto seen." He would adopt the Moravians as his tutors in the faith.[64]

The sermons Wesley wrote on shipboard begin to show an increasing acknowledgment of the Holy Spirit in his understanding of the spiritual pilgrimage. The sermon on "A Single Intention" continues his theme of singularity: "Your one end is to please and love God." But a new dynamic begins to be more evident: "His Holy Spirit shall dwell in you and shine more and more upon your souls unto the perfect day; . . . he shall establish your souls with so lively a hope as already lays hold on the prize of your high calling, and shall fill you with peace, and joy, and love."[65] These fruits of the Spirit will come to play an important role as evidence of the internal state, revealing the beginning of a shift from an emphasis on sincerity to a reliance upon the witness of the Holy Spirit and the concomitant evidence.

The following month, Wesley wrote another sermon on love, using a phrase he had often quoted from Romans 5:5, "the love of God shed abroad in our hearts," but now adding the final phrase, "by the Holy Ghost given unto us."[66] The development of a more vital doctrine of the Holy Spirit (pneumatology) in Wesley's thought was to have important consequences for his epistemology, especially regarding the question of assurance, how one might *know* that one is a Christian.

The question of assurance was pressed home to Wesley in Georgia by August Gottlieb Spangenberg, whose advice Wesley had sought. Spangenberg first asked him: "Do you know yourself? Have you the witness within yourself? Does the Spirit of God bear witness with your spirit that you are a child of God?" Wesley's silence was met by further questions: "Do you know Jesus Christ? . . . Do you know he has saved you? . . . Do you know [this for] yourself?" Wesley's weak answers to these questions led Spangenberg to give Wesley several directions to follow.[67] When Spangenberg described to Wesley the fruits of faith, Wesley later recalled responding, "If this be so, I have *no* faith." To which the German tutor responded, *"Habes fidem, sed exiguam"* ("You have faith, but insufficient [faith]").[68] What he needed was *more* faith, a stronger faith.

On the trip back to England in December and January of 1737–38, Wesley's lack of faith became evident to him again in his fears and doubts, confirming in his mind the dangerous state of his soul. The imminent danger of death made him very uneasy, and he was strongly convinced that the cause of his uneasiness was unbelief.[69] At this point, he saw unbelief as being the result of either a want of faith or a want of right tempers.[70] He was definitely beginning to swing toward the Moravian view of *sola fide*. In a moment of self-examination on shipboard he wrote: "By the most infallible of proofs, inward feeling, I am convinced . . . of unbelief; having no such faith in Christ as will prevent my heart from being troubled, which it would not be, if I believed in God, and rightly believed also in him." True faith would eliminate doubt. The evidence upon which assurance would be based included not only the presence of positive fruits, including faith and certain virtues, but also the elimination of all contrary and troubling indications. A continuing confession of several other shortcomings is followed by Wesley's plea: "Lord, save, or I perish! Save me . . . by such a faith as implies peace in life and in death; . . . by such humility as may fill my heart . . . ; by such a recollection as may cry to thee every moment . . . ; by steadiness, seriousness, [honesty], sobriety of spirit."[71] His conviction of unbelief relied upon inward feeling. His understanding of the cure for his doubt and fear was also inward: "the one thing needful," a true, living faith.[72]

A New Gospel and Heightened Expectations

Wesley's close friends could not agree with his assessment of unbelief. Thomas Broughton, an Oxford Methodist, could not imagine that John, "who had done and suffered such things," did not have faith. Charles felt such talk from John was mischievous. A blunt exchange with them in the spring of 1738 had a positive result in John's perception: "It did please God then to kindle a fire which I trust shall never be extinguished."[73] But the sure evidence of such a confident faith was not yet constantly present in Wesley's life, and the presence of doubt and fear continually placed his small degree of confidence in jeopardy [question]. The proof of belief would have to be as sure as the proof of unbelief—inner feeling. Wesley had begun a manner of speaking that was clear to him: I feel, therefore I know—it is inwardly evident to me in my own experience.[74] This was a new twist on his desire for evidence as a basis of knowledge, a variation on the empirical method that relied on less than traditional empirical evidence and more on direct inner knowledge. This inner knowledge was, nevertheless, expressed in terms of sensation, feeling.

Within this developing framework, Peter Böhler had a fairly easy time during the early months of 1738 convincing Wesley that *true* faith eliminated all doubt. Wesley's reflections at the end of his journal account of the voyage back to England in January 1738 betray the hindsight of his later encounters with the Moravians in England, which confirmed him in two important points: (1) "I knew not that I was *wholly void of this faith*, and thought *I had not enough* of it."[75] This implies that there are *no degrees of faith*. (2) "I want [lack] that faith which none can have without *knowing* that he hath it . . . ; for whosoever hath it is 'freed from sin' . . . is freed from fear . . . and is freed from doubt."[76] Thus true faith is always accompanied by assurance and evidenced by freedom from sin, fear, and doubt, three fruits which inseparably attend assurance and attest to a proper faith.

Upon hearing Böhler outline his view of faith, Wesley remarked that he was amazed and "looked upon this as a new gospel."[77] Once again, Wesley faced another "new view" of religion and the prospect of redefining his conception of true Christianity. The consequences were clear: if Böhler was right that assurance necessarily accompanies true faith, then it was clear that Wesley (who was not free from doubt and fear, much less sin) did not have true faith and was therefore not a real Christian. On 5 March 1738, Wesley became convinced of the necessity of this faith alone for salvation (*sola fide*) and of his own state of unbelief. He began preaching salvation by faith the following day.[78] In Georgia, Wesley had been impressed by the Moravians as a contemporary exhibit of apostolic Christianity[79] and now accepted the validity of their theological presuppositions as well. Only one thing prevented him from being able (with them) to claim with confidence his own status as a child of God, and that was the lack of an experience of assurance that would eliminate sin, doubt, and fear and thereby bring true holiness and happiness through love, peace, and joy in the Holy Ghost.[80]

Salvation in a Moment

Wesley now dropped his objections to Böhler's comments on the nature of faith and assurance, understood by Wesley within the framework of the definition in the *Homilies*: "a sure trust and confidence in God." Böhler highlighted the radically experiential aspect of this concept in terms of *Christus pro me*: "that through the merits of Christ *my* sins are forgiven and *I* am reconciled to the favor of God."[81] Faith was not simply a matter of agreeing with this belief, a rational assent to propositional truths; faith entailed a personal experience of divine forgiveness, confirmed by the witness of the Holy Spirit and made evident in a life without sin.

Böhler also convinced Wesley that this true faith "converts at once." John was introduced to the idea of instantaneous conversion on April 22 and became convinced of it the following day by the testimony of several "living witnesses that God *can* . . . give that faith whereof cometh salvation in a moment."[82] Thus, the experience that Wesley was expecting and for which he was hoping and praying was to be an experience of faith, inevitably attended by an assurance of pardon, which would necessarily result in freedom from sin, doubt, and fear, and be accompanied by a full measure of peace, joy, and confidence—all this in a moment, and altogether understood as conversion, the moment at which he would become a real, genuine Christian.[83]

Experience and Evidence

The pressure upon John became even greater on Whitsunday, 21 May 1738, when, after hearing a sermon on "They were all filled with the Holy Ghost," he received the "surprising news"that his younger brother Charles "had found rest to his soul." Charles Wesley's experience of assurance in the Moravian manner served to confirm John even further in his own expectations.[84] Therefore, what happened on 24 May 1738 in the meeting of "a society in Aldersgate Street" was naturally understood by him at the time in the light of those expectations. He testified on the spot to those about him what he felt in his heart. He felt a trust in Christ alone for salvation (essential to the definition of faith as sure trust and confidence), and at that instant he did receive an assurance that Christ had taken away *his* sins and saved *him* from the law of sin and death.[85] He was now a Christian and could claim that a week previous he had not been.[86]

Wesley celebrated the exuberance of the moment with an immediate testimony to those present; later that evening the celebration continued in Charles's rooms with the singing of a hymn.[87] The real test, however, of the authenticity of this experience was to be found, not in terms of whether or not he felt his heart "strangely warmed,"[88] but whether or not the expected and necessary fruits of faith and assurance (as he was taught by the Moravians to expect) would be in evidence: freedom from sin, doubt, and fear, and the fullness of peace, confidence, and joy in the Holy Ghost (otherwise called "holiness and happiness").

Questions began to develop almost immediately, raised by Wesley's quest for positive evidence or the problem of evidence to the contrary. The "enemy" soon suggested that what he had experienced could not be faith: "for where is thy joy?" He was at least comforted by the awareness that, although still buffeted with temptations, he had the sense that he was now "always conqueror."[89] The following day, Wesley's empiricism got the better of him: "If thou dost believe, why is there not a more sensible change?" Again, comfort came in the form of a measure of "peace with God." The matter of fears (which he had been taught to equate with unbelief) was pushed aside for the moment by a text from St. Paul—"Without were fightings, within were fears." He resolved to go on and simply try to tread them under his feet. The same was true concerning "heaviness because of manifold temptations"— the Moravians advised not fighting them but fleeing from them.[90] Four days after Aldersgate, he was still bothered by waking "in peace, but not in joy."

During the following days, he was constantly troubled by one problem after another relating to his only partially fulfilled expectations. One area that would trouble him rather consistently was the matter of degrees of faith, which was brought vividly to his attention by simply being in the presence of Peter Böhler. Wesley perceived Böhler to be in so much higher a state of salvation than he was that he wondered if they could possibly have the same faith (that one true faith that was necessary for salvation). The clear light of such evidence caused him to fall back upon a previous assumption that there are *degrees* of faith—"Though his be strong and mine weak, yet that God hath given some degree of faith even to me, I know by its fruits."[91] Wesley could not discard the concept of degrees of faith. The evidence of his own experience, viewed in the light of Scripture, confirmed for him that although he did *not* have a constant abiding joy, he *did* at that point have constant peace and freedom from sin and therefore some measure of faith.

The issue concerning degrees of faith was highlighted by a letter he soon received from Oxford, which drew out the dichotomy of faith versus unbelief in the form Wesley had most feared: "No doubting could consist with the least degree of true faith; that whoever at any time felt any doubt or fear was not *weak in faith*, but had *no faith* at all."[92] Wesley could no longer accept this position. Against this assertion, he again posited the testimony of Scripture: 1 Corinthians 3 speaks of "babes in Christ." Certainly these had some degree of faith, though perhaps weak.

Experience and Doctrine—The Moravians in Germany

Wesley decided to visit the Moravian community in Germany to converse with "those holy men who were themselves living witnesses of the full power of faith and yet able to bear with those that are weak."[93] What he discovered, however, was that they were not all willing to tolerate Wesley's lack of full confidence and joy. On one occasion they barred him from participating in the Lord's Supper with them because it was evident to them that he was still *homo perturbatis*, a perturbed person not clearly evidencing the marks of full assurance.[94] The confusion of that occasion was compounded by his discovery that some of the Moravian views in Herrnhut differed remarkably from those of Böhler and the English Moravians on crucial points.

Nikolaus von Zinzendorf, the head of the community, claimed that assurance could be separate in time from the moment of justification—one might not *know* or be assured of one's justification until long afterward. This notion countered Böhler's argument that one could not have forgiveness of sins without experiencing an immediate sensation of it. In addition to questioning the necessity of assurance as a prerequisite for claiming justification, Zinzendorf also qualified the requisite nature of other evidences of justification: peace *may* be evident, but joy is frequently *not* present.[95] For Wesley, this view of salvation seemed closer to his earlier experience and understanding of Scripture: a view that would allow for degrees of faith and sequential development, a view that might allow for a more satisfactory analysis of his own experience as well.

The German Moravians made several distinctions that Wesley would find crucial: distinguishing between justification and assurance (both theologically and chronologically), between faith and assurance, and between the beginning and the fullness of salvation. Wesley noticed especially four sermons by Christian David, who repeatedly spoke of "those who are 'weak in faith,' who are justified but have not yet a new, clean heart; who have received forgiveness through the blood of Christ but have not received the indwelling of the Holy Ghost."[96] Since his discussions with Böhler in the spring, Wesley had spoken generally in terms of "salvation by faith," as in his sermon of that title. From this point, Wesley begins to use the more precise concept of "justification" much more frequently.

While he was in Germany, Wesley met and interviewed several persons who could testify that their experience matched their doctrines. Wesley wrote careful notes on these interviews and later published them in his *Journal* as evidence of the true doctrines of the Moravian Church in order to clear the Moravians from any aspersion arising from the teachings of the English brethren. Among those he questioned was Arvid Gradin, whose personal account of "the full assurance of faith" was (as he later noted) "the first account I ever heard from any living man, of what I had before learned myself from the oracles of God and had been praying for (with the little company of my friends) and expecting for several years."[97]

The conflict between the German and English Moravian positions represented the nub of the problem for Wesley at this point. He had been taught by the English Moravians of the necessity of an experience of the type Böhler described, with its absolute requirements and necessary evidences and allowing for no doubt or fear. Wesley's confusion in his attempt to understand his own experience in the light of those expectations was caused in part by the difficulties inherent in the Moravian position. The English Moravians had, in Lutheran fashion, collapsed sanctification into justification and, in Pietist fashion, extended forgiveness of sins (imputed righteousness) into freedom from sin (infused righteousness). This approach resulted in the expectation of a sinless perfection (including a full measure of the fruits of the Spirit) as the necessary mark or evidence of salvation (genuine conversion).[98]

This tendency to equate faith with assurance and correlate sanctification with justification did not match Wesley's own theological background: he was trying to understand (and experience) a Lutheran theology in the context of his own Anglican and Arminian assumptions. The English Moravians looked for marks of salvation that Wesley would more naturally understand (within his own tradition) as evidence of sanctification.[99] They were propounding a view that essentially equated conversion with perfection, an understanding of salvation as sanctification that Wesley was never able to accept fully, even in the light of his own experience under Moravian tutelage. But it took Wesley several years to work out not only the finer distinctions between justification and sanctification, but also the various nuances of his own doctrines of faith and Christian perfection. For a while, though, he maintained his ties with the Moravians and tried to work out his spiritual quandary and theological problems in fellowship with them.

Working Out Your Own Salvation; Assurance and Faith

Back in England after his trip to Germany, Wesley began immediately to work on clearing up several matters of confusion in his own mind and experience: the nature and necessity of assurance, the problems of doubt and fear, the question of degrees of faith and assurance, the meaning of freedom from sin, the distinction between beginning and full salvation, and the role of good works and the means of grace. As he continued personally to press home several questions in his own mind in these areas over the next two years, he began to qualify many of his views and found himself increasingly in conflict with the Moravians. It is interesting to note that during the several months that Wesley was working on these issues (in growing conflict with the Moravians), although he personally dealt quietly with the questions of degrees of faith, the presence of doubt, and using the means of grace, he continued publicly by and large to preach the necessity of full assurance of faith and actual freedom from sin as the true ground of a Christian's happiness.[100] These questions all had a bearing on Wesley's attempt to understand what had happened in May 1738.

In the midst of Wesley's attempts to work out these questions in the autumn of 1738, two other important developments helped shed some light on his developing ideas. First, he read Jonathan Edwards's "surprising" narrative of the conversions in New England.[101] In this work he could plainly see the influence of the Holy Spirit in the revivals in New England. This reading confirmed for him the significance of the spiritual dynamic in the story and the pneumatological dimension in the theological explanation; it set the stage for his understanding of the movement of the Spirit among the people.

Secondly, Wesley rediscovered the *Homilies* on that "much controverted point of justification by faith."[102] In the homilies on salvation, faith, and good works (numbers 3, 4, and 5), Wesley discovered (within the authoritative doctrinal statements of his own tradition) the sum of what he had been putting together on his own and the answer to some of the problems raised by the Moravians. Although he could not then sense how close he would eventually come to reiterating the doctrine of the Church of England, he immediately recognized that the answer to most of his theological problems with the English Moravians were contained in those homilies, of which he hastened to publish an extract.[103]

These discoveries did not immediately solve either his spiritual or his theological problems. The last few months of 1738 were a period of intense self-scrutiny and questioning for Wesley.

Self-examination and the Fruits of the Spirit

Wesley was put in a quandary by the Moravians *requiring* the plerophory (fullness) of faith (assurance) evidenced by the *full* measure of fruits thereof (love, joy, peace) as the *necessary* expectation of the *true* (i.e., the only "real") Christian. Questions were raised by his own experience (and the experience of others), his own church's tradition, and Scripture. Nevertheless he continued to accept the Moravian position throughout his own struggle with its definition of the genuine Christian (and the evidence thereof). The tension can be seen clearly in several memoranda of self-examination Wesley wrote between October 1738 and January 1739. The first came shortly after reaching Oxford in October, in consequence of being disturbed by a letter he received:[104]

> Considering my own state more deeply . . . what then occurred to me was as follows: "Examine yourselves, whether ye be in the faith." Now the surest test whereby we can examine ourselves, whether we be indeed in the faith, is that given by St. Paul: "If any man be in Christ, he is a new creature: old things are passed away; behold, all things are become new." First, his judgments are new: his judgment of himself, of happiness, of holiness. . . . Secondly, his designs are new. . . . Thirdly, his desires are new. . . . Fourthly, his conversation is new. . . . Fifthly, his actions are new.[105]

With regard to holiness, Wesley judges that he is indeed a new creature, based on the evidence: "He no longer judges it to be an *outward* thing—to consist either in doing no harm, in doing good, or in using the ordinances of God."[106] He equates holiness with "the life of God in the soul; the image of God fresh stamped on the heart; an entire renewal of the mind in every temper and thought, after the likeness of Him that created it." On the second point, his designs being new, Wesley also considers himself to be a new creature. On the third point, his desires being new, he dares not claim success, but sees that God has begun, (though not finished) the work. As to his conversation and actions, he also is able to measure the evidence positively.

But there is one final criterion against which he falls short. On the matter of the "fruits of the Spirit," Wesley's evidence is somewhat disheartening: he does find some measure of peace, long-suffering, gentleness, meekness, temperance; yet in other areas he is definitely lacking but still full of hope and with some confidence that he is a child of God:

> I cannot find in myself the love of God, or of Christ. . . . I have not that joy in the Holy Ghost; no settled, lasting joy. Nor have I such a peace as excludes the possibility either of fear or doubt. . . . Yet upon the whole, although I have not yet that joy in the Holy Ghost, nor the full assurance of faith, much less am I, in the full sense of the words, "in Christ a new creature"; I nevertheless trust that I have a measure of faith, and am "accepted in the Beloved"; I trust . . . that I am "reconciled to God" through his Son.[107]

The absolute demands of the Moravians were beginning to crumble in Wesley's mind. He was beginning to accept the idea that there were degrees of both faith and assurance. And he began to sense that full assurance of faith (which he now felt he had never experienced) was not necessary to the new birth, but a "measure of faith" was adequate for reconciliation through Christ.

In the matter of assurance, Wesley began to distinguish further between assurance and faith as two distinct realities. The Moravians had related these so closely as practically to correlate them. Wesley's own post-Aldersgate experiences continued to raise variations of the question of degrees of faith first posed in conversation with Spangenberg in Georgia—whether one could speak of weak faith and strong faith, and whether faith could admit any doubt or fear. As long as faith was equated with full assurance (as in the Böhler/English Moravian understanding), doubts and fears plainly indicated a lack of faith, which was to say, no true faith at all but rather the sin of unbelief. But faith must surely be able in many cases to subsist with doubt and fear.[108]

Wesley recognized that "some measure of this faith" had resulted in "peace and trust in God through Christ" in his own life. And he also was convinced that freedom from sin, which he had claimed since 24 May, surely must be understood as freedom from the *reign* of sin rather than from the *remains* of sin. And although he now realized that he had yet to experience what he had seen many others receive, full assurance through the witness of the Spirit (evidenced by the fruits of the Spirit), he could see himself and others in his condition as being Christians, even though in an "imperfect sense."[109]

Wesley also distinguished between the assurance of *faith* and assurance of *salvation*. The former, a conviction of present pardon, he still felt was important and perhaps necessary as a normal expectation for the Christian, but the latter, based on the expectation of perseverance and the promise of final salvation, was rare and not necessarily to be expected, much less required. The "plerophory of faith," he pointed out to Arthur Bedford, is "nothing more nor less than hope: a conviction, wrought in us by the Holy Ghost, that we have a measure of the true faith in Christ, and that as he is already made justification unto us, so *if* we continue to watch and strive and pray, he will gradually become 'our sanctification here, and our full redemption hereafter.'"[110] He goes on to point out that "this assurance . . . is given to some in a smaller, to others in a larger degree." Assurance, then, for Wesley was also a matter of degrees and not to be confused with final perseverance; assurance was a daily confidence (more or less) that one is a child of God. The real possibility of backsliding never left Wesley's frame of thinking.[111]

On 29 October, Wesley noted that he was again "doubtful of my own state," especially concerning faith. Some relief, in keeping with developing inclinations, was provided by his method of bibliomancy, for he opened his Bible upon James's description of Abraham (in 2:22): "Seest thou not how faith wrought together with his works? And by works was faith made perfect."[112]

Whatever comfort he might obtain from such self-examination, however, was tested by his friends, especially those associated with the Moravians. Charles Delamotte, who had accompanied him to Georgia but was now back in England and under Moravian influence, told Wesley in November that Wesley was now better off than when he was in Savannah because Wesley now recognized that he was wrong in Georgia. But, Delamotte went on, "You are not right yet; you know that you was then blind, but you do not see now." Delamotte tried to convince Wesley that he was still trusting in his own works and did not believe in Christ; that his freedom from sin was only a temporary suspension of it, not a deliverance from it; and that his peace was not a true peace—"if death were to approach, you would find all your fears return."[113]

In December 1738, Wesley wrote some notes[114] that provide a sequel to the memorandum of October 14, in which he measures himself on some of the same evidences as before. As for happiness, "I still hanker after creature-happiness," which he explains in terms that are again reminiscent of his sentiments in 1726—"I have more pleasure in eating and drinking, and in the company of those I love, than I have in God."[115] He refers to the degree of his progress with a scriptural phrase that is telling and will become a familiar metaphor: "The eyes of my understanding are not yet fully opened."[116] On the second point, as to the design of his life, his eye is not yet single. And on the third point, his desires are not all new; his affections in general are mixed between spiritual and natural.[117]

Shortly after another experience of the power of God (during a lovefeast on 1 January 1739), Wesley again took an opportunity for writing notes of self-reflection. This memo, however, reveals more serious self-critical doubt on the questions of love, peace, and joy; in it, he holds himself up to the strict definition of Christian that admits no degrees of perfection in measuring the evidence:[118]

> My friends affirm I am mad, because I said I was not a Christian a year ago.[119] I affirm I am not a Christian now. . . . That I am not a Christian at this day I as assuredly know as that Jesus is the Christ. For a Christian is one who has the fruits of the Spirit of Christ, which (to mention no more) are love, peace, joy.[120] But these I have not. I have not any love of God. . . . I feel this moment I do not love God; which therefore I know because I feel it. . . . Again, joy in the Holy Ghost I have not. . . . Yet again, I have not "the peace of God." . . . From hence I conclude . . . , though I have given, and do give, all my goods to feed the poor, I am not a Christian. Though I have endured hardship, though I have in all things denied myself and taken up my cross, I am not a Christian . . . . My works are nothing, my sufferings are nothing; I have not the fruits of the Spirit of Christ. Though I have constantly used all the means of grace for twenty years, I am not a Christian.[121]

Wesley seems again to assume the necessity of full assurance of faith, which not only excludes all doubt and fear concerning present salvation but also excludes all sin as shown by the full presence of peace, love, and joy as the fruits of the Spirit. Wesley now understands the explicit role of the Holy Spirit as central, both as a source of self-knowledge (direct internal evidence—witness of the Spirit, the basis for claiming assurance) and as a source of the fruits (indirect external evidence—fruits of the Spirit, the basis for confirming assurance). The genuine Christian is the perfect Christian, and Wesley is not hesitant during this period to define the character of a Methodist (i.e., a "genuine Christian") in these same terms, namely, as one "who has the love of God shed abroad in his heart by the Holy Spirit."[122]

Although Wesley is beginning at times to allow for some qualitative distinctions and levels within the definition of Christian, the general sense of his preaching is that the "altogether Christian" is the "real" Christian and the "almost" Christian is not really a Christian at all. To put it differently (in terms Wesley was not yet using), the hard question still is whether the only "true" Christian is the fully sanctified Christian. Wesley still has not worked out the full implications of his ideas in this regard nor the careful use of his terminology.[123]

In January 1739, he makes a crucial distinction between being born again "in the lower sense" and in "the full sense of the word." What he describes, without using the terminology, is the difference between justification and sanctification: remission of sins as distinguished from a thorough, inward change by the love of God shed abroad in the heart.[124] The implication is that the latter, being born again in the higher sense, is the genuine Christian. But it is significant that Wesley is beginning again to allow for gradations ("the lower sense") rather than to hold a simple either/or position. His mature theology will come to rest upon the "both/and" of justification and sanctification, which he is here only beginning to sense and develop.

The Witness of the Spirit—Living Arguments

Wesley nevertheless continued to preach the central significance of the "witness of the Spirit" in the societies at London and Oxford. In fact, he developed an increased measure of confidence in its truth through what he will come to call "living arguments." The work of the Spirit was beginning to be evident in the lives of his hearers. He mentions several women in particular who responded to the work of the Spirit in consequence of his preaching at Oxford. In December 1738, one at St. Thomas's Workhouse was delivered from her raving madness, and another woman at Mr. Fox's society "received a witness that she was a child of God."[125] In March 1739, Mrs. Compton, who was "above measure enraged at this new way and zealous in opposing it," was further inflamed by Wesley's arguments, but when he began praying with her, she soon experienced the witness of the Spirit and cried out, "Now I know I am forgiven for Christ's sake."[126]

Spiritual inspiration of this sort, however, brought controversy. Wesley was not simply credulous in every case but was inclined to "try the spirits" in the scriptural manner, testing "to see whether they be of God." In January 1739 he visited a meeting led by one of the "French prophets." But after over two hours of observation, he felt the evidence was inconclusive and pointed out that "anyone of a good understanding and well-versed in the Scriptures" might have said the same things and the motions could easily have been "hysterical or artificial."[127] His advice in such situations was that "they were not to judge of the spirit whereby anyone spoke either by appearances, or by common report, or by their own inward feelings . . . all these were, in themselves, of a doubtful, disputable nature . . . and were therefore not simply to be relied on . . . but to be tried by a farther rule to be brought to the only certain test—the Law and the Testimony."[128] This advice would become increasingly more important as Wesley continued to emphasize the work of the Holy Spirit in the lives of true believers while trying at the same time to determine whether the outward signs were authentic, how the inward signs could be discerned, and just what these both signified. These questions were all soon to be magnified as the Methodist movement began to leave the society room and took to the streets and fields.

This New Period of My Life

Wesley's growing tendency to develop some confidence in his views by the response to his preaching soon gained a tremendous boost. At the beginning of April 1739, Wesley began field preaching. It was not his idea. Whitefield had set the example on Sunday morning, 1 April, at the Bowling Green in Bristol. That evening at the Nicholas Street Society, Wesley expounded on the Sermon on the Mount. This "pretty remarkable precedent of field-preaching" was not lost on him. The following day Wesley "submitted to be more vile" and "proclaimed in the highways the glad tidings of salvation" to about three thousand people gathered around a little eminence in the Brickyard at the edge of town.[129]

Wesley's hesitance to begin such a ministry was soon swept aside by the remarkable response to his preaching. His own journal account of this outdoor preaching occasion at Bristol reveals the significance of this development by referring to "this new period of my life."[130]

Even preaching to small groups in the past had encouraged John in the quandaries of his own spiritual pilgrimage and had served to confirm the truth of the gospel he was preaching.[131] Now he was preaching to thousands and seeing a marvelous work of God in their midst. The story of Wesley's quest for assurance takes an unexpected turn—it becomes less singularly personal as he begins to sense the work of the Holy Spirit in the midst of the people, a phenomenon not unlike what he had read about in Jonathan Edwards' writings.

After preaching to a little society in Bristol on Sunday evening, 2 April, he spoke Monday afternoon to three or four thousand on the text, "The Spirit of the Lord is upon me because he hath anointed me to preach the gospel to the poor."[132] On eight occasions during the following fortnight, he spoke to large groups ranging from one to six thousand people in the Bristol area, a total attendance of some twenty-five thousand. On 29 April alone, he preached outdoors in three places to a total of fourteen thousand people, married four persons, preached to a full church at Clifton, held a society meeting at Mrs. England's, followed by a lovefeast in Baldwin Street. He closes his account of the day in his *Journal* with the remark, "Oh how has God renewed my strength! who used ten years ago to be so faint and weary with preaching twice in one day!"[133] Equally significant, however, is his remark that, during his sermon at the Bowling Green on "Free Grace," "one who had long continued in sin . . . received a full, clear sense of His pardoning love and power to sin no more."

Such confirmations of God's action bolstered his own faith to a great extent. His busy days, indeed, may have given him little time to worry about his own condition, but his continuing concern for his own spiritual condition in the midst of his "success" in preaching is evident in a comment to James Hutton and the society at Fetter Lane: "Dear brethren, pray that when I have preached to others, I may not myself be a castaway!"[134]

Wesley was still at this time claiming publicly that the full assurance of faith is the true ground of a Christian's present happiness. On 28 April, his sermon on "Free Grace," which was his first major attack on predestination (and effectively declared his independence from Whitefield), reiterated his conviction that assurance of faith excludes all doubt and fear.[135] Aiming directly at Whitefield's Calvinism, Wesley also continued his assault upon its corollary, antinomianism, pointing out that predestination cuts off any zeal for good works.[136] This Arminian view, clearly stated and strongly held, would provide the snag that would start unraveling his relationship with the Moravians as well as the Calvinists.[137]

Wesley also continued to see evidence of the Holy Spirit working in the lives of the people, now on a somewhat larger scale. And many more were offended by the cries of those on whom the power of God came.[138] In a letter to his brother Samuel, in response to his question "How can these things be?" and his cautions not to regard outward signs of remission of sins, John wrote:

> You deny that God does now work these effects; at least, that he works them in such a manner. I affirm both, because I have heard those facts with my ears and have seen them with my eyes. I have seen (as far as it can be seen) very many persons changed in a moment from the spirit of horror, fear, and despair, to the spirit of hope, joy, and peace. . . . These are matters of fact, whereof I have been, and almost daily am, an eye- or ear-witness. . . . These are my living arguments for what I assert.[139]

Inevitably, this matter caused disruptions and divisions among the societies in Bristol and London.[140] Most controversial were the *outward signs* that accompanied the *inward work* of the Spirit. Although Wesley was hoping that everyone would "suffer God to carry on His own work in the way that pleaseth Him,"[141] he also wanted to provide some guidelines for interpreting and understanding the movement of the Spirit among the people. To the Methodists in Bristol, he suggested that when "appearances, common report, or inward feelings" resulted in controversy, the spirit whereby anyone spoke or acted should be tried by "the only certain test—the Law and the Testimony."[142] The inward work of the Spirit itself really held Wesley's attention, however, and his longtime inclination was that it could in some way be verified through certain evidence.

On 22 May 1739, John preached on "Awake, Thou that Sleepest" (Ephesians 5:14).[143] The published text of Charles's sermon on the same topic presents an intriguing metaphor that may have significance for the Wesleyan anthropological assumptions that underlie both soteriology and epistemology. Grace does not destroy or overcome nature, which is diseased and distorted, but rather perfects (awakens, restores, heals) it to its original image and design. This is no minor transformation, however. The disease of sin results in the person's being effectively dead unto God. And being thus dead in sin, natural man has not "senses exercised to discern spiritual good and evil" (Heb. 5:14)—having eyes, yet he sees not; he hath ears, and hears not (Mark 8:18); he has no spiritual senses, no inlets of spiritual knowledge.[144]

How can such a one be awakened and know that he is alive to God? "Faith is the life of the soul," and the Spirit of God is sufficient evidence, the *elenchos pneumatos* (divine consciousness, evidence), the witness of God that is "greater than ten thousand human witnesses."[145] The claim that one could sense the indwelling of the Holy Spirit, which was not only "the common privilege of all believers," but also "the criterion of a real Christian," led to charges of enthusiasm. Wesley, however, was attempting to develop a way to explain how one senses this divine revelation in a manner analogous to other sense perceptions that might be verified.[146] The Wesleys were quick to claim that by holding such a view of "perceptible inspiration," they taught nothing contrary to the doctrines of the Church.[147]

Wesley and the Church of England; Distinctive Emphases

By the autumn of 1739, Wesley was preaching to thousands of people every Sunday in London.[148] Contrary to his critics, who saw him as an enthusiast and fanatic, Wesley claimed that he was simply preaching "the fundamental doctrines of the Church" as clearly laid down in the Articles, Homilies, and Book of Common Prayer.[149] He further proclaimed that Methodism, although everywhere spoken against, was simply "the true old Christianity."[150] It was propagating, in Wesley's view, the true Church of England doctrine. For a clerical friend, he outlined the difference between what generally passes for Christianity in the Church of England (among those who in fact did not adhere to its doctrines) and what he himself was preaching:

> 1. They speak of justification either as the same thing with sanctification or as something consequent upon it. . . .
>
> 2. They speak of our own holiness, or good works, as the cause of our justification. . . .
>
> 3. They speak of good works as a condition of justification, necessarily previous to it. . . .
>
> 4. They speak of sanctification, or holiness, as if it were an outward thing. . . .[151]
>
> 5. They speak of the new birth as an outward thing, as if it were no more than baptism, or at most a change from outward wickedness to outward goodness.[152]

His own views are easily distinguished from these, as he points out in each case: justification is *distinct* from and antecedent to sanctification, *Christ's* active righteousness and passive righteousness are the cause of our justification, the condition of justification is faith *alone* without works,[153] sanctification is an *inward* renewal of the heart, and the new birth is an *inward* change of our inmost nature resulting in new tempers of the soul.[154] Having sorted these points out in his own mind with regard to his own tradition, Wesley was now ready to clarify the other side of his position with respect to the Moravians, especially regarding *sola fide*: he certainly did not accept the implication that such a doctrine implied discarding the means of grace. This practical point of contention would provide the issue over which Wesley finally broke with the Moravians.

Subverting the Souls of the Justified; Crisis in the Societies

Wesley soon began to notice that requiring full assurance of faith as a necessary mark of the Christian (as the Moravians did) threw many into idle reasonings, doubt, and fear, and even led some to cast away their faith. The question of true faith had practical implications that were not lost on Wesley. He began to challenge those who claimed not only that *weak faith* is unbelief, but also that only true believers (having received the full assurance of faith) should use the means of grace, in particular, receive the Sacrament. Some of the Moravians were saying that no person who does not truly believe should use any of the means of grace (sacraments, prayer, etc.). Although Wesley was certainly not yet willing to say that "good works" were necessary prior to justification, he was sure that some activity was appropriate on the part of the person desiring salvation.[155]

The Fetter Lane society began to experience problems again as the autumn of 1739 approached. On September 9, Wesley discovered that a want of love was the general complaint; during the next few days he pressed the members to love each other and to keep close to the Church and to all the ordinances of God. John and Charles went to Oxford at the beginning of October to discover that only a few had not "forsaken the assembling themselves together." John also had occasion to examine the "shattered condition" of the work at the University, where Methodism had begun. Even the remnants of their program had nearly disappeared—no one visiting the prisons, no one visiting the workhouses, the school (formerly helping about twenty poor children at a time) on the point of breaking up for lack of students or teachers. The society in the town was not much better, having been "torn asunder and scattered abroad." After a quick tour to Wales and the West Country, during which he confronted several controversial situations associated with his preaching and extraordinary exercises that attended it, Wesley returned to London to discover the society there in disarray.

Wesley's crisis with the Moravians intensified in October 1739 after Philip Henry Molther appeared among the Moravians in London. Molther's "quietism" sharpened the differentiating issues between Wesley and the English Moravians. As a result of Molther's teachings, which in effect required full assurance as a prerequisite for receiving the Sacrament, many of the Fetter Lane group were thrown into turmoil.[156] They continued to believe that any fear or doubt indicated that they had no assurance and therefore no faith at all. This assumption was not new. But Molther added a new twist: such persons should cease from all outward works and "be still." Many, including Spangenberg, were won over to this position, which simply extended the basic approach of Böhler that faith in Christ was the only means of salvation. Wesley now began to see clearly the drastic consequences of such a view, the challenge that it represented to his emphasis on Christian discipline and using the means of grace, before as well as after justification. He also began to see clearly that the Moravians were proclaiming a view of the "way of salvation" (*via salutis*) that, Wesley said, "I cannot reconcile to the Law and the Testimony."[157] For Wesley, their view represented a perverse form of antinomianism that put the requirements for justification too high and at the same time took away the normal channels of divine assistance, the means of God's grace.

Wesley had special difficulties with many of the new ideas that were spreading despair in the Fetter Lane society, especially the claim that the ordinances (the Lord's Supper, in particular) are not means of grace—that the only means of grace is Christ. Wesley began to counter Molther's teachings with what he saw as a better method of trying the spirits, that is through "true stillness"—"patient waiting upon God, by lowliness, meekness, and resignation, in all the ways of his holy law and the works of his commandments."[158] Susanna Wesley may have supplied one of the best arguments against the Moravian position. In spite of their attempts to persuade her that she had no faith, Susanna seems to have convincingly testified that she had recently experienced assurance of forgiveness while receiving the Sacrament.[159]

For the better part of a week, Wesley tried to heal the wounds in the society. But by the second week of November, he and some of his friends began to meet separately in the old Foundery in Moorfields.[160] This split was the beginning of their final separation with the Moravians. On the last day of 1739, after continual controversy over these points, Wesley wrote down the differences between himself and the English Moravians at that point. He begins to outline Molther's views as follows:

> 1. There are no degrees of faith and that no man has any degree of it before all things in him are become new, before he has the full assurance of faith, the abiding witness of the Spirit, or the clear perception that Christ dwelleth in him.
>
> 2. Accordingly you believe there is no justifying faith or state of justification short of this.[161]

In 1738, these ideas (expressed at that point by Peter Böhler) had furnished the rationale for and urgency behind Wesley's desire for (and expectations of) an experience of assurance, which he finally had at Aldersgate. These ideas also supported the framework of his attempts to explain that experience for some time thereafter. His own position on these matters was now clear at the end of 1739: there *are* degrees of faith, and there is a degree of justifying faith short of (and antecedent to) full assurance. And now he saw some of the additional problematical consequences which the Moravian position entailed. He continued to spell out Molther's views:

> That gift of God which many receive . . .—viz. "a sure confidence of the love of God to them"—was not justifying faith. And that the joy and love attending it were from animal spirits, from nature, or imagination; not "joy in the Holy Ghost" and the real "love of God shed abroad in their hearts."
>
> As to the way to attain it is to wait for Christ, and be still—that is, not to use (what we term) the means of grace; not to go to church; not to communicate; not to fast; not to use so much private prayer; not to read the Scripture; . . . not to do temporal good; nor to attempt doing spiritual good.[162]

Wesley disagreed with these positions, especially when the implication is that nothing is valid unless it agrees with Molther's own personal judgment of whether or not it is valid.[163] In an almost sarcastic use of Molther's own terminology, Wesley outlined his own understanding of the way to attain faith: "to wait for Christ and be still"; that is, "in using all the means of grace" (which he proceeds to list in great detail).[164]

By the end of 1739, then, Wesley had in effect come to the point of disentangling himself theologically from the English Moravians who had been his spiritual tutors for the previous two or three years. The next few months saw Wesley completely disavow the English Moravians as holding views with which both the Church of England and the true Moravian Church disagreed.[165] After another long interview with Molther at the end of April 1740, the Fetter Lane Society was irreparably split. On 11 June 1740, Wesley visited the Fetter Lane society and, as he said, plainly told the "poor, confused, shattered society wherein they had erred from the faith—they could not receive my saying. However, I am clear from the blood of these men."[166] During the following month, Wesley was banned from preaching at Fetter Lane, and a week later he and a small group of Methodists moved their meetings entirely to the Foundery in a final separation from the Moravians.

Summary of Situation in 1739

By the spring of 1739, Wesley had begun in some small ways to soften the sharp dichotomy that the Moravians seemed to draw between the Christian and the non-Christian, while still defending his claim that he himself was only beginning to move across the gap. In a letter to a friend, he pointed out that two years earlier, he had "told all on the ship, all at Savannah, all at Frederica, and that over and over, in express terms, 'I am not a Christian; I only follow after, if haply I may attain it.'" He is at this point, however, beginning to appreciate the struggle of those who are searching but who have not yet received the witness of the Spirit. Rather than denigrate their efforts, as the Moravians seemed to do, Wesley tried to encourage those who had "a desire to be a Christian."[167] At the same time, he was beginning to distinguish between "young converts" and those who had "already attained or were already perfect," comparable to his distinction between those born again in a "lower" and a "higher" sense.[168] This insight continues a very significant theological development. Wesley was clearly differentiating between justification and sanctification and becoming more positively inclined to value the experience of the "almost" Christians (those without full assurance, i.e., not fully sanctified), a crucial step in his growing independence from the English Moravian perspective.

Explaining his principles of actions in pursuing his own desire to be a Christian, Wesley said that he had long acted on the conviction "that whatever I judge conducive thereto, that I am bound to do; wherever I judge I can best answer this end, thither it is my duty to go."[169] But such constant "doing" and "going" bothered the Moravians, who continued to press hard on the matter of *sola fide*, increasingly requiring the witness of the Spirit to the virtual exclusion of the means of grace. Wesley was willing to grant the necessity of *sola fide* but was not ready to give up the means of grace or other works of piety and mercy, all of which he viewed as central to the Christian life and helpful even in pursuing the desire to be a Christian (crucial to sanctification, important to justification). Wesley was also willing to grant the importance of the witness of the Spirit as an assurance of faith but was beginning to distinguish between assurance of pardon (justification) and assurance of perfection (sanctification), while still generally associating the "witness of the Spirit" with the latter.

The English Moravians had tried to convince him that assurance of redemption was accompanied by freedom from sin (entire sanctification, in Wesley's terminology) as well as freedom from doubt and fear. But he was coming to realize that the "young convert" should not expect to be perfect; that a person, though justified, was yet a sinner.[170] And, contrary to the Moravian view, one who has not received the plerophory of faith and assurance (a sign of complete freedom from sin, fear, and doubt) should not despair of not having any faith whatsoever and certainly should not cease using the means of grace.

The relationship between the inward and outward signs of spiritual experience also continued to widen the breach between Wesley and the Moravians. Generally, Wesley continued to distinguish between the indications of "religion commonly understood" (outward: avoiding evil, doing good, using the means of grace) and those of "real religion" (inward: righteousness, peace, and joy in the Holy Ghost) but felt the two must be integrally related in the life of the believer.[171] *Outward* indications of Christian deportment must be accompanied by an *inward* experience of a living faith, which is "a sure trust and confidence in God that, by the merits of Christ, his sins are forgiven and he reconciled to the favour of God,"[172] and its inward evidence, "the love of God shed abroad in the heart, the peace of God which passeth all understanding, and joy in the Holy Ghost."[173] These are some of the inward "fruits of the Spirit" that must be *felt* wherever they are. Without these very "*sensible* operations," we cannot *know* that one is born of the Spirit.[174]

The tensions inherent in this definition of faith from the *Homilies* when understood from a Moravian perspective posed considerable difficulties for Wesley. If faith was understood as a necessary prerequisite condition for justification, then faith was "a sure trust which a man hath that Christ hath loved him and died for him."[175] This faith was a trust that God has acted in Christ to redeem him (the atonement) and that his sins *will be* forgiven. This faith accompanies repentance and is a necessary condition for justification. On the other hand, if (as the Moravians said) faith also entailed assurance, then the phrase from the *Homilies* would have a quite different sense—a "confidence in God that, by the merits of Christ, his sins *are* forgiven and he *is* reconciled to the favor of God." This faith is an assurance that Christ has, in fact, redeemed him and that his sins *have been* forgiven. This faith of assurance is accompanied by an evident sense of pardon at the least (if not a fuller sense of freedom from all sin), and the personalized *Christus pro me* becomes one's motto.

In 1739, Wesley was coming to realize that these different definitions of faith, both of which might be read into the phrasing of the *Homilies* definition, represent at least two and perhaps even three different stages in the spiritual pilgrimage. And faith in each of these instances would be evidenced in a different manner, some harder than others to perceive. This developing understanding represents a direct challenge to the Moravian's unitary concept of faith. Another fairly obvious question that begins to emerge from this distinction is, How can faith, a prerequisite for divine forgiveness, also be the subsequent evidence of it?[176]

At this point, the definition of the "real" Christian for Wesley turns on the issue of whether the true child of God can be justified without being sanctified (forgiven of sin and able not to sin, or freed from sin and not able to sin? converted or perfected?). The *German* Moravians had suggested that such was the case. The matter of relying upon both outward and inward signs further sharpened the issue—what are they signs of: conversion or perfection? By late 1739, Wesley had begun to see that the external visible evidence of good works generally applies to sanctification (a real change but not necessarily entire; an internal change with external evidence), while justification (a relative change, also internal) is harder to verify by external evidence, especially in others. Wesley felt an increasing need to develop a way to explain the sensation of divine evidence for justification: spiritual senses to discern the operations of the Spirit.[177]

In this context, the Wesleys began using the definition of faith in Hebrews 11—faith is the "evidence of things unseen."[178] Generally, this phrase was used to refer to the witness of the Spirit in the sense of assurance; but if faith is also preliminary to justification, the evidence is more difficult to perceive. In either case, this divine evidence was not perceived by the unbeliever. It was presented only to the spiritual senses—the eyes of the believer were opened, the ears of faith could hear.

Further Developments, 1740 and Beyond

By 1740, then, Wesley had severed his association with the Moravians, unable to accept their position on several key issues. He does not agree that there are no degrees of faith, that there is no justification without full assurance of faith, that persons should not use the means of grace until they have received full assurance, and that good works are not part of faith. He has begun to realize that the *definition* of a Christian is more complicated than the either/or explanation presented by the Moravians, which required full assurance of faith, complete freedom from sin, doubt, and fear, and a perfect manifestation of love, peace, and joy. He is beginning to distinguish between justification and sanctification (and soon entire sanctification) as significantly distinct steps in the *via salutis* and thereby to allow that there is opportunity for growth within a range of Christian experience from infancy to maturity.[179]

His understanding of the process by which a person *becomes* a Christian has also undergone some development beyond the simple teaching of Böhler (exaggerated by Molther) that only a proper faith alone, without works, would instantaneously bring conversion to a new state of sinless perfection. He is expressing some ambiguity regarding the nature of real religion, holiness, which he is inclined to think necessarily includes good works.

The ground of Wesley's certainty of salvation, how believers *know* they are Christians, is still basically the witness of the Spirit, which the Moravians had taught him, but he is beginning to develop that doctrine in different directions. He not only allows for degrees of assurance and exceptions to the normal expectations that all will experience it, but is beginning to disentangle the correlation of assurance with both faith and sanctification so as to allow also for repentant faith and assurance of justification. And Wesley's attempt to explain the doctrine in scriptural terms has resulted in hints at the notion of spiritual senses.

In each of these areas, Wesley refines his views even further during the 1740s and beyond, in many cases falling back upon ideas and methods that he had been using since his Oxford days. Surveying the change should not cause us to lose sight of the continuity, as Wesley continued to press many of his themes from the early days at Oxford—Christian perfection, prevenient grace, repentance, sincerity, doing one's best, avoiding evil, the importance of the virtues—though now within a more vital spiritual context and a more dynamic theological rationale, and with an increasingly evangelistic and pastoral concern.[180]

Although early in the 1740s Wesley draws a very sharp distinction between the "almost Christian" and the "altogether Christian"[181] (with only the latter being a true Christian), by the conference of 1745 he is aware that such preaching is not fully adequate. He realizes that the Methodist preachers must take care not to depreciate justification "in order to exalt the state of full sanctification."[182] The question even came up as to whether or not the Methodists had changed their doctrine in this regard, no longer preaching "as we did at first?" Wesley pointed out that at first they had preached mostly to unbelievers and therefore spoke almost entirely of forgiveness of sins. But now, recognizing that in many of their listeners a "foundation is already laid," they can exhort to go on to perfection. This distinction, Wesley says, "we did not see so clearly at first."[183] Wesley now begins to distinguish between being saved from the guilt of sin and being saved from the power of sin.[184] This distinction will become more useful to him as he continues to develop the distinction between justification and sanctification more fully. He will later add a third step, being saved from the root of sin, which is essential to entire sanctification.[185]

Wesley also extends the idea of being saved from the guilt and power of sin into another biblical comparison—having not only the *form* but the *power* of godliness.[186] In the early sermons such as "The Almost Christian," Wesley used this comparison to distinguish between the would-be and the real Christian. As time goes on, however, he is less prone to denigrate those who exhibit simply the *form* of godliness. In 1741, the "almost Christians," who are no better than honest heathens, are described as having only the form of godliness—trying to be honest, avoiding evil, and using the means of grace.[187] In 1744, when he published *The Nature, Design, and General Rules of the United Societies*, Wesley chose this phrase to describe a Methodist society—"a company of men 'having the form and seeking the power of godliness.'"[188] The rules themselves were the three guidelines that he tended to use so often in the late 1730s to denigrate a false view of real religion: avoiding evil, doing good, and using the means of grace. And the persons who qualified for continuing membership in the societies were given class tickets, which were as good a recommendation, said Wesley in 1749, as if he had written thereon, "I believe the bearer hereof to be one that fears God and works righteousness."[189] By 1768, Wesley applies this phrase to those Christians who have received assurance: "I believe a consciousness of being in the favour of God . . . is the common privilege of Christians fearing God and working righteousness."[190] By 1785, he openly uses this phrase to refer to the "real Christians," those who are contained within the inner circle of God's providence.[191]

In 1787, Wesley explains the distinctions among the faithful a bit further by describing what he calls "two orders of Christians": (1) those who do many good works, abstain from gross evils, and attend the ordinances of God; and (2) those who spared no pains to arrive at the summit of Christian holiness. He goes on to say, "From long experience and observation I am inclined to think that whoever finds redemption in the blood of Jesus, whoever is justified, has then the choice of walking in the higher or the lower path."[192]

All of these categories undergo significant modifications in the maturing Wesley. In 1744, one who is seen by Wesley as a "*servant* of God" ("one who sincerely obeys him out of *fear*") is "a Jew, inwardly," e.g., still under the Jewish dispensation. However, a "*child* of God" is one who sincerely obeys him out of *love*.[193] Whereas in the late 1730s, Wesley had viewed "half-Christians" in terms of their *lack* of being fully Christian, by the 1780s, they are viewed with more hope in terms of their being *at least* "nominal" Christians. By that time,Wesley applied this latter phrase ("fearing God," associated with those who only have the form of godliness) in a positive sense to those who *at least* have the faith of a servant and are seeking the faith of a son.

Deprecation of the person who has the "faith of a servant," who "fears God," who has "the form of godliness," begins to disappear in later years as the emphasis turns to encouraging those who are in a state that falls short of the fullness of faith. Thus, in 1788 he can say,

> Whoever has attained this, the faith of a servant, . . . "feareth God and worketh righteousness," in consequence of which he is in a degree (as the Apostle observes), "accepted with him." . . . Even one who has gone thus far in religion, who obeys God out of fear, is not in any wise to be despised, seeing "the fear of the Lord is the beginning of wisdom." Nevertheless he should be exhorted not to stop there; not to rest till he attains the adoption of sons; till he obeys out of love, which is the privilege of all the *children* of God.[194]

This rather remarkable development seems to emerge from a maturing pastoral sensitivity as well as a more sophisticated theological perspective. By this time, Wesley can look back on his life and remark with candor,

> Indeed nearly fifty years ago, when the preachers commonly called Methodists began to preach that grand scriptural doctrine, salvation

> by faith, they were not sufficiently apprised of the difference between a servant and a child of God. They did not clearly understand that even one "who feared God, and worketh righteousness, is accepted of him."[195]

Most remarkable of all was Wesley's radical turnabout on the matter of assurance, which the Moravians had said was essential to the Christian. Once Wesley had seen the damage such teaching had done in the community of believers and had begun to dismantle this seemingly monolithic doctrine into its various parts, it became a much more effective element in the dynamic of his theology. Assurance was related to both justification and sanctification but no longer equated with faith or required as an essential experience.[196] Once again, looking back from the 1780s, he would be able to remark in all honesty to his friend Melville Horne,

> When fifty years ago my brother Charles and I, in the simplicity of our hearts, told the good people of England that unless they *knew* their sins were forgiven they were under the wrath and curse of God, I marvel, Melville, they did not stone us![197]

The definition of faith itself also undergoes an interesting development during this period. Besides formulating the distinction between the faith of a servant and of a child of God, Wesley also begins to shift away from the definition of faith in the *Homilies* ("a sure trust and confidence") to the definition in Hebrews 11:1—"the evidence of things not seen."[198] He initially understood this definition of faith essentially as the witness of the Spirit, frequently explained in the terminology of Romans 8:16—"The Spirit itself beareth witness with our spirit that we are children of God."[199]

Wesley relies upon his empirical inclinations to develop this idea of "spiritual senses," eventually including not only the sense of sight and hearing (eyes and ears that see and hear divine evidence), but also the sense of taste and feel.[200] In this fashion, Wesley combines an empiricist approach with an intuitionist sense to provide a description of how the "new creature in Christ" has a transformed capacity for knowing and understanding spiritual truth that is more than simply "analogous" to sense perception.[201] This epistemological perspective was another reflection of Wesley's constant attempt to relate the inner and outer aspects of religion in a rather precarious balance that tried to emphasize both vital spiritual experience and responsible Christian living while avoiding the pitfalls of subjective enthusiasm on the one hand or legalistic moralism on the other. This development and the manner of his combining human experience with revelation of spiritual truths were the culmination of his search for human certainty within a lively pneumatology in the process of working out his own salvation.

Conclusion

Wesley's Aldersgate experience on 24 May 1738 was a significant step in his spiritual pilgrimage. It was a step that Wesley had been led to expect and for which he had been carefully prepared by his English Moravian friends. Their basic teachings on the matter were:

(1) Faith alone is necessary to salvation.

(2) Good works (of piety or mercy) are not required before salvation and in fact are not possible.

(3) There are no degrees of faith; there is only one proper faith; a weak faith is no faith but rather unbelief.

(4) A proper faith will immediately bring with it an assurance of faith which will be unmistakably known.

(5) The assurance of faith will bring freedom from sin, doubt, and fear.

(6) Assurance will be accompanied by perfect love, peace, and joy in the Holy Ghost.

(7) Without this assurance, one is not a Christian.

(8) Assurance brings perseverance unto final salvation.

The urgency of Wesley's situation was prompted by the seventh proposition in this list, along with two corollaries to propositions five and six: (1) Any doubt or fear indicates an absence of faith and assurance; (2) A lack of perfect love, peace, and joy indicates an absence of faith and assurance. Under these requirements, Wesley was becoming convinced in 1737 and early 1738 that he was not a Christian. To anxiety was added frustration, since Wesley saw his use of the means of grace (going to church, reading the Bible, taking the Sacrament, prayer, fasting, etc.) as ineffectual because he had not received assurance (no good works before salvation).

Wesley's experience of assurance on 24 May did not, however, solve all his problems. Within the Moravian understanding, he expected thenceforth to have a freedom from sin, doubt, and fear, that would be accompanied by perfect love, peace, and joy. Such was not the case. For several months, Wesley's periodic self-examinations came to the same conclusion: since he has not the fruits of the Spirit and still manifests doubt and fear, he is still not a true Christian.

Within two years, however, Wesley had noted several basic problems in the Moravian position and altered his own thinking accordingly. His differences with the Moravians were basic enough that he left the fellowship of the society he had co-founded with Peter Böhler. By the summer of 1740, he disagreed with every Moravian proposition listed above except the first. His main challenges were based on the following propositions of his own: (1) there are degrees of faith; (2) there are degrees of assurance; (3) the means of grace should be encouraged prior to assurance; (4) justification does not necessarily result in assurance; (5) assurance of justification does not necessarily bring complete freedom from doubt or fear; (6) assurance of justification does not necessarily bring full love, peace, and joy; (7) assurance is not of final salvation.

Two key developments in Wesley's own theology during this period were his recognizing the distinction between justification and sanctification, disentangling faith and assurance, and his qualifying the subjective norm of experience by appeals to the Scripture, the teachings of the Church (primitive and contemporary), and reason. Having made the break with the Moravians, he could then continue to develop his understanding of salvation by faith according to these norms and in the light of his own experience. He could further clarify his ideas on justification and sanctification, Christian perfection, faith, assurance, the witness of the Spirit, good works, eschatology, and other matters essential to the Christian life.

Through all the subsequent developments, two ideas from 1738 continued to find a central place in Wesley's theology even though he modified their explanation: salvation by faith alone and the witness of the Spirit. These were both the result of Wesley's having felt the power of the Holy Spirit in his life on that spring evening in London; his subsequent attempts to understand the theological dynamics and implications of that experience were crucial to the development of a Wesleyan theology. Wesley's affirmation of justification by faith, expectation of assurance, and the possibility of perfection became hallmarks of his theology. But these crucial concepts (learned, borrowed, observed, experienced) were necessarily altered by Wesley so as to fit within an understanding of justification and sanctification that was quite different from the Moravian theological framework [soteriology] that he had assumed in 1738.

In this light, we can say that Aldersgate is especially significant for Wesley in two ways. (1) It is the point in his spiritual pilgrimage at which he experiences the power of the Holy Spirit and at which his theology is confronted by a dynamic pneumatology. From that point on, the Holy Spirit has a central role in Wesley's definition of the "true Christian," his understanding of how one becomes a Christian, and his explanation of how one knows he or she is a Christian. (2) It is also the point from which Wesley's theology begins to develop its own characteristic shape, a cast distinguished from the Moravian view by some of its basic doctrines and distinguished from the popular Church of England view by its characteristic constellation of emphases.

Theology, for Wesley, was primarily an explanation of the *via salutis*. For him, theological reflection is inexorably tied to the spiritual pilgrimage, and both are dynamic and developmental. In this sense, Aldersgate certainly was not an inconsequential event in Wesley's life. It is best viewed, however, within the context of a man trying both to live "the scripture way of salvation" and to explain it as well. His experience often outran his understanding. Four days after Aldersgate, he was claiming that he had previously not been a Christian. According to the Moravian assumptions under which he was operating at the time, that was a true perspective. It is significant, however, that every subsequent comment of that sort (even within weeks of the experience) can be understood within Wesley's later theology as saying, "I was previously not (or am not now) a fully sanctified Christian."[202] His later distinctions between two orders of Christians, between the faith of a servant and of a child of God, between the young convert and the mature Christian, between faith and assurance (and allowing for various degrees of both), are all the result of his finally differentiating between justification and sanctification as theologically and experientially distinguishable steps on the spiritual pilgrimage. And crucial to the whole shape of his theology is the assumption that Christians can expect the privilege of knowing that they are children of God through the divine evidence of the witness of his Spirit with their spirits.

Aldersgate was for Wesley a significant step in his spiritual pilgrimage wherein he experienced an assurance of faith. It is clear that in 1738 he defined that experience of the witness of the Spirit as his conversion because he then accepted the Moravian theological framework for anticipating and explaining such instantaneous experiences. It is equally clear that he subsequently rejected many of the equations built into that Moravian theology, including the necessary correlation of faith with assurance, of assurance with salvation, of salvation with conversion, of sanctification with justification, of justification with sinless perfection, of doubt with sin. He continued, however, to stress the possibility of assurance of justification through the witness of the Holy Spirit (with modified expectations as to its necessary fruits and consequences) as a privilege to be desired by all Christians and to be known (evident) through the spiritual senses.

The irony of Aldersgate, however, is that its theological significance rests in Wesley's eventual modification of nearly every aspect of his perception and explanation of the event at the time. The Moravians had led him to great expectations that his own experience and reflection did not confirm as an appropriate or adequate understanding either of true Christianity or of what happened to him that evening. It is not surprising, in this light, that Wesley himself did not hearken back to Aldersgate as a model experience to be universalized. Rather, his subsequent attempts to explain that evening in the context of his continuing spiritual pilgrimage led to significant theological developments that eventually helped shape his own mature understanding and explanation of the Scripture way of salvation.

Chapter 7

EARLY SERMONS OF JOHN AND CHARLES WESLEY[1]

John Wesley's Early Sermons

On 16 October 1771, John Wesley noted in his *Journal,* "I preached at South Leigh. Here it was that I preached my first sermon, six-and-forty years ago." From this one entry, a number of differing accounts have developed concerning Wesley's first preaching. One particular tradition interprets the account as an anniversary notice and places the first preaching by the newly ordained Wesley on 16 October 1725.[2] More recently, historians have followed the picturesque account that Nehemiah Curnock gives in his introduction to the "Standard Edition" of John Wesley's *Journal.* Assuming that Wesley preached on the Sunday following his ordination as deacon, Curnock presents the following account of 26 September 1725:

> On Sunday morning he rides alone through Oxfordshire lanes towards Witney and, halting at the quaint old church at South Lye with frescoed walls, he presents his authority signed by Bishop Potter, and preaches, from an exquisitely neat little MS, on "Seek ye first the kingdom of God and His righteousness."[3]

This rather romanticized portrayal is admittedly the result of "historical imagination," which is often the child of assumptions and the mother of legends. Curnock himself introduces his remarks by stating: "Strange to say, no record of the sermon or of its preaching appears in the Diary."[4]

The diary to which he refers is the first in a series of diaries that John Wesley wrote while at Oxford. A careful examination of this first Oxford diary, however, reveals references not only to this sermon, but also to most of the sermons that John Wesley wrote between 1725 and 1735. Comparison with the extant manuscripts of the sermons and other early documents allows us to make the following observations: John Wesley's "first sermon" is really his second; most of Charles Wesley's published sermons were written by John; and many of John's early sermons are abridgments from other authors. The key that unlocks this storehouse of confusing data is a listing of sermon texts and titles found in the first Oxford diary.

The five notebooks known as the"Oxford diaries" are much more than simply daily accounts of the life of their author. The daily entries usually start several pages into the volume and stop before the last page is reached, leaving several opening and closing pages free for additional notes. In the first diary, the daily entries are made only on the recto of the page; the versos are left empty for further miscellaneous entries.[5] The diaries were not simply filled and then put aside. Although the daily entries in the first diary cover only the period from 25 April 1725 to 19 February 1727, the monthly financial accounts (which begin from the back) include September 1726 to December 1731. Other miscellaneous entries scattered throughout the blank pages contain notes dated as late as 21 June 1734.[6]

It is on one of these pages, the verso immediately preceding the first diary entry, that Curnock noticed "a list of texts and topics for pulpit preparation, written roughly, at various times, and here and there rudely erased."[7] Curnock does not mention, however, another similar list further along in the volume, opposite a page dated 24 September 1726. The particular significance of this latter list (which we shall refer to as "list A") is that many of the entries have numbers affixed to them. A careful reading of the diaries and a comparison with the extant manuscripts of the early sermons confirm the suspicion that here we have a listing of John Wesley's early sermons numbered in the order that he wrote them.

This numbering scheme can be verified in several ways. The manuscripts give various types of clues. The holograph of the sermon that has usually been referred to as Wesley's "first sermon"[8] has at the top center of its cover in John Wesley's hand the numeral "2," which corresponds with the numbering in the diary list. On the back cover, Wesley has noted in cipher the places (and in some cases the dates) where he preached this sermon, the first mentioned being Binsey in 1725. The daily record in the diary reveals that he began working on a sermon on 7 November 1725 and finished it the morning of his preaching in Binsey, 21 November (which was the only time he preached there in 1725). Further down the list there is a record of his having preached this sermon in South Leigh, but the probable date is 1727.[9]

There are, nevertheless, diary notations of his having preached on five Sundays between his ordination on 19 September 1725 and the writing and preaching of this sermon at Binsey. The sermon most probably preached on these occasions is the one listed as number "1" in the diary "list A," on Job 3:17—"There the wicked. . . ." A holograph of this sermon also exists,[10] and in John Wesley's hand on the cover is the inscription, "The first sermon I ever wrote," with the number "1" carefully inscribed at the top of the page. Again on the back cover are listed some of the places and times of preaching this sermon; these references correspond to several diary entries for his preaching during the period 1725–27. Of particular interest is a notation that he preached this sermon also at South Leigh in 1727. This notation verifies his statement made many years later that "Here it was that I preached my first sermon," although it was not the first preaching of that sermon nor his first preaching at South Leigh! As was frequently the case, his memory was less than precise as to the date.

Another bit of evidence that corroborates the numbering scheme is found on the holograph copy of a sermon on 2 Corinthians 2:17—"For we are not as many which corrupt the word of God." The seemingly insignificant number "12" scratched at the top center of the first page coincides with the number for this text in the diary listing. At the end of the manuscript, Wesley also noted the date on which he finished transcribing his pulpit copy from the rough draft; this dating also falls into chronological sequence with the other numbered sermons.[11] In February 1730 Wesley began to note more regularly, in his daily diary entries and the monthly summaries (in *MS Oxford Diary* 2), the subjects and/or texts of the sermons he was writing. These begin to follow the entries on the list Curnock noticed ("list B"), starting with some of the titles that Wesley had underlined. One of these underlined entries, "What I do thou canst not know," is the text for the sermon that Wesley noted as his fiftieth sermon in his diary on 26 September 1730. This reference is the first *daily* diary entry that designates a sermon by number, and from this evidence we can determine the numbering sequence for some of the immediately preceding sermons that are also found on "list B." Subsequent mention in the daily diary entries of sermon-writing seldom refers to the text or title, but usually indicates only the number of the sermon. In most cases, we have no manuscripts of the sermons mentioned only by number in the daily entries or the monthly diary summaries.

At this point, help comes from a rather unexpected source—the manuscripts in Charles Wesley's handwriting that are the basis for the published edition of his sermons.[12] Six of these manuscript sermons are on texts found in John Wesley's diary lists, and the shorthand notes that Charles made at the beginning or end of the sermons indicate that these, along with three others, were indeed "transcribed from my brother's copies" at various times during Charles's excursion to America in 1735–36. It is easy to imagine that Charles, having been rather hastily ordained deacon by Bishop Potter and priest by Bishop Gibson less than a month before embarking for America, felt the need for some assistance from his older brother, who by that time had been writing sermons for over ten years. The prospect of being assigned to different parishes in Georgia might have made it possible for the brothers to use the same sermons, had they not each preached in both places. This may have been the plan for John's sermon on Matthew 6:22–23, which he mentions on 29 January 1736 in his first Georgia diary, "began sermon on Single Eye." Finishing the sermon on 3 February, he reworked ("corrected") it the next morning before meeting Charles at noon. The manuscript of this sermon in Charles's handwriting, with the title "A Single Intention," ends with a note written in Byrom's shorthand: "from my brother's copy; transcribed February 4, 1736."[13]

Other sermons by John were similarly copied by Charles during his stay in America and on his trip back to England in the autumn of 1736.[14] In some cases Charles took the pains to copy the dates and places of preaching that John had noted at the end of the sermons (changing John's cipher into Byrom's shorthand). In every case, these dates and places fit the preaching references in John's Oxford diaries and help to fill in some of the gaps in the numbering scheme.

The system of numbering has more than a simple chronological significance. John Wesley seems to have numbered only those sermons that he himself wrote. He did, however, preach some sermons that were not his own, just as Charles obviously did. One whole volume of manuscript sermons in John Wesley's handwriting belongs in the category of unnumbered sermons "collected," transcribed, or abridged from other authors.[15] From his diary entries and the dating on the manuscripts, we learn that four of these sermons were collected from Benjamin Calamy[16] and four from William Tilly.[17] A fifth sermon abridged from Tilly was noted in the diary, but no manuscript has survived.[18] These sermons appear in the following table because, although not original with Wesley, they do indicate theological interests that were sufficiently close to his own that he could feel comfortable using them as his own.

Another significant example of literary appropriation is Wesley's abridgment of Robert Nelson's *The Great Duty of Frequenting the Christian Sacrifice*, in January and February 1732. The resultant essay was then further abridged into the form of a sermon, "The Duty of Constant Communion."[19] Although he and others did refer to this as *his* "sermon on the Sacrament," Wesley did not include the text in his diary lists, and (like the Tilly and Calamy items) neither the essay nor the sermon is in his numbering sequence.

The following list of John Wesley's early sermons ends with the sermon he preached on 21 September 1735 just before leaving for America. The text for this sermon is the same as that for his first sermon (Job 3:17) nearly ten years earlier, although it is a completely different sermon. The latter version was published by Charles Rivington in 1735 and was the first of his sermons to appear in print. The diary lists, incidentally, do contain two references to this text: on "list A" as "There the wicked" and on "list B" as "There the weary."

Although there are two major gaps in the manuscript diaries for this ten-year period, presumably most of the texts for the sermons we know only by number are included on the two diary lists. The listed entries for which we have no dates or numbers are therefore included in the following table in order to give a more complete picture of the topics upon which John Wesley was preaching (or thinking about preaching) in the early period of his ministry.[20]

Charles Wesley's Early Sermons

As we noted earlier, Charles Wesley was ordained a deacon and presbyter in September of 1735, just a month prior to his sailing with John for Georgia. As the ship *Simmonds* left Gravesend, Charles was busy preparing for his preaching duties, finishing the manuscript of a sermon on Phillippians 3:13–14 on 21 October.[21] His first recorded preaching occasion was about a month later (30 November) on board the ship as it was anchored off Cowes, the Isle of Wight, waiting for favorable winds. The sermon was based on an Old Testament text: "No longer halt between two opinions" (1 Kings 18:21).[22] There is no evidence of the sermon's author or date of writing on the MS; since there is no positive evidence that John ever wrote a sermon on that text, we might assume that this sermon was written by Charles.

Charles's next recorded preaching was his inaugural sermon at Frederica. He had copied his brother's sermon on "A Single Eye" (Matt. 6:22–23) during the ocean crossing.[23] It begins,

> The good providence of God hath at length brought you all unto the haven where you would be. This is the time which you have so long wished to find; this is the place you have so long desired to see.[24]

It appears that John had written this sermon specifically for his brother since Charles also used it in Savannah on his first preaching occasion there, 23 May 1736.[25]

Besides these two sermons, Charles mentions by name three other sermons that he preached in Georgia: "Keep innocency, take heed" (on 1 Clement 14); "Children of Light" (on Luke 16:8); and "He that now goeth" (on Ps. 126:6). The first of these, taken from a non-canonical text, was preached on 4 April 1736 and has not survived in any form.[26] The second one Charles transcribed from his brother's copy on 6 May 1736 and preached that following Sunday at Frederica, then again on 25 July in Savannah.[27] The third, perhaps of his own composition, he preached both places as well, on 18 April and 6 June 1736. On 20 June he preached a revised version of the sermon "Between two Opinions" that he had preached on board the *Simmonds*.

Although these five references comprise the explicit record of the sermons Charles preached in Georgia, we do know that he preached more often than five times and that he had more sermons available to use. From the Wesley brothers' journals, we know that Charles was in Frederica during March, April, and May 1736 and might have preached there as many as seven Sundays (two Sundays being supplied by his brother John and Benjamin Ingham). He went to Savannah in May and may have preached there as many as six Sundays, possibly using the same sermons.[28] Eight sermons would have more than satisfied Charles's needs during his stay in Georgia, and we do know of eight sermon manuscripts in Charles's handwriting that are dated prior to his departure from the colony. Of those eight, four are most certainly John Wesley's compositions, one other is likely John's (it is dated prior to Charles's ordination), and the other three have no specific evidence to verify authorship.[29]

When Charles left the colony, John gave him a further supply of sermon manuscripts to take along to England for his use. John accompanied his brother to the port of Charleston and immediately returned to Savannah before the ship sailed. The Sunday after John left Charleston, Charles preached from his brother's manuscript of the sermon, "The One Thing Needful." A month later, on board the *London Galley*, Charles made his own transcript of this sermon, along with at least three others written and previously preached by John.[30] During September and October 1736, the ship was moored at Boston for four weeks, during which Charles preached at both Christ Church and King's Chapel each Sunday, using John's sermons on at least four of the eight occasions (including, for the first time, John's sermon on Job 3:17).[31]

Having arrived back in England in 1737, Charles continued to use his brother's sermons. Combining the citations on the manuscript sermons and the references in Charles's *Journal,* we know that he preached the following sermons from his Georgia list during the following year: "The One Thing Needful,"[32] "The Love of God," "The Circumcision of the Heart,"[33] "He that winneth souls," "He that now goeth" (at least four of them John's).

On 28 May 1738 (the week after his "strange palpitation of heart"), Charles began writing what he called his "first sermon in the name of Christ my Prophet." There is no way to know whether that was truly his first sermon, or whether this phrase implies the first of a new type of sermon His borrowing from John did not cease, in any case. Within the next two months, Charles noted, "I preached my brother's sermon upon faith" on at least four occasions.[34] He seemed to have no qualms about using sermonic material of John's creation. At the same time, he was beginning to put together more sermons of his own (one presumes) that have survived only in shorthand copies.[35]

The history of Charles's early preaching reveals what appears to be his heavy reliance upon John for homiletical material. It may be that all of these early sermons in Charles's hand are actually John's. In any case, it is almost certain that Charles felt so comfortable using sermons of John's creation that, even if the few other early manuscript sermons in Charles's hand from 1736 are actually Charles's, they no doubt reflect a pattern of thinking that was nearly identical to John's. Although in later years there may have been some significant differences of emphasis and interpretation, it is important to recognize that at the beginnings of Charles's ministry during the "second rise of Methodism" in Georgia (and even a year or two beyond), he seemed to be in total agreement with his brother as to "The One Thing Needful" and most other basic points of the newly developing Wesleyan theology.

John Wesley's Early Sermons

No.	Title, text, or subject	Written
1.	There the Wicked (Job 3:17) (Sermon 133)	25 Sept–1 Oct 1725
2.	Seek Ye First (Matt. 6:33) (Sermon 134)	7–21 Nov 1725
3.	I am not ashamed (Rom. 1:16)	7 June–25 July 1726
4.	Ye know not what (Luke 9:55: "On Universal Charity")	14–24 Aug 1726
5.	There is One Lawgiver (James 4:12: "Against Rash Judging")	13–15 Sept 1726
6.	On Guardian Angels (Ps. 91:11) (Sermon 135)	[Pr'd 29 Sept 1726]
7.	Now He is Gone (2 Sam. 12:23) (Sermon 136)	10–12 Jan 1727
8.	So God loved the World (John 3:16)	
9.	Rivers of Water Run (Ps. 119:136)	
10.	Acquaint Thyself with Him (Job 22:21)	
11.	Fools Make a Mock at Sin (Prov. 14:9)	
12.	For We are not as Many (2 Cor. 2:17) (Sermon 137)	6 Oct 1727
13.	I am a Stranger and a Sojourner as all (Ps. 39:12)	
14.	Of Affliction	
15.	Hear, O Heavens (Isa. 1:2)	
16.	Behold an Israelite (John 1:47)	
17.	Behold an Israelite (John 1:47) (Sermon 138)	17 Jan 1728
18.	Behold an Israelite (John 1:47)	
19.	Died Abner (2 Sam. 3:33)	
20.	James 5:14; Genesis 3:19	
21.	Decently and in Order (1 Cor. 14:40)	
22.	What shall a Man Give? (Matt. 16:26)	
23.	On the Sacrament	
24.	On Fasting	
25.	Self-Denial	
26.	Evil Thoughts	
27.	When the Unclean Spirit (Matt. 12:43, or Luke 11:24)	
28.	Psalm 1:3 ("What is Man?")	
29.	On Christ	
30.	Humility[36]	
30.	Good Friday	

No.	Title, text, or subject	Written
31.	On Easter Day	
32.	Anger	
33.	Do it with thy Might (Eccles. 9:10)	
	Lovers of Pleasure more (1 Tim. 3:4)[37]	
	I preach not myself, but — (2 Cor. 4:5)	
	The Unprofitable Servant (Matt. 25:14–30)	
	Ezekiel 18	
	Verily Every Man Living	
	Poison of Asps (Rom. 3:13)	
	O the Depth (Rom. 11:33)	
	Whitsunday	
	Trinity	
	Luke 12:19 ("Eat, drink, and be merry")	
	Luke 13:24 ("Enter in at the strait gate")	
	Luke 15:10 ("Joy . . . over one sinner that repenteth")	
	Ephesians 5:15 ("Redeeming the time")	
	No resistance	
	Suffering	
46.	On Providence	7–22 Aug 1729
47.	On Pride	2 Jan 1730
48.	Negative Goodness	23–27 Feb 1730
48a.[38]		21–26 June 1730
49.	On the Sabbath (Exod. 20:8) (Sermon 139)	1–4 July 1730
50.	What I do, Thou canst not Know (Sermon 140: John 13:7)	26 Sept–13 Oct 1730
51.	In the Image of God Made He Man (Sermon 141: "On Original Sin," Gen. 1:27)	27–31 Oct 1730
52.		3–14 Mar 1731
53.		20–27 Mar 1731
54.	He that Winneth Souls is Wise[39] (Sermon 142: "Sermon for Ordination," Prov. 11:30)	5–12 July 1731
55.	Known unto the Lord are All (Acts 15:18)[40]	10–29 Aug 1731
56.	Where the Worm Dyeth Not (Mark 9:46)	24–25 Sept 1731
*	The Duty of Receiving the Lord's Supper (from Nelson and Beveridge)	31 Jan–19 Feb 1732[41]
*	Let me die the death of the righteous (Num. 33:10; from Calamy, #7)	11–12 Mar 1731
*	And they went out and preached that men should repent (Mark 6:12; from Calamy, #10)	1–2 Apr 1732

No.	Title, text, or subject	Written
*	Who went about doing good (Acts 10:38; from Calamy, #1)	2–5 June 1732
*	But some men will say, How are the dead raised up? (1 Cor. 15:35; from Calamy, #11)	5–7 June 1732
57.	Consecration Sermon ("for Mr. B.")	17–19 July 1732
*	("Collected a sermon of William Tilly")[42]	15–20 July 1732
*	Work out your own salvation (I) (Phil. 2:12, 13; from Tilly, #8)	12–14 Aug 1732
58.	On Public Diversions (Amos 3:6) (Sermon 143)	2–3 Sept 1732
*	Work out your own salvation (II) (Phil. 2:12, 13; from Tilly, #9)	29 Sept–1 Oct 1732
*	Grieve not the Holy Spirit (Eph. 4:30; from Tilly, #11)	27–28 Oct 1732
*	If any man thinketh he knoweth anything (1 Cor. 8:2; from Tilly, #13)	17–18 Nov 1732
59.	The Circumcision of the Heart (Rom. 2:29)	26 Nov–31Dec1732
60.[43]		10–17 Feb 1733
[60a]		19 Apr–3 May 1733
*	["Planned sermon," extemporaneous?]	26 May 1733
61.	Love of God and Neighbor (Mark 12:30) (Sermon 144)	2–15 Sept 1733
62.	Thy Will be Done (Matt. 6:10) (Sermon 145)	19–20 Apr 1734
63.	Martha, Martha ("The One Thing Needful") (Luke 10:42; Sermon 146)	—May 1734[44]
64.		—Aug 1734
65.		15–29 Oct 1734
*	[Extemporaneous sermon? Matt. 5:12]	[Pr'd 10 Nov 1734]
66.		6–9 Jan 1735
67.	Sermon for Sister Molly	24–27 Feb 1735
	Perfect Freedom (James 2:12)[45]	
	A Good Understanding (Ps. 111:10)[46]	
	And in Hell he Lift (Luke 16:23)[46]	
	Be Ye Angry (Eph. 4:26)	
	Thou art not far from the Kingdom (Mark 12:34)	
	Psalm 19:8 ("The precepts of the Lord are right")	
	Denying the Power of it (2 Tim. 3:5)[46]	
	Who teacheth like Him (Luke 12:12)	
	Man is born to Trouble (Job 5:7)[46]	
	Whence hath it the Tares? (Matt. 13:27)	

No.	Title, text, or subject	Written
	By their Fruits ye shall Know Them (Matt. 7:20)	
	God no Respecter of Persons (Acts 10:34)	
	Ye are not your own (1 Cor. 6:19)	
	Supererogation	
	Vain Philosophy (Col. 2:8)	
	Whoso mocketh the poor (Prov. 17:5)[46]	
	Faith, Hope, Charity (1 Cor. 13:13)[46]	
	He has ordained his arrows against the persecuters (Ps. 7:13)	
	Thou art unto them (Ezek. 33:32)	
	Grow in grace (2 Pet. 3:18)	
	Be not righteous over much (Eccles. 7:16)	
	A Reasonable Sacrifice (Rom. 12:1)	
	Though an Angel from Heaven (Gal. 1:8)	
	Wiser than the Children of Light (Luke 16:8; Sermon 147)[47]	
	Left us an Example that we tread (1 Pet. 2:21)	
	Dead, alive in God (Rom. 6:11)	
	A New Creature (Gal. 6:15, or 2 Cor. 5:17)	
	Other foundation than this can no man lay (1 Cor. 3:11)	
	Laodicea (Rev. 3:14f.)	
	There the weary (Job 3:17)[48]	[Pr'd 21 Sept 1735]

Charles Wesley's Early Sermons

No.	Title, text or subject	Written
[1]	Though your righteousness exceed (Matt. 5:20) (JW pr'd?)[49]	5 Jan 1735
[2]	Press toward the MarkTr'd (Phil. 3:13–14)	21 Oct 1735[50]
[3]	Between two Opinions (1 Kings 18:21)	Pr'd 30 Nov 1735
[4]	A Single Intention (Matt.6:22–23; JW sermon)	Tr'd 4 Feb 1736
[5]	Keep innocency, take heed (1 Clement 14)	Pr'd 4 Apr 1736
[6]	On the Sabbath (Exod. 20:8; JW sermon, #49 above)	Tr'd 6 April 1736
[7]	He that now goeth (Ps. 126:6)	Pr'd 18 Apr 1736
[8]	Wiser than Children of Light (Luke 16:8; JW sermon, see n. 47 above)	Tr'd 6 May 1736

No.	Title, text, or subject	Written
[9]	What I do, Thou knowest not now (John 13:7; JW sermon, #50 above)	Tr'd 7 May 1736
[10]	The One Thing Needful (Luke 10:42; JW sermon, #63 above)	Pr'd 8 Aug 1736 Tr'd Sept 1736
[11]	He that Winneth souls (Prov. 11:30)	Tr'd Sept 1736
[12]	Guardian Angels (Ps. 91:11; JW sermon, #6 above)	Tr'd Sept 1736
[13]	Love of God (Mark 12:30; JW sermon, #61 above)	Tr'd 4 Sept 1736
[14]	He that is faithful (Luke 16:10)	
[15]	Whoso drinketh of the water (John 4:14, unfinished or incomplete)	

Chapter 8

SPIRIT AND LIFE: JOHN WESLEY'S PREACHING[1]

John Wesley preached most of his sermons without the assistance of any notes or manuscripts. As a result, his oral sermons often gave the appearance of spontaneous expositions of Scripture. The only record we have of most of these preached sermons is a brief notice in his *Journal,* a cryptic entry in his preaching register, or a passing remark in the notes of an observer. But these brief references to such preaching occasions usually provide little help either to elucidate the content of his preached sermons or to clarify the relationship between Wesley's oral preaching and his published sermons. The reports, even in Wesley's own *Journal,* rarely indicate the basic outline of the sermon, much less the full text of what he said.

The impression that emerges from the descriptions of Wesley's preaching is that the oral presentations were more or less extemporaneous and were intended to edify and nurture his listeners, who in most cases were members of a Methodist society. Such a context would also seem to indicate that, by and large, the two homiletical forms, preached and printed, were rather different in form if not content. Many of his printed sermons were carefully developed treatises written specifically for publication and intended to be theological in nature. Nevertheless, in spite of this seeming contrast of form and function, one would naturally expect Wesley's preached and published sermons to fall within the same universe of homiletical discourse.

A small number of reports, by observers of Wesley's preaching, preserve samples of Wesley's extempore "field-preaching" and furnish a sampling by which to test the relationship of Wesley's preached and published sermons. These accounts of his oral sermons are best understood in the light of firsthand accounts of Wesley's preaching in general.

Wesley as a Preacher

If Wesley's stature as a theologian has been underestimated, his reputation as a preacher has probably been overestimated. Wesley's primary skill was not in the techniques of preaching; he certainly did not have the homiletical flair of a Whitefield. A visiting Swedish professor reported home in 1769 that Wesley "has not great oratorical gifts, no outward appearance; but he speaks clear and pleasant."[2] Thomas Haweis commented that Wesley's "mode of address in public was chaste and solemn."[3] An observer in Lincolnshire in 1788 remarked that "There was so little effort in the preacher, that but for an occasional lifting of his right hand, he might have been a speaking statue."[4] And yet, Wesley is also said by a another contemporary observer to have preached "with an eloquence and force which were irresistible."[5] The power seems to have been more in the message than the manner of delivery.

Wesley's preached sermons seem to have followed the design laid out in the preface to his published sermons: "plain truth for plain people." John Whitehead, a contemporary biographer of Wesley, noted that his style was "neat, simple, and perspicuous, and admirably adapted to the capacity of his hearers."[6] Charles Atmore testifies to this sense of propriety in his report of Wesley's preaching to a Sunday school gathering in 1790; Atmore remarks that the sermon "was literally composed and delivered in words of not more than two syllables."[7] George Story confirms the personal level of Wesley's manner of preaching when he states that "Mr. Wesley's sermons were, in a peculiar manner, calculated for establishing me in what I had lately experienced."[8]

Many eyewitnesses noticed one special characteristic of Wesley's preaching style: his frequent use of illustrations. George Burder, a Congregational minister who heard Wesley several times, remarked that "he illustrates almost every particular with an anecdote."[9] Sir Walter Scott characterized Wesley's sermons as "colloquial" and agreed with several other firsthand observers: "He told many excellent stories."[10] Even a critical viewer confirmed this same general impression in remarking that Wesley's sermons "consisted of nothing more than a string of mystical raptures about the new birth . . . richly interlarded with texts of Scripture and childish anecdotes about his own life and conversation."

Alexander Knox mentioned that Wesley's published sermons "bear the impress and breathe the spirit of John Wesley."[12] On occasion, the preached and published sermons seem to have been quite similar. In a few instances in the latter part of his career (as in the early years) he did use a manuscript (e.g., Sermon 111, "National Sins and Miseries," reported in his *Journal*, Nov. 12, 1775, with the comment, "Knowing how many would seek offence, I wrote down my sermon"). On occasion, he also seems to have used notes, especially in his old age, as reported by an eyewitness at Haworth in 1790, who noted that Wesley was accompanied by Joseph Bradford, who had the leading thoughts of Wesley's discourse written on slips of paper. When he found the memory of the venerable preacher at fault, he put before him the slip containing the thought he intended to express, which was at once taken up and the discourse continued in its appointed order.[13]

Overall characterizations as well as evaluations of Wesley's preaching range from strong approbation to gentle criticism, as might be expected. Mrs. Mary Bosanquet Fletcher mentioned that "each sermon was indeed spirit and life."[14] Another eyewitness referred to a Wesley sermon as "a combination of terror and tenderness."[15] John Nelson found Wesley's preaching to be effective and personal.[16] Dr. Beattie of Aberdeen, after hearing Wesley preach in 1776, remarked that it was "not a masterly discourse, and yet only a master could have delivered it."[17] At times, however, Wesley's busy schedule overextended his capacity for good preaching; Samuel Bradburn stated that occasionally Wesley's third or fourth sermon in a day "would be far beneath what he could have made them, had he preached but twice."[18]

Wesley's style of preaching does not seem to be inherently incongruent with or inhospitable to the form and content of his published sermons. The reports which preserve samples of Wesley's extempore "field-preaching" help elucidate the nature of this relationship. The following sections present accounts of Wesley sermons recorded at the scene by firsthand observers. While they add substantially to our knowledge of Wesley's preaching and we can have a certain degree of confidence in the integrity of these reports, they should be read with caution appropriate to the problems outlined above. The first and last accounts are particularly helpful since they are reports of preached sermons that are also available in published form. The second is unusual in that it only records theological concepts and contains virtually no anecdotal material, perhaps reflecting the interests of the recorder. Two of George Story's transcripts include the only record of the substance of two of Wesley's favorite preaching texts; no published versions of the texts exist.

Clerkenwell Charity Sermon

Wesley's *Journal* for December 16, 1787 records that after preaching at Spitalfields at eight in the morning, he "hastened to St. John's, Clerkenwell, and preached a charity sermon for the Finsbury Dispensary; as I would gladly countenance every institution of the kind." Charity sermons were occasions for raising money for specific charities, and in this case, the appeal raised over twenty pounds for the rather new public dispensary.[19] The substance of the sermon was reported in a manuscript now in the library of the Theological School of Drew University, Madison, New Jersey. The manuscript is headed, "Minutes of a Sermon preached at St. John's, Clerkenwell, by Mr. John Wesley, Dec. 16, 1787. Mr. Wesley was then eighty-five years of age" [nearly right; he was eighty-four]. In a note at the end of the manuscript, the observer/reporter indicated that "Mr. Wesley's sermon was forty-five minutes in delivering; he preached without any notes."[20]

It is characteristic that Wesley preached the sermon without using notes. But the sermon was not extempore in the true sense of being a totally unprepared discourse delivered on the spur of the moment. Wesley had written a sermon "On Charity" in 1784 and had published it in the *Arminian Magazine* in 1785.[21] He preached on the same text nearly two dozen times between writing the sermon and this occasion in 1787 and apparently was in the habit of following the text of the published sermon rather closely in spite of his extempore style. This fact was not lost on one observer, William Gurley, who heard Wesley preach this sermon in Ireland on May 1, 1785, and noted that "It was a most able discourse, just the same as is printed."[22]

The matter of delivery time (reported to have been forty-five minutes) is an important factor in comparing the report and the published text. John Whitehead, Wesley's personal physician in his later years, reports that in Wesley's old age, "his sermons were always short: he was seldom more than half an hour in delivering a discourse."[23] The text of the published sermon can be read in slightly over thirty minutes, but the report of the 1787 oral preaching of the sermon includes two additional sections: an anecdote about St. George's Hospital and a concluding appeal for the specific charity of the day, the Finsbury Dispensary:

> Having summed up all by saying that whatever we do, whatever we hope, whatever we believe, yet if love be wanting, we shall not be

> meet partakers of the Kingdom of Heaven, he adverted to the subject of the day (it was a charity sermon). When he was a boy, he said there were only two hospitals in London: St. Thomas's and St. Bartholomew's. A child, going along Dean's Yard [Westminster], picked up a French book giving an account of the great hospital at Paris [L'Hôtel de Dieu]. He carried it to his father, who showed it to Mr. Wesley's father (or uncle)[i.e., his brother, Samuel], who was then head usher at Westminster School. "Come," says Mr. Wesley, "let us found an hospital." The other gentleman said, "You are jocular." Mr. Wesley assured him he was serious, and the very next day they went about soliciting contributions in which they succeeded so well that the Hyde Park Hospital [i.e., St. George's] was soon after built.
>
> Wesley then briefly mentioned the number of charitable institutions which are now established, and concluded with a few exhortations to induce his audience to contribute upon the present occasion.[24]

These concluding comments, if added to the full text as published, would have extended the time to nearly forty-five minutes. One further observation made by the anonymous listener on this occasion may also account for some lengthening of the delivery time:

> Soon after Mr. Wesley had begun his discourse, he made a pause and said, "This I learned of a good man, Mr. Romaine: to pause every now and then, especially in the wintertime, that those who happen to be troubled with coughs may have an opportunity of easing themselves without interrupting the congregation."

The report of the Clerkenwell observer, however, omits major sections of the sermon as published two years earlier. That does not necessarily mean that Wesley had preached a shortened or radically altered text of the sermon on that occasion. The reporter's version of the forty-five minute sermon, including the added anecdote and appeal, can be read in less than ten minutes. The reported version obviously has left out a major proportion of the sermon. In this particular case, we can presume that the omitted material is in the published version, if Gurley's observation ("it was . . . the same as is printed") holds true for the Clerkenwell occasion as well.

Wakefield Preaching-House Sermon

On Thursday, 28 April 1774, John Wesley "opened the new [preaching-]house at Wakefield." In his *Journal*, Wesley added a further comment on the event, recalling the earlier grim days of his ministry there: "What a change is here since our friend was afraid to let me preach in his house, lest the mob pull it down?" On that earlier occasion in August 1748, he had preached "pardon for sinners"; a quarter century later he could note, "then was sown the first seed which has since borne so plenteous a harvest."[25]

His sermon for the occasion in 1774 was subsequently printed at Leeds.[26] The title page indicates that the sermon was "taken down in shorthand at the time of delivery by Mr. Williamson, a teacher of that art, and published at the request of many of the hearers." The price of the twelve-page pamphlet was threepence, more than the usual cost of a Wesleyan tract of that size. This suggests that the publication was a private project of Mr. Williamson, of whom nothing else is known. That he was not a Methodist might be inferred from his use of "meeting-house" on the title-page, a dissenting label that Wesleyans would have avoided.

Wesley does not refer to the printed sermon, but both its form and substance are close enough to his other published writings on the familiar linked themes of justification and sanctification to support the impression of authenticity. As in the case of other reports of oral sermons, however, it is unlikely that we have here a verbatim transcript—the text is less than half the usual length and, in most places, more concise than the published texts of other sermons that were preached. This transcript, unlike those mentioned above, is nearly barren of anecdotal illustrations and focuses almost entirely upon theological explanations and illustrations. The question of accuracy is accentuated by the form of the material in the published tract—the text is filled with dashes and semicolons, requiring extensive revision of the punctuation for modern publication. In one or two places the scribe had garbled the text in such a fashion as to create grammatical or theological problems.

What is noteworthy, however, are the summary distinctions between formal religious observance and the power of the Spirit, the "common calls" and the "effectual" call of God, the relative change in justification and the new creation in sanctification. There is also the clear suggestion, typical of John Wesley, that sanctification begins with justification, as the planting of a seed that requires the nurturing growth processes of grace to bring love to flower and fruition. The implied attribution to his critics of the definition of enthusiasm as extravagant biblicism and regenerationism is also significant and typical.

Plymouth Dock Sermon on Backsliding

One of the most striking examples of Wesley's oral preaching is found in the papers of George Story. Shortly after becoming a Methodist preacher, Story was named Wesley's "assistant" for the East Cornwall circuit. During his year in that position, he went to hear Wesley preach at Plymouth Dock. Wesley's *Journal* for Monday, 1 September 1765, contains a short reference to this occasion: "I came to Plymouth Dock, where, after heavy storms, there is now a calm. The house, notwithstanding the new galleries, was extremely crowded in the evening. I strongly exhorted the backsliders to return to God, and I believe many received 'the word of exhortation.'" This occasion is one of eighty-seven times he preached on this topic; in 1757, Hos. 14:4 had been one of his most frequently used texts, along with 1 Cor. 1:23–24.

Story carefully wrote the basic content of the sermon into a small paperbook, using Macauley's shorthand to assist him in the process; about one-third of the material is in shorthand.[27] Story's notebooks also contain more sketchy notes on three other Wesley sermons (see below, pp. 169-72), on Mark 4:3 (also preached at Plymouth Dock the following day), and on Matt. 10:30 and Phil. 4:7 (preached at Salisbury in October 1784). A Wesleyan preacher who itinerated for twenty-nine years beginning in 1762, Story later became the editor and printer for the connexion and was the publisher for Vol. IX of Wesley's *Sermons on Several Occasions* (1800).

Wesley's published sermons are often more instructive than converting, more nurturing than chastising. This sermon, however, though preached to a Methodist society, is remarkable for its powerful call to the sinners, those members who have slipped. This sermon has the same theological framework as two other sermons written during this decade, "On Sin in Believers" and "The Repentance of Believers."[28] The transcript is sketchy at best, often containing only main ideas, cemented by semicolons. The text amounts to about one-fourth the normal length of a Wesley sermon. Apparently the most memorable part of the sermon for George Story, the part which he records most expansively and in greatest detail (accounting for nearly a third of the transcript), is an anecdote about a backsliding Methodist preacher. The end of that story provides a natural transition to Wesley's concluding call to the backslider, which juxtaposes the familiar biblical assurance that Christ's blood can wash sins "as white as snow," with the less familiar but equally powerful motto of the medieval mendicants, "Come naked to a naked Christ":

> In the North of England, a wretched man heard my brother first at Newcastle. He was healed at once and continued so for two years; at length, he was called to preach; he came to me to consult about it, and was much discouraged because he was a tinker. I told him, it was no blame at all. He came to London, but was rejected by the people; from thence he went to Carlisle and then to Newcastle. He then fell into all manner of wicked ways and wandered into the vales of Cumberland. At a little inn, there were a parcel of lead miners drinking and swearing and they fell of abusing the Methodists, calling them a parcel of damned rogues that went about the country deceiving people; and this man was one of them and [they] hath found it out. Speak, man, speak. He answered, "I know you are all a parcel of villains, and I am more a child of the Devil than any of you; and I am afraid that all of you will have a better place in Hell than me." As I happened to be in those parts and hearing of him, found him out, and gave him in charge to one of our brethren; coming again into those parts, I found him full of faith and full of God.
>
> Look unto him that hath died for thee; though your sins be as red as crimson, his blood shall wash them white as snow. The Lord make you as at first; come naked to a naked Christ.

Story's notes on this sermon conclude with fragments from two Charles Wesley poems which John either quoted at the end or lined out for the people to sing:

> ["Thy sins are forgiven!] Accepted thou art!"
> I listened, and heaven springs up in my heart.[29]
>
> Thy love, [let it my heart o'erpower,]
> And all my simple heart devour.[30]

Other George Story Transcripts of Wesley Sermons

George Story's shorthand notebooks contain the outline of three other sermons that he heard Wesley preach. The first was a sermon on "Hearken: a sower went out to sow" (Mark 4:3, cf. Matt. 13, Luke 8). This sermon was preached at Plymouth Dock on Tuesday morning, presumably September 2, 1766, the morning after the sermon on backsliding. It is found in the same notebook with the latter, and in the same form of combined shorthand and longhand. Wesley was still in town on that day, and it is likely that this is another of his sermons, though it is not mentioned specifically in his *Journal* (and there is no extant sermon register or diary for that period). He preached on this text many times, at least fifty-five of them noted in his sermon register, *Journal*, and papers. Story's transcript contains only the first part of the sermon, stating the question to be dealt with, the structure of the sermon, and the beginning of the first part.

The question raised for Wesley by the parable is, Why should the same Word have no effect on some people? The sermon outline is simple: "I. The meaning of these words. II. Apply them to ourselves."

The main terms are lined out: "The seed is the Word, the sower is the preacher, and the soil or ground is the heart and soul of man." The sower is defined as "anyone that speaketh the Word of God." Christ is the principal Sower; after our Lord, the twelve apostles; then the seventy, and then all the rest—"every preacher of the gospel is a sower . . . ; all that are not his ministers sow not seed but chaff." The notes end with the explanation of the Word: "the Word preached is like seed sown in the furrows of the field." The rest of the sermon is missing.

The second of the additional Story transcripts is a sermon on "The peace of God, which passeth all understanding" (Phil. 4:7). The text is headed "Phil. 4:5," but the title and the subject matter are obviously from verse 7. Although there is no date or place listed on the manuscript, the sermon can be dated precisely in conjunction with another sermon that is adjacent to this one in his notebook. Wesley records in his diary that he preached on this text Tuesday, October 5, 1784, at 5 p.m. in Salisbury, immediately preceding the sermon on Luke 12:7 (below). Story had been appointed to the Salisbury circuit at the conferences in both 1783 and 1784. His pencilled shorthand entry of this sermon into his notebook is still in its rough fragmentary form. If Story intended to transcribe the text, as he began to do with the notes of the other Wesley sermon preached that day, he apparently never followed through on that intention.

After some introductory comments about the Platonic nature of St. Paul's language and a quotation from Abraham Cowley ("and thence the truth is truest poetry"), Wesley goes on to provide the general design of the sermon:

I. What is the peace of God.
II. How it passeth all understanding.
III. How it will keep our hearts.

The definition of the peace of God includes in outline form the three marks of that peace: calmness of manner, serenity, contentment. The basis of Wesley's view is reiterated in his typical trinitarian formulation: "God is the object of it, [God] is our Father, God the Son is our Redeemer, God the Spirit is our Sanctifier." One sure characteristic of such peace in a person's soul is that he is not afraid to die. This point is illustrated by a story about Colonel Gallatin who, though "his knees smote," was "not afraid of death" at the battle of Fontenoy.[31]

The second point of the sermon enters the arena of spiritual epistemology. In describing how this peace passes all understanding, Wesley uses one of his favorite concepts: "to say that it passeth all our senses" implies that "it is deep in the understanding of the spirit." Even the brute animals, he points out, "have some shadow of a human understanding." But the peace of God exceeds normal human understanding. He points out that "we have spiritual senses to discern spiritual good and everlasting life; the wisdom of God requires it." To support his point "that [God's] peace surpasses their understanding" he refers to a saying of Mr. Selby "at the University": for a man "to comprehend the peace of God with his understanding is to think with his ears."

The third part of the sermon is essentially a development of "that phrase, Christian life." The peace of God, Wesley says, "garrisons the spirit" after the manner of garrisoning a city. This peace "will keep our hearts, i.e., all our passion," on the one hand, and will also keep "all the wondering of the manner, reason, and imagination." It is, in the end, "the common bond of all the branches of Christian Perfection." This leads Wesley to conclude on one of his favorite themes: this peace of God comes from giving your life to God, and results in "having the mind of our Lord."

The last of the Story transcripts reports on Wesley's preaching on a text on which he had already published a sermon in 1786: "The very hairs of your head are all numbered" (Luke 12:7).[32] He had preached upon this text frequently; there are forty-five recorded instances after 1744, sixteen of them during the year 1784 (three of them in October).

The notes at the heading of this sermon indicate that it was preached on "Tuesday night" in "Sarum." Wesley's diary indicates that he preached at Salisbury, on this text, on Tuesday, October 5, 1784, at 6:30 in the evening, following the sermon on Phil. 4:7 (above).

Story took down rapidly scribbled shorthand notes in pencil. He began the process of transcribing these (in ink) into longhand, palimpsest style (overwriting), but managed to transcribe less than one-fifth of his notes. That transcribed portion reads as follows:

> The expression is figurative;[33] it means that the providence of God is extended to small things as well as to great things.[34]

> I. We allow that men see but a little way, a few miles; an angel may take in the whole earth at one view; God takes in all space at every moment.[35]
>
> Theocritus: *Joviis omnia pleno*—all things are full of God.[36] You know what is said and done in this room. God knows every creature, every angel, whether it be good or evil, every beast of the field, every bird, fish, insect.[37]

The manuscript then goes on in fragmented shorthand, dealing with several typical Wesleyan themes, many of which are found in the published sermon on this text: the relationship of animate and inanimate nature, the souls of brutes, the three widening circles in which Providence can be perceived, the assertion that God "can see one thousand years as one moment," the care of the Lord for both hero and sparrow alike,[38] and the need for diligence, meditation, reconciliation.

Conclusion

On the basis of these contemporary firsthand reports, it appears that Wesley's oral preaching does not seem to be radically different from the form and content of his published sermons. There are a few obvious dissimilarities, some of which can be explained by the difference between the channels of communication being employed, whether oral or written. The disparity in length between the reports and written sermons can be partially attributed to the problem of note-taking. One could not expect to write fully the complete body of the sermon, even using shorthand in an amateur fashion. These observations do not, however, fully explain the differences between what might have been said and what was reported. Two factors would seem to be of primary importance in explaining why the reports of Wesley's preaching varied from the published versions we have and in every case seem to be abbreviated: selectivity and attentiveness.

Aside from the question of how full or accurate the observer's hearing of the sermon might have been, comparison of the text and the report of two of the sermons indicates that *selectivity* on the part of the reporter is an important consideration. Some selection would be necessary simply from an inability to write as fast as Wesley could talk. Even shorthand notation would most likely not have been full or accurate. Further selection might depend upon the observer's level of interest in what was being said or level of understanding of the concepts being presented. Not everyone would find every comment as memorable as another. In some accounts, the observer records anecdotes from the sermon in great detail, while noting theological concepts only by key phrases or in outline form. In one case, however, the record is nearly void of anecdotal references, and the focus is almost entirely on the basic concepts being developed in the sermon.

The *attentiveness* of the observer could also influence what was recorded—a person whose mind was either wandering from or intent upon the oral presentation might easily have had occasional lapses in note-taking. The records of firsthand observers would differ to some degree not only from the actual preached sermon but also from other firsthand accounts, depending upon different canons of concern as well as different levels of intellectual ability and scribal efficiency among the observers.

The main observation from such a comparison of these records of preached and published sermons is that there is a definite congruency between the two. The examples we have examined would seem to indicate that there was more than likely a consonance of form and a consistency of message between the broader range of Wesley's preaching and the typical forms of Wesley's published sermons, even though in some ways the latter were designed to serve a more narrow didactic purpose. The basic difference in the records we have of the two homiletical forms, preached and printed, is an expected one of occasional omissions of published material in the former, but also the inclusion of more anecdotes and informal timely comments. It is not surprising, then, that the reports of Wesley's oral preaching in these cases, though perhaps not dramatic or eloquent in themselves, point toward homiletic presentations that have more spirit and life than their published counterparts.

Chapter 9

Plain Truth: Sermons as Standards of Doctrine[1]

John Wesley's comment in the preface to his *Sermons on Several Occasions* has become a favorite (though often misquoted) Wesleyan catchphrase: "I design plain truth for plain people."[2] What is not often recognized is that this declaration echoes the language and sentiment surrounding the use of the Homilies of the Church of England, which were (as their title explains and canon law proclaims) designed to be "read plainly and aptly . . . for the confirmation of the true faith and . . . for the better understanding of the *simple* people."[3] Wesley had a certain genius for abridgment.

As United Methodists, we have been increasingly concerned of late to clarify our doctrinal stance and our theological task. This concern is reflected in the action of the 1984 General Conference that requested the formation of a committee with the mandate "to prepare a new [doctrinal] statement [for the discipline] that will reflect the needs of the church [and] define the scope of our Wesleyan tradition in the context of our contemporary world. . . ."[4] Sooner or later in that enterprise, Wesley's *Sermons* enter the discussion, especially since the last theological study commission (1968–72) included in its report the statement that Wesley's *Sermons on Several Occasions* and *Notes Upon the New Testament* were to be understood ("by plain historical inference") as part of "our present existing and established standards of doctrine" referred to in the first restrictive rule of the constitution of 1808 (and still contained in the 1984 *Book of Discipline*).[5] Our purpose in this paper is to examine the role and function of Wesley's *Sermons* vis-à-vis doctrinal standards in the England of his day and subsequently in the early days of Methodism in America.

The question of doctrinal standards is not one that usually arises in the incubation period of a new religious group. Christianity began as a faith witness to the life and message (dare I say, sermons) of Jesus

Christ, proclaiming the coming of the Kingdom of God. This proclamation, the heart of the apostolic witness, the life-blood of the early church, the pulse of the writings to be canonized in the New Testament, was not without need for clarification and explanation in the face of philosophical challenges from without and differing interpretations from within the church. Thus the need for definitive *teaching* (or *doctrine,* in its simple etymological sense) became a fixture in the ecclesiastical history of Christendom. The tension between *kerygma* and *didache,* though not a necessary one, was a natural development within a religious institution which had leadership with both prophetic and teaching roles. As early as St. Paul, the problem of doctrinal standards arose, as we can see in his comments to the church at Rome concerning the "form of doctrine which was delivered you" (Rom. 6:17); and in the words of encouragement in 1 Timothy to those who would be "good ministers of Jesus Christ, nourished up in the words of faith and of *good* doctrine" (1 Tim. 4:6; my italics). These value judgments and implied criteria for determining the proper form of doctrine speak to the question of doctrinal standards.

We will not rehearse here the development of creeds and doctrine within the church, nor examine the long history of preaching the gospel in confessional and prophetic settings; rather, we will jump immediately to the eighteenth century to look at the various expressions of doctrinal statements and doctrinal standards in Wesley's time, both in the Church of England and in Methodism. Wesley says many times over that the Methodists preach the doctrines of the Church of England, as clearly laid down in her Articles of Religion, Homilies, and Book of Common Prayer.[6] In the light of his own use of sermons as a teaching instrument, let us examine the role of the Homilies within his own church, the Church of England.

The Reformation in England produced a church that formulated its basic doctrinal standards in the form of Articles of Religion—the Ten Articles of 1536, the Six Articles of 1739, the Forty-two Articles of 1552, and finally the Thirty-nine Articles of 1562, published, as the title says, "for the *avoiding of the diversities of opinions,* and for *the establishing of consent touching true religion.*"[7] The same movement of reform, under the leadership of Thomas Cranmer, also produced a book of Homilies, first in 1543 (published in 1547), and completed in 1563 (published in 1572). The Thirty-fifth Article of Religion (of the Thirty-nine) pertains directly to this book of Homilies (or rather these two books of homilies), which, it says, "doth contain a godly and wholesome doctrine and necessary for these times." This Article is only a minor alteration of the previous Thirty-fourth Article in the

Edwardian set (1552) that says the Homilies "be godly and wholesome, *containing* doctrine to be received of all men and therefore are to be read to the people diligently, distinctly and *plainly*."[8]

The Homilies were to some extent authoritative within the Edwardian church, as also can be seen in the injunction of Edward VI to his bishops in 1547, "that the preachers should not at any time or place preach, or set forth unto the people any doctrine *contrary or repugnant to the effect and intent contained* or set forth in the king's highness' homilies."[9] The wording here is important: "contrary to," "effect," "intent," "contained in." These words were not to be taken lightly; but, on the other hand, there was no provision for enforcement of an injunction. Fifty-five years later, the Canons of 1603 spelled out the role and function of the Homilies more fully. The Homilies were prescribed "for the confirmation of the true faith, and for the good instruction and edification of the people."[10] To this end, preachers were required to read a Homily every Sunday, "unless a sermon be preached,"[11] in which case the homily could be put off until the next Sunday (and so forth from Sunday to Sunday, presumably). The actual criterion for correct doctrine in preaching was specified in Elizabethan law, with provisions for enforcement: "if any person ecclesiastical . . . shall advisedly maintain or affirm any doctrine directly contrary or repugnant to any of the said Articles [of Religion], and . . . shall persist therein or not revoke his error [or later affirm such untrue doctrine], such maintaining or affirming, and persisting, or such eftsoon affirming shall be just cause to deprive such person of his ecclesiastical promotions" (Methodists would call it "involuntary location").[12]

The Articles of Religion, therefore, are the standards of doctrine for the Church of England, the measure by which orthodox doctrine is to be judged. What actual role then do the Homilies play in the propagation of true doctrine? James I provides some help in clarifying the function of the Homilies in this setting in a letter to George Abbot, the Archbishop of Canterbury (in 1622); in the letter he refers to the Homilies as "a *pattern* and a *boundary*, as it were, for preaching ministers, and for their further instruction for the performance thereof."[13] The two functions of pattern and boundary apply to the Homilies in two specific and different types of circumstances. The educated clergy (ordained, with a Master of Arts degree) were allowed to preach sermons, as we have seen, in place of reading a homily. For these, the Homilies served as a *pattern* of doctrine, a model of exposition, a resource that might or might not be used, so long as the doctrines in the sermon were "not directly contrary or repugnant to any of the said

Articles," which would make them "erroneous" and "untrue" (the clergyman presumably was able, from his training, to discern such correlation).[14] On the other hand, the Elizabethan Admonition of 1563, repeated in Canon 49, stipulates that "no parson, vicar, or curate do preach, treat, or expound of his own voluntary invention, any matter of controversy in the scriptures, if he be *under* the degree of a master of arts, . . . but only for instruction of the people read the Homilies already set forth"[15] (or as canon law states it with regard to the unlicensed preacher, "shall only study to read *plainly* and aptly, *without glossing or adding*, the Homilies already set forth"). In this case, for the less educated parson or curate, the Homilies become a boundary, not a pattern. Such a person is essentially limited to preaching no other doctrine (in fact, no other word) than is contained in the book of Homilies.

The distinction between Articles as *standards* of true doctrine and Homilies as *containing* godly and wholesome doctrine is further described in the works of such canonists as Edmund Gibson and Thomas Bennet, both of whose expositions of the Thirty-nine Articles Wesley read (Gibson's edition of the *Codex iuris ecclesiastici Anglicani* was the current codification of canon law in Wesley's day). Bennet, in his advice to aspiring ordinands, follows Gibson's main argument and makes the point that a person subscribes to the *Articles* as the basic *standard of doctrine*, and to the *Homilies* only insofar as the Thirty-fifth Article says they "*contain* godly and wholesome doctrine."[16] He goes on to point out that the determination of *what* those doctrines are in the Homilies, to which one professes approbation and belief, is accomplished by the same rule one uses with regard to other writings: looking for "those points which the author lays down and sets about the proof of, and giving his judgment and determination concerning them."[17] Subscription to the Thirty-fifth Article therefore does not mean agreement "that every argument therein urged is in our opinion valid, that every proposition in the declamatory part is strictly true, that every illustration is exactly just and home; these, I say, and the like particulars are by no means implied in our saying that the Book *contains* sound doctrine."[18] In fact, Bennet points out that the clergy are not ever required to study them, much less preach them (unless they are uneducated or unlicensed). "Subscribing to the Homilies" therefore means subscribing to the Article that says they *contain* sound doctrine, without putting a *nihil obstat* on the whole of them or making them a *standard* of doctrine. (A similar argument, by implication, could be made relative to the Book of Common Prayer, but that raises a whole new set of legal and theological connections with which we will not deal at this point.)

One problem in misinterpreting the role of the Homilies as authorized standards of doctrine is illustrated explicitly by Bennet, who refers to those who would claim that subscription to the Thirty-fifth Article implies such: "'Tis a common practice for [some] men to catch at every expression in the Homilies, which they think favorable to their own private notions, and thereby to drag the Church into the controversy, merely to cast an odium upon their adversaries, as apostates from what they have *subscribed*."[19] And yet, he goes on, when *that* person is pressed upon *other* points, they tend to interpret their own subscription to the Thirty-fifth Article more loosely (and thus to their own advantage) as not binding them to everything in the Homilies as a standard measure of correct doctrine. Such is human nature on matters of law and freedom.

Bennet also follows Gibson in a second point regarding the Article on the Homilies; namely, he indicates that its phrase "necessary for these times" is to be read "necessary for those times" ("these" times only for those who wrote the Articles). Gibson points out that while the doctrine in any homily, "if *once true*, must be always *true*, yet it will not be always of the same *necessity* to the people. . . . Those doctrines were necessary for that time, [but] we cannot say that it is as necessary for the present time to dwell much on those matters, as it was for that time to explain them once well."[20] The logical conclusion of this line of somewhat ambivalent thinking is reflected in the xeroxed bibliographical note attached to the inside cover of a nineteenth-century edition of the Homilies in the Bridwell Library at Southern Methodist University—"Although *unsuitable* for modern use, these Homilies retain *a measure of authority* in view of Article 35."

The question before us now, however, is how does all this relate to Wesley's use of sermons, as preached, or published, or designated as standards of doctrine in his movement? As the Methodist movement grew, Wesley was pressed to provide instruments of guidance and leadership. The conference, begun by Wesley in 1744, was his organizational means of giving advice, answering questions, and generally keeping control of what was going on. You remember that the conferences in Wesley's day were not deliberative or legislative bodies; Wesley invited selected preachers to come and talk with him (as reflected in the title of their yearly minutes: *Minutes of Some Late Conversations between the Rev. Mr. Wesley and Others*). And those early minutes reveal that the conversations were as likely to be about *doctrine* as about discipline. The form of the *Minutes* was question and answer. And you know who was giving the answer—there were no motions, no roll call votes. No one had to ask "who speaks for Methodism" in those days—everyone knew: Mr. Wesley. And generally speaking, the preachers were eager for his advice and guidance. In fact, it appears that the publication of Wesley's first collection of sermons was the result of the preachers' request for further doctrinal assistance in their preaching.

Sermons on Several Occasions began appearing in 1746; vol. 2 in 1748; vol. 3 (of three) in 1750. In the preface, Wesley writes, "The following sermons *contain* the substance of what I have been preaching for between eight and nine years last past [since 1737–38]. . . . Every serious man who peruses these will therefore see in the clearest manner what those doctrines are which I embrace and teach as the *essentials* of *true* religion."[21] The gist, as well as the wording, of this statement is important: The following sermons *contain* the substance of my preaching, those doctrines which I have been teaching as the essentials of true religion. To use the Edwardian phraseology regarding the Homilies, it would appear here that Wesley considered the *Sermons* to be a *pattern* for his preachers to follow, *containing* the essentials of true religion (sound doctrine). But the actual function of the *Sermons* within Methodism soon became much more explicit.

In the late 1740s, Wesley began to draw up model deeds upon which to fix his preaching houses; the deeds contained stipulations that would guarantee their use for Methodist preaching. In 1763, after he had published yet another volume of sermons (unnumbered, but fourth in the series) and a commentary on the New Testament (*Explanatory Notes upon the New Testament*), he decided to be more specific in the Model Deed then published in the *Minutes*. In the Model Deed printed in the "Large Minutes" of 1763, the trustees of the preaching houses are given explicit authority not only to see that only those preachers appointed by Mr. Wesley were to preach there, but also, as the Deed states, to see "that such persons preach no other Doctrine than is contained in Mr. Wesley's Notes upon the New Testament, and four volumes of Sermons."[22] The wording again is important: the Methodist preachers (unlicensed to be sure, and mostly uneducated) were required to preach "no other doctrine" than that contained in the *Sermons* and *Notes*. These two documents then acted as *boundaries*, not patterns; they provided the limits beyond which the Methodist preachers were not to preach. Wesley was using the *Sermons* with regard to his preachers in a similar fashion to the way the Church of England used the Homilies with regard to its unlicensed and uneducated preachers. The intention was to guarantee, as far as possible, sound doctrine, to be sure. But we should point out that his purpose was different from the Church's to the extent that his doctrinal emphases were distinguishable from the Church's—he was more interested in *edification* that would promote *holiness* of life than in *enforcement* that would simply guarantee *uniformity* of doctrine.

In Wesley's mind, however, these sermons were not at variance with the accepted doctrines or established standards of the Church. He constantly protested that the doctrines he taught were simply those of the Articles, the Homilies, and the Book of Common Prayer. This assertion, repeated in his journals, his sermons, his letters, and his treatises, is borne out in one sense by the fact that his published abridgment of the first five Homilies (1739) went through twenty printings in his lifetime, more than most any other Wesleyan publication.[23] In fact, the Wesleyans became closely identified with the Homilies (at least in some people's minds) to the extent that one Church of England priest refused to let his curate read the Homilies in church because "if he should do so, all the congregation would turn Methodists."[24]

But Wesley and the Methodists were not completely satisfied with the precise form or emphases of the basic doctrinal documents of the Church. In 1775, Joseph Benson and John Fletcher proposed a method by which to organize Methodism into a distinct denomination. They included the suggestion "that a pamphlet be published containing the 39 articles of the Church of England rectified according to the purity of the gospel." They also suggested that some "needful alterations" be made in the liturgy and homilies, and proposed that a book containing the "most spiritual part of the Common Prayer," together with the Thirty-nine [rectified] Articles and the Minutes of the conferences (which they refer to as "the Methodist canons"), should be, next to the Bible, "the *vade mecum* [constant companion or handbook] of the Methodist preachers."[25] This proposal is not only an interesting anticipation of what will happen in America; its particular shape also suggests that the *Sermons*, as important as they were, were not seen in the same legal role as the Articles, Minutes, or even prayerbook as official constitutive documents of this proposed Methodist "church." It should be pointed out, however, that while needful alterations were proposed for the Homilies, they were not proposed as supplanting Wesley's four volumes of *Sermons* as the practical measure of proper *Methodist* preaching. And finally, we should note, Wesley did not accept this proposal, so that Methodism did in fact continue as a group within the Church of England during the remainder of his lifetime. The Model Deed was still in effect even though it was not given the force of English law until the Deed of Declaration (1784) established the conference as a legal entity. Until that time, Wesley's stipulations regarding doctrine and discipline were as the *regula* of an unrecognized Order within the Church; in this setting the *Sermons* (and the Doctrinal Minutes) formed the heart of the *regula fidei*. This approach might be seen as less denominational than sectarian, as was perhaps fitting and appropriate for the Methodist societies at that time, an approach that continued at least a generation past Wesley's death, as British Methodism was hesitant to take on the trappings of a church, even in the face of their ecclesial independence (Plan of Pacification, 1795). Ordination was not implemented on a wide scale for many years after 1791; communion was not allowed in all Methodist chapels; ministers were asked to refrain from using the title "Reverend." Articles of Religion proposed by Thomas Coke, Joseph Benson, and Adam Clarke in 1806 at the request of the previous Conference "for the security of our doctrines" were not enacted by the Conference, which was occupied with other pressing business, "a multitude of weighty matters which were *necessary* to be considered and decided upon."[26]

Only as British Methodism entered the 1830s did it begin to look like a church. And, interestingly enough, at that precise time the wording of the Model Deed regarding the *Sermons* and *Notes* was changed. Whereas it had said the preachers must "preach *no other doctrine than* is contained in" the *Sermons* and *Notes*, it was then changed to read "No person . . . shall be permitted to preach . . . who shall maintain, promulgate, or teach any doctrine or practice, *contrary to what is contained in* Notes on the New Testament commonly reputed to be the Notes of the said John Wesley, and in the first four volumes of Sermons commonly reputed to be written and published by him."[27] The shift, one might say, represents a move from using the Wesleyan documents as *boundaries* to using the *Sermons* and *Notes* as *patterns* (as one might also distinguish between the use of the Homilies by the unlicensed preachers and by the ordained/educated clergy, as we saw above). Methodism in Great Britain was beginning in some ways to see itself as a church with a qualified (as well as called) ministry.

The *Sermons* were actually quite adaptable to either role as boundary or as pattern, as were the Homilies. They certainly were sermons (though not really designed for or preached on several occasions as the title implies). But they were not so much published preaching texts from Wesley's pulpit manuscripts as they were published homilies that Wesley had written for the doctrinal guidance of his preachers.[28] They are in most cases theological treatises in sermon form, model expositions of scriptural themes, which make them quite useful as doctrinal statements not unlike the Homilies of the Church. They are not the evangelistic documents that some might expect from an early Methodist preacher. There are few anecdotal illustrations, common in Wesley's extemporaneous preaching; there is no evangelistic call for decision at the end. There is a persistent focus on nurture and Christian living, with a combination of theological and practical themes, not unlike the Homilies (whose table of contents includes such topics as An Homily Of Salvation; Of Faith; Of Good Works; Of Repentance; Concerning the Sacrament; along with other works Against Excess of Apparel; Against Gluttony and Drunkenness; Against Idleness; Against Disobedience and Wilful Rebellion).

But there is a difference in the Methodist setting. The *Sermons*, along with the *Notes*, had become doctrinal standards for the British Wesleyans—they were, along with the *Minutes*, the official statements of doctrine that the church defined as the measure of proper preaching, the focus of proper teaching, and (by implication and practice) the source of proper doctrinal preparation for ministry. They were in any sense of the term doctrinal standards for British Methodism.[29]

An interesting problem arose in this regard, however. The Model Deed of 1763 originally specified *the four volumes* of Wesley's sermons as the only source of proper Methodist doctrine. In 1763, that would have meant the forty-three sermons in the original four volumes (or forty-four sermons, if you include the sermon "Wandering Thoughts," added in a second edition of volume three published also sometime in 1763). But in 1771–72, Wesley began the publication of his collected works with the four volumes of *Sermons on Several Occasions*. In this edition, however, he included nine additional sermons that he had written in the 1760s, after the appearance of the original fourth volume. "*The four volumes* of Wesley's Sermons" in the *Works* thus contained fifty-three sermons. The picture becomes even more complicated in the 1780s when Wesley decided to publish a new collection of sermons that would include those additional sermons he had written for publication in the *Arminian Magazine* during the previous decade. This third collection (eight volumes) includes a republication of the previous four volumes plus four new volumes. But the first four are not the fifty-three sermons from the 1772 *Works*, but rather the forty-three sermons from the original four volumes plus the extra one from a later edition of volume three, making forty-four sermons in these "four volumes."[30]

In the eighteenth century, no one seems to have had a problem with the phrase in the Model Deed. By 1810, however, the Conference revised the wording slightly to read "the *first* four volumes of Sermons," in the light of their publishing history.[31] Inevitably, however, the question arose—does that phrase mean the first four ever published, or the first four in the *Works*, or the first four in the edition of eight volumes? (i.e., 43, 53, or 44 sermons?) Thomas Jackson, when he published Wesley's *Works* in the 1820s and 30s, simply stated that this phrase referred to the first four volumes of the *Works* published in the 1770s (53 minus the one on the death of Whitefield equals 52). But persistent questions during the rest of the nineteenth century eventually forced the matter into the hands of Chancery Lane lawyers, who in 1914 finally decided (for better or worse) that "the first four volumes" specified in the Model Deed were in fact volumes 1–4 in the edition of 1787–88 and included forty-four sermons.[32] The irony of that decision was that several of Wesley's best doctrinal sermons, written in the 1760s, were omitted from the sermons which provided the "standard" for British Methodist doctrine. "The Lord Our Righteousness," "The Scripture Way of Salvation," "On Sin in Believers," "The Witness of the Spirit (Discourse II)," "The Repentance of Believers"—these are in the fifty-three sermons in the first edition of the *Works* (and republished as such in Jackson's now-familiar fourteen-volume set) but not in the first four volumes of 1788, and therefore not *standards* in Great Britain according to that decision.

We will not even attempt here to trace the problems in British Methodism that accompany the attempt to see Wesley's *Sermons* (by and large patterned after the Homilies as expositions of Scripture doctrines) as official doctrinal standards. Suffice it to say that the problems anticipated by Bennet and Gibson in Wesley's day of using the Homilies as standards of doctrine (rather than expositions of doctrine) were easily recognized in nineteenth-century Methodism and might be seen as one reason why British Methodism today, while still affirming the legal position of Wesley's *Sermons* and *Notes* as standards of doctrine, in fact generally ignores Wesley from the pulpit as though he were an embarrassment to modern theological and ecumenical endeavors.

The fate of Wesley's *Sermons* in America is a different story in many ways. The doctrinal stance of American Methodism during the colonial period is quite expectedly identical to that in Great Britain, since the Methodists were by and large located in English colonies and operated within the Church of England. Pressures for separation (ecclesiastical independence) were apparently as real here as in England, however, for the earliest conferences found it necessary to declare their allegience to the Wesleyan scheme of things, including their adherence, as stated in 1781, to the "old Methodist doctrine" as contained in the *Sermons, Notes,* and *Minutes* ("Large Minutes" of the British Conference).[33] With the conclusion of the War of Independence, however, a new situation arose. The pressures to obtain an ordained clergy in order to administer the sacraments cried for an ecclesial resolution to their problem as societies. Wesley's response, slow in coming (apparently due more to practical problems than theological scruples), was definitive and recognizeable in its proposed form.[34] His proposed scheme of organization for American Methodism, brought over by Thomas Coke in 1784, included Articles of Religion, a prayerbook, and ordination of clergy. When Coke and Asbury tried at the last minute to effect a union with the Anglicans in America (who were also moving toward independence from the parent church in England) and showed Wesley's scheme to William West and John Andrews, the latter were impressed that "the people called Methodists were hereafter to use the same liturgy that we make use of, to adhere to the same Articles, and to keep up the same three orders of clergy."[35]

It is interesting that the Anglican clergy saw no basic differences between Wesley's proposed documents and the Church of England's Articles and prayerbook. There *are* some basic differences, not least of all by deletion. We might notice in passing that the Article 8, "Of the Three Creeds," disappears from this Wesleyan canon. For our purposes in this discussion, however, a noticeable omission is that of Article 35 "On the Homilies." One might expect that Wesley would see his *Sermons* functioning in tandem with his new version of the Articles in similar fashion to the way the Homilies functioned in tandem with the Anglican Articles, that is, as "containing godly and wholesome doctrine" and providing proper exposition of that doctrine (should we add "necessary to those times"?).

It is clear that the Christmas Conference accepted the Articles of Religion as the doctrinal standards for their new church, the Methodist Episcopal Church. The preface to these Articles, as published in 1788, states: "These are the doctrines taught among the people called Methodists. Nor is there any doctrine whatever, generally received among that people, contrary to the articles now before you."[36] The terminology echoes that of the Anglican canons.[37] In the American revision of the British Methodist canon law (i.e., "Large Minutes" into the *Form of Discipline*), the Articles become the only stipulated measure by which proper Methodist preaching is determined and enforced. The Model Deed (with its doctrinal stipulations) was omitted from the earliest disciplines, and when it was reinserted in 1796, the phrase concerning the *Sermons* and *Notes* was deleted entirely. Doctrinal protection of Methodist pulpits in America was guaranteed by requiring that the preachers using them be persons regularly appointed *by the conference*. And the examination of candidates for ministry by the conference simply asks if they have read the *Form of Discipline*, which itself carries no doctrinal requirements vis-à-vis the *Sermons* or *Notes*.

The more explicit protection of doctrine for American Methodism is stipulated in a section of the Discipline that appears in 1788 under the question, "What shall be done in cases of improper tempers, words or actions, or a breach of the articles, and discipline of the church?" This is the question of maintaining proper doctrine, and the *measure* is the Articles, as one might expect. The following year, the question respecting doctrine is rephrased to say, "What shall be done with those Ministers or Preachers who hold and preach doctrines which are *contrary to* our Articles of Religion?" It is clear that the established rule for measuring proper doctrine is the Articles, in a manner (and using terminology) not dissimilar from their Anglican heritage (though the term "repugnant" is dropped). This terminology anticipates the change of terminology in British Methodism by some forty-five years (1832) but applies in this instance to the Articles, not the *Sermons* and *Notes*. The Methodist societies in America were not as hesitant as the Wesleyans in England to take on the ecclesial forms of a denomination. And they did so in more traditional forms.

It is therefore impossible to say, on the basis of the church's own official documents (or any other explicit evidence that I am aware of), that the Methodist Episcopal Church ever "established" anything but the Articles of Religion as their "standards or rules of doctrine" in the eighteenth or nineteenth century. This is not to say that American Methodists disregarded Wesley—far from it. They had not only accepted his scheme of organization for their church; they also declared themselves to be his "Sons in the Gospel, ready in matters *belonging to church government*, to obey his Commands." This "binding minute" from the first Discipline does not say "in matters of doctrine," but I have no doubt but what American Methodists also continued to read his *Sermons* and *Notes*, even though they did not have an overabundant supply of these materials from American publishers for several years. The publishing history of these two documents is a bit spotty in America before 1825.[38] In the thirty-five years of organized Methodism in America from the first conference of 1773 (when they first regulated the printing of books) to the General Conference of 1808, the *Sermons* and *Explanatory Notes* had each appeared in only two printings. It is the appearance of the first edition of Wesley's *Works* in America in 1826 and 1831 that seems to have sparked a vital interest in, and consequent publication of, Wesley's *Sermons, Notes,* and other writings.

In reflecting upon the nature and function of doctrinal standards in early American Methodism, and particularly the role of the *Sermons* in this connection, we might simply try to draw some conclusions based on our comparison of the Methodist Episcopal Church in America with the Church of England and Wesley's Methodism. In the Methodist Episcopal Church, Wesley's *Sermons* functioned differently from their role in British Methodism since they were not required standards of preaching. American preachers after 1785 were no longer limited to preaching "no other doctrine than is contained in" the *Sermons*; the sermons were no longer a boundary, but a pattern, and a voluntary one at that. A *boundary* that limits in any fashion must be carefully *defined*; the only definition of doctrinal limitations in the Discipline (in the section on trials) listed only the Articles. The fact that Wesley's sermons have not been considered a doctrinal standard in the manner of British Methodism explains why there has been no attempt in the two hundred years of American Methodism to *define* officially the meaning of the term, "the first four volumes of Mr. Wesley's Sermons"; Americans have no reason to get excited over the question of 43, or 44, or 52, or 53 "standard" sermons. A close examination of the course of study over the years will disclose that those "four volumes" have never formed the required doctrinal core of ministerial training in America as they have in English Methodism; they have never been officially specified as a criterion for determining what it means to disseminate doctrines contrary to our doctrinal standards. In short, this comparison reveals, among other things, that American Methodists have not let the British decide their doctrinal standards for them since 1785.

In the Methodist Episcopal Church, the *Sermons* also had a status somewhat different from that of the Homilies of the Church of England. The *Sermons* were never accorded any official place in or by the Methodist Articles of Religion. They have not been stipulated as required preaching by unlicensed preachers. They have not been listed in any official canon of the church. But they have *functioned* in ways remarkably similar to the Homilies (perhaps more like the Homilies in fact than the *Sermons* in British Methodism). They have functioned outside of the realm of canonical or constitutional doctrinal standards (which in the Church of England and American Methodism were Articles of Religion, 39 and 25 respectively). But in both cases, they were widely recognized as *containing* godly and wholesome doctrine to be used for the edification of the people. The British saw the Homilies as good expositions of the scriptural truths in the Articles; the Americans saw Wesley's *Sermons* as containing a good explanation of the scripture doctrines of Methodism, most of which were in the Articles.

The similarities and differences, both constitutional and functional, are striking and perhaps not accidental. The legal place of Wesley's *Sermons* in Great Britain has not, as we have mentioned, guaranteed their vital appropriation in the continuing life of the church. The relationship of the official status of the Homilies to their actual role in the Church of England is betrayed by a note I mentioned earlier, found inside the cover of the Book of Homilies I used for this study: "Although *unsuitable* for modern use, these Homilies retain *a measure of authority* in view of Article 35."

I would like to assert that Wesley's *Sermons* also retain "a measure of authority" within American Methodism without being referred to by any Article or being listed in any canon of the Church.[39] That authority is not constitutional, in spite of claims to the contrary; nor should it be. The authority of the *Sermons* rests in the realm of *tradition*, an authority which United Methodists profess to take seriously. The wisdom of the English canonists vis-à-vis the Homilies should remind us that documents like homilies and sermons are by nature not designed to be standards of doctrine, to be picked over word by word, to be used as measure and proof-text for doctrinal orthodoxy. If we want the *Sermons* in that manner, we must take the *Notes* as well, for they hang together in the historical argument. Do we really want to specify Wesley's note on Ephesians 5:22 as a United Methodist doctrinal standard?—"in all indifferent things, the will of the husband is a law to the wife." Or likewise his note on Acts 17:4?—"women lie naturally under a great disadvantage, as having less courage than men." And the very doctrines that make up the distinctive emphases of the Wesleyan tradition (assurance, Christian perfection, the witness of the Spirit) find quite different expression in sermons from different times in Wesley's life. Are we to declare them all (even with some internal contradictions) as constitutionally binding standards of doctrine by which we protect the soundness of our preaching and teaching?

You have to believe me when I say, I am not very excited about seeing the Articles of Religion fastened upon as operative standards of doctrine under the usual definition of the term; they need to be updated at the very least and combined with the Confession of Faith at the earliest possible opportunity in order to be taken seriously by

United Methodists and other Christian churches *in our day*. You also have to believe that I am not excited about seeing Wesley's *Sermons* placed in the same coffin with the anti-Roman Articles as constitutional standards of doctrine. There is no one in the world who is more interested than I am in having Wesleyan theology become and remain a vital and essential expression of our United Methodist witness of faith and a key component of our continuing theological heritage. But I am not ready to slip Wesley's *Sermons* into the arena through the back door by some historical fiction in order to effect this, nor ready to risk their being officially declared and then universally ignored, as have other official standards (when was the last time you measured your life-style by the General Rules?).

I am simply here stating the facts as they appear to me as a historian using certain critical tools of my trade. Wesleyan theology as contained in the *Sermons* was, is, and hopefully always will be an essential element of what it means to be (or have been) United Methodist. Wesleyan theology *is* a constitutive element of our *tradition*. As long as we are mindful of that tradition and appropriate it for our present age, we do not have to worry about the status of "plain truth" that speaks to "plain people"—it *will* be clearly heard where the Scripture way of salvation is preached and lived.

Chapter 10

At Full Liberty: Doctrinal Standards in Early American Methodism[1]

> The distinction between doctrines and the standards used to enforce them can be understood as a tension between the weight of tradition and the force of law.

American Methodism has never been characterized by a strong inclination toward careful doctrinal definition. That is not to say that Methodism has had no concern at all for matters of doctrine. From the beginning, the Methodist preachers referred to "our doctrines" with a sense of pride; they likewise expressed concern about the dissemination of erroneous doctrines in their midst. As American Methodism shifted from a movement to an institution (from a society to a church), it quite naturally developed structures and procedures to protect and perpetuate its traditional identity. Such a process included not only the establishment of legal and constitutional means by which to guard the "standards of doctrine," but also the preservation of traditional doctrinal emphases to perpetuate the distinctive, if not well-defined, Methodist proclamation of the gospel that lay at the heart of the movement. The growing desire for order and discipline, in tension with a seeming ambivalence toward doctrinal formulation, provided the setting for a unique development in the constitutional history of Methodism in America that to this day has not received an interpretation that commands a consensus.

The General Conference in 1808 passed a set of rules for "regulating and perpetuating" the conference. Among the provisions that became recognized as constitutionally binding upon Methodism was the stipulation that the General Conference have "full powers to make rules and regulations for our Church," subject only to a list of six "restrictions" subsequently called the "Restrictive Rules." The First

Restrictive Rule, still in effect in the United Methodist Church today, states that

> the General Conference shall not revoke, alter, or change our articles of religion, nor establish any new standards or rules of doctrine, contrary to our present existing and established standards of doctrine.[2]

Questions of doctrinal standards[3] in Methodism are determined in large part by the interpretation of this rule. The issue of interpretation is often focused on the meaning of the last phrase ("our present existing and established standards of doctrine"), giving rise to no small amount of debate among Methodist theologians during the past hundred years or so.

The interpretation that has prevailed over the last century has been incorporated into the official documents of the United Methodist Church. The *Plan of Union,* approved in 1966–67, noted that, although the last phrase of the First Restrictive Rule had never been formally defined, the "original reference" would include, "as a minimum," Wesley's "forty-four *Sermons on Several Occasions* and his *Explanatory Notes Upon the New Testament.*"[4] That assumption provided the basis for subsequent interpretive statements passed by the General Conference in 1972. The "Historical Background" statement, contained in Part II of the 1984 *Book of Discipline,* reiterates the claim that Wesley's *Sermons* and *Notes* were "by plain historical inference" among the "present existing and established standards of doctrine" specified by the framers of the First Restrictive Rule in 1808.[5] This view, however, like nearly every comment on the question during the last century, overlooks two key sources of evidence: the *Discipline's* own historical stipulations for enforcing doctrinal standards (beginning in 1788) and the manuscript journal of the General Conference of 1808 that passed the first constitutional rules. Careful consideration of this evidence challenges the current view and calls for a reconsideration of the assumptions that have prevailed regarding doctrinal standards.

The question of doctrinal standards in early American Methodism has taken on added significance with the decision of the 1984 General Conference to establish a study committee on "Our Theological Task." The committee's charge is "to prepare a new statement [*Book of Discipline,* ¶69] that will reflect the needs of the church [and] define the scope of our Wesleyan tradition in the context of our contemporary world." The First Restrictive Rule, of course, remains in force, and therefore a clear understanding of the intent of its framers (and thereby the meaning of its language regarding doctrinal standards) is crucial to the constitutionality of any updating of disciplinary statements concerning United Methodist doctrine. Of particular concern in this essay is the relationship between matters that bear the force of law and those that rely on the weight of tradition.

The matter of ascertaining the meaning of the phrase "our present existing and established standards of doctrine" in the 1808 document hinges upon two questions: What do the official documents of the Methodist Episcopal Church from 1785 to 1808 stipulate (legally establish by definition or implication) as the doctrinal standards of the denomination at that time? and What did the persons who drew up those documents intend by their language? Two related, but different, questions are, What are the distinctive doctrinal emphases of early Methodist preaching? and What documents best exhibited those distinctive doctrines? The developments during the period from 1785 to 1808 are of primary interest in answering these questions regarding law and tradition, but the ideas and actions of the generations of American Methodists before and after that period also help illuminate the issues.

The constitutional developments at the turn of the nineteenth century have never been fully outlined or adequately examined in the light of material now available. These events are crucial to a full understanding of the issues today, however, and deserve our careful attention. We will therefore look at the constitutional activities of early American Methodism step by step with an eye toward discerning the tension and interplay between the force of law and the weight of tradition in an attempt to contribute to a better understanding of the scope of the Wesleyan tradition in relation to doctrinal standards in the United Methodist Church.

Wesley and the Christmas Conference

The organizing conference of the Methodist Episcopal Church met in Baltimore in December, 1784, to consider the scheme of organization proposed by Wesley, as filtered through Francis Asbury and Thomas Coke. Its main concern was to establish a workable polity for American Methodists, separate from their former British connections yet still to some extent reliant upon Wesley during his lifetime.

The question of doctrine remained largely in the shadows during those days of rewriting the *Minutes* of the British Methodist Conference (also known as the "Large Minutes") into a form of discipline for the American Methodist connection. In fact, the official minutes of the Christmas Conference do not refer at all to any action concerning doctrine as such. One oblique reference appears in a letter from Wesley "To Dr. Coke, Mr. Asbury, and our brethren in North America" that is prefixed to those minutes. The letter spells out Wesley's rationale for allowing the organization of a separate church in the American states in the light of the "uncommon train of providences" by which they had become independent. Wesley concludes by proclaiming that the American Methodists, being totally disentangled from the English state and church, "are now at full liberty, simply to follow the scriptures and the primitive church."[6]

Lest anyone think, however, that he was casting his American followers adrift into a sea of doctrinal tumult, Wesley sent to the new world, with Dr. Coke, a document that provided the liturgical and doctrinal framework for American Methodism. *The Sunday Service of the Methodists in North America*, received and adopted by the Christmas Conference, contained Wesley's abridgment of the Book of Common Prayer and his distillation of the Thirty-nine Articles. Wesley may very well have conceived of these materials, along with the "Large Minutes," as providing the basic design for the organization of a Methodist church in America, much as John Fletcher and Joseph Benson had proposed to him in a nearly identical scheme for England in 1775.[7] The Methodist preachers in America not only adopted Wesley's revision of the Articles, but also apparently assumed that these materials from Wesley's hand furnished the necessary doctrinal framework for an ecclesiastical organization, similar to the way the Thirty-nine Articles provided doctrinal standards for the Church of England.[8] The acceptance of these documents per se did not diminish the American Methodists' regard at that time for Wesley's continuing leadership in matters of government or for his writings as a traditional source of doctrine.[9] In fact, their high regard for Wesley's scheme seems to have convinced them that the specific documents he had drawn up and sent over were deliberately conceived for the purposes of establishing the new church, which now stood in a new and separate relationship to both the Church of England and British Methodism.[10]

The preachers meeting in Baltimore clearly understood themselves to be establishing an independent organization that superseded any previous arrangements that had existed. The minutes of the Christmas Conference point out that "at this conference we formed ourselves into an Independent Church." Also, the answer to Question 3 in their first *Discipline*, which they drew up in Baltimore, makes this point very clearly:

> We will form ourselves into an Episcopal Church under the Direction of Superintendents, Elders, Deacons and Helpers, according to

> the Forms of Ordination annexed to our Liturgy, and the Form of Discipline *set forth in these Minutes* [my italics].[11]

The British "Large Minutes," which formed the basis for these American "Minutes" as revised at the Christmas Conference, were thus superseded and no longer had any binding effect on the American Methodists after January 1785.[12]

There is no reason to suspect that the traditional distinctive doctrines preached by Methodists in America would have changed as a result of any action of the organizing conference. The preachers in the newly organized Methodist Episcopal Church would certainly be expected to preach the same message that had given life to their movement over the previous decade. No one would expect that Wesley's *Sermons* and *Notes* would suddenly be discarded by the Americans; they had long been an important resource for solid Methodist doctrinal preaching.

After 1784, however, a new legal situation had been established in which the *Sermons* and *Notes* would appear to function quite differently than previously. During the decade prior to the Christmas Conference, the American Methodist conference had on several occasions pledged itself to the Wesleyan scheme in both doctrine and polity. It had followed the stipulations of the British *Minutes* to the letter, as was appropriate, given their status as part of British Methodism, under leaders appointed by Wesley. Their chapels were secured by the "model deed" contained in those *Minutes*, which, among other things, (1) required that the preachers be appointed by Mr. Wesley, (2) "Provided always, that such persons preach no other Doctrine than is contained in Mr. Wesley's Notes upon the New Testament, and four Volumes of Sermons."[13] These guidelines for measuring the doctrinal soundness of Methodist preaching were certainly, by any definition, "doctrinal standards." As such, they applied equally in America up through 1784 and were reinforced by specific actions of the conferences of Methodist preachers in America.[14] But the Christmas Conference had established American Methodism as a separate organization with its own set of constitutive documents, similar in form but significantly different in content from the British counterparts. The differences in the legal situation and the tensions with the traditional understandings became evident in the development of American Methodism subsequent to 1784.

From the Christmas Conference to the General Conference of 1808

After 1784, the Methodist preachers in America no doubt remained committed to their traditional doctrines. But the question remains, what did the Methodist Episcopal Church understand their "established *standards* of doctrine" to be? The fate of the "model deed," which stipulated those standards in Britain, helps answer that question. As noted previously, the Christmas Conference spent a large part of its time revising the "Large Minutes" into the new American form of discipline, published as the *Minutes* of 1785. A comparison of the two documents indicates that, although some sections were altered, many sections were either omitted totally or adopted without change, depending on their applicability to the American scene. The section which contained the "model deed" was omitted.[15] The new *Discipline* therefore specified no doctrinal standards.

The Conference had, however, received and adopted another document, *The Sunday Service*, that did contain a specifically designed formulation of doctrinal standards, the Articles of Religion (printed at the end, in the same manner that the Anglican Thirty-nine Articles appeared at the end of the Book of Common Prayer). These "rectified" Articles, as we have said, had been drawn up specifically by Wesley for the American Methodists. There seems to have been no need in the minds of the American preachers, given Wesley's intentional provision of these Articles, to specify any other standards of doctrine. This assumption is further supported by the fact that the "model deed," which the Methodist Episcopal Church did insert into its *Discipline* beginning in 1796, not only (1) designated a new source of authorization for the preachers (the American conferences instead of Wesley), but also (2) specifically deleted the proviso concerning the *Sermons* and *Notes*, thus consciously deleting their force as legally binding standards of doctrine.[16]

A more direct clue to the Methodist Episcopal Church's understanding of its doctrinal standards can be found in the disciplinary provisions for maintaining and enforcing those standards. The *Form of Discipline* for 1788 introduces a section on the trial of "immoral ministers and preachers," in which Question 2 is "What shall be done in cases of improper tempers, words or actions, or a breach of the articles, and discipline of the church?"[17] (This same edition of the *Discipline*, coincidentally, also has "some other useful pieces annexed,"[18] one of which contains the Articles of Religion.) The first General Conference of the Methodist Episcopal Church, meeting in 1792, divided that question (the second in the section on trials of ministers) into two questions that distinguish between matters of discipline and matters of doctrine. The new Question 3, dealing with doctrine, reads, "What shall be done with those Ministers or Preachers, who hold and preach doctrines which are *contrary to* our *Articles of Religion*?" (emphasis mine).[19] It is clear from this question that the only official measure or test of doctrinal orthodoxy within the Methodist Episcopal Church at that time was the Articles of Religion. In the same *Discipline* (1792) that contains this new question, the Articles were moved to a more prominent position at the front of the book, §II. The sacramental services were added to the volume, and the title was changed to *The Doctrines and Discipline of the Methodist Episcopal Church in America*.

At no point in the early history of American Methodism were the Articles of Religion designated as standards that demanded positive subscription. Although not a creedal formula in that sense, they did function like the creeds of the primitive church in another way—they were used as standards by which to protect orthodoxy by determining heresy or erroneous doctrines, i.e., those doctrines that were "contrary to" the standards as found in the Articles.[20] No American Methodist candidate for ministry was required to make any positive doctrinal subscription, either to the Articles, or to Wesley's *Sermons* and *Notes*, or to any other documents. The Articles served the purpose, then, of providing minimal norms or standards by which to measure the orthodoxy (not necessarily the adequacy) of doctrines held and preached by the Methodists.[21] The Wesleyan Articles of Religion provided a churchly doctrinal foundation for the new American Methodist ecclesiastical organization. They also presented an explicit doctrinal tie to the church universal and as such were a more appropriate standard of doctrine for such a church than the earlier British Methodist standards, Wesley's *Notes* and *Sermons*. In their original context, these British Wesleyan standards outlined what might be seen as a sectarian emphasis (for a movement rather than a church) under the larger umbrella of the Articles of Religion of the Church of England.

So far we have been looking at standards of doctrine as found in the Articles. That is not to say that good Methodist or Wesleyan doctrines are not to be found other places. The *Discipline* itself, beginning with the first edition, contained two sections on doctrine (on perfection and against antinomianism) and explicitly recommended several other writings for specific purposes.[22] Beginning with the edition of 1788 (the "useful pieces annexed"), the *Discipline* contained several doctrinal tracts in addition to the two doctrinal sections already mentioned.[23] These were apparently not considered to be standards of doctrine in the same sense as the Articles since the provisions for the trial of a preacher on matters of doctrine were not altered in any way so as to take these doctrinal writings into account. These treatises certainly contained sound Methodist (if not, strictly speaking, Wesleyan) doctrine, as did many other writings, but they were clearly never considered to be standards of doctrine.[24] The same can be said of the *Sermons* and *Notes*. Whether or not the American Methodists understood all the ecclesial implications of their separate establishment, they apparently did accept Wesley's intention that their organization be grounded upon a doctrinal statement (the Articles of Religion) that had obvious ties to the larger church universal in both form and content.

The General Conference of 1808

Twenty-three years after the Christmas Conference, only a dozen or so of the preachers from 1785 remained active in the Methodist connection in America. At about the same time, the passing of the earlier generations had led the British Methodist Conference in 1806 to ask, "Can anything be done for the security of our doctrines?" The answer in their *Minutes* was that Adam Clarke, Joseph Benson, and Thomas Coke were to "draw up a Digest or Form, expressive of the Methodist Doctrines." Their efforts resulted in two documents, both entitled *Articles of Religion*.[25] In America, a similar desire to protect and perpetuate the established doctrines and discipline of the church was apparently on the minds of Asbury and some of the other preachers at the General Conference in Baltimore in 1808.

On the fourth day of the conference, a committee was established to set rules for "regulating and perpetuating General Conferences in the future."[26] This "committee of fourteen," formed by two members elected by each conference, included all seven of the preachers in attendance (excepting Asbury) who had been in active connection since 1785: Philip Bruce, Ezekiel Cooper, Jesse Lee, John M'Claskey, William Phoebus, Nelson Reed, and Thomas Ware. The subcommittee designated to write the proposal was made up of three persons: Bruce, Cooper, and Joshua Soule, a young preacher who would soon make his mark on Methodism. Their report to the conference came from the hand of Soule and proposed the following as the first "restrictive rule": "The General Conference shall not revoke, alter, or change our Articles of Religion, nor establish any new standards of doctrine, contrary to our present existing and established standards of doctrine."[27]

The report of the "committee of fourteen" also contained, as its first item, a controversial proposal to establish a delegated General Conference. The defeat of that part of the report, over the question of how the delegates would be selected (largely because Jesse Lee opposed the committee's proposal of seniority as a basis), seemed to doom the whole report, which was then laid aside. As the conference drew to a close, however, the question of designating a time and place for the next conference allowed for the reintroduction of the question of delegation, and Soule's motion that delegates be selected by the annual conferences "either by seniority or choice" broke the logjam and allowed for the rest of the report to be brought up and carried, item by item.

Along with the other rules for governing the conference, the First Restrictive Rule was then passed, including the important phrase in question, "nor establish any new standards or rules of doctrine, contrary to our present existing and established standards of doctrine."[28] The primary impact of that second part of the statement seems to be to allow for new standards or rules of doctrine so long as they are *not contrary to* the existing ones ("present existing and established"). The main intention, then, of the conference's adoption of the phrase seems not to have been to incorporate an additional body of material, such as Wesley's *Sermons* and *Notes*, to their "present and existing standards," the Articles. The primary intent was rather to protect the present standards, the Articles, and to stipulate narrow restrictions under which new standards could be developed.

The intention of the conference in the face of the tension between the force of legal standards and the weight of traditional ideas is made more evident in the actions taken almost immediately after the passage of the Restrictive Rules on the morning of May 24. The first action of the afternoon session was an attempt to clarify any ambiguity caused by the phrasing of the first rule. Francis Ward moved

> that it shall be considered as the sentiment of this Conference, that Mr. Wesley's Notes on the New Testament, his four first Volumes of Sermons and Mr. Fletcher's Checks, in their general tenor, contain the principal doctrines of Methodism, and a good explanation of our articles of religion, and that this sentiment be recorded on our Journal without being incorporated in the Discipline.[29]

Three things are significant about this motion: first, it indicates a willingness among some preachers to specify particular writings that "contain" the core of traditional Methodist doctrine and exposit the "standards" found in the Articles; second, that such sentiment was not inclined to rely solely upon Wesley's *Sermons* and *Notes* but to include also John Fletcher's *Checks Against Antinomianism*; and third, that this sentiment was somewhat hesitant, resulting in a desire for a "memorandum of understanding" only, that would be recorded in the journal of the proceedings but not explicitly stated in the *Discipline*. The most startling thing about this guarded and carefully worded motion is that it lost. The General Conference was *not* willing to go on record defining its standards of doctrine in terms of documents other than the Articles, not even Wesley's *Sermons* and *Notes*.

The rationale for the conference's negative vote on this motion is nowhere explicitly indicated. Nevertheless, in the light of the wording of the motion as well as the action taken, it seems obvious that the majority of the members present did not consider Wesley's writings to be "rules or standards of doctrine" in the same sense as the Articles of Religion. If the members of the conference had generally assumed such a correlation, the motion would not have been made in the first place, much less defeated.

But what is confusing to the present observer is the conference's reticence to specify that the writings of Wesley and Fletcher "contain the principal doctrines of Methodism." This vote seems to be continuing evidence of a spirit of independence among the American Methodists that was more than simply anti-British sentiment, although that spirit can be seen flaring up at several points during the early years of the new denomination, including this period leading up to the hostilities of 1812.

The tension between dependence upon and independence from Wesley had long been a mark of the Methodists in America, as illustrated clearly in the life and thought of Francis Asbury himself, who played a major leadership role in the conference of 1808. Asbury was apparently satisfied that the conference had sufficiently protected its Methodist heritage. Three days after passage of the Restrictive Rules, he reflected upon the actions of that conference in a letter to Thomas Rankin, noting in particular that "we have . . . perpetuated in words the good old Methodist doctrine and discipline." Although this phrasing echoes the minutes of 1781, when the colonial conference reiterated its allegiance to the British Wesleyan standards, this comment by the bishop can be seen as an indication on his part that the actions of the conference had, without a literal return to their pre-1785 legal condition, preserved the original Methodist spirit in the face of new challenges from both heresy and sloth. Although the Articles of Religion seem to bypass some distinctively Wesleyan ideas, it appears that the Methodists in America accepted Wesley's design for protecting doctrinal orthodoxy through a brief and basic symbol of catholic doctrine, purged of Calvinist and Roman errors.

The intent of the 1808 General Conference thus seems to be clear. The majority desired to restrict Methodism's "established standards of doctrine" to the Articles of Religion that Wesley had provided in 1784 and to avoid even implying, by association or otherwise, that there were other specific writings that were authoritative *in the same manner*. The motion itself is, of course, an expression of the weight of the Wesleyan tradition coming to the fore, howbeit in a form considered inappropriate by most of those present and voting at the conference. The defeat of the motion seems to be conclusive evidence that the General Conference did not understand its standards of doctrine to include Wesley's *Sermons* and *Notes*. The Methodist Episcopal Church was left with a constitutional statement in the wording of the First Restrictive Rule, which refers specifically only to the Articles of Religion and reiterates and reinforces the crucial importance of the Articles by referring to them as "our present existing and established standards of doctrine."

In the light of those actions of the 1808 General Conference, it is by no means strange that for two successive generations, no one ever seems to have raised the question as to what the "present existing and established standards of doctrine" were. The Articles of Religion were the only standards of doctrine that had been "established" by the Methodist Episcopal Church, that is, adopted between 1785 and 1808 with provisions for enforcement as a measure of Methodist doctrine in America.

The fact that writers in the last half of the century began to raise the question, and in fact make inaccurate speculations about the intentions of the framers of the First Restrictive Rule, can be partially explained by the absence of any mention of this motion (or attempted "memorandum of understanding") from the published version of the manuscript journal of the conference. A note in the margin of the manuscript journal explains the omission: "N. B. It was voted that this motion be struck out of the Journal." The whole paragraph mentioning the defeated motion regarding the *Notes*, *Sermons*, and *Checks* is struck through with a huge "X" and consequently deleted from the printed version of the journal. That entry is the only instance of such an action in the whole manuscript volume, which covers the general conferences from 1800 to 1828. The conference did not want to specify its Wesleyan measures for orthodoxy beyond the Articles, but it also did not want the public to know that it had been unwilling to go on record in that matter.

The General Conference of 1808 manifested in its actions the continuing tension between dependence and independence, and, in its careful maneuvering, highlighted the distinction that is occasionally evident between the force of law and the weight of tradition.

The General Conferences of 1816 and 1828

The evidence outlined above would seem to be adequate to make the point that the doctrinal standards of early American Methodism were understood from a legal and constitutional point of view to be located solely in the Articles of Religion (though perhaps traditionally understood to be illustrated in other Wesleyan writings as well). However, further evidence to corroborate that view can be found in the actions of the General Conferences during the two decades following the establishment of the Restrictive Rules of 1808. Two incidents in particular relate to this question, and they are both coincidentally connected with Joshua Soule.

In the first case, the General Conference of 1816 decided to appoint a "Committee of Safety," which was assigned the task of inquiring "whether our doctrines have been maintained, discipline faithfully and impartially enforced, and the stations and circuits duly attended."[30] This committee consisted of Enoch George, Samuel Parker, and Soule (a most appropriate person to be in this group, providing continuity from the Conference of 1808). The report of the Committee of Safety, apparently drawn up by the chairman, Soule,[31] was approved two weeks later. It begins with the following statement:

> After due examination, your committee are of opinion that, in some parts of the connexion, doctrines contrary to our established articles of faith, and of dangerous tendency, have made their appearance among us, especially the ancient doctrines of *Arianism*, *Socinianism*, and *Pelagianism*, under certain new and obscure modifications.[32]

The term "established articles of faith" is not precisely the same as "articles of religion," but the committee seems to have had those articles in mind since the three erroneous doctrines listed are specifically contradictory to Articles II, I, and IX respectively of the Articles of Religion.

In the second incident, the General Conference of 1828 exhibited again the relationship that some persons within Methodism saw between the Articles as doctrinal standards and the other doctrinal writings accepted and used by the preachers as containing good Methodist doctrine. The conference heard the appeal of Joshua Randall, a preacher from the New England Conference, who, according to the wording in the *Journal*, "had been expelled from the Church, upon a charge of holding and disseminating doctrines contrary to our articles of religion." The charges were upheld by an overwhelming majority of 164 votes to 1. Encouraged by the tone of the conference, Lawrence M'Combs introduced a proposal that accused Bishop Soule (who was presiding at that session!) of preaching erroneous doctrine the previous year in a sermon at the South Carolina Conference. The motion claimed that in the sermon there was "in the opinion of some an apparent departure from several points of doctrine held by the Methodist Episcopal Church."[33] The matter was referred to the Committee on the Episcopacy, on which M'Combs sat. The committee's report was brought to the floor the following day by its chairman, Stephen Roszel, the only member of the group who had been at the General Conference of 1808. The report, adopted by the conference, cleared the bishop of the charges. It concluded by saying, "There is nothing in the sermon, fairly construed, inconsistent with our articles of religion, as illustrated in the writings of Messrs. Wesley and Fletcher."[34]

The conference thus stated its understanding of the relationship between the legal standards of doctrine and the traditionally accepted doctrinal writings. This statement is particularly illuminating in four ways: first, it demonstrates the position of the Articles of Religion as *the* standards of doctrine; second, it shows that the doctrinal material found in certain other writings in the Methodist tradition did actually function at that time in a supplemental and illustrative role in relation to the doctrinal standards in the Articles of Religion, similar to the manner expressed by the defeated motion of 1808; third, it reveals that, among these other writings, the broad range of Wesley's works was considered useful in illuminating matters of doctrine, rather than just the *Sermons* and *Notes*; and fourth, it clearly indicates that materials other than the writings of Wesley, in this case (again) the writings of Fletcher, were also considered to be important in this illustrative role. While the Articles of Religion functioned as juridical standards of doctrine, these other doctrinal writings, traditionally accepted as containing sound Methodist doctrine, were seen as exemplary illustrations of the Methodist doctrinal heritage.

Concluding Observations

The developments within early American Methodism indicate very clearly that the "historical inferences" that are "apparent" from the available evidence all tend to confirm the Articles of Religion alone as the "present existing and established standards of doctrine" that the "committee of fourteen" had in mind when it drew up the First Restrictive Rule. The founders of the Methodist Episcopal Church were not legally bound by any action previous to the Christmas Conference and seem to have taken Wesley's words to heart in considering themselves "at full liberty." At every point where the Methodist Episcopal Church had an opportunity to reiterate and reaffirm its allegiance to Wesley's *Sermons* and *Notes* specifically as doctrinal standards after 1785, it either consciously deleted the references, failed to mention them, or voted to the contrary. At every point where doctrinal standards are referred to, it is the Articles of Religion that are specified as the basic measure of proper Methodist doctrine.

That American Methodism was firmly grounded in the broader Wesleyan doctrinal heritage, however, can hardly be denied. Wesley had not only provided the new church with its Articles of Religion; even after 1808 his writings continued to provide the traditional exposition of the principal doctrines of Methodism, despite the General Conference's reticence to make that relationship explicit. The *Sermons* and *Notes* were quite likely alongside the Bible in the saddlebags of many preachers in America, along with *Primitive Physick*, the *Doctrines and Discipline*, and other basic resources of the circuit rider. Just as likely, Fletcher's *Checks* could be found in those same saddlebags, and, shortly, even Watson's *Institutes* and *Apology* would be considered appropriate baggage for a Methodist preacher. The relationship between these traditional doctrinal *statements* (accepted patterns of doctrinal *exposition*) and the established doctrinal *standards* (minimal measures of doctrinal *orthodoxy*) soon became confused as the constitutional distinctions became blurred in the minds of later generations.

By the middle of the nineteenth century, commentators began to read mysterious inferences into that phrase, "present existing and established standards of doctrine," and shortly began to alter the *Discipline* to conform to their new readings. Bishop Osmond Baker, in his 1855 manual of church administration,[35] was one of the first to claim that the Articles of Religion "do not embrace all that is included in 'our present existing and established standards of doctrine.'" His rationale was quite simple: "Many of the characteristic doctrines of our Church are not even referred to directly in those articles." He therefore suggested that "usage and general consent would probably designate Mr. Wesley's Sermons, and his Notes on the New Testament, and Watson's Theological Institutes" as "established standards of doctrine."

This line of reasoning, confusing traditionally accepted doctrinal statements with officially established doctrinal standards, was continued in southern Methodism by Bishop Holland N. McTyeire, who comments in his manual on the *Discipline* that "the phrase, 'doctrines which are contrary to our Articles of Religion,' is evidently elliptical." He goes on to mention those works which "usage and general consent" would include in the "established standards of doctrine" and adds to Bishop Baker's list the Wesleyan Methodist Catechisms and the Hymnbook.[36]

In the 1880s, this broadened reading of the meaning of "established standards" was incorporated into the *Discipline* of the northern church in the section on the "Trial of a Preacher." The charge of disseminating "doctrines contrary to our Articles of Religion" was amended to add the phrase "or established standards of doctrine," thereby referring to a separate body of material.[37] The Ecclesiastical Code Commission that proposed this change to the 1880 General Conference was chaired by James M. Buckley. Buckley's published explanations of doctrinal standards confuses the clear distinctions of legal establishment and traditional acceptance, resulting in continual references to "*other* established standards of doctrine" (my italics).[38] Buckley, along with others who used this frame of reference, was forced into making distinctions between the way the Articles could be enforced and the manner in which these "other" standards functioned. He noted, for instance, that such a range of material provides for "substantial unity" while allowing "circumstantial variety" within Wesleyan Methodism.

The incorrect assumption (as well as the new wording) of these constitutional historians became explicitly implanted in the 1912 *Discipline* of the northern church, which referred to "doctrines which are contrary to our Articles of Religion, or our *other* existing and established standards of doctrine" (¶245; my italics). This wording was subsequently carried over into the *Discipline of The Methodist Church* after 1939. In the meantime, the First Restrictive Rule had remained unchanged, though by now its original context and intent were fully misunderstood.[39]

The terminology for the section on trials in the present *Book of Discipline* (1984) is less precise, though perhaps more accurate (if understood properly) in its simple reference to "the established standards of doctrine of the Church" (¶2621.g.). The phrase should be understood historically and constitutionally as referring to the Confession of Faith (from the Evangelical United Brethren tradition) and the Articles of Religion (from the Methodist tradition). These are the standards of doctrine that have been established as juridical standards and carry the force of law within the church. Any attempt to enumerate *other* "standards of doctrine" confuses the distinction between the constitutional history of the church and the development of its doctrinal heritage. To say that our doctrinal standards are not "legal or juridical instruments" (1984 *Discipline*, p. 72) is to ignore our own provisions for enforcing those standards. To say that a particular list of other historical doctrinal statements should in some way be considered "established standards of doctrine" is to confuse the weight of tradition with the force of law.

The task of defining "the scope of our Wesleyan tradition in the context of our contemporary world" includes much more than defining or redefining legal standards of doctrine, although that is also involved. Minimal legal standards of orthodoxy have never been the measure of an adequate witness to the tradition, be it Christian or United Methodist. The heart of our task is to discover how seriously we take our distinctive doctrinal heritage and how creatively we appropriate the fullness of that heritage in the life and mission of the church today.

Chapter 11

JOHN WESLEY AND THE HISTORIAN'S TASK[1]

Many people recognized John Wesley as a significant man in his own day, even referring to him as "one of the most extraordinary characters this or any age ever produced."[2] During the following two centuries, this evaluation was reinforced in part by the sheer volume of writing about the man. Since Wesley's death, nearly two thousand books have been written about him.[3] His place of prominence in eighteenth-century European history has long since been assured. By this time, one would think that everything worth saying about Wesley had already been said. And yet, more books than ever continue to pour off the printing presses; the nature of his significance continues to be carefully scrutinized, and with good reason.

The writers who have analyzed Wesley over the years have exhibited a curious mixture of approaches in their use of his writings as a source for their studies. There are those, on the one hand, who assume that Wesley himself provided the first and the last word of any consequence. After all, it was he who had said, "As no other person can be so well acquainted with Methodism, so called, as I am, I judge it my duty to leave behind me, for the information of all candid men, as clear an account of it as I can."[4] Therefore, Wesley's own words need only to be repeated, inaccuracies and contradictions notwithstanding.[5] Let the great man speak for himself and his movement. On the other hand, most historians presume that Wesley can *not* be fully understood without a *broader* knowledge of his historical context and sources as well as an *accurate* understanding of his writings. The first approach tends to put Wesley on a *pedestal*, simply displaying the famous man; the second tends to put Wesley under a *microscope*, examining him carefully.

The trend in Wesley studies in recent years has been to move away from the "pedestal" approach (which characterized the first 150 years of work) and toward the "microscope" approach. Nevertheless, both approaches are still evident today, often waging a quiet "battle of the books" on the shelves of many unsuspecting owners. The differences in these two types of magnification often result in some confusion to the person who is simply looking for a "good book" on Wesley. The problem becomes somewhat more understandable, however, if we look at some basic distinctions that can be made between various levels of research and writing.

Levels of Study

The material that is currently available on Wesley can be placed into four general categories or levels of study. These represent four basic levels of research and writing that comprise the process of discovering and disseminating knowledge based on historical investigation. These levels of study are common to all fields of historical inquiry. In this essay, we will illustrate how they apply to Wesley studies.

The first level of research might be called *primary studies*. The basic task of this level is to provide *reliable texts* of primary resources, the essential foundation for the historian's task. This process requires the discovery, collection, comparison, and critical investigation of documents (published and unpublished) that are contemporary with the subject under study. This level of research also attempts to present the documents in the light of the events and thought patterns of their own time, which is the historical matrix within which the documents must be understood.

The second level is comprised of *specialist studies* that analyze and interpret particular topics. These works investigate the specific political, scientific, literary, theological, social, economic, or cultural aspects of the topic under examination. This process may operate with different angles of focus, examining a single idea, event, or structure, or perhaps studying a whole group or class of things. The main characteristic of this level of work is the *scholarly analysis and interpretation* of a selected topic—one must look carefully and critically at the background, the historiography, the documents, the context, and the implications of the specialized topic under consideration. Such studies at this second level depend very heavily upon the results of adequate primary research at the first level.

The third level of work consists of comprehensive studies that summarize and synthesize the studies done at the second level. These comprehensive works attempt to survey eras, movements, or individuals in such a fashion as to provide a thorough analysis of the subject. Works of this sort often present an interpretation that, with wide acceptance, claims to be the "standard" view. Challenging such a viewpoint once it has become widely accepted as a "standard" view is sometimes difficult, the more so as time passes. A competing interpretation must adopt a different interpretive stance that relies upon a new insight derived from newly discovered primary research materials or revised views of specialist studies. Therefore, new research and writing at the first and second levels can and should result in *new* interpretations and revisions of "standard" viewpoints at this third level of work.

The fourth level in this process is made up of the *popular studies*, works written for the general public. These works usually rely heavily upon the comprehensive studies of level three, some parts of which are summarized, simplified, edited, and produced in such a fashion as to appeal to a wide audience. (Some people would say they are easy to identify because they usually have larger size print and often have pictures.) These works play an important part in the broad dissemination of ideas. Quite often, the main considerations of the writers at this level are didactic (to teach), hagiographic (to honor), or aesthetic (to appreciate). But scholarly adequacy, essential to the work of levels one and two, and important in level three, is (unfortunately) often overlooked or set aside in the production of work in level four.

These four levels of study are all going on at the same time. Ideally, they should all build upon the foundation of primary studies, each level then building upon the best work of the others as we have listed them. From a scholarly point of view, the problem for the last two centuries in Wesley studies has been that no adequate base of primary research has been present to undergird the work of the other levels. There has never been a solidly reliable text of Wesley's writings available to scholars. One explanation for this situation can be found in the history of historical scholarship in general. It was not until well into the nineteenth century that modern critical [analytical] historical studies became prevalent in European scholarship with the work of Leopold von Ranke and other careful historians. Even then, their idea (that it was necessary both to go back to the primary sources and to analyze them critically) was not easily or readily accepted by some writers, especially when religious ideas or traditions were a part of the subject to be examined. This hesitance to accept *critical scholarship* in the realm of religious ideas is evident also in the study of sacred scriptures, where such work has only gradually been accepted during the last century (and not without a great deal of controversy).

The lack of a critical base upon which to build an adequate program of Wesley studies, thus explained but not excused, has had predictable results. Many comprehensive and popular studies (that is, at levels three and four) of Wesley's life and thought have been produced that are not founded upon adequate historical research at the primary and specialist levels of study.

It would be easy to disparage the works of many nineteenth-century Wesleyan writers in this regard, perhaps too easy from our modern critical perspective. We must recognize that only recently have two important developments taken place. First, more and more persons who are interested in Wesley studies have begun to see the *value* of (rather than fear the "danger" of) critical historical methods in helping to discern the significance of Wesley's life and thought. Second, the scholarly world (including specialists in non-religious fields) has begun to recognize the value of Wesley studies as a *respectable* sub-field of the *academic* study of religion, politics, literature, and several other fields. As a result, a noticeable renaissance of Wesley studies has occurred in the last two or three decades, fostered in part by a rising historical consciousness associated with various anniversary celebrations, such as those in American Methodism from 1966 to 1984. The question that arises at this point is whether or not the solid work that has begun in this field can maintain its momentum and whether its results can be felt in all four levels of study mentioned above.

It is not our purpose here to list or review the recent works that have been published in Wesley studies.[6] Rather, we will look at the present state of affairs in the four levels of study, noting in particular the agenda that lies before us in order to best satisfy the needs of those who are interested in a better understanding of the past.

Primary Studies

Of first importance in the study of the Wesleys (John and Charles in particular) is a complete and reliable text of their writings. It is a revealing comment on the present state of Wesley studies to note, as we did, that the standards of modern critical scholarship are only beginning to be applied to the publication of the Wesleys' works. For the better part of two centuries, writers have had to rely on less than adequate editions of the Wesleys' writings as a basis for their work.

The early commentators on John Wesley's life and thought relied heavily upon the first edition of his *Works* published by the printer

William Pine in Bristol, England, in the 1770s. That edition was filled with typographical errors, an accumulation of unwarranted editorial insertions and deletions, a host of hasty corrections, and even major omissions of material due to the printer's oversight (two years of the Journal were inadvertently omitted). That collection perpetuated many errors made in previous printings. In 1745, for example, a whole line was inadvertently omitted from a crucial passage in his *Farther Appeal to Men of Reason and Religion*. This mistake deleted the reference to "faith" as one of the three essential factors Wesley felt was necessary for justification; it was never reinserted in any subsequent edition (until the new edition in 1976).[7] In preparing his works for the collected set in the 1770s, and in correcting them as they came off the press, Wesley himself does not seem to have checked the text against the earlier editions. Therefore, in some cases, when Wesley attempted to correct obvious errors in the printer's proofs, his on-the-spot correction often resulted in a wording that only complicated the problem rather than restored the original text.[8]

Subsequent editions of Wesley's writings were based upon this inadequate "Pine" edition. The second and third editions (ed. by Joseph Benson and Thomas Jackson in the early nineteenth century) did improve somewhat upon the previous edition; they still, however, included no manuscript sources and provided no annotations or comparative textual analyses. They also mistook some works to be original with Wesley that were not and continued the practice of using later editions of Wesley's writings without comparing them with earlier or first editions. They thus perpetuated many typographical and editorial corruptions that had crept into the text.

Jackson's edition, which reached its final form in the "fourth" edition of 1872, was the last "complete" collection of Wesley's works to be published and has been the basis for all the recent reproductions of Wesley's *Works* in fourteen volumes. However, that edition and even the so-called "standard" editions of the *Journal* (eight volumes, 1909–13, ed. Curnock), *Letters* (eight volumes, 1935–37, ed. Telford), and *Sermons* (two volumes, 1921–22, ed. Sugden) do *not* reflect the standards of critical textual or historical work expected by the present generation. Nor do they contain much of the manuscript material that has become available only recently and that sheds important light on the development of the early Wesleyan movement. It is rather astounding to realize that the first ten years of Wesley's private diary, which should be ready for publication in another three or four years, will be coming out for the *first* time in the two-hundred and fifty years since it was written!

There is also a lack of Wesley writings in translation. As far as I am aware, his complete works are not available in any non-English publication. Most writings that are presently in translated form are usually edited selections and abridgments (often based on early inadequate editions) and therefore do not begin to meet the basic expectations of modern textual and historical scholarship.

As a first major step in correcting this situation, the new thirty-five-volume edition of Wesley's works now in production will overcome the lack of a reliable text of Wesley writings in English.[9] This edition is carefully annotated and incorporates the best scholarship available in a number of disciplines to help the reader understand the sources and context of the material. The new edition includes *introductory material* to provide the background of the work and citations that locate the sources of Wesley's quotations (or more often, misquotations). *Footnotes* also shed further light upon many of the ideas, events, or individuals mentioned in the text. *Manuscript material* is included when appropriate to illuminate the published texts, and lists of *variant readings* reflect each particular item's changes during its publishing history. The new edition will also include the previously unpublished Wesley *diaries*, a storehouse of information about the private Mr. Wesley. One of the most important scholarly tools in the whole project will be the two-volume *bibliography* of the writings of Wesley. It will provide a definitive listing of descriptive information relative to the various Wesley publications.

Over the next several years, this project, called the "Wesley Works Editorial Project," will produce a thirty-five-volume critical edition of Wesley's writings, a core of foundational materials necessary for first-rate specialist studies on Wesley's life and thought.

In the meantime, the writings of the rest of the Wesley family remain in a relative state of obscurity and chaos. Of particular concern are Charles Wesley's works, both his prose and poetry. Charles was, in many ways, the co-founder and co-leader of the Methodist movement in the eighteenth century. The only major attempt to collect the *poetical* works of the Wesleys is a thirteen-volume work in the mid-nineteenth century, which has serious limitations as a source for careful scholarship. Several other smaller anthologies of Charles's poetry have been published over the years, but most of them simply present a selection of favorite Wesleyan hymns. Two recent works have begun to set the stage for a fuller treatment of Charles's poetry.[10] A great deal of work remains, however; much of the poetry is largely untouched at this basic level of primary textual studies.

Similar textual work remains to be done on the prose works of Charles Wesley. The basic edition of his *Journal and Letters* published in 1849 omitted those portions of the journal that Charles had written in shorthand (some of the most interesting entries). A new edition of the journal that incorporated those sections was begun in this century by John Telford, but only one of the proposed three volumes was ever completed.[11] A new collected edition of Charles Wesley's letters is also desired, the rather meager collection of 1849 being the only one ever published. The sermons of Charles Wesley are also in a state of disarray. The only edition every published, in 1816, was based on sermons in Charles's handwriting, but we now know that they are mostly (if not entirely) sermons written by John Wesley and subsequently copied by Charles, the manuscripts then published posthumously as Charles's by his widow.[12] A group of sermons that were written by Charles in shorthand (and *are* apparently of *his* creation) have only recently been published.[13] A critical edition of these sermons, along with a new edition of Charles's letters and journal, could provide the public the valuable core of his prose works. Next summer, two hundred years after the death of Charles, a convocation of interested scholars will mark the beginning efforts of a Charles Wesley's Works Project, which hopefully will begin to rectify this situation.

Much work therefore remains to be done at the level of primary studies in order to provide complete, reliable, and annotated texts, not only of John Wesley's works, but also of Charles Wesley's works, edited in such a fashion as to reveal both the sources of their thought and the context of their activities. Such foundational primary studies as these are necessary as an adequate base for the second level of work, the specialist studies.

Specialist Studies

For many years after Wesley's death, "Wesley studies" consisted solely of biographies. These were generally *by* Methodists and *for* Methodists; the triumphalist tone was inevitable. The first appearance of more specialized topical studies occurred in the latter part of the nineteenth century, when several writers (primarily Anglican and Methodist) began to examine Wesley's relations with the Church of England. Studies of Wesley's theology, in some instances comparing Wesley with other Protestants, such as Calvin, Swedenborg, and Whitefield, began to appear before the end of the century. The early twentieth century brought more studies of special aspects of Wesley's life and thought—evangelism, romance, philanthropy, socialism, science, patriotism, ethics, etc. The tendency of these studies, however, was simply to describe a special facet of Wesley's biography, selected from his own writings and isolated from the larger background and context of his times. These works exhibit a partisan preoccupation on the part of Methodists with their founder and show little interest in the *sources* of Wesley's own thought and action, much less the broader historical *context* in which Wesley was writing and acting.

A few theological studies in the second quarter of the twentieth century began to call for and exhibit a wider approach. Maximin Piette's study, *Réaction de John Wesley dans l'Evolution du Protestantisme* (1925), and George Croft Cell's book, *The Rediscovery of John Wesley* (1935), opened up new areas of investigation, not only specific doctrines within Wesley's thought, but also the relationship of these ideas to traditional Reformation theology. In the last half century, many works have helped illuminate major themes in Wesley's life and thought. In keeping with the growing ecumenical tendencies in religious thought, the more recent theological studies have by and large begun to free Wesley from his Methodist closet. In addition, Wesley has been discovered by writers from a variety of disciplines, such as political science, literature, music, science, psychology, medicine, and philosophy.

The result has been a growing body of books and articles that demonstrate the wide variety of Wesley's own interests and involvements. Many of these works are done by scholars with competence in their own special academic field of inquiry but with only a limited acquaintance with Wesley. The major problem at this point is that the available Wesley resources at the textual and contextual level often do not give adequate support for the scholar's task. It is precisely at this point that the incomplete nature of the work at the primary level begins to effect subsequent endeavors at every other level.

Take, for example, the study of Wesley and medicine. Basic to that endeavor would be an understanding of the background and development of Wesley's popular little publication, *Primitive Physick*. It is one thing to say that it is a quaint collection of home remedies and folk medicine. It is quite another thing to document the origins of these prescriptions and the process by which Wesley came to include them in his collection. That information is still largely elusive at this point, awaiting the sharp eye of some patient researcher. A further requisite for such a study would be a good understanding of the status of medical theory and practice in the eighteenth century, a field of study that is itself just beginning to emerge.

Another good example of the work that remains to be done at this level can be seen in the prerequisites necessary to write an adequate study of Wesley's theology. No one has ever done a study that not only considers the various *topics* essential to an understanding of Wesley's theology, but also examines the chronological *development* of each of these topics as expressed in the full collection of Wesley's own *writings*. His theology should also be analyzed in the light of his *sources* (as seen in an analysis of his reading patterns over the years), the various *controversies* in which he participated, as well as the larger *historical context* within which Wesley was acting and thinking—the developments in politics, science, music, theology, economics, philosophy, technology, biblical studies, transportation, and other areas that would contribute to a better understanding of the living matrix of Wesley's life. By such means, one could examine Wesley's theology more thoroughly, thereby beginning to comprehend the *richness* of its background, the *complexities* of its development, and the *urgencies* of its rhetoric.

Many valuable specialist studies have already been completed that could contribute to a further sharpening of work at this level. There are still many other areas that need further careful investigation besides specific aspects of his theology—such as the place of women in the Wesleyan organization, the nature of Wesley's work among the poor, the character of the political and economic philosophy that guided his thought and actions, and his approach to the major scientific questions of his day. Any good study of Wesley in these areas must exhibit the principles of good historical investigation. It would consider the *whole* of Wesley (early and late periods as well as the middle), would consider the *change* as well as the *continuity* in his development, would take seriously the *criticisms* of anti-Wesleyan views as part of the whole picture, would recognize the *incongruities* and analyze the resulting *tensions*, and would look for the *precursors* and precedents of his thoughts and actions.

Much work remains to be done in many areas of contextual studies that provide necessary support for Wesley studies. Such a predicament should not, however, discourage the student of Wesley from making effective use of the supporting material that is presently available.

Comprehensive Studies

The two previous sections have repeatedly illustrated the point that there is much yet to be done at the first two levels of Wesley studies. We have just barely begun to approach Wesley with the appropriate critical tools and the breadth of outlook that are necessary to build a solid foundation and sturdy framework to house our endeavor; adequate work at these two levels is a necessary prerequisite to the production of biographies and historical surveys that measure up to modern critical standards. The same criteria that are indispensable at the first two levels of study are also essential to the production of adequate comprehensive studies.

The biography has been the most common form of surveying the Wesleyan story. In spite of the prolific production of such works, a definitive biography of Wesley has never been written and perhaps could not yet be written. However, some good biographies have been produced; several well-written, credible works have presented enlightening portraits of Wesley. Even a quick survey of the literature, however, will reveal that none of the biographies presently available provides a full narrative of Wesley's life in its many-faceted complexity. They do not take into account, for instance, the *full range of his theological development* that furnished not only the ideological context for his own spiritual pilgrimage but also the doctrinal agenda for his revival movement (a typical aversion of most current biographical writers). Neither do they fully notice the broad scope of his *many energetic activities* that made up the curriculum of a long and productive life (including his involvement in politics, medicine, prisons, poetry, and economics, as well as the quirks of his personal relationships with women which seem to be a particular fascination of many present authors). These and a host of other areas require treatment within any fully *comprehensive* look at the man.

Historical surveys of the Wesleyan movement in the eighteenth century generally display many of the same shortcomings as the biographies. There are not as many histories as there are biographies, to be sure—one would be hard-pressed to find in a bookstore these days *any* narrative history of Wesley *and his movement*, in any language. Such a situation may simply represent the current state of Wesley studies in general. The older, out-of-print works seem insufficient and yet the basic material is not quite fully in hand yet for definitive new works. However, the revisionist work of the specialist studies is beginning to provide a growing body of new material, and as that information builds up, it calls for a new synthesis to be reflected in subsequent surveys of the Wesleyan movement. The demands of critical scholarship obviously apply at least as much to these historical endeavors as to the biographies. The tendency of writers in this century to rely on the twice-told tales (often-repeated stories that come to be accepted as true simply by repetition) passed on in the books of the nineteenth-century simply demonstrates how much work remains to be done at this level.

Popular Studies

The work of the first three levels is essentially scholarly. But much of what is written about Wesley is intentionally non-scholarly, designed to reach a non-academic audience. While the area of popular studies is only one of four points for our consideration here, the material in this category probably makes up at least half the total bulk of current publications about Wesley. This category would include Sunday school literature, devotional publications, novels, newspaper and magazine articles, and works about Wesley that attempt to reach a wide popular audience.

The self-consciously non-academic approach of some of this literature reminds me of the speaker who starts a speech by saying, "Now I'm not really a scholar or expert in the field, but . . ." and then launches out upon a discourse that represents a very firmly held personal interpretation of some controversial issue. Disclaiming academic credentials does not, however, excuse a person from being responsible in making truth-claims. Unfortunately, many popular studies tend to keep repeating the old stereotypes long after the specialists have made important new discoveries and insights that have begun to cause revisions at the third level, of comprehensive studies.

The production of popular works does *not* necessitate compromising the academic integrity of the topic in order to make it attractive or interesting to a particular audience. A striking example of this is a children's book in the "Ladybird" series in England, a biography of Wesley that is simple, well-written, illustrated, and uses the latest research on the life and thought of Wesley and his times.[14] The fact that a book is written with a literary flair, or that it has illustrations, or that it is designed for a specific group should not exempt it from the normal expectations of accuracy and integrity.

We are still in the infancy of our knowledge of how to use pictorial illustrations relative to Wesley and Methodist studies. Graphic (and iconographic) materials have been used so indiscriminately for so long that one almost presumes that "pictures" lower the academic integrity of a work. There is no reason why that should necessarily be the case. Appropriate illustrations, if selected carefully and produced well, *can* provide very helpful insights that complement the written or spoken word. At this point, the tendency seems to be for (1) the books with good pictures and fluid writing to be lacking in historical scholarship, and (2) the works that represent the best in scholarship to be more difficult to read and without good illustrations. With new technologies and new information, however, and a willingness to use all available resources, the best of scholarship, writing, and the graphic arts might be brought together more frequently.

The Purpose and Future of Wesley Studies

The seeming divergence between *scholarly* and *popular* approaches to Wesley studies might be seen by some as a reflection of the different character and methods of the *academy* and the *church*. Such an explanation, while plausible, need not be understood as defining an essentially divergent goal of the church and the academy with regard to the Wesleyan heritage. Both the church and the academy are grounded in a concern for truth. In the academy, the search for truth through a *critical investigation* of the past defines the character of historical inquiry. The historian's task is to understand the past on its own terms before interpreting or appropriating its meaning for the present. In the church, the *critical temper* is also essential to the continuing practice of "an historically authentic Christian tradition."[15] The ongoing practice of a viable tradition depends upon critical reflection to maintain its vitality and integrity. Historical inquiry in the academy *and* in the church is important to the future of careful and meaningful studies of the Wesleyan heritage.

Within the last several years, major international conferences have given special opportunities for investigating and reflecting upon the Wesleyan tradition. Six years ago, the American Academy of Religion incorporated a Wesleyan Studies working group as one of its officially recognized study areas. The Oxford Institute of Methodist Theological Studies, a meeting every five years at Oxford University, has spent its last two sessions (1982 and 1987) looking in particular at "The Future of Wesleyan Theology." A special consultation on

"Methodism and Ministry" at Drew University in April 1983, and the another on "Wesleyan Theology and the Next Century" at Emory University in August 1983, were held with the expressed purpose of examining critically various elements within the Wesleyan tradition. The World Methodist Historical Society meets every five years on a global scale and sponsors regional meetings at more frequent intervals.

Participants at these events have included members of the church and the academy, preachers and teachers, clergy and laity, men and women, of all races and ethnic groups, and from around the globe. These participants represented a variety of academic disciplines and religious perspectives. On such an interdisciplinary and ecumenical base, the level of interest in Wesley that was sparked on those occasions has encouraged many to think that a new day has dawned in Wesley studies. The working groups on those occasions approached the Wesleyan tradition from all sides, approaching a host of new issues from a variety of new directions, including many insightful perspectives from non-English-speaking cultures.[16] They seriously reexamined the possible Wesleyan resources that might inform human self-understanding as we move into the twenty-first century on an ever-shrinking globe.

With the recognition that much basic work presently remains incomplete at every level of Wesley studies (as we have seen), the participants of the conferences were eager to move forward using the highest standards of critical scholarship presently available, aware at the same time of the need to be more openly cautious in making broad generalizations and to be more modest in stating final conclusions. Many participants expressed the strong feeling that Wesley is an important resource for religious self-understanding today. They also sensed that Wesley, rightly understood and creatively appropriated, could lend a vision of the potentialities of human existence that could continue to reform and renew individuals and institutions in our world.

These conferences have been an important step in the process of implementing a new approach to Wesley studies. They were especially significant, in each case both as a symbol and as an opportunity, for the manner in which they allowed the church and the academy to work together as partners in the process of rediscovering Wesley. The goal of Wesley studies properly conceived, then, as seen in these recent developments, is not to recapture or perpetuate a sectarian "Wesleyan" self-consciousness, but rather to understand and appropriate the Wesleyan heritage in ways that will guide and invigorate our conscientious attempts to think and live as vital and authentic human beings in our own day in our own way.

To the question, Why study Wesley? What is the underlying purpose of examining the Wesleyan heritage? we propose an ancient answer: we seek knowledge, and, not being born with it, we seek it in the past.[17] Thucydides, the ancient Greek historian, said that he wrote his great work for those "who desire an exact knowledge of the past as an aid to the interpretation of the future, which in the course of human things must resemble if it does not reflect it."[18] This point of view may lead to the narrow and negative sense that if we do not learn from history, we are doomed to repeat its mistakes. The more positive sense of Thucydides seems, however, to suggest a more useful perspective on our goals for looking at history and a more promising goal of studying the Wesleyan heritage—an attempt to understand who we are as human beings, as we try to live with authenticity in the present and to move with identity and purpose into the future to create a better world for all of us.

Notes

Preface

1. The dates of these discoveries were as follows: (1) July, 1969; (2) August, 1969; (3) April, 1973; (4) September, 1984; (5) October, 1986.

2. John Telford, ed., *The Letters of the Rev. John Wesley*, 8 vols. (London: Epworth Press, 1931); Nehemiah Curnock, ed., *The Journal of the Rev. John Wesley, A.M.*, 8 vols. (London: Epworth Press, 1938); Thomas Jackson, ed., *The Works of the Rev. John Wesley*, 3rd ed., 14 vols. (London: Mason, 1829-31; reprinted many times).

Chapter 1: What's In A Name? The Meaning Of "Methodist"

1. This paper was first presented as one of the Merrick Lectures at Ohio Wesleyan University in October 1984 and subsequently revised for presentation as the inaugural lecture of the Albert C. Outler Chair in Wesley Studies, Southern Methodist University, in October, 1985.

2. William Shakespeare, *Romeo and Juliet*, II.ii.43–44.

3. The argument among the Aristotelians, Platonists, and nominalists was still alive in the Renaissance England of Shakespeare's day. See Basil Willey, *The Seventeenth Century Background* (New York: Columbia, 1934), esp. pp. 27–28, 97–98; see also the development of this theme in the best-selling novel of monastic intrigue by Umberto Eco entitled *The Name of the Rose* (New York: Harcourt, Brace, Jovanovich, 1980; Warner Books Edition, 1984).

4. *Romeo and Juliet*, II.ii.33.

5. Thomas Ware, who was present at the "Christmas Conference" at Baltimore in 1784, later reflected that he would have been satisfied with the name, "The Methodist Church." John Dickins, later to become the first book editor of the new denomination, seems to have proposed the name "Methodist Episcopal Church" at the conference, and as Ware recalled, it was adopted without a dissenting voice. Thomas Ware, *Sketches of the Life and Travels of Rev. Thomas Ware* (New York: Mason and Lane, 1839), p. 106.

6. This anonymous letter was written on November 19, 1732, as part of the reaction at the university to the death of William Morgan, one of Wesley's friends and part of the Wesleyan movement. It appeared in *Fog's* on December 9. See Heitzenrater, *The Elusive Mr. Wesley* (Nashville: Abingdon, 1984), 2:28–31.

7. Although this attention to practice over theology was also typical in many of Wesley's own descriptions of the movement, he occasionally takes pain to notice both sides of this issue, as can be seen in his comment in the introduction to the *Plain Account of the People called Methodists:* "I send you this account, that you may know not only their *practice* on every head, but likewise the *reasons* whereon it is grounded . . . "; in *The Works Of John Wesley*, 34 vols. (Nashville: Abingdon, 1976–), 9:254 (hereinafter cited as *Works*). See also his comment in the preface to *The Character of a Methodist* (1742), §1, repeated in a letter to William Warburton (1763): "Many have been at a loss to know what a

'Methodist' is; what are the *principles* and the *practice* of those who are commonly called by that name" (*Works*, 9:32; 11:481).

8. *Webster's Third New International Dictionary of the English Language, Unabridged* (Chicago: Encyclopaedia Britannica, 1981), *s.v.* The word could also be used in a more general sense, such as in the verse,

Though Sorrow's an ill
Methodist, yet we
(Like him we treat) will grieve
more orderly.

Edward Sparke, *Scintillula altaris; or, A Pious Reflection on Primitive Devotion* (London, 1652), p. 97. For other general uses of the term, see Fred C. Wright, "On the Origin of the Name Methodist," *Proceedings of the Wesley Historical Society* 3 (1900):110–13 (hereinafter cited as *Proceedings WHS*); see also n. 10 below.

9. Wesley's Oxford diaries reveal a penchant for developing methods; see n. 71, below; see also *The Elusive Mr. Wesley*, 1:50–74.

10. Susanna Wesley, letter to John, 22 April 1727, responding to his description of his new scheme of study; in *Works*, 25:215 (reprinted in his *Journal* at 1 August 1742, the date of his mother's funeral). In her later description of her child-raising methods, Susanna explained to John that "the children were always put into a regular method of living, in such things as they were capable of, from their birth." Nehemiah Curnock, ed., *The Journal of the Rev. John Wesley* (London: Epworth, 1938), 2:34; hereinafter cited as *Journal* (Curnock).

11. First read by Wesley in April 1733; published and distributed by the Society for Promoting Christian Knowledge (SPCK) well into the following century. See also *Diary of an Oxford Methodist; Benjamin Ingham, 1733–34* (Durham, N.C.: Duke University Press, 1985), 5 February 1734, and p. 12n.

12. The handbook or "method" genre of writings was evident in many fields; other publications were also available at the time which promoted the use of particular methods to effect specific goals, such as *A Certain Necessary Method for Regulating the Press* (1711); *A Method for the Regular Management of those Societies called Box Clubs* (London, 1728); *A True Method for Raising Soldiers and Seamen* (1703), or *A Short Method to Prevent the Desertion of Army Recruits* (1710); *The Methodist; or, A New Method of Reading, Writing, and Printing all Languages in Short-Hand, by a New and Universal Alphabet* (1741); Elizabeth Burnet's *A Method of Devotion; or Rules for Holy and Devout Living* (1709); Thomas Blackwell's *Methodus Evangelica; or, Discourses concerning the Right Method of Preaching* (1712); in theology, see such works as August Hermann Francke, *Methodus Studii Theologici . . . accedit methodus exercitationum biblicarum autea seorsum excusa* (Magdeburg, 1723), and Richard Baxter, *Methodus theologiae Christianae* (London, 1681) and *The Right Method for Peace of Conscience and Spiritual Comfort* (London, 1653).

13. Wesley himself had been called "Primitive Christianity" by his friends as early as April 1730 (see letter of Mary Pendarves in *Works*, 25:246n). The first contemporary reference to their being called "Methodist" appears in a letter from John Clayton to John Wesley, 6 September 1732 (*Journal* [Curnock], 8:281). Clayton was responsible for heightening Wesley's interest in the life and thought of the early church. See Heitzenrater, "John Wesley and Oxford Methodists" (Durham, N.C.: Duke University dissertation, 1972), pp. 160–66, and below, pp. 74–75.

14. *Character of a Methodist* (1742), §3 (*Works*, 9:32), repeated in his open letter to William Warburton, Bishop of Gloucester (1763; in *Works*, 11:481–82). This claim was directly challenged by Bishop Warburton; see n. 25 below.

15. *A Letter to the Author of The Enthusiasm of the Methodists and Papists Compar'd* [Bishop George Lavington] (1750; in *Works*, 11:375). If Lavington had focused his scurrility less on the emotional fears of outward appearances of enthusiasm and had been a bit more familiar with the esoteric theological polemics on the continent in recent generations, he might have seen an even more direct connection between these Meth-

odists and the theological methods of the "Popish Methodists" of the previous century; see below, pp. 19–20, 25.

16. Preface to *The Character of a Methodist*, §3, in *Works*, 9:32–33; the phrasing is repeated in Wesley's *Short History of Methodism* (1765), §5, in *Works*, 9:368. The phrase, "new set of Methodists," may have been more than accidental in its construction; see also a letter (22 February 1733) from James West to Thomas Hearne, *Remarks and Collections*, ed. H. E. Salter (Oxford: Clarendon, 1921), 11:162n: "Your new set of Methodists or Sacramentarians are much talked of here, tho' I think we have no true account of them."

17. *Character of a Methodist*, in *Works*, 9:32; cf. Sermon 112, *On Laying the Foundation of the New Chapel*, in *Works* 3:581; *Second Letter to Dr. Free*, in *Works*, 9:324; and *Short History of Methodism*, in *Works*, 9:368. The reference in Sermon 112 uses the term "set" instead of "sect" when referring to the group of physicians.

18. See "The Methodists," in *Ancient Medicine; Selected Papers of Ludwig Edelstein*, ed. by Owsei Temkin and C. Lilian Temkin (Baltimore: Johns Hopkins, 1967), pp. 173–91. The founder of the school is thought by some to be Themison of Laodicea, a pupil of Asclepiades of Bithynia, whose ideas he took over; the completion of the system of Methodist teaching then being accomplished by Thessalos about the time of Nero. Edelstein follows Galen and others, however, in crediting Thessalos as the more likely founder of the school, at the beginning of the first century A.D. (ibid., pp. 173–79); see also "Methodists," *Encyclopaedia Britannica*, 3rd ed. (Edinburgh, Bell and MacFarquhar, 1797), 9:630.

19. *A Second Letter to the Rev. Dr. Free* (1758) in *Works*, 9:324. Free's explanation of the derivation of the term was just as incredible: "your being nick-named from the whimsical method of keeping a diary of all your actions." *Dr. Free's Edition of the Rev. Mr. John Wesley's Second Letter* (1759), p. 39; cf. at n. 24 below.

20. See *Short History of Methodism*, §5 (*Works*, 9:368); and Sermon 112, *On Laying the Foundation*, in *Works*, 3:581.

21. Whitefield, *Journals* (London: Banner of Truth Trust, 1960), p. 48. John Wesley provided a further refinement of this definition of "Methodist" in his *Complete English Dictionary* (1753): a Methodist is "one that lives according to the method laid down in the Bible." Cf. other more extensive definitions, such as "By Methodist I mean a people who profess to pursue (in whatsoever measure they have attained) holiness of heart and life; inward and outward conformity in all things to the revealed will of God; who place religion in a uniform resemblance to the great object of it; in a steady imitation of him they worship, in all his imitable perfections; more particularly in justice, mercy, and truth, or universal love filling the heart and governing the life." *Advice to the People Called Methodists* (1745), §2, in *Works*, 9:123–24.

22. Letter to Dr. Chandler (28 April 1785); see Frank Baker, *Charles Wesley as Revealed by his Letters* (London: Epworth, 1948), p. 14; cf. Frederick C. Gill, *Charles Wesley, the First Methodist* (New York: Abingdon, 1964), p. 36. This letter, in which Charles implies that he was first given the name Methodist, is often seen as a basis for calling Charles the founder of Oxford Methodism. It was, however, a very late recollection at a time when he and John were both contending for leadership among the Methodists and trying to support their claims of priority by asserting their own significant role at the origin of the movement. Cf. John's account in Sermon 112, *On Laying the Foundation* (1777), where he describes the origins of the movement in terms of his own solitary pilgrimage, unable to find companions in the way, for several years constrained to travel alone, until 1729 when he found one (Charles) who had the same desire. *Works*, 3:581.

23. *A Short History of Methodism*, §1, in *Works*, 9:367; cf. *Journal*, 5 June 1749, and *A Letter to the Rev. Mr. Baily of Cork*, II.4, in *Works*, 9:301, where the same sentiment is expressed in terms of wearing "long whiskers."

24. *Second Letter to Dr. Free*, §9, in *Works*, 9:324. His answer to Dr. Free also harkened back to the Greek doctors: "not one line is true. For (1) it was from an ancient sect of

physicians, whom we were supposed to resemble in our regular diet and exercise, that we were originally styled Methodists." Ibid., 9:324.

25. *A Letter to the Right Reverend the Lord Bishop of Gloucester* (1763), I.15, in *Works* 11:481; cf. n. 28 below. Warburton also claims that Wesley should best know the meaning of the term since it was not a *nickname* imposed on the sect by its enemies, but an appellation of honour bestowed upon it by themselves. *The Doctrine of Grace* (London: Millar, 1763), p. 167.

26. John Spencer, *Things Old and New* (1658), p. 161; "plain pack-staffe Methodists." Richard Watson refers to this phrase as being from a sermon preached at Lambeth in the year 1639: "Where are now our Anabaptists, and plain pack-staff Methodists, who esteem all flowers of rhetoric in sermons no better than stinking weeds, and all elegances of speech no better than profane spells?" (*Life of Wesley*, [New York: Phillips & Hunt, 1831], p. 16n). An article in *The Gentleman's Magazine* 58 (1788, 2nd part):688, quotes the passage as being in a batch of sermons printed at London in 1640.

27. "Peter Ramus and the Naming of Methodist; Medieval Science through Ramist Homiletic," *Journal of the History of Ideas* 14 (1953):235–48.

28. Wesley himself provides the answer to this claim as well as Warburton's comment about the Methodists' preaching by pointing out that "this nickname was imposed upon us before this 'manner of preaching' had a being" in their movement. *Works,* 11:482. Outler's general evaluation of these early sermons is that they are "clearly unmemorable," the style being "markedly more turgid than we are accustomed to in the later sermons." *Works,* 4:201–2.

29. Preface to the first volume of his *Sermons on Several Occasions* (1746), §3; in *Works* 1:104.

30. "Sadoleto's Letter to the Genevans," in John C. Olin, ed., *A Reformation Debate* (New York: Harper, 1966), p. 31.

31. "Calvin's Reply to Sadoleto," in ibid., p. 62.

32. Ibid., pp. 63–77.

33. Published in Charenton, 1634; English translation, *Faith Grounded upon the Holy Scriptures; Against the New Methodists. By John Daillé . . . and now Englished by M. M.* (London: Benj. Tooke, 1675).

34. Ibid., pp. 5–7.

35. Ibid., pp. 24–25.

36. Ibid., p. 42.

37. Ibid., pp. 14, 65ff.

38. Ibid., pp. 144–45. See also comments throughout which emphasize holy living, such as, "we are obliged to live holily and righteously," p. 9; "those who believe *and live* according to the Gospel of Jesus Christ shall have eternal salvation," p. 12.

39. Ibid., Part III.

40. John Lawrence Mosheim, *An Ecclesiastical History, Ancient and Modern* (London: Tegg, 1826), 3:482–84 (XVII, II.i.xv). Véron's *Règle générale de la foy catholique* (1660) appeared posthumously and was translated as *The Rule of Catholic faith; Sever'd from the Opinions of the Schools, Mistakes of the Ignorant, and Abuses of the Vulgar* (Paris, 1660); Nihus wrote *Ars nova dicto Sacrae Scripturae* (Hildesheim, 1632); Nicole wrote *Préjugez légitimes contre les calvinistes* (Paris, 1671); Bishop Bossuet had published *Exposition de la doctrine de l'Église catholique sur les matières de controverse* (Paris, 1671) which was translated into English, *Exposition of the Doctrine of the Catholique Church in the Points of Controversie with those of the Pretended Reformation* (Paris, 1672), and *Histoire des Variations des Églises Protestantes* (Paris, 1688), two works that William Wake would answer a decade later.

41. Mosheim, 3:480. Mosheim's account is the basis for the article on "Popish Methodists" in the *Encyclopaedia Britannica* (3rd ed., 1793), *s.v.*

42. That is, by the Protestants "refusing to believe those doctrines which the Church of Rome professes to have received with the grounds of Christianity, or the Papists in maintaining their possession." William Wake, *A Defence of the Exposition of the Doctrine of*

the Church of England against the Exceptions of Monsieur de Meaux, Late Bishop of Condom, and his Vindicator (London: Richard Chiswell, 1686), p. 3. Wake restates the question a bit more precisely for his own purposes: "The state of the question is this: 'That we who have been so often charged by the Church of Rome as Innovators in Religion, are at last by their own confession allow'd to hold the antient and undoubted foundation of the Christian Faith; and that the question therefore between us is not, Whether what we hold be true? But whether those things which the Roman Church has added as superstructures to it and which as such we reject, be not so far from being necessary Articles of Religion, as they pretend, that they do indeed overthrow that truth which is on both sides allowed to be divine, and upon that account ought to be forsaken by them'" (ibid., p. 3).

43. Ibid., pp. 4, 85–86.

44. This development can be seen in the discussions between Protestants and Roman Catholics at the colloquies of 1539–41, summarized in the *Regensburg Book* of 1541; see *Liber Ratisponensis*, §v, in B. J. Kidd, *Documents Illustrative of the Continental Reformation* (Oxford: Clarendon, 1911), pp. 343–44. The mediating position reached on the issues of free will, justification, and good works were also reflected in the theological position of the Henrician Reformation, especially in *The King's Book* of 1543 and the subsequent definitions of the doctrine of justification, faith, and good works in the Articles of Religion. See *The King's Book, or A Necessary Doctrine and Erudition for any Christian Man, 1543* (London, SPCK, 1932), pp. 147–63.

45. Phrase taken from the subtitle: *Wherein the nature of divine predetermination is fully explicated and demonstrated, both in the general as also more particularly, as to the substrate matter, or entitative act of sin: with a vindication of Calvinists and others from that blasphemous imputation of making God the author of sin* (London: John Hill, 1678), 4:t.p.

46. Gale, 4:1–2 and *passim*. Gale uses scholastic (especially Scotist) terminology to argue his position that God effectively causes (by efficacious predeterminative concurse, i.e., necessarily effective divine concurrence with human activity) the underlying constitutive actuality of human sinful acts (the material entitative act, i.e., the substrate matter of sin as distinguished from the form or the specific act of sin itself) but is not thereby the "author of sin." He thereby tries to defend the Calvinist doctrine of double predestination against the advocates of free will.

47. Ibid., 4:40.

48. Baxter, *Catholick Theologie: Plain, Pure, Peaceable, for Pacification of the Dogmatical Word-Warriors* (London: White, 1675), Pt. 3, p. 80; quoted in Gale, *Court*, 4:10.

49. Gale, *Court*, 4:142.

50. Ibid., 4:30, 149.

51. Ibid., 4:143.

52. Ibid., 4:144–49. LaPlace (Placeus) published *Syntagma thesium theologicarum in Academia Salmuriensi variis temporibus disputatarum* (1664); Strang wrote *De interpretatione & perfectione scripturae* (Amsterdam, 1663).

53. At Theophilus Gale's death in 1678, his library passed to Harvard College in New England. It is no surprise then that the orthodox Calvinist theology of Gale was shared by the then president of Harvard, Increase Mather, who is quoted by his son Cotton inveighing against Arminianism as Neo-Pelagianism. The elder Mather considered Amyrald as *Arminium Redivivum*, and the Amyraldists as *Novatores* and *Methodistas* ("innovators" and "methodists"). Cotton Mather, *Magnalia Christi Americana: or, The Ecclesiastical History of New England, 1620–98* (London: Parkhurst, 1702), Book IV, p.132.

54. "*Haec nove Methodus corrumpat doctrinam de Justificatione ex sola fide.*" *Dissertationes Trias: de Dei operum & pacis foederibus, atque de justificatione* (Amsterdam: Blankard, 1689), p. 241. This work has apparently never been published in English translation.

55. Ibid., pp. 186–91, 360, 417–21.

56. Ibid, p. 415.

57. Ibid., pp. 415–17. The work of Pitcarne was typical of those that focused the dispute on faith and works, as can be seen also in the similar title of one of Bull's

publications: *Harmonia apostolica: or, Two Dissertations, in the Former of which the Doctrine of St. James on Justification by Works is explained and Defended; in the Latter, the Agreement of St. Paul with St. James is Clearly Shown* (1670).

58. Crisp's works were first published in 1643.

59. Williams took up Baxter's cause upon the latter's death in December 1791, his main work being *Gospel Truth Stated and Vindicated* (1692). For an account of the "war," see David Bogue and James Bennett, *History of Dissenters, from the Revolution in 1688 to the Year 1808* (London: Printed for the author, 1808), 1:399–409.

60. The subtitle is *Also a Form of Prayer according to those Principles; with The Orthodox Doctrine about a believing Sinners Actual Justification, wherein is the Country-mans Method represented to view; as also A Form of Prayer for Actual justification, according to those Principles* (London: Jaye and Baldwin, 1693). The author, speaking for himself of this "New Divinity" under debate, "saith for himself, that it's a Method he dare not espouse, fearing he should lose his own hopes; . . . that all hope of his being saved is almost taken away" (p. iii).

61. Ibid., p. 6.

62. Ibid., pp. 6–7. Goodwin was one of Wesley's main sources for his doctrine of justification. Wesley published an abridgment of Goodwin's *Imputatio Fidei* (1642) as *A Treatise on Justification* in 1765; he also published extracts of several of Baxter's works, including his *Aphorisms*.

63. *War Among the Angels*, pp. 4, 7.

64. Ibid., p. 8.

65. Ibid., p. 8.

66. Ibid., p. 8. The nature of the distinction between the Covenant of Works and the Covenant of Grace was one of the points of contention in this dispute. Many Calvinists resisted any implication that the New Covenant implied obedience, as implied by any variation of the phrase, "Do this and live." (see below, at n. 76) They characterized the New Methodist position, emphasizing holy living, as being a new moralism or legalism teaching that "we are now to be justified by our own Evangelical Righteousness, made up of Faith, Repentance, and sincere Obedience, though imperfect" (ibid., p. 11). The Calvinist solifidian position outlined in this publication emphasized that Christ's active righteousness (active obedience to the moral law), not our own, is the material cause of justification, and that the sufferings of Christ as a propitiatory sacrifice (his passive righteousness) was the meritorious cause of justification; God's grace is the efficient cause, faith the instrumental cause (ibid., pp. 14–18).

67. "For a believing, coming, repenting Sinner, in his first uniting to Christ (as he is in Christ) is as really and perfectly justified as he ever shall be." Ibid., p. 19.

68. Ibid., p. 14. Wesley at Oxford would have been very comfortable with this perspective, as we shall see below, pp. 28–30.

69. One reference to the New Methodists, nearly contemporary to Wesley's experience at Oxford, was by Robert Wodrow, a Scottish ecclesiastical historian (and apparently a good Scots Presbyterian), who wrote in September 1717 to a friend about to visit Leiden: "I would know the state of doctrine among the professors of Geneva, and other Calvinist places in Germany, how far Arminianism has crept in among them, or the opinions of the New Methodists. I have heard suspicions that Turretin, Ostervald, and some others are venting new schemes of doctrine, and discover themselves favourable to the hierarchy and are quitting many of Calvin's tenets." *Wodrow's Correspondence*, 3 v. (Wodrow Society, 1842–43), quoted in *Proceedings WHS* 2 (1900): 112.

70. *Journal* (Curnock), 8:281.

71. Talk of method with pupils, *MS Oxford Diaries*, 2:109 (6 December 1731); method for Castle, ibid., 2:133 (22 May 1732); method for acquaintance, ibid., 3:30 (19 November 1733), method of reading, ibid., 3:56 (1 March 1733); method of reading the Scriptures, ibid., 4:92 (9 March 1734).

72. See Wesley's references to this important step in the development of Oxford Methodism in his letter to Richard Morgan, Sr., 19 October 1732, prefixed to the first extract of his published journal (*Journal and Diaries I*, in *Works*, 1:131–32) and in his *Short History of the People Called Methodists* (*Works*, 9:427).

73. See Albert C. Outler's comments on Wesley's early preaching, *Works*, 1:36–37, including the observation that the early sermons include "a radical emphasis on human freedom and responsibility."

74. Methodist theologians subsequent to Wesley's time have almost universally overlooked these theological connections to the "New Methodists" and have never attempted to relate the seventeenth-century ideas to the theology of the Oxford Methodists. Richard Watson is one of the few who even mentions the theological similarity, noting that the nonconformist New Methodists in 1693 held views "somewhat similar to those of the Wesleyan Methodists on the imputation of faith for righteouness." *Life of Wesley*, p. 17. See also Albert C. Outler, "John Wesley: Folk Theologian," *Theology Today* 34 (July 1977):159.

75. *John Wesley MS XX*, Colman Collection, in the Methodist Archives, The John Rylands University Library of Manchester. This later became the basis for his sermon commonly known as "The Duty of Constant Communion" (Sermon 101, in *Works*, 3:426–39).

76. *John Wesley MS XX*, Colman Collection, fols. 18r–20r; see also Appendix C, "Sermons Abridged from Other Authors," in *Works*, 4:527.

77. *Journal* (Curnock), 8:280–81.

78. Sermon 17, in *Works*, 1:401.

79. Ibid., p. 402.

80. Rom. 13:10, 1 Tim. 1:5; in ibid., 1:407.

81. Ibid., 1:407, 411, 413.

82. Wesley's methods and rules gave the outward impression of a works-oriented theology grounded in an obligation theory of ethics. His writings for the Oxford period, the height of this lifestyle, disclose a quite different, inward orientation that is focused on inward intentions and the virtues; at the root, his ethical theory is more virtue-oriented than obligation-oriented. All the rules, self-examination, good works, etc., were means by which the inner disposition of the soul could be measured. The counterpart in Wesley's later thought is his further development of the idea of the assurance of faith, grounded in "divine evidence" as perceived by the spiritual senses (see below, ch. 6, "Great Expectations"). Even the mature Wesley viewed good works as being in some sense necessary for salvation, but avoided a works-righteousness by making faith the only immediate and direct necessity, and viewed good works in terms of "faith acting in love," possible only by the grace of God (as also was faith).

83. See also other phrases such as "Obey him thou lovest." Sermon 144 (1733), in *Works*, 4:332, 336.

84. Ibid., 4:336–37.

85. Sermon 145 (1734), in *Works*, 4:348–50.

86. Sermon 142, "The Wisdom of Winning Souls," in *Works*, 4:313, 315.

87. *De imitatione Christi*, I.vii.1. Wesley's use of this phrase in terms of an active sincerity as the basis for hope of assurance is seen in a note he penned in the front pages of *MS Oxford Diary* 5; see below, pp. 102, 118. The phrase is often cited in the form *facere quod in se est*. For the significance of this concept in the late medieval understanding of justification, see Heiko A. Oberman, *The Harvest of Medieval Theology: Gabriel Biel and Late Medieval Nominalism* (Cambridge, MA: Harvard University Press, 1963), esp. pp. 128–45, and "*Facientibus quod in se est Deus non denegat Gratiam*: Robert Holcot O.P. and the Beginnings of Luther's Theology," *Harvard Theological Review* 55 (1962):317–42.

88. Letter to Mrs. Pendarves, 12 August 1731, in *Works*, 25:304.

89. Letter of 3 October 1731, in ibid., 25:318.

90. Pp. iv, vii.

91. See above, n. 16.

92. We have dealt with a selected but certainly representative sampling of theologians who participated in these complex developments, as well as a few contemporary historians, lexicographers, and encyclopedists who were aware of these developments and terminology. Although these events have subsequently faded into the obscure crevices in the history of Christian thought, they were certainly more familiar to those who were closer in time and perspective to these polemics of the seventeenth century. It is somewhat surprising that Wesley himself seems not to have been aware of this fairly evident theological precedent for the naming of his movement.

93. *MS Oxford Diaries*, 3:36. In terms of the development of nicknames, it is probably fortunate that the *Fog's* critic's references to them also as "sons of sorrow," "shameless gut-gazers," "madmen and fools," were forgotten in the discussions that followed.

94. *The Oxford Methodists: Being some Account of a Society of Young Gentlemen in that City, so Denominated; Setting Forth their Rise, Views, and Designs, with some Occasional Remarks on a Letter Inserted in Fog's Journal of December 9th, Relating to Them. In a Letter from a Gentleman near Oxford to his Friend at London* (London: Roberts, 1733); cf. letter to Mr. Morgan, 19 October 1732, in *Works*, 25:335–44; also prefixed by Wesley to his *Journal*, see *Works*, 18:123–33.

95. Eco, p. 611.

96. Preface to *The Character of a Methodist* (1742), §4, in *Works*, 9:33.

97. Several of the comments in the section on "Distinctive Wesleyan Emphases" in the current United Methodist doctrinal statement are directly tied to the historic emphases of the seventeenth century "New Methodists" as well as persistent themes of Wesley from his Oxford days onward, especially the comments on human freedom and responsibility, on the synergism of divine grace and human activity, on the relationship of faith and good works within an all-encompassing theology of grace, and the goal of a faith active in love—holiness and happiness of heart and life. *The Book of Discipline* (Nashville: United Methodist Publishing House, 1988), pp. 45–48.

Chapter 2: The Church and the Religious Societies

1. This essay first appeared as chapter 1 of the author's Ph.D. dissertation, "John Wesley and the Oxford Methodists, 1725–35" (Duke University, 1972).

2. [Richard Steele, Joseph Addison, *et al.*] *The Spectator* (10th ed.; London: Printed for J. Tonson, 1729), 6:238 (#458).

3. M. Dorothy George, *Hogarth to Cruikshank: Social Change in Graphic Satire* (London: The Penguin Press, 1957), p. 13.

4. Rupert Davies and Gordon Rupp, ed., *A History of the Methodist Church in Great Britain* (London: Epworth Press, 1965), 1:xxiii.

5. Charles John Abbey and John H. Overton, *The English Church in the Eighteenth Century* (London: Longmans, Green and Co., 1878), 1:38.

6. "Tendencies of Religious Thought in England, 1688–1750," in *Essays and Reviews* (London: J. W. Parker, 1860), p. 259.

7. Quoted in W. K. Lowther Clarke, *Eighteenth Century Piety* (London: Society for Promoting Christian Knowledge, 1944), p. 16.

8. Thomas Coke and Henry Moore, in one of the earliest biographies of John Wesley, portray post-Restoration England in this same light: "Ungodliness of every species overflowed the whole land, and it became the very fashion of the day to imitate the most corrupt courts in all its vices. So sudden an overthrow of all that is righteous and good, is not to be paralleled in the history of any nation under heaven." *The Life of the Rev. John Wesley, A.M.* (London: G. Paramore, 1792), p. 5.

9. See the works of W. K. Lowther Clarke, Norman Sykes, and particularly Wickham Legg, *English Church Life from the Restoration to the Tractarian Movement*

Considered in some of its Neglected or Forgotten Features (London: Longmans, Green and Co., 1914). Arthur Wilfred Nagler comments on Legg's work by saying that "All the author proves is that there were some redeeming features in an otherwise exceptionally decadent age." *Pietism and Methodism; The Significance of German Pietism in the Origin and Early Development of Methodism* (Nashville: Smith & Lamar, 1918), p. 75.

10. The report of a committee of both houses of Convocation in 1711 noted that "tho' it may with truth be affirm'd that the good Christians among us were never better than now; yet can it not withal be deny'd, that the bad were never worse." Francis Atterbury, *et al.*, *A Representation of the Present State of Religion with Regard to the Late Excessive Growth of Infidelity, Heresy, and Profaneness* (London: Printed for Jonah Bowyer, 1711), p. 5 (hereinafter cited as *Present State of Religion*).

11. This is the view of A. S. Turberville, *English Men and Manners in the Eighteenth Century* (New York: Oxford University Press, 1964), pp. 10ff., Sir Leslie Stephen, *History of English Thought in the Eighteenth Century* (3rd ed.; New York: Peter Smith, 1949), 2:332ff., and Nagler, *Pietism and Methodism*, p. 75.

12. Basil Willey, *The Eighteenth Century Background* (Boston: Beacon Press, 1964), p. 55.

13. A. D. Godley, *Oxford in the Eighteenth Century* (London: Methuen & Co., 1908), pp. 4, 5.

14. *The Spectator*, 6:238 (#458).

15. *Present State of Religion*, pp. 4, 9.

16. Ronald Paulson, ed., *Hogarth's Graphic Works* (New Haven: Yale University Press, 1965), 2:plate 127. This print was first published by Hogarth in the spring of 1730. Ibid., 1:141.

17. Ibid., 2:plate 134 (March 1733); in sharp contrast with Marshall Claxton's portrayal of Wesley and his friends at Oxford in the 1730s (see pp. 64, 81 below).

18. Gerald R. Cragg, *The Church and the Age of Reason* (Baltimore: Penguin Books, 1966), p. 128.

19. Abbey and Overton, *The English Church*, 1:32.

20. The combination of devotional practice and practical divinity evident in the method and structure of the religious societies can be seen as parallel to the "general disposition of theological method" in seventeenth-century Anglicanism. Harry R. McAdoo, *The Spirit of Anglicanism* (New York: Charles Scribner's Sons, 1965), p. 327.

21. This phrase comes from *Orders Belonging to a Religious Society* (London: [n.p.] 1724), p. 3 (hereinafter cited as *Orders*).

22. Legg, *English Church Life*, p. 292. The societies' rules usually had some stipulation to the effect that "no alteration, or addition be made to these Orders, without the consent of some pious and learned divine of the Church of England." *Orders*, p. 9; cf. Legg, pp. 308, 312.

23. We shall not attempt to trace the history of the societies. This may be obtained from the monograph of Garnet Vere Portus, *Caritas Anglicana; or, An Historical Inquiry into those Religious and Philanthropical Societies that Flourished in England between the Years 1678 and 1740* (London: A. R. Mowbray & Co. Ltd., 1912), or from the early view of Josiah Woodward, *An Account of the Rise and Progress of the Religious Societies in the City of London* (3rd ed.; London: Sympson, 1701). Major attention is given to these developments in many other works also, such as Abbey and Overton, *The English Church*, and John S. Simon, *John Wesley and the Religious Societies* (London: The Epworth Press, 1921).

24. Samuel Wesley in his "Letter Concerning the Religious Societies" notes some parallels between the English societies and the groups established by Marquis de Renty in France. Appendix to *The Pious Communicant Rightly Prepar'd* (London: Printed for Charles Harper, 1700), p. [181]. Portus notes also some similarities with the societies of Vincent de Paul in Paris but comments that "Horneck's organizations were so perfectly natural under the circumstances, that we need not strain after an evolutionary explanation of them based on foreign models." *Caritas Anglicana*, p. 26. Arthur Nagler points out

however that Horneck himself was steeped in continental pietism. *Pietism and Methodism,* p. 147. Clarke emphasizes the spontaneity of Horneck's movement. *A History of the SPCK* (London: SPCK, 1959), p. 2.

25. Elie Halévy, *England in 1815* (2nd ed.; London: Ernest Benn, Ltd., 1949), p. 410. This should not be taken to infer that the societies drew upon the upper classes for members. Records of several societies indicate that except for an occasional clerk or schoolmaster, the members were lower and middle-class workers: glaziers, perukemakers, wiredrawers, butchers, silversmiths, etc. "The Names, Places of Abode, Employments, and Occupations of the Several Societies in and about the Cities of London and Westminster Belonging to the Church of England, 1694," Bodleian Library, Oxford (Rawl. MS. D. 1312), fol. 2–18. Robert Nelson, a strong supporter of the religious societies, tried to encourage broader participation from the upper levels of society, observing that if the persons already involved could do so much for religion, certainly persons of "quality and character [could] do abundantly more for reviving the piety and charity of the primitive times." *An Address to Persons of Quality and Estate* (London: R. Smith, 1715), p. 136.

26. See Herbert B. Workman, *The Place of Methodism in the Catholic Church* (New York: Methodist Book Concern, 1921), and Charles Brockwell, "Methodist Discipline: From Rule of Life to Canon Law," *Drew Gateway* 54 (Winter/Spring, 1984):1–24.

27. *Orders*, pp. 4, 6. To promote their designs, members were expected to be loyal to the Church of England, to attend the services of the Church, to bear allegiance to the monarch, and "withal to express due Christian charity to all men." Ibid., p. 3; cf. Legg, *English Church Life,* p. 310.

28. *Orders,* p. 4; Legg, *English Church Life,* p. 309.

29. *Orders*, pp. 6–8. A similar list, from the "Rules of the Religious Society of St. Giles' Cripplegate" is found in Legg, *English Church Life,* p. 311.

30. Legg, *English Church Life,* p. 310.

31. Ibid., p. 312.

32. *Orders*, p. 5.

33. Legg, *English Church Life,* p. 310.

34. *Orders*, p. 9.

35. Ibid.

36. "An Account of the Origin and Designs of the Society for Promoting Christian Knowledge," appended to John Heylyn, *A Sermon Preached at St. Sepulchre's Church* (London: Printed by Joseph Downing, 1734), p. 15 (hereinafter cited as "Origin and Designs of the SPCK" [1734]).

37. *An Account of Several Work-Houses for Employing and Maintaining the Poor* (London: Printed by Joseph Downing, 1732), p. ix.

38. Portus, *Caritas Anglicana*, pp. 36ff.

39. "An Agreement of Divers Gentlemen &c Citizens in and about London for Promoting the execution of the Lawes made against profaneness and debauchery," Bodleian Library, Oxford (Rawl. MS. D.129), p. 8.

40. Ibid., p. 15b.

41. Clarke, *History of the SPCK,* p. 13.

42. It should be pointed out that while their interests and methods were oriented toward areas outside of their own group, the impetus for their action arose from the same desire to overcome immorality in the country which motivated the religious societies in general, and the power of their program lay primarily in the qualities of charity, virtue, and piety which the religious societies promoted and which characterized the lives of the members. Samuel Wesley commented that "Persons must be first truly and deeply concerned for religion themselves, before they are likely to be concerned for others." "Letter Concerning the Religious Societies," p. [185].

43. *A Letter From a Member of the Society for the Propagation of Christian Knowledge in London, to a Correspondent in the Country* (London: n.p., 1701), p. 3 (hereinafter cited as *SPCK Circular Letter, 1701*).

44. Ibid., p. 2.

45. "Origin and Designs of the SPCK" (1734), pp. 5, 27ff. A single-stitched copy of an *Abridgment of the Bible* could be purchased for one penny.

46. *The Standing Rules and Orders of the Society for Promoting Christian Knowledge* (London: Printed by Joseph Downing, 1732), p. 15.

47. *SPCK Circular Letter, 1701*, p. 1.

48. See below, p. 75.

49. W. O. B. Allen and Edmund McClure, *Two Hundred Years: The History of the Society for Promoting Christian Knowledge, 1698–1898* (London: SPCK, 1898), pp. 87–88 (Samuel Wesley to SPCK, July 10, 1700; June 10, 1701).

50. "An Account of the Religious Society begun in Epworth in the Isle of Axholme, Lincolnshire, Feb. 1, An. Dom. 1701–2," in Allen and McClure, *Two Hundred Years*, pp. 89, 90. The following description of the Epworth society is based on Samuel's "Account," with all quotations taken from the document as it appears in Allen and McClure, pp. 89–93.

51. This provision prefigures the general pattern of organization which John Wesley followed with his company of friends at Oxford three decades later. See below, pp. 75, 82–84.

52. Pp. 176–77.

53. Portus, *Caritas Anglicana*, pp. 194–95. See also *Orders*, p. 3; *Rules and Orders of SPCK, 1732*, p. 5; *The Spectator*, 1:44; and Thomas Hearne, *Remarks and Collections of Thomas Hearne*, ed. by C. E. Doble, *et al.* (Oxford: At the Clarendon Press, 1885–1921), 6:63.

54. T. Salmon, *The Present State of the Universities and of the Five Adjacent Counties, of Cambridge, Huntingdon, Bedford, Buckingham and Oxford* (London: J. Roberts, 1744), p. 410.

55. V. H. H. Green, *The Young Mr. Wesley* (London: Edward Arnold Ltd., 1961), pp. 13ff. Godley, in a typical understatement, notes that a "comfortable slackness prevailed." *Oxford in the Eighteenth Century*, p. 100. Even Salmon, the optimistic observer quoted above, found cause to mention that some members of the academic community of his day failed to live up to the standards of exemplary virtue and scholarly industry that had historically characterized the institution. He pointed out in particular that some tutors provided ill examples with respect to abstemiousness, early rising, and study. In addition to poor leadership among the scholars, he discerned the main problems to be poor rearing in the homes, immoderate use of intoxicating liquors and keeping of ill company. *Present State of Universities*, pp. 412ff.

56. *A Short History of the People Called Methodists*, §9, in *Works*, 9:430.

Chapter 3: The Search for the "Real" John Wesley

1. This essay first appeared as part of the Introduction to *The Elusive Mr. Wesley*, 2 vol. (Nashville: Abingdon, 1984), hereinafter cited as *EMW*. The footnotes in this edition are added to the original text, in many instances citing the location of material in that particular work.

2. *Gentleman's Magazine* 61 (March 1791):284.

3. See W. Reginald Ward, "Introduction," *Journal and Diaries I*, in *Works*, 18:105–19. Ward notes that the style of the *Journal* was based on past autobiographical models and did not anticipate the new romanticism of Rousseau and Goethe.

4. For the wide range of his publications, see Frank Baker, comp., *A Union Catalogue of the Publications of John and Charles Wesley* (Durham, NC: Duke University, 1966).

5. *EMW*, 1:119–24, 2:28–31, 55–58.

6. Ibid., 2:161–73.

7. Philip Thickness, signed "The Wanderer"; *Gentleman's Magazine* 62 (January 1792):23–24. See *EMW*, 2:58–61.

8. The Hebrew scholar, Benjamin Kennicott; *Wesleyan Methodist Magazine* 89 (1866):47. See *EMW*, 2:85–87.

9. The portrait hangs at Wesley College, Bristol.

10. See the illustrated article by Joseph G. Wright, "Some Portraits of John Wesley," in *Proceedings WHS* 3 (1902):185–92; 4:1–5; see also John Telford, ed., *Sayings and Portraits of John Wesley* (London: Epworth, 1924).

11. See *EMW* 2:181; in spite of its generally acknowledged shortcomings, this portrait was used in Great Britain as the frontispiece for the Wesleyan Methodist hymnbook and many other prominent Methodist publications worldwide through most of century.

12. The tradition that John Wesley had a middle name, Benjamin, is false, and is contradicted by copies of the baptismal record in Samuel Wesley's own hand. *EMW*, 1:37–38; see Frank Baker, "Investigating Wesley Family Traditions," *Methodist History* 26 (April 1988):160.

13. For many generations, anti-Methodist publications were rarely studied seriously by students of Wesley except as examples of scurrility or hostility. Richard Green published the first bibliography of these writings, *A Bibliography of Anti-Methodist Publications* (London: Kelly, 1902); see the more recent studies by A. M. Lyles, *Methodism Mocked; The Satiric Reaction to Methodism in the Eighteenth Century* (London: Epworth, 1960), and Donald Kirkham, *Pamphlet Opposition to the Rise of Methodism* (Ph.D diss., Duke University, 1973).

14. See "Early Sermons of John and Charles Wesley," chapter 7 below.

15. These simple procedures of modern historical investigation, initiated by historians of the nineteenth century, have only recently been applied even-handedly to some areas of church history. See John Dolan, *History of the Reformation* (New York: Desclee, 1965), pp. 32–34.

16. The statistics of Wesley's industriousness were already a matter of universal fascination by the time of his death (*EMW*, 2:154, 165). The estimations of his preaching and traveling can easily be substantiated by a quick analysis of his *Journal*, sermon register, and bibliography.

17.Wesley noted in his *Journal* for 17 November 1783 that his weight was the same as it had been fourteen years earlier, 122 pounds, and added, "I doubt whether such another instance is to be found in Great Britain." Wright quotes John Hickling as saying, "It is well known that [Wesley] was of small stature, being only 5 ft. 3 in. in height and spare in build." *Proceedings WHS* 3 (1903):185.

18. The many eulogies of Wesley in 1791 spin out a common thread—his amazing energy during such a long life (*EMW*, 2:163–67); see also his obituary in *Gentleman's Magazine* 61 (March 1791):283.

19. W. Reginald Ward also notes that the *Journal* is essentially a defensive work that at times slips into the mode of trite moralism. *Works* 18:38–39, 63.

20. Sermon 93, in *Works*, 3:325.

21. In July 1726 he resolved to rise at 7 a.m. (*MS Oxford Diaries*, 1:63); in March 1727 he told his mother he was rising "an hour sooner in the morning,", but that still appears to be 7 a.m. (*Works*, 25:214); during 1729–31, the time gradually moves back (with fluctuations) to a fairly regular time of 4 a.m. by 3 February 1732 when he paid for an alarm and also noted in the front of his diary, "If in bed at 11, rise at 4" (ibid., 2:iv, 1–117, and *John Wesley MS XVIII* (Financial Accounts), Colman Collection, p. 17.

22. *EMW*, 1:126–30, 2:72–73.

23. E.g., compare his positive comments in Sermon 11, "The Witness of the Spirit, II" (April 1767), II.2–3, in *Works*, 1:287, with his despairing letter to Charles, 27 June 1766 (*EMW*, 1:198–200).

24. See John Gambold's "family picture" of Wesley, *Methodist Magazine* 21 (March/April 1798):117–21, 168–72; see also *EMW*, 2:37–44.

25. See especially charges of Wesley being "a Jesuit in disguise," "a fanatic saint," "an Arminian fox," and "a pretending physician"; *EMW*, 2:97–138.

26. Wesley's obituary in the *Gentleman's Magazine* 61 (March 1791):283, noted that "he never treated his opponents with the ill-breeding and abuse that he received from them"; that "he has been known to receive into even his confidence those who have basely injured him"; and that he was "one of the few characters who outlived enmity and prejudice, and received, in his latter years, every mark of respect from every denomination." *EMW*, 2:152–54.

27. *MS Oxford Diaries*, 3:66–69, 98.

28. E.g., Charles sided with Samuel Taylor against John on the matter of lay-preachers in Methodism; see "A Charles Wesley Letter on Separation," *Methodist History* 22 (April 1984):200–02.

29. See *EMW*, 2:65–66, 87–89, 96–102, 111, 114.

30. This has been observed by many persons, e.g., Colin Williams, *John Wesley's Theology Today* (Nashville: Abingdon, 1960), pp. 13–17; and Albert C. Outler, "John Wesley, Folk Theologian" *Theology Today* 34 (July 1977):150–51, and *John Wesley* (New York: Oxford University Press, 1964), pp. 26–27; but cf. Mark Horst, "Experimenting with Christian Wholeness: Method in Wesley's Theology," *Quarterly Review* 7 (Summer 1987):11–23.

31. Ronald Knox, *Enthusiasm* (Oxford: Clarendon, 1950), p. 447. Even observers friendly to Wesley have not been hesitant to repeat this general evaluation.

32. For Wesley as a mediating theologian, see Albert C. Outler, "The Place of Wesley in the Christian Tradition," in Kenneth E. Rowe, ed., *The Place of Wesley in the Christian Tradition* (Metuchen, NJ: Scarecrow, 1976), pp. 14–16, 31–33.

33. See Frank Baker, "The Real John Wesley," *Methodist History* 12 (July 1974):183–97.

34. Preface to *Sermons on Several Occasions* (1746), §3, in *Works*, 1:104.

35. "For Children" ("Come Father, Son, and Holy Ghost"), Hymn 461, st. 5, lines 25–26, *The Hymnbook: A Collection of Hymns for the Use of the People called Methodists*, in *Works*, 7:644.

36. Sermon 39, "Catholic Spirit," wherein he also speaks of the need to be "fixed as the sun in his judgment concerning the main branches of Christian doctrine" (III.1), *Works*, 2:93; see also such comments as "Keep close to these good, old, unfashionable doctrines, how many soever contradict and blaspheme." Sermon 53, "On the Death of George Whitefield," III.5, in *Works*, 2:343.

37. More often than not, Wesley tried very hard to claim a lifetime of continuity in many of his teachings; W. Reginald Ward points out that Wesley's *Journal*, which spanned over fifty years, illustrates his incapacity to show growth or development in his life-story. *Works*, 18:46, 55–60.

38. See the otherwise excellent study of Martin Schmidt, *John Wesley: A Theological Biography* (Nashville: Abingdon, 1962–73), 2 (Pt. 1):7; when the author reaches mid-1738 in the story, he begins to treat the material by subject rather than chronological development, claiming that "John Wesley's course remained constant after his conversion on 24th May 1738."

39. "Wesley Studies: Working Group Paper," in M. Douglas Meeks, *The Future of the Methodist Theological Traditions* (Nashville: Abingdon, 1985), p. 61.

40. Albert C. Outler stresses that the later Wesley is the neglected Wesley who must be studied in order to redress the traditional imbalance in the agenda of Wesley studies. *Works*, 1:54–55.

41. See below, ch. 6, "Great Expectations."

42. See below, p. 146–149.

43. This development is reflected in the presence of a Wesleyan Studies Working Group in the American Academy of Religion since 1984, with participation by a broad representation from the various academic fields—English literature, philosophy, history, science, medicine, in addition to the traditional field of theological inquiry.

44. See below, pp. 209–10.

45. See above, n. 1.

Chapter 4: The Quest of the First Methodist: Oxford Methodism Reconsidered

1. Appreciation is extended to Dr. John Walsh, Jesus College, Oxford, for the invitation to present this paper during Trinity Term 1976 to his graduate seminar on "Evangelicalism in English History" while the author was in England as a Fellow of the American Council of Learned Societies.

2. Sermon 93, "On Redeeming the Time," in *Works*, 3:325–26; see above, p. 52 and n. 21.

3. "A Short History of Methodism," §6, in *Works*, 9:368.

4. Luke Tyerman gives typical expression to this perspective in several of his works on Wesley and the Oxford Methodists; see particularly *The Oxford Methodists* (London: Hodder and Stoughton, 1873), pp. 43, 58, 81.

5. Curnock has taken a statement from Wesley's later journals and through misreading, lack of adequate information, and wrong assumptions, has conjured up this picture of Wesley preaching for the first time, on the Sunday after his ordination; from "an exquisitely neat little MS" on Matthew 6:33. That sermon was not, in fact, the first sermon he wrote; nor did he preach in South Leigh until 1727, at which time he delivered (for at least the tenth time) the "first sermon" he had ever written (on Job 3:17). See below, p. 152. See also Ralph Bates, "John Wesley's First Preaching Sunday," *Proceedings WHS* 40 (February 1975):7–16.

6. Simon builds his quaint anecdote around the assumption that William Law was the author of the first published defense of the Wesleyan movement, *The Oxford Methodists* (London: J. Roberts, 1733), a groundless conjecture proposed by Thomas Marriott in 1844 that has, through persistent repetition, taken on the aura of historical fact. The problem is outlined, though not solved, by F. F. Bretherton in "The First Apology for Methodism," *Proceedings WHS* 20 (June 1935), 20ff.

7. This inscription was included on the copy engraved by Samuel Bellin. Reproductions of varying quality can be found in several illustrated volumes on Wesley and Methodism, with the usual caption, "The Holy Club."

8. Letter of 28 April 1731, in *Works*, 25:278.

9. ". . . if it deserves so honourable a title." Letter to Richard Morgan, Sr. (17 December 1733), in *Works*, 25:360.

10. *Oxford Methodists*, p. 31.

11. *Journal* (Curnock), 1:39–40.

12. Ingham's diary follows precisely the same format as the Wesley diaries, but contains much fuller comments on many aspects of the Methodists' life at Oxford. *Ingham MS Diary* (C. 203), Methodist Archives, Rylands; see *Diary of an Oxford Methodist; Benjamin Ingham, 1733–34* (Durham: Duke University Press, 1985) and chapter 5 below. A twenty-page fragment of George Whitefield's diary from this period also confirms many aspects of the cipher and provides a third example of the Wesleyan diary-keeping scheme that was adopted by at least a dozen other Methodists at Oxford. *Whitefield MS Diary* (1735), Congregational Trust Hall, London. As a result of these discoveries and twenty years of research in the manuscripts, the present author is editing Wesley's Oxford diaries

for publication as volume 32 of the thirty-four volume *Bicentennial Edition of the Works of John Wesley*.

13. Gambold wrote this in 1736, noting that Wesley "never assumed any thing to himself above his companions; any of them might speak their mind, and their words were as strictly regarded by him as his were by them." "The Character of Mr. John Wesley," *Methodist Magazine* 21 (1798), 118f.

14. Sermon 17, "The Circumcision of the Heart" (1733), in *Works*, 1:402.

15. These phrases are quoted from two sermons that Charles transcribed from his brother's copies—"The One Thing Needful," *CW MS Sermonbook*, p. 39, and "A Single Intention," *CW MS Sermon* on Matthew 6:22, p. 3 (both in the Methodist Archives, Rylands); see Sermons 146 and 148 in *Works*, 4:351–59, 371–77.

16. This development was encouraged (and typified) by such works as Frederick C. Gill, *Charles Wesley, the First Methodist* (Nashville: Abingdon, 1964). Others have also been proposed as founders of the movement. John Godley, Lord Kilbracken, an Irish journalist, argued in 1978 that William Morgan, one of his ancestors, was the possible founder of Methodism; his article is a combination of misconstrued evidence and misunderstood developments. "Origins of Methodism; the Leitrim Connection," *Leitrim Guardian Magazine* (1978), pp. 81–82. John Evans , anti-Methodist cleric of Eglwys Cymyn, claimed that Griffith Jones was not only in contact with the Methodists at Oxford but even "that it is highly probable that he was the great and chief instrument in setting Methodism on foot in England, that he first formed the Methodist club in Oxford and put into their heads to go up and down the country preaching, as himself had done before them and they have done ever since." *Some Account of the Welch Charity Schools* (London, 1752), p. 119.

17. "A Short History of Methodism," in *Works*, 9:367.18. Letter of 19 October 1732, in *Works*, 25:336. This letter has been prefixed to most editions of Wesley's *Journal* under the title, "The Rise and Design of Oxford Methodism."

19. "Three or four young men at Oxford," in "The Character of a Methodist" (1742), *Works*, 9:32; "Two or three young men, desiring to be scriptural Christians, met together for that purpose," in "Thoughts Upon a Late Phenomenon" (1788), *Works* (1872), 13:265; "In 1729, two young men, reading the Bible, saw they could not be saved without holiness, followed after it, and incited others so to do," in the "Large Minutes" (1753), *Works* (1872), 8:300.

20. Sermon 112, "On Laying the Foundation" (1777), in *Works*, 3:580–81.

21. Letter to Thomas Taylor (January 1780), *Letters* (Telford), 6:375; cf. letter to Samuel Sparrow (December 1773), ibid., 6:61. John's own recollection of the number of folks originally involved in the movement narrows down from four to one with the increased challenges to his own authority within the developing movement—showing his own primary role in the beginning is used to strengthen his position of authority.

22. The same is true with Charles's statement, made late in life, that he gathered together some friends and was called a Methodist before John came back to the University in 1729. At the time of his comment, in a letter to Dr. Chandler in the 1780s, Charles was contending with his brother over several issues within the movement, and an implicit claim to historical priority within the movement was most useful to gain support for a disputed position at that moment.

23. Frank Baker, *John Wesley and the Church of England* (Nashville: Abingdon Press, 1970), p. 15.

24. Wesley's first diary contains several lists of rules in cipher, ranging from very specific injunctions ("Avoid drunkards and busybodies") to rather general principles ("Whenever you are to do an action, consider how Christ did or would do the like, and do you imitate His example"). These resolutions provided the basis for his regular periods of self-examination, which not only resulted in a listing of particular failures, but often inspired new resolutions, as can be seen in an entry for 29 January 1726: "I have loved women and company more than Christ. Resolve—Never to let sleep or company hinder

me from going to prayers." *MS Oxford Diaries*, 1:viii, 35, in the Methodist Archives, Rylands.

25. Kirkham's frivolous wit is evident in his surviving correspondence, including the lines he wrote to John on 20 February 1726/27:

For, when you write, smooth elocution flows;
But when Bob scrawls, rough ignorance he shows.

In July of that year, John and Charles rode, as they had done many times before, to the Kirkham home in Stanton, but this time for the purpose of accompanying Bob back to Oxford to enroll at the University.

26. MS Letter, 6 January 1727/28 (Methodist Archives, Rylands).

27. Letter of 20 January 1728, *Works*, 25:230.

28. "I would willingly write a diary of my actions, but don't know how to go about it. What particulars am I to take notice of? Am I to give my thoughts and words, as well as deeds, a place in it? I'm to mark all the good and ill I do; and what besides? Must not I take account of my progress in learning as well as religion? What cipher can I make use of? If you would direct me to the same or a like method with your own, I would gladly follow it, for I'm fully convinced of the usefulness of such an undertaking." Letter of 22 January 1729, in *Works*, 25:236.

29. At John's request, Charles had sent him a transcription of the broadside issued by the Vice Chancellor, Heads of Houses, and Proctors of the University which called upon the tutors to "discharge their duty by double diligence" in explaining the Articles of Religion, recommending the careful reading of the Scriptures and "such other books as may serve more effectually to promote Christianity, Sound Principles, and Orthodox Faith" to counteract those "ill-designing persons" who were "introducing Deism, profaneness, and irreligion." Letter of 5 January 1728/29, in *Works*, 25:235.

30. Letter of 5 May 1729, in *Works*, 25:238

31. Ibid., 25:237.

32. *MS Oxford Diaries*, 2:6 (1 July 1729).

33. At this point, Wesley was still enjoying one of his favorite pastimes, card games. On one day in June he lost money three times at cards, his pleasures costing him twelve shillings. *MS Oxford Diaries*, 2:5; 1b:41. The games he mentions in the diaries include Loo, Pope Joan, Ombre, Quadrille, and Brag (Poker).

34. Letter to Susanna Wesley (28 February 1730), in *Works*, 25:245–46: cf. *MS Oxford Diaries*, 2:33 (19 February 1730), where Wesley notes that Kirkham came to "talk of his studies."

35. Letter to Richard Morgan, Sr. (19 October 1732), in *Works*, 25:338.

36. The sermon is "Circumcision of the Heart," preached on 1 January 1733; the *apologia* is Wesley's letter to Richard Morgan, Sr. (19 October 1732), which was published without Wesley's previous knowledge or permission as the heart of a pamphlet, *The Oxford Methodists* (1733), defending the little society against charges that had appeared in *Fog's Weekly Journal* (see above, pp. 13, 31–32).

37. See ch. 1 above, "What's in a Name?"

38. *Journal* (25 January 1738), in *Works*, 18:212–13n.

39. "Now that you are gone [to London] we have in good part lost the honourable appellation of Methodists," Letter of 6 September 1732, in *Journal* (Curnock), 8:281; see above, p. 26. Although the name seems thus to have been closely associated with Wesley himself, the rationale for its application may well have had some grounding in the perspective which Clayton brought to the group.

40. *MS Oxford Diaries*, 3:3. A note in the prefatory pages of *MS Oxford Diaries*, 2 (p. ii), indicates Wesley's own schedule at about this time: Monday, Pupils; Tuesday, Castle; Wednesday, Bocardo; Thursday, Castle; Friday, Pupils, Saturday, Children, Castle. On the next page, a slightly altered schedule includes visiting the poor (Mr. Eagle) on Sundays.

41. Letter to John Wesley (4 September 1732), in *Journal* (Curnock), 8:281.

42. *Works*, 9:368, 427

43. Most of the anti-Methodist literature before 1744, when directed against a specific individual, is aimed at George Whitefield, whose powerful preaching style and extrovert character attracted the attention of the public. See Richard Green, *Anti-Methodist Publications of the Eighteenth Century* (London: Kelly, 1902).

Chapter 5: The Meditative Piety of the Oxford Methodists

1. This essay was published as part of the introduction to *Diary of an Oxford Methodist: Benjamin Ingham, 1733–34* (Durham: Duke University Press, 1985) and is used here with permission (hereinafter cited as *Diary*).

2. Even the anticipation of recording one's actions might help, as James Boswell noted in the preface to his journal: "Knowing that I am to record my transactions will make me more careful to do well. Or if I should go wrong, it will assist me in resolutions of doing better." *Boswell's London Journal, 1762–63*, ed., Frederick A. Pottle (New York: McGraw-Hill, 1950), p. 39. An anonymous diarist in 1680 noted at the beginning of the fifth book of his record, "The particular grace I will endever to obtain duering the righting this Booke is spirituall recolection or the constant consideration of the presence of God. The Lord give me his grace that at the end I may perceive some incres in this vertue." MS., Rawlinson Collection, Q.e. 26–28, Bodleian Library, Oxford.

3. John Free attacked the Methodists in 1758, describing their origins in this manner: "The name was first given to a few persons who were so uncommonly *methodical* as to keep a diary of the most trivial actions of their lives, as how many slices of bread and butter they ate" (quoted in Wesley's letter to Dr. Free, 24 August 1758, in *Works*, 9:324); see above, pp. 16–17.

4. Letter of 22 January 1728/29, in *Works*, 25:236.

5. Whitefield's diary MS for 1736 is in Add. MS 34068, British Library, London; a fragment from his diary for 1735 is in the Congregational Trust Hall Library, London.

6. One minor variance is Ingham's frequent use of James Weston's shorthand method, which Wesley did not begin to use in his diary until early 1735.

7. Wesley regularly used abbreviations for frequently used words, such as prepositions and pronouns, and occasionally listed these in the front of manuscript volumes that might be read by other persons, such as his commonplace book containing poetry (*John Wesley MS I*, Colman Collection, Methodist Archives, The John Rylands University Library of Manchester).

8. See the description of the "exacter" diary method in Ingham, *Diary*, Appendix 1, pp. 275–76 and plates 12–15.

9. These diaries are neither absolutely precise nor totally exhaustive, however. Most entries are listed to the nearest quarter hour; in many instances the activity may have taken slightly more or less time than that noted, and in some cases may not have been the sole focus of that time period. Cf., for example, Ingham, *Diary*, pp. 93, 116 (10 December and note 121; 23 February, note 209).

10. The currently popular version of the story has Charles Wesley as the "first Methodist" organizing "the Holy Club" in May 1729, then turning the leadership of the "Methodists" over to his brother John on 22 November of that year. In fact, however, there was no group in May 1729 (Charles Wesley and William Morgan were simply studying and attending the Sacrament together); John Wesley returned to Oxford for two months in June 1729 (and engaged in the same activities he did later on his return in November); the term "Holy Club" was not coined until November 1730 (and dropped six months later); and the name "Methodist" does not appear until the summer of 1732. See above, pp. 15, 31, 70–74, and n. 24 below. For a survey of the literature on this topic, see Heitzenrater, *The Elusive Mr. Wesley*, vol. 2, part 2, especially pp. 204–7.

11. Marshall Claxton's misleading painting, done in the 1850s, has been reproduced many times, often with the caption "The Holy Club" or "The Rev. John Wesley and his Friends at Oxford." See *Proceedings WHS* 2 (1899):28. Major errors include the number of persons portrayed, the particular combination of persons at one place and time, and the location of the group in John Wesley's room as the meeting place.

12. Letter of 19 October 1732, in *Works*, 25:335–44. This letter to Richard Morgan, Sr., contains a description and defense of Wesley's activities up to that point; it is prefixed to most editions of Wesley's *Journal*, sometimes under the title, "The Rise and Design of Oxford Methodism."

13. *MS Oxford Diaries*, 2:5–66; see also Richard P. Heitzenrater, "John Wesley and the Oxford Methodists, 1723–1733" (Ph.D. diss., Duke University, 1972), pp. 46–125.

14. Letter of 14–15 January 1734, in *Works*, 25:365, 368.

15. Clayton encouraged his friends to engage their acquaintances in the work, "by which means," he told Wesley, "I hope in God we shall get at least an advocate for us, if not a brother and a fellow labourer, in every College in town." One of Clayton's pupils (William Nowell?) "promised to try what he can do with a cousin of his at Queen's" (Ingham?). *Journal* (Curnock), 8:281 (letter of 6 September 1732).

16. *MS Oxford Diaries*, 3:66 (15 April 1733), 67 (19 April 1733).

17. Letter of [25] July 1733, in *Works*, 25:352.

18. See Heitzenrater, "Oxford Methodists," pp. 35–45.

19. Letter, Samuel Wesley to John Wesley (28 September 1730), in *Works*, 25:338.

20. *The Fothergills of Ravenstonedale*, ed. Catherine Thornton and Frances McLaughlin (London: William Heinemann, 1906), p. 67.

21. Ambrose Bonwicke, whose life of piety was one of several models imitated by the Oxford Methodists, wrote to his father shortly after arriving at St. John's College, Cambridge, "My tutor did not talk to me about a Method, etc., as I hear is customary; but I have (thinking it convenient) proposed to myself one." A schedule of weekly studies follows. Theological and homiletical "method" was the subject of many treatises, and the general concern for promoting Christian virtues through disciplined living is epitomized in the tract, *The Way of Living in a Method, and by Rule*, first published in 1722 and widely distributed by the Society for Promoting Christian Knowledge (S.P.C.K.) well into the next century.

22. Ingham adopted the convention of referring to the Eucharist as "the Sacrament," a practice followed throughout this essay. Wesley frequently noted the attendance at St. Mary's for the Sacrament at the beginning of each term; the number was usually very low. See Ingham, *Diary*, pp. 74, 179 (9 October, note 50, and 23 April, note 38).

23. Instructions given in a broadside beginning "At a General Meeting of the Vice-Chancellor, Heads of Houses, and Proctors of the University of Oxford, on Monday, Dec. 2nd, 1728." It should be remembered that most of the students at Oxford were preparing for holy orders; the university statutes required the tutor "to imbue the scholars committed to his tuition and rule with virtuous morals, and to instruct them in approved authors, and most of all in the rudiments of religion, and the articles of doctrine that were published in the Synod at London in the year 1562; and to the utmost of his power he is to make them conform to the discipline publicly received in the Church of England." *Statutes*, III.2, in G. R. M. Ward, *Oxford University Statutes* (London: Pickering, 1845).

24. The earliest use of the term "Methodist" in relation to the Wesleyans in any contemporary document is in a letter of 5 September 1732 from John Clayton to John Wesley. *Journal* (Curnock), 8:281. See above, pp. 15, 31. The term was also used in the first published attack on Wesley and his comrades in *Fog's Weekly Journal* on 9 December 1732, and became fixed as their common title after the publication in February 1733 of an anonymous apologetic tract entitled *The Oxford Methodists*, which quoted at length Wesley's letter to Richard Morgan of October 1732 (see note 12 above).

25. See Ingham, *Diary*, Appendix 2 (pp. 180–87) for books read by Ingham. Ingham read through the *Country Parson's Advice* (1680) at least six times, sometimes alone, at other times with friends. His "resignation" to a holy life during Holy Week of 1734 was accompanied by a series of resolutions, largely "in the Country Parson's words," carefully transcribed into his diary (see *Diary*, pp. 165–69).

26. See Ingham, *Diary*, p. 198 (16 May, note 128) and *MS Oxford Diaries*, 3:iii ("Resolutions as to Times"). These two diaries contain the only references to this treatise I have been able to find.

27. Wesley was supported on this point by the opinion of John Clayton; letter of 2 August 1734, in *Works*, 25:391.

28. Ingham's confession on 7 August 1734 of having "indulged vain thoughts of being a fine poet" seems directed more against vanity than poetry.

29. This "sermon" was for the most part extracted from the works of Robert Nelson and William Beveridge on the necessity of frequent attendance upon the Sacrament, composed in 1732, as Wesley later said, "for the use of my pupils at Oxford." He later abridged his own extract even further, publishing it in his collected edition of sermons in 1766 as "The Duty of Constant Communion" (Sermon 101, in *Works*, 3:427–39). Ingham also made copies of John Clayton's sermons; see Ingham, *Diary*, p. 117 (24 February 1734).

30. *A Collection of Forms of Prayer for Every Day in the Week*, John Wesley's first published book. See *MS Oxford Diaries*, 4:46 (17 January 1733/34).

31. A scholarly composition that inquires into first principles; often focused upon a topic (*genesis thematica*) or a question (*genesis problematica*).

32. The agenda of a typical Methodist meeting, never fully outlined in the diaries, can be deduced from the descriptions of Richard Morgan, Jr., in a letter to his father, 14 January 1734 (in *Works*, 25:365), and of John Gambold in "The Character of Mr. John Wesley," *Methodist Magazine* 21 (March 1798):119.

33. Richard Morgan, Jr., attended only the reading and study portion of Wesley's meetings since he was "so little experienced in piety and charity," as Wesley explained to the boy's father (or until he "had acquired a pretty good stock of religion," to quote the son's report to his father). Letters of 17 December 1733 and 15 January 1734, in *Works*, 25:360, 365.

34. *Country Parson's Advice*, p. 81. In a letter to the editor of the *London Magazine* in 1760, John Wesley noted his having first read this work some thirty years before, quoting this passage and adding that "a few young gentlemen then at Oxford approved of and followed the advice. They were all zealous Church-men, and . . . for their exact regularity they were soon nicknamed Methodists" (letter dated 12 December 1760).

35. The idea that persons "become such as the company they keep" is a theme found in several works the Methodists read, such as Richard Lucas's sermon *The Influence of Conversation* (1707), sec. 1, and Robert Nelson's *Practice of True Devotion* (1696), I.vi.

36. See Louis Martz, *The Poetry of Meditation* (New Haven: Yale University Press, 1954), pp. 4–13.

37. Wesley was careful to include Hall's observation that it was more possible "to live without a heart than to be devout without meditation." *John Wesley MS VII*, Colman Collection, p. 29, Methodist Archives, Rylands. Cf. Joseph Hall, *The Art of Divine Meditation* (1607), ch. XXXVII.

38. Wesley had set times for meditation during this period; Ingham was less regular, but generally meditated early in the morning or before his daily self-examination in the afternoon. John Gambold advised Ingham that meditation on God's omnipresence and peculiar care of us was one of the "best means to acquire all the virtues." Ingham, *Diary*, pp. 148–49 (1 April 1734).

39. See Ingham, *Diary*, p. 224 (20 June) and letter of 1 January 1734, in *Works*, 25:364.

40. *MS Oxford Diaries*, 2, contains rough notes and resolutions at the front and back from which John Wesley drew up his list of General Questions; revisions of that list he subsequently transcribed into Diaries 3 and 4. Ingham's list, copied from Charles Wesley's and almost identical to John's, is found in his *Diary*, pp. 119–20. Whitefield's MS diary for 1736 also contains this list of fifteen questions (fol.2; cf. Arnold Dallimore, *George Whitefield* [London: Banner of Truth Trust, 1970], 1:80); see also Ignatius of Loyola, *Spiritual Exercises* (1548), secs. 24–31, "Particular and Daily Examen."

41. Wesley's lists can be found in *MS Oxford Diaries* 3, 4, and 5. Ingham seems not to have stressed this aspect of self-examination to the same extent that John Wesley did, although he certainly would have been familiar with the process from using the Wesleyan method and from having read William Law's *A Serious Call to a Devout and Holy Life* (1729), ch. XXIII.

42. The questions for Wednesday served also for Friday. See *MS Oxford Diaries*, 3:vii, 4:iii, the pages preceding Wesley's November summary, 5:v, and John Wesley, *A Collection of Forms of Prayer for Every Day in the Week* (1733).

43. For a discussion of the theology that underlies this practice, see the section on theology below, pp. 98–105.

44. Sermon 107, "On God's Vineyard," I.I, in *Works*, 3:504.

45. Ingham, *Diary*, p. 149; Wesley's version in *MS Oxford Diaries*, 4:ix, reads "actions" in place of "human writings"; see also his *Address to the Clergy* (1756), I.2.2.

46. The asterisked verses in Leusden contained all the words used by the sacred writers; see Ingham, *Diary*, p. 232–33 (10 July 1734), note 32. Francke's handbook outlined a method for studying Scripture both as respects the "letter" (grammatical, historical, and analytical) and the "spirit" (expository, doctrinal, inferential, and practical) of the Word.

47. *Statutes*, III.1.

48. Letter from Richard Morgan, Jr. (25 September 1735), in *Works*, 25:433. This is reminiscent of Wesley's own comment to his brother Samuel that if he could have given up early rising, "not one man in ten of those that are offended at me as it is would ever open their mouth against any of the other particulars." Letter of 17 November 1731, in *Works*, 25:320.

49. See, for example, Ingham, *Diary*, pp. 71ff. (1–2 October 1733, notes 40, 43, et seq.).

50. See note 29 above.

51. George Whitefield, *A Short Account of God's Dealings with the Reverend Mr. Whitefield* (London: W. Strahan, 1740), p. 26.

52. See Wesley's letter to Samuel Wesley, Sr. (10 December 1734), *Works*, 25:406-7. Wesley also commented to his brother Samuel in February 1753, "No one is a Christian till he is despised." *Works*, 25:417.

53. The opening rubric for the Communion of the Sick stipulates that "at least two" others should receive the Sacrament with the sick person. *B.C.P.*

54. *Country Parson's Advice*, p. 81.

55. Letter from Clayton to John Wesley (1 August 1732), in *Works*, 25:334 .

56. The Hamel is a street in Oxford west of the Castle, about halfway to St. Thomas's church, leading to the ruins of Osney Abbey. David Loggan's map of Oxford (1675) shows it as a rather broad, though short, thoroughfare lined with small houses and marked by a cross toward the north end. The derivation of "Hamel" is unclear, though it seems this area in medieval times was a hamlet inhabited by workmen associated with the abbey. See Thomas W. Squires, *In West Oxford* (London: A. R. Mowbray, 1928).

57. The founder's statutes at Queen's College stipulated that thirteen poor persons were to be fed in the Hall daily. John Richard Magrath, *The Queen's College* (Oxford: Clarendon Press, 1921), 1:58. There seems to be no evidence that this act of charity had persisted into the eighteenth century.

58. Letter of John Wesley to his father (11 June 1731), in *Works*, 25:282. Ingham also attended a "charity sermon" at St. Mary's on the Thursday after Easter; these occasions provided the opportunity to extol the values of such schools and raise funds for their support.

59. For examples of this polemic see Jean Daillé, *Faith Grounded upon the Holy Scriptures; against the New Methodists* (1675); Johannes Vlak, *Dissertationum trias: de Operum & pacis foederibus, atque de justificatione* (1689); and an anonymous work, *A War Among the Angels of the Churches, Wherein is Shewed the Principles of the New Methodists on the Great Point of Justification* (1693). Wesley seems to have been unaware of the term "New Methodist" and its theological connotations even though he adopted the basic position they represent (see above, pp. 15–16, 32).

60. The anonymous "Country Professor of Jesus Christ" who wrote *A War Among the Angels* recognized that "the real design" of all these groups was "to promote holiness," to which he could not object, observing nevertheless that the point of disagreement was "at what door to bring in works and holiness" (p. 8).

61. Studies of the Oxford Methodists have usually portrayed them in the same terms that Luke Tyerman used to describe Ingham at this point: "He was a conscientious, earnest Pharisee, seeking to be saved by works of righteousness rather than by penitential faith in Christ." *The Oxford Methodists* (London: Hodder and Stoughton, 1873), p. 59. Cf. Ingham's conversation with John Gambold concerning the Solifidians and "morality," in *Diary*, pp. 148–49 (1 April 1734).

62. In *The Poetry of Meditation*, Louis Martz examines the definition of "meditation" among the writers of the seventeenth century, typified by Francis de Sales's view that "meditation is an attentive thought iterated, or voluntarily intertained in the mynd, to excitate the will to holy affections and resolutions," to which might be added Richard Gibbons's comment ". . . from whence doth arise in our affectionate powers of good motions, inclinations, and purposes which stirre us up to the love and exercise of vertue and the hatred and avoiding of sinne" (pp. 14f.).

63. The best expression of Oxford Methodist theology is found in the early sermons of John Wesley, published in *Works*, 4:201–388 (Sermons 133–49). See Sermon 146, "The One Thing Needful" (I.5), which Wesley designates as "to be born again, to be formed anew after the likeness of our Creator" (ibid., p. 357).

64. See Sermon 141 on Gen. 1: 27, "So God created man in his own image." *Works*, 4:290–303.

65. See Sermon 146, "The One Thing Needful," III.3: "Be it our one view to regain the highest measure we can of that faith which works by love." *Works*, 4:359.

66. This goal is first stated by Wesley in 1733 in Sermon 17, "The Circumcision of the Heart," and constantly repeated in his subsequent delineations of the doctrine of Christian perfection.

67. See Sermon 144, "Love of God," §3, in which Wesley states that "love is still the fulfilling of the Law," which includes the positive commandments of Christ; these "either enjoin the use of the means of grace, which are only so many means of love, or the practice of those particular virtues, which are the genuine fruits of love." *Works*, 4:332.

68. See Sermon 17, "The Circumcision of the Heart," I.3: "We are convinced that we are not sufficient of ourselves to help ourselves; that it is he alone who worketh in us by his almighty power, either to will or to do that which is good; it being as impossible for us even to think a good thought, without the supernatural assistance of his Spirit, as to create ourselves, or to renew our whole souls in righteousness and true holiness." *Works*, 1:403–4.

69. Wesley and his companions used the exercise of meditation to lead them to a life of devotion and action rather than a state of mystical contemplation and union, although the two processes cannot always be completely distinguished or severed from each other. See Martz, *Poetry of Meditation*, p. 20.

70. See above, p. 91.

71. As this question indicates, the Wesleyan position at this point allowed for no "indifferent acts"—every action had either good or evil implications. See the correspondence with brother Samuel (17 November, 11 December 1731), in *Works*, 25:322, 325.

72. L. Bouyer notices this particularly in the way Hall and Baxter adapted the Ignatian system; see A History of Christian Spirituality (London: Burns & Oates, 1969), 3:159.

73. In noting the similarities between Puritan exhortations and Jesuit practices, Martz tries to shift attention away from the question of influences in one direction or another by making the important observation that "all these practices arose from a central preoccupation of the entire age, shared by Christians of every creed." *Poetry of Meditation*, p. 123. Bouyer also acknowledges this ecumenical tendency when he explains how Anglican spirituality, in attempting to recuperate some of the tradition of the ancient Church, reconciled the positive elements of both Protestantism and modern humanism with Catholicism, "not by abandoning its principles but by sifting and renewing all that was most positive in their origins." *History of Christian Spirituality*, 3:62. See also C. F. Allison, *The Rise of Moralism* (New York: Seabury Press, 1966). Gordon Wakefield admits that the piety of the Puritans has much in common with the great devotional traditions of the past but is careful to distinguish some essential differences between Protestant and Catholic devotion he feels Martz overlooked; see *Puritan Devotion* (London: Epworth Press, 1957), pp. 5, 160. This same willingness to categorize has led many historians to view any tendency among Protestants to use meditative exercises as an *invasion* or *infiltration* of mysticism into the Protestant traditions, a rather parochial view that overlooks the deeply ecumenical nature of meditative piety. See, for example, F. Ernest Stoeffler, *The Rise of Evangelical Pietism* (Leiden: E. J. Brill, 1965), pp. 15, 81; R. Newton Flew, *The Idea of Perfection in Christian Theology* (Oxford: Oxford University Press, 1934), p. 277.

74. The theme of unity, grounded in a discernible "consensus," was not only basic to these writers' view of the Primitive Church but may also be seen in Wesley's often repeated (and also somewhat idealistic) reflections upon the Oxford Methodists as being "all precisely of one judgment," "all of one heart and of one mind," "exactly of the same mind," and other hyperbolic terms. Sermon 112, "On Laying the Foundation of the New Chapel," I.3, in *Works*, 3:582; Wesley, *A Short History of the People Called Methodists* (1781), 3, in *Works*, 9:427: letter from Wesley to Henry Brooke, 14 June 1786.

75. Jean Orcibal, "The Theological Originality of John Wesley," in *A History of the Methodist Church in Great Britain* (London: Epworth Press, 1965), 1:88.

76. See, for example, Jean Baptiste de Saint-Jure, *The Holy Life of Monsr de Renty* (1658); cf. John Wesley's *Extract of the Life of Mons. de Renty* (1741). William Cave, in the preface to his *Apostolici*, claims that the lives of these saints "acquaint us with the most remarkable occurrences of the Divine Providence, and present us with the most apt and proper rules and instances that may form us to a life of true philosophy and vertue; history (says Thucydides) being nothing else but 'philosophy drawn from examples.'" Vol. I (1677), "To the Reader." Wesley not only read many such biographies but included spiritual biographies in his fifty-volume *Christian Library* (1749–55) and, later in the century, incorporated many autobiographies as a regular feature in his *Arminian Magazine* (1778–), many being the lives of his preachers written by themselves.

77. This term was used by Pierre Poiret, an indefatigable propagator of the Catholic mystics among the Protestants, who seems to have influenced some of the Oxford Methodists on the matter of the *ordo salutis*. John Byrom, *The Private Journal and Literary Remains of John Byrom* (Manchester: Chetham Society, 1856), 2:230. See also Orcibal, "Theological Originality of John Wesley," p. 111.

78. "Our hope is sincerity, not perfection, not to do well, but to do our best." Letter of John Wesley to Anne Granville (3 October 1731), in *Works*, 25:318.

79. *De imitatione Christi*, I.vii.1 (with a footnote citing Augustine, *Sermones ad fratres in eremo*, 27). Wesley's edition was entitled *The Christian's Pattern* (1735). This perspective can also be seen in Wesley's contrast of the Old Covenant and its absolute demand, "Do

this and live," with what he saw in 1732 as the tempered conditions of the New Covenant, "Try to do this, and live." *John Wesley MS XX*, Colman Collection, "The Duty of Receiving the Lord's Supper," fol. 18 verso, Methodist Archives, Rylands. See above, pp. 28–30.

80. William Law, *A Practical Treatise Upon Christian Perfection* (1726), ch. IX, "Of the Necessity of Divine Grace and the several Duties to which it Calleth all Christians."

81. Saint-Jure, *The Holy Life of Mons[r] de Renty*, p. 356 (quoting St. Ambrose).

82. See Ingham's resolution dated 1 February 1733, followed by the comment,"therefore ever distrust thyself." *Diary*, p. 109.

83. Bouyer, *History of Christian Spirituality*, 3:155; Wakefield, *Puritan Devotion*, p. 157.

84. Orcibal notes that Wesley claimed after 1770 to have remained "as tenacious a champion of inner holiness as any mystic and of outward holiness as any Pharisee." "Theological Originality of John Wesley," p. 102. See also Albert C. Outler, ed., *John Wesley* (New York: Oxford University Press, 1964), pp. 119, 423.

85. The spirituality of the holy living tradition shares some of the pietist aversion to theological disputation, their occasional lack of solid theological reinforcement deriving more from indisposition than inability. See Bouyer, *History of Christian Spirituality*, vol. 3:58f.

86. Cell's familiar dictum that Wesley's teaching exhibited a synthesis of "the Protestant ethic of grace and the Catholic ethic of holiness" is based on the sort of categorizing tendencies that we have tried here to avoid, recognizing instead the more basic significance of the common elements that undergird the ecumenical nature of the holy living tradition. See George Croft Cell, *The Rediscovery of John Wesley* (New York: Henry Holt, 1935) p. 361.

Chapter 6: Great Expectations: Aldersgate and the Evidences of Genuine Christianity

1. A summary of this essay appeared in *Circuit Rider* 12 (May 1988):4–6.

2. *Journal and Diaries I* (24 May 1738, §14), *Works*, 18:250.

3. See, e.g., Wesley's comment in 1745 that "from 1738 to this time, . . . the 'Word of God ran' as fire among the stubble." *The Principles of a Methodist Farther Explained*, VI.1, in *Works*, 9:222–23.

4. In fact, he told one critic that "conversion" was a term "which I very rarely use, because it rarely occurs in the New Testament." *A Letter to the Author of The Enthusiasm of the Methodists* (1749), in *Works*, 11:368.

5. Wesley's own editorial corrections in subsequent editions of his *Journal* and *A Plain Account of Christian Perfection* make it clear that he changed some of his earlier evaluations of his own spiritual condition during the period surrounding Aldersgate, as we shall see below.

6. This caution should apply also to Wesley's *Journal* accounts, many of which benefit from a normal four or five year delay between the last events described and the preparation of the material for publication. *Works*, 18:82. Wesley is also notoriously inaccurate as to historical details in many of his retrospective flashbacks.

7. "The way of salvation." It is no surprise that one of the finest summaries of his mature theology is his sermon entitled "The Scripture Way of Salvation" (Sermon 43, *Works*, 2:153–69).

8. See especially *Letters I* (1721–39), vol. 25 in *The Bicentenniel Edition of the Works of John Wesley* (Nashville: Abingdon, 1980); *Oxford Diaries* (1725–35), forthcoming as *Works*, vol. 32; *Journal and Diaries I* (1735–39), in *Works*, vol. 18; early sermons (1725–41)in *Sermons IV*, *Works*, 4:201–419.

9. Several works have appeared recently that emphasize and analyze this point; see especially Richard E. Brantley, "Young Man Wesley's Lockean Connection," ch. 1 of *Locke, Wesley, and the Method of English Romanticism* (Gainesville: University of Florida

Press, 1984); Frederick Dreyer, "Faith and Experience in the Thought of John Wesley," *American Historical Review* 88 (February 1983):12–30; Rex D. Matthews, "'Religion and Reason Joined': A Study in the Theology of John Wesley," Th.D. dissertation, Harvard University, 1986, and "'We Walk by Faith, not by Sight': Religious Epistemology in the Later Sermons of John Wesley," paper presented to the Wesley Studies Working Group of the American Academy of Religion, 25 November 1985.

10. Letter to Susanna Wesley (18 June 1725), *Works*, 25:169–70.

11. Letter from Susanna Wesley (23 February 1725), *Works*, 25:160. "The one thing needful" will become a useful imperative for Wesley, defined in a number of ways throughout the years.

12. Letter from Susanna Wesley (8 June 1725), *Works*, 25:165–66. These comments came in the midst of a continuing discussion of Thomas à Kempis.

13. Letter to Susanna Wesley (29 July 1725), *Works*, 25:174–75; cf. 25:186–87. See Wesley's later use of this maxim in Sermon 117, "On the Discoveries of Faith." §1, and Sermon 119, "Walking by Sight and Walking by Faith," §7, *Works*, 4:29, 51; see also Rex D. Matthews, "Religious Epistemology," pp. 17–23.

14. Letter to Susanna Wesley (29 July 1725), *Works*, 25:175. This letter is an early manifestation of his opposition to the idea of "perseverance of the saints."

15. Susanna also used familiar imagery when commenting upon zeal: "Yet after all that can be said, though prudence and charity should correct the irregular motions of our zeal, they must by no means extinguish it. But we must keep that sacred fire alive in our breasts" (18 August and 10 November 1725), *Works*, 25:179, 185.

16. Letter from Samuel Wesley, Sr. (1 September 1725), *Works*, 25:181.

17. Letter to Susanna Wesley (22 November 1725), *Works*, 25:188.

18. Letter from Susanna Wesley (30 March 1726), *Works*, 25:193–94.

19. See §§1–2 of his autobiographical reflections, 25 January 1738: ". . . having from the very beginning valued both faith, the means of grace, and good works, not on their own account, but as believing God, who had appointed them, would by them bring me in due time to the mind that was in Christ." *Works*, 18:212n.

20. *Journal* (24 May 1738, §2), in *Works*, 18:243. This formula was not necessarily distinctive with Wesley but will become familiar to later Methodists as the guidelines in the *General Rules* (1743): avoid evil, do good, attend to the ordinances of God. Wesley's respective view of his "sins" during this period is qualified by the understatement, "which I knew to be such, though they were not scandalous in the eye of the world."

21. *Journal* (24 May 1738, §3), in *Works*, 18:243.

22. Ibid., §4.

23. See letter of 8 June 1725 from Susanna Wesley, who argues that perfection is essentially internal and centered on the virtues. *Works*, 25:165–66. Wesley soon came to hold this view himself. He published this letter in the first issue of the *Arminian Magazine* in 1778, pp. 33–36. See above, n. 12. Sincerity also became a consistent theme for Wesley throughout his lifetime; see below, at nn. 39, 59, 180.

24. "So that now, doing so much and living so good a life, I doubted not but I was a good Christian," *Journal* (24 May 1738, §4), *Works*, 18:244.

25. "When it pleased God to give me a settled resolution to be not a nominal but a real Christian (being then about two and twenty years of age). . . ." Sermon 81 (1781), "In What Sense we are to Leave the World," §23, *Works*, 3:152. See also his later comment that his resolve "to dedicate all my life to God" as a result of reading Jeremy Taylor, Thomas à Kempis, and William Law, came from a recognition of "the absolute impossibility of being half a Christian," and he determined, "through his grace (the absolute necessity of which I was deeply sensible of), to be all-devoted to God." *Plain Account of Christian Perfection*, §2, *Works* (Jackson), 11:366–67. These early and late evaluations bracket a contrasting account of his condition at Oxford found in Sermon 2 (1741): "I did go thus far for many years. . . : using diligence to eschew all evil; . . . buying up every opportunity of doing all good to all men; constantly and carefully using all the public and

all the private means of grace. . . [*viz.*, the *General Rules*]. Yet . . . all this time I was but 'almost a Christian'" (which, in his understanding of 1741, was none at all). *Works*, 1:136–37; and see pp. 142–44, below.

26. Wesley speaks in terms of "the happiness God has promised to his servants," which he always links with holiness and defines in terms of the Great Commandment, here in 1725 and throughout his life. Sermon 134 (1725), "Seek First the Kingdom," §4, *Works*, 4:218; see below, pp. 144–45.

27. *Journal* (24 May 1738, §5), *Works*, 18:244–45. In a correction added in 1774, Wesley himself confirms this sentiment, saying "And I believe I was"; ibid., 18:245n. Albert C. Outler views the "radical change" that occurred in Wesley at this point as "a conversion if ever there was one." *John Wesley* (New York: Oxford University Press, 1964), p. 7.

28. *Journal* (24 May 1738, §6), *Works*, 18:245.

29. Sermon 140 (1730), *Works*, 4:284–287. Wesley here lists three of his traditional authorities.

30. Ibid., 4:287–88; an early use of this text (2 Cor. 5:7) that will become central to his mature views. One of his later critics turns Wesley's own early sentiments back upon him by claiming that Methodists who claim to be wholly sanctified upon the instant of their justification show a lack of humility. See *A Letter to the Right Reverend Lord Bishop of London* (1747), §7, in *Works*, 11:338.

31. Sermon 141 (1730), *Works*, 4:294.

32. Ibid., 4:299–302.

33. *John Wesley MS V*, "The Procedure, Extent, and Limits of Human Understanding" (Colman Collection, Methodist Archives, Rylands), pp. 1–2.

34. Peter Browne, *The Procedure, Extent, and Limits of Human Understanding* (London: Innys, 1729), p. 250.

35. MS "Procedure," p. 49; in the end, Wesley will ignore Browne's use of "analogy" to make the connection between the human and divine realms, that as reason perceives what the senses grasp, so faith apprehends the things of God; Wesley will draw a more direct parallel between the two, using the idea of "spiritual senses."

36. Eph. 1:18; letter to Ann Granville (3 October 1731), in *Works*, 25:318. The "seeing" metaphor has several variations with different implications: the eyes are opened, renewed, or new eyes are given; the sight is restored, renewed, enlightened, or new sight is given. See below, n. 116.

37. *John Wesley MS XX*, "The Duty of Receiving the Lord's Supper" (Colman Collection, Methodist Archives, Rylands). This extract was the basis for Wesley's "sermon on the Sacrament," used heavily by the Oxford Methodists and later revised as "The Duty of Constant Communion" (Sermon 101, in *Works*, 3:427–39; see also 4:525–28 for a comparison of the manuscript and printed versions).

38. MS, "Duty," f.v. 18.

39. See below, at n. 58.

40. This tendency is encouraged, of course, by Wesley's own comments in the months following his experience in May 1738, describing his present and previous condition in the light of his perspective at that time.

41. Sermon 17, in *Works*, 1:407, 414. See Wesley's comment in his *Plain Account of Christian Perfection* fifty years later: "This was the view of religion I then had, which even then I scrupled not to term 'perfection.' This is the view I have of it now, without any material addition or diminution." *Works* (Jackson), 11:369.

42. *Works*, 1:402.

43. "Such as faith as is 'mighty through God.'" Ibid., 4:404.

44. By this time, Wesley had begun to delineate the distinction between "half-Christians" or "common" Christians, and "true" Christians, as seen in the contrast between those who simply "use God and enjoy the world" (Pascal's phrase) on the one hand and those who are evangelists and martyrs on the other hand. Sermon 142 (1731), "The Wisdom of Winning Souls," *Works*, 4:310–14.

45. *Works*, 1:405.

46. In his later revision of this sermon for publication in 1748, Wesley incorporates the personal language, "loved *me*," "reconciled *me*," etc., noting that this material "is not added to the sermon formerly preached." Ibid., 1:405.

47. Ibid., 1:409–11. One must be cautious in assuming that this whole sermon, save for the one passage that Wesley explicitly acknowledges was later added, stands as it was preached in 1733. This phrase may be a later interpolation.

48. Love (of God and neighbor) is the primary virtue, evident in the presence of other virtues, which are evidenced by good works. See n. 56 below.

49. Wesley began to test his many rules, including early rising and fasting, by casting lots in order to discern God's providence in these matters. See *MS Oxford Diaries*, 5:152 (Friday, 7 February 1735), where he cast lots ("as to sleep") between 5 and 6 a.m. to see if he might go back to bed, and between 9 and 10 a.m. ("as to eating") to see if he might have breakfast (break the Friday fast early).

50. See his autobiographical reflections in his *Journal* (25 January and 24 May 1738), *Works*, 18:213, 245–46.

51. Sermon 144 (September 1733), "The Love of God," in *Works*, 4:329–45. Love of God and neighbor (the great commandment) will be a major focus of Wesley's mature theology. The ascription at the end of this sermon reveals that the twofold basis of the Wesleyan soteriology was present in seminal form at that point: redemption by the blood of Christ and a heart filled with love by the grace of the Holy Spirit.

52. Sermon 146, *Works*, 4:354–58. The concept of "the one thing needful" (Luke 10:42) had arisen in this discussion as early as 1725 (see above at n. 11) and would continue to be a useful concept well past 1738 with a succession of different goals seen as the "one thing."

53. Matt. 6:22, Sermon 148 ("A Single Intention"), *Works*, 4:374; Charles Wesley transcribed this sermon and referred to it as "A Single Eye"; see ch. 7 below.

54. Richard P. Heitzenrater, ed., *Diary of an Oxford Methodist; Benjamin Ingham, 1733–34* (Durham: Duke University Press, 1985), p. 109 (1 February 1734).

55. Whitefield, *A Short Account of God's Dealings with the Rev. Mr. Whitefield* (London: Strahan, 1740), p. 44; *MS Oxford Diaries*, 5:159–60.

56. "Love is the end of every commandment of Christ . . . ; the positive [commands] are only so many means of love, or the practice of those particular virtues which are the genuine fruits of love." Sermon 144, "The Love of God" (September 1733), *Works*, 4:332.

57. *Journal* (25 January 1738), §6, *Works*, 18:213.

58. *MS Oxford Diaries*, 5:vi; cf. Thomas à Kempis, *Imitatione Christi*, I.vii.1 (cited as from Augustine, *Sermones ad fratres in eremo*, 27), translated by Wesley in his 1735 edition of Kempis (*The Christian's Pattern*) as "Do what lieth in thy power, and God will assist thy good will." Although some solifidian opponents would characterize Wesley's position as "works-righteousness" or "trusting in his own works," the synergism that Wesley espoused was based on a view of God's grace perfecting human nature. For a discussion of the background and development of this idea, see H. A. Oberman, *The Harvest of Medieval Theology* (Cambridge: Harvard University Press, 1963), pp. 120–45.

59. See Ingham's comment that he was "resolved, God's grace assisting me, . . . never to depend upon my own strength because I can do nothing without God's assistance; therefore ever distrust thyself." *Diary* (1 February 1734), p. 109. Although some of the tension resulting from this reliance on sincerity was resolved for Wesley in 1738, he continued to reiterate the necessity of "doing one's best" within the context of human/divine synergism. See Albert C. Outler, "Methodism's Theological Heritage," in Paul M. Minus, Jr., ed., *Methodism's Distiny in an Ecumenical Age* (Nashville: Abingdon, 1969), pp. 51–63.

60. Sermon 147, "Wiser than Children of Light," *Works*, 4:367.

61. This comment by Samuel was recalled thirteen years after his death, in a letter to John Smith after Smith had suggested that, if assurance were a prerequisite for

salvation (as Wesley was preaching in the early 1740s), then Wesley himself at Oxford stood in jeopardy of damnation as well as his father, who died before John started preaching this doctrine. Letter (22 March 1748), *Works*, 25:288. The dialogue with Smith was the occasion for a good deal of clarification in Wesley's thinking (accompanied by some evasive rhetoric that reveals intellectual uncertainty).

62. Letter to John Burton (10 October 1735), *Works*, 25:439.

63. *Journal* (23 November 1735, 23 January 1736), *Works*, 18:140, 142.

64. *Journal* (25 January 1736), *Works*, 18:143. Clifford W. Towlson is careful to point out that Wesley's becoming a pupil of the Moravians was more complicated than simply a reaction to their demeanor during this storm. *Moravian and Methodist* (London: Epworth, 1957), p. 39.

65. Sermon 148, *Works*, 4:377. This sermon was begun on 29 January and finished on 4 February 1736, the day they first saw land; Georgia Diary I, in *Works*, 18:346–49.

66. Sermon 149 (1736), "On Love," *Works*, 4:385; cf. Sermon 144 (1733), "The Love of God," *Works*, 4:334.

67. *Journal* (8 February 1736), *Works*, 18:145–46.

68. Conversation recalled in a letter to Joseph Benson (11 October 1771), *Letters* (Telford), 5:281. Spangenberg's differing evaluation of Wesley is further noted in his own diary at the time: "I observe that grace really dwells and reigns in him." Quoted in Martin Schmidt, *John Wesley; A Theological Biography* (Nashville: Abingdon, 1962–73), 1:153.

69. In the midst of his fearfulness and unease, he found it useful to preach to others, perhaps not unlike his resolve to go to Georgia in the hope of saving his own soul, hoping at the same time to learn the "true sense of the gospel of Christ by preaching it to the heathens." Letter to John Burton (10 October 1735), *Works*, 25:439. See *Journal* (2 and 9 January 1738): "Being sorrowful and very heavy . . . in the evening, therefore, I began instructing the cabin-boy, after which I was much easier." "I had resolved, God being my helper, not only to preach it to all but to apply the Word of God to every single soul in the ship. . . . I no sooner executed this resolution than my spirit revived." *Works*, 18: 207–10.

70. *Journal* (28 December 1737), *Works*, 18:207.

71. *Journal* (8 January 1738), *Works*, 18:208–9.

72. Ibid. (24 May 1738, §11), *Works*, 18:247.

73. Ibid. (25 April 1738), 18:235; notice the pietist and Moravian fire imagery.

74. This view will be clearly expressed in his memo of 4 January 1739: "I *know* because I *feel* it." *Journal* (Curnock), 2:126. Wesley, never able to sever completely inward and outward religion (or later the direct and indirect witness of the Holy Spirit), was also never able completely to swing fully to an intuitionist perspective which is in part what preserved him from falling into the trap of "enthusiasm." See Lycurgus M. Starkey, Jr., *The Work of the Holy Spirit* (New York: Abingdon, 1962), pp. 64–77.

75. *Journal* (24 May 1738, §11), *Works*, 18:247.

76. *Journal* (epilogue following 2 February 1738), *Works*, 18:215. Böhler gave new meaning to the phrase "sure trust and confidence" in the Homilies' definition of faith by seeing it in terms of full assurance.

77. *Journal* (24 May 1738, §11), *Works*, 18:248. Wesley's logical mind was operating with two syllogisms at this point, the first element in each coming from the Moravians: (1) One cannot have forgiveness of sins and not feel it; I feel it not; therefore, I do not have forgiveness; and (2) there is no true faith without a sense of forgiveness; I feel no sense of forgiveness; therefore, I have no true faith.

78. On 5 March, he was "clearly convinced of unbelief." His inclination was to "leave off preaching," but he reports that Peter Böhler then said to him, "Preach faith till you have it, and then, because you have it, you will preach faith." *Works*, 18:35, 228; but cf. Böhler's own account, which reports that Wesley's attitude on this occasion was simply "if that is true which stands in the Bible, then I am saved." W. N. Schwarze and

S. H. Gapp, "Peter Böhler and the Wesleys," *World Parish* 2 (November 1949):6. Preaching and speaking to others always seemed to make him feel better about his own problems; see on shipboard, and later. *Journal* (2 and 13 January 1738), *Works*, 18:208, 210. James Hutton recalled that "Wesley preached this Gospel everywhere as soon as he believed it and many received it. Wesley's manner and the Gospel itself . . . made much ado in the Societies." "The Beginning of The Lord's Work in England," tr. by J. N. Libbey, *Proceedings WHS* 15 (1926):185.

79. *Journal* (28 February 1736), *Works*, 18:151. Wesley was no doubt attracted to the Moravians' self-conscious attempt to recapture and preserve the traditions of Apostolic times. See Towlson, *Moravian and Methodist*, p. 32.

80. *Journal* (23 March, 22 April 1738), *Works*, 18:232–34.

81. *Homilies*, "Of Salvation," Pt. III; *Works*, 18:215–16, 233–34; cf. 250. One of the strongest restatements of this in the Wesley corpus is found in the comments on faith he later added to his Oxford sermon on "Circumcision of the Heart," I.7: "a confidence whereby every true believer is enable to bear witness, 'I know that my Redeemer liveth'; that I 'have an advocate with the Father,' that 'Jesus Christ the righteous is' my Lord and 'the propitiation for my sins.' I know he 'hath loved me, and given himself for me.' He 'hath reconciled me, even me to God'; and I 'have redemption through his blood, even the forgiveness of sins.'" Sermon 17, in *Works*, 1:405.

82. Böhler's Moravian friends in the first instance, followed by Mr. Hutchins of Pembroke College and Mrs. Fox in Oxford; *Journal* (23 and 26 April 1738), *Works*, 18:234–35, 576 (diary entry for 23 April, "convinced that faith converts at once"). Böhler reported that Wesley and his friends were "as though struck dumb" at the narratives of the four Moravian witnesses, and while singing a hymn, Wesley frequently dried his eyes, then asking Böhler how he should attain to such faith, saying that "if he once had *this*, he would then certainly preach about nothing other than faith." "Peter Böhler and the Wesleys," p. 8.

83. Though the Moravians would have seen no reason for any qualifying adjective—anything less than this state is not Christian at all. Having been convinced of this position, Wesley wrote to William Law twice during May 1738, criticizing his former spiritual mentor sharply (and probably unjustly) for not having advised him of his lack of a true faith in Christ. *Works*, 25:240–50.

84. "I felt a strange palpitation of heart. I said, yet feared to say, 'I believe, I believe!' . . . I found myself convinced . . . I now found myself at peace with God." Charles Wesley, *The Journal of the Rev. Charles Wesley* (London: Culley, 1910), 1:147. Thorvald Källstad, viewing John Wesley's situation in psychological terms, sees Charles's experience as further reinforcing John's own anticipations and strengthening his susceptibility to a similar experience, which Källstad interprets as a stage in the "reduction of cognitive dissonance between the Anglican and the Moravian models of faith." *John Wesley and the Bible; A Psychological Study* (Stockholm: Nya Bokförlags, 1974), pp. 234, 238. Sydney G. Dimond views these developments within what he calls "the psychology of suggestion" and "the resolution of pathogenic conflict." *Psychology of the Methodist Revival* (Nashville: Whitmore, 1926), p. 87–99.

85. See above, at nn. 74, 81; see also his subsequent refinements in the definition of the "witness of the Spirit." Albert Outler points out that "whatever psychological account one may prefer, the theological import of Aldersgate was largely *pneumatological*." "A Focus on the Holy Spirit: Spirit and Spirituality in John Wesley," *Quarterly Review* 8 (Summer 1988):9.

86. Mrs. Hutton considered him to be "turned a wild enthusiast or fanatic" because of his claims on 28 May: "Mr. John got up and told the people that five days before, he was not a Christian." Her response was: "If you was not a Christian ever since I knew you, you was a great hypocrite, for you made us all believe you was one." *Journal* (28 May 1738), *Works*, 18:252n. The point is rather obvious (as we have seen) but crucial: Wesley would not have disclaimed his Christian standing during his earlier years, nor would he

be so critical of himself during that period from the perspective of later years; but the Moravian framework of his experience of 24 May 1738 led him to hold this view at that time.

87. "Towards ten, my brother was brought in triumph by a troop of our friends, and declared, 'I believe.' We sang the hymn with great joy, and parted with prayer." Charles Wesley, *Journal*, 1:153.

88. Traditional pietist and Moravian terminology associated with variety of experiences; see, e.g., 21 December 1740: "Our hearts were warmed." *Journal* (Curnock), 2:409. The noteworthy word in Wesley's phrase is "strangely," implying "unusually," "inexplicably," or somehow "different from other times."

89. *Journal* (24 May 1738, §§15, 16), *Works*, 18:250.

90. *Journal* (25 and 26 May 1738), *Works*, 18:251.

91. *Journal* (29 May 1738), *Works*, 18:253.

92. *Journal* (6 June 1738), *Works*, 18:254.

93. Ibid.

94. "His head had gained an ascendency over his heart." Daniel Benham, *Memoirs of James Hutton* (London: Hamilton, Adams, & Co., 1856), p. 40. The insulting rejection was apparently heightened by their willingness to allow Ingham to partake. Hutton goes on to say that Wesley "unhappily concealed and brooded over" this offence.

95. *Journal* (12 July 1738), *Works*, 18:261, where Wesley lists eight main ideas outlined by the Count and six contrasting views that had been taught by Peter Böhler. Zinzendorf's ideas were confirmed by Christian David's sermons a few days later. *Works*, 18:270–71. See his letter to brother Charles (28 June 1738), *Works*, 25:554.

96. *Journal* (10 August 1738), *Works*, 18:270. This distinction confirmed a crucial point in Wesley's own developing theology. See also his comments in the second published extract of his *Journal* (Preface), §§7–10, *Works*, 18:219–20

97. *A Plain Account of Christian Perfection*, §8, *Works* (Jackson), 8:370. See also *Journal* (11–14 August 1738), *Works*, 18:291. It is especially interesting that Wesley here in retrospect (1763) is saying in effect that he himself had not experienced this full assurance of faith at Aldersgate, even though in 1738 that is what he had been led to think he had experienced, since within the English Moravian framework there was only one type and degree of assurance.

98. Martin Schmidt questions whether Wesley really understood what Böhler had taught him, saying that Wesley interpreted what he heard in terms with which he was familiar. Schmidt's own analysis of the theological basis of Wesley's conversion also combines Pietist and Reformed ideas in a Lutheran fashion that would be problematic from an Anglican point of view. *John Wesley*, 1:238–39.

99. The English Moravian doctrine of freedom from sin also tended to overlook (or failed to develop) an important element of their own Lutheran background, the crucial concept of *simul iustus et peccator*—the Christian is at the same time justified and a sinner. Böhler records that on the evening that the Fetter Lane society had been organized (1 May 1738, three weeks before Aldersgate), Wesley "feels himself justified and is a seeking poor sinner," adding his own comment, "May the Saviour receive him on his arm and lap." "Peter Böhler and the Wesleys," p. 12.

100. "An assurance that excludes all doubt and fear," Sermon 110 (1739), "Free Grace," §14, *Works*, 3:549; "A Christian is so far perfect as not to commit sin," Sermon 40 (1741), "Christian Perfection," II.20, *Works*, 2:116. James Hutton reported that after John's return from Germany, "he and his brother were also not grounded, but still at that time they did much, and protested against the 'Inspired,' etc." "Beginning of the Lord's Work," p. 186.

101. *A Faithful Narrative of the Surprizing Work of God . . . in New England* (London: John Oswald, 1737).

102. 10 October 1738, *Journal* (Curnock), 2:84.

103. *The Doctrine of Salvation, Faith, and Good Works: Extracted from the Homilies of the Church of England* (Oxford: n.p., 1738). The tract was republished at least twenty times during Wesley's lifetime. When the revival started in Bristol in 1739, the Wesleys gave away these pamphlets by the hundreds, John remarking to James Hutton that this pamphlet was "better than all our sermons put together." Letter of 8 May 1739, *Works*, 25:645.

104. The letter received on 14 October may well have been by William Delamotte (10 October), who commented on the question of assurance in response to Wesley's observations on "weak faith." *Works*, 25:567–68; see also *Journal* (Curnock), 2:88–89. Wesley wrote the following notes ("wr.n.") between 2 and 3 p.m.; *MS London Diary*, 1:91.

105. 14 October 1738, *Journal* (Curnock), 2:89–90.

106. Here he is reiterating his decade-long rejection of external actions (summarized by the trilogy of the later *General Rules*) as the essence of real (internal) holiness; see at nn. 18, 20, 23 above. See also *Journal* (13 September 1739), where he also denigrates the typical clergy emphasis on sanctification as "an outward thing" in terms of the threefold outward activities (*General Rules*), and instead emphasizes internal renewal and holy tempers; see also Sermon 2 (1741), "The Almost Christian," I.13, *Works*, 1:136: an honest heathen follows those three outward rules, as he did while at Oxford for so many years, but that does not make one "an altogether Christian."

107. 14 October 1738, *Journal* (Curnock), 2:91; see also letter to Samuel Wesley, Jr. (30 October 1738), *Works*, 25:576–77.

108. As early as 29 May 1738, Wesley had been "tempted to doubt" whether he and Böhler had the same faith; *Works*, 18:253. In early June, he was becoming settled in his mind that degrees of faith were possible; *Works*, 18:254. By October, his recollection of 24 May indicated that he himself had then received "such a sort or degree of faith as I had not till that day"; letter to Samuel Wesley, Jr. (30 October 1738), *Works*, 25:576.

109. Letter to Samuel Wesley, Jr. (30 October 1738), *Works*, 25:575–77. Although not an experience of "full" assurance, Aldersgate did represent for Wesley an assurance of pardon which provided an experiential confirmation for his developing doctrine of the witness of the Spirit. See Colin W. Williams, *John Wesley's Theology Today* (Nashville: Abingdon, 1960), p. 104–5, and cf. Arthur S. Yates, *The Doctrine of Assurance* (London: Epworth Press, 1952), p. 11. Yates refers to the "witness of the Spirit" as "a theological name for 'the heart strangely warmed.'"

110. Letter (25 September 1738), *Works*, 25:564; see also Sermon 110 (1739), "Free Grace," §16, *Works*, 3:550.

111. "Saved from the fear, though not from the possibility, of falling away from the grace of God." Sermon 1, "Salvation by Faith," II.4, *Works*, 1:122; on 27 December 1738, Wesley preached at Whitechapel on "I will heal their backsliding." *Journal* (Curnock), 2:119.

112. *Journal* (Curnock), 2:97.

113. Conversation of 26 or 27 November 1738, recorded by Wesley in his *MS London Diary* 1:113.

114. Indicated by the usual abbreviation "wr.n." in his diary.

115. 16 December 1738, *Journal* (Curnock), 2:116; cf. self-examination of 29 January 1726: "I have loved women and company more than God"; *MS Oxford Diaries*, 1:35.

116. The question of whether the renewal of one's nature in the image of God results in *new* eyes or *renewed* sight has interesting implications for the doctrine of the Fall and the condition of "natural man." Although Wesley does not deal with this metaphor in a consistent fashion that would indicate a well-considered approach, he does tend to opt for the "renewed" and "enlightened" eyes most often, implying a higher anthropology (and assuming a different relationship between nature and grace) than if the eyes needed to be replaced.

117. 16 December 1738, *Journal* (Curnock), 2:116; cf. 2:90.

118. In effect, requiring entire sanctification as evidence of genuine Christianity, i.e., collapsing sanctification into justification, a typical approach for the Moravian Lutherans, as we saw above. These bouts with despair through self-questioning cannot simply be ignored or disregarded, as James Richard Joy has suggested in *John Wesley's Awakening* (Memphis: Commission on Archives and History, 1937), p. 70.

119. See at n. 71 above.

120. Cf. the requirements for the "altogether Christian": love of God, love of neighbor, and a faith that works through love. Sermon 2 (1741), *Works*, 1:137–139.

121. Again the formula: avoiding evil, doing good, using the means of grace—these do not suffice to make one a Christian. *Journal* (Curnock), 2:125–26. Recall Charles Wesley's and Thomas Broughton's confusion on this a year before (at n. 73 above).

122. See *Character of a Methodist* (1742), §5, in *Works*, 9:35, where he consciously uses the model of the perfect Christian from Clement of Alexandria; see also Sermon 40 (1741), "Christian Perfection" (*Works*, 2:105–21), where he explains that a Christian is cleansed from all sin and therefore "in such a sense perfect as not to commit sin," although later he denies that he ever uses the term "sinless perfection" (*Plain Account*, §19, *Works* [Jackson], 11:396); see Sermons 13 and 14, "On Sin in Believers" and "The Repentance of Believers," *Works*, 1:314–52; Sermon 43, "The Scripture Way of Salvation," III.11, *Works*, 2:166). The correlation between Methodism and genuine Christianity is straightforward in Wesley: "These are the marks of a true Methodist. . . . If any man say, 'Why, these are only the common, fundamental principles of Christianity'—'Thou hast said.' So I mean." *Character*, §17. See also his *Plain Account of Genuine Christianity* (1749), also used to defend Methodists. *Works*, 11:527–38.

123. He was at this time beginning to refer to himself and others who had not received full assurance as being Christians in an "imperfect" sense. Letter to Samuel Wesley, Jr. (30 October 1738), *Works*, 25:577.

124. Most of those who are baptized are born again only in a "lower sense", i.e., receive the remission of their sins (some in neither sense). See 25 January 1739, *Journal* (Curnock), 2:135. Later, Wesley will disentangle new birth or regeneration from justification in a theological sense, stressing that it is the "gate" or "threshold" of sanctification. Sermon 45, "The New Birth," IV.3, *Works*, 2:198; Sermon 107, "On God's Vineyard," §§6–7, *Works*, 3:506–7.

125. 5 and 10 December 1738, *Journal* (Curnock), 2:107, 113. At that point, such responses do not generally occur when Wesley was doing some occasional preaching at parish churches, but rather when he was with the societies, in workhouses, or speaking in private. Almost a year after Aldersgate, the same phenomenon will begin to occur in a greatly expanded context as he starts "field-preaching" to large groups out-of-doors.

126. 2 March 1739, *Journal* (Curnock), 2:147.

127. 28 January 1739, *Journal* (Curnock), 2:136–37. Five months later, he provided similar advice to the women of the Fetter Lane society, among which many misunderstandings and offenses had crept in: "not to believe every spirit, but to try the spirits, whether they were of God" (1 John 4:1). 13 June 1739, *Journal* (Curnock), 2:220.

128. 22 June 1739, *Journal* (Curnock), 2:226. This reference to the Old and New Testaments reiterates his lifelong reliance upon Scripture as the primary authority for theological and spiritual questions, especially as a test for individual experience. See above, p. 92 at n. 45.

129. 2 April 1739, *Journal* (Curnock), 2:167–73.

130. 28 March 1739, *Journal* (Curnock), 2:159.

131. See above, nn. 69, 124, 125.

132. The journal account reports three thousand (2 April 1739), *Journal* (Curnock), 2:173; a letter to James Hutton (4 April 1739) reports three or four thousand; *Works*, 25:625.

133. *Journal* (Curnock), 2:185–86. According to the diary, the field preaching was at 7 and 10:30 a.m. and 4:30 p.m.

134. Letter (7 May 1739), *Works*, 25:644. John wrote regular journal letters to "the brethren" in London, reporting on his activities in Bristol. C. J. Podmore has shown rather persuasively that the Fetter Lane society was quite thoroughly Moravian in its foundation and character and that Wesley's role in its leadership has been exaggerated. "The Fetter Lane Society, 1738," *Proceedings WHS* 46 (1988):137–40, 144–48.

135. Assurance did not necessarily imply a full assurance of our future perseverance but does indeed imply a full assurance that all past sins are forgiven, that you are now a child of God. Sermon 110 (1739), §§14, 16, *Works*, 3:549–50. He prepared this sermon in response to pressure to preach against "the decrees" and as a result of casting lots on April 26 (result, "Preach and publish").

136. Sermon 110, §18, *Works*, 3:550–51. Harald Lindström claims that Wesley was caught up in 1738 with the doctrines of "present justification" and "present salvation" and overlooked the importance of good works (as anything other than the result of faith) until he later began emphasizing final salvation. *Wesley and Sanctification* (Nashville: Abingdon, 1946), pp. 208–9. This view ignores the controversy with the Moravians over the use of the means of grace by the repentant or seeking person; see below, at n. 155.

137. Not all German Pietists denigrated active obedience or leaned toward antinomianism. Halle and Herrnhut represented two quite different approaches, and the more energetic and active Hallensian piety of August Hermann Francke and the Salzburgers in Georgia had already impressed Wesley. In June 1739, Wesley published *Nicodemus; or, A Treatise on the Fear of Man*, an extract of a work by Francke (*MS London Diary*, 30 May–1 June 1739). See Arthur W. Nagler, *Pietism and Methodism*, pp. 153–54; and Martin Schmidt, "Wesley's Place in Church History," in Rowe, ed., *The Place of Wesley in the Christian Tradition*, pp. 87–88.

138. 30 April, 1 May, 30 July 1739, etc., *Journal* (Curnock), 2:186–87, 232, 248, etc.

139. Letter to Samuel Wesley, Jr. (4 April 1739), *Works*, 25:622–23. Samuel's critical perspective had swayed Susanna to become critical of John. When she had seen his account of Aldersgate in June 1738, she approved it and "blessed God who had brought him to so just a way of thinking." A year later, with an account from Samuel intervening, she had fears that John "had greatly erred from the faith." 13 June 1739, *Journal* (Curnock), 2:219.

140. 11–18 June 1739, *Journal* (Curnock), 2:216–25.

141. 7 July 1739, *Journal* (Curnock), 2:240.

142. 22 June 1739, *Journal* (Curnock), 2:226.

143. Also on 24 August 1739. Charles later preached a sermon at Oxford on the same text, 4 April 1742, which was published as Sermon 3 in John Wesley's *Sermons on Several Occasions* (1746). John had written several sermons that Charles was still preaching at this time, and although there is no evidence that John wrote this published sermon on Ephesians 2:5, one can assume for a variety of reasons that John certainly agreed with the content. See *Works*, 1:142–58.

144. Sermon 3, "Awake, Thou That Sleepest," I.3–11, *Works*, 1:145–46.

145. Sermon 3, I.3–11, *Works*, 1:146. John begins using "divine evidence or conviction" (Heb. 11:1) at least by 24 August 1744 (Sermon 4, "Scriptural Christianity," *Works*, 1:161)

146. In 1746, Wesley would equate "the inspiration of the Holy Ghost" with assurance and "the revelation of Christ in us." *Minutes* (13 May 1746), *Works* (Jackson), 8:290.

147. Sermon 3, *Works*, 1:155. The question of "perceptible inspiration" also led to controversies surrounding the "extraordinary gifts of the Spirit," a topic which John Wesley usually tried to channel into discussions of the "ordinary gifts of the Spirit." See Sermon 4, "Scriptural Christianity," §5, *Works*, 1:151.

148. By his own account, Wesley preached to ten thousand on 2 September, to thirty thousand on 9 September, to thirty thousand on 16 September, and to thirty thousand

on 23 September; the diary reports him preaching to twenty-seven thousand on 30 September. *Journal* (Curnock), 2:266–83.

149. 13 September 1739, *Journal* (Curnock), 2:275. This became a consistent argument for Wesley as part of his continual claim that the Methodists were not separating from the Church of England.

150. 16 September 1739, *Journal* (Curnock), 2:278. See also *Character of a Methodist*, §17, *Works*, 9:41, and n. 122 above.

151. Wesley explains this point by yet another reference to religion in terms of the outline of the *General Rules*: "as if it consisted chiefly, if not wholly in . . . : the doing no harm; the doing good; . . . the using the means of grace." See above, n. 106.

152. 13 September 1739, *Journal* (Curnock), 2:275.

153. His sermon on "Salvation by Faith" (1738) had said, "We speak of a faith which is necessarily inclusive of all good works and all holiness." A critic writing to the *Gentleman's Magazine* pointed out the inherent contradiction of this position with his *sola fide* views, so that in subsequent editions, Wesley changed the wording to read "faith which is necessarily productive of all good works and all holiness." See *Elusive Mr. Wesley*, 1:91. But Josiah Tucker, an Anglican priest and critic from Bristol, wrote to him in November 1739 after hearing him preach: "I must confess, sir, that the discourse you made that day, wherein you pressed your hearers in the closest manner . . . not to stop at *faith* ONLY, but to add to it *all virtues* and to show forth their *faith* by every kind of *good works*, convinced me of the great wrong done you by a public report, common in people's mouths, that you preach *faith* without *works*." *Journal* (Curnock), 2:304. Wesley spent much of the rest of his life trying to explain a view of "faith alone" that also necessarily entailed good works "in some sense"; e.g., *A Farther Appeal to Men of Reason and Religion* (1745), II.11, *Works*, 11:117; Sermon 43 (1765), "The Scripture Way of Salvation," III.2, III.13, *Works*, 2:162–63, 167.

154. This language of "tempers" hearkens back to the meditative piety of his Oxford days and will come highly visible in his common vocabulary again in the 1780s. *E.g.*, real religion as "holy tempers" or "right tempers," 24 March and 11 December 1785, *Journal* (Curnock), 7:59, 130; see also Sermon 107 (1787), "On God's Vineyard," I.9: "Who then is a Christian? . . . He in whom is that whole mind, all those holy tempers, which were also in Christ Jesus." *Works*, 3:507–8

155. Wesley exhibits some ambibuity on this point during this period. In his sermon *Salvation by Faith* (1738), III.1, Wesley had first said, "We speak of a faith which is necessarily inclusive of all good works and all holiness" ("inclusive" was changed to "productive" in later editions); *Works*, 1:125. In his Preface to *Hymns and Sacred Poems* (1739), he refers to "faith contradistinguished from all holiness, as well as from good works." Between these two works, in the sermon on "Free Grace" (April 1739, §18), Wesley argued against predestination because it is destructive of holiness and good works. *Works*, 18, 3:550–51.

156. In the preface to the second extract of his *Journal*, Wesley speaks of those who had found "the beginning of that salvation, being 'justified freely'"; but in the fall of 1739, while he and Charles were at Oxford, "certain men crept in among them unawares, greatly 'troubling and subverting their souls.'" *Journal* (Preface), §§8–9, *Works*, 18:219.

157. *Journal* (Curnock), 2:310. From the Moravian view, Wesley was appealing to "those who were unsound and wished to remain so." Hutton, "Beginning of the Lord's Work," p. 188.

158. 9 November 1739, *Journal* (Curnock), 2:316. Wesley continued to attack this problem head-on, as seen by his preaching to the society on 1 January 1740 on the text, "Be still and know that I am God." *Journal* (Curnock), 2:331.

159. The story is told by Wesley without names, but the person is most likely his mother. See 3 September and 10 November 1739, *Journal* (Curnock), 2:267, 315.

160. 11 November 1739, *Journal* (Curnock), 2:319n. From the Moravian perspective (James Hutton's view), "Wesley became hostile, partly through our imprudent behaviour

towards him, partly from inablility to bear that he should be less thought of amongst us than Brother Molther. In short he broke off from us, contradicted our teaching publicly, but we contradicted his only quietly. He took away from us almost all the women folk who then belonged to us but only some fourteen men. He became our declared enemy." "Beginning of the Lord's Work," p. 188. Wesley's final organizational break with the Moravians came on 23 July 1740; *Journal* (Curnock), 2:369–71. Hutton sarcastically refers to the separated group as rapidly forming "a 'sect' in which the Saviour does not hinder them." "Hutton's Second Account," *Proceedings WHS* 15 (1726):211.

161. 31 December 1739, *Journal* (Curnock), 2:329. Towlson claims that doctrinal differences between Wesley and the Moravians would not have resulted in such controversy and disruption if not for the personal friction between Wesley and the Moravian leadership. *Moravian and Methodist*, pp. 116–17.

162. *Journal* (Curnock), 2:329.

163. Wesley was beginning to sense the worst side of "enthusiasm," the subjective judgmentalism that cannot be challenged. In this context, he continually falls back upon his more traditional authorities as guides to measure the validity of personal experience: Scripture, the primitive church, and the teachings of the Church of England.

164. *Journal* (Curnock), 2:329–30. Wesley also points out in his memorandum against Molther that, as for propagating the faith, we should not use guile, deception, or "describing things a little beyond the truth in order to their coming up to it"; much hurt has been done by this method, many "now wholly unsettled and lost in vain reasonings and doubtful disputations," many brought into "unscriptural stillness," "many being grounded on a faith which is without works, so that they who were right before are wrong now."

165. See the second extract of his *Journal* published in the fall of 1740 to show that the Church of England and the "true" Moravians both disagreed with these false teachings perpetuated by some Moravians, under whose influence he had been in May 1738. *Journal* (Preface), *Works*, 18:218–20, 260–61; *Letters* (5 August 1740), *Works*, 26:24–30.

166. *Journal* (Curnock), 2:351.

167 Letter to John Clayton? (28 March 1738?), *Works*, 25:615.

168. 23 July 1739, *Journal* (Curnock), 2:246; cf. 25 January 1739, ibid., 2:135.

169. Letter to John Clayton? (28 March 1738?), *Works*, 25:615. Later in this same letter he draws a larger picture on the same principles, using the familiar phrase, "I look upon all the world as my parish," explained thusly, "that in whatever part of it I am, I judge it meet, right, and my bounden duty to declare unto all that are willing to hear the glad tidings of salvation." Ibid., 25:616. Earlier, Wesley had used a similar rationale in a letter to his father explaining his reasons for staying at Oxford rather than taking the Epworth living, and to John Burton explaining his reasons for going to Georgia; ibid., 25:399, 439.

170. This idea of *simul iustus et peccator* is not yet clearly or consistently developed by Wesley at this time but is reflected in his idea that justification and sanctification free the person from the guilt and power, though not the remains, of sin. *Works*, 1:123n, 124; 25:318, 575. Cf. Sermon 43 (1765), "The Scripture Way of Salvation," III.6, *Works*, 2:164–65 (this sermon is one of the best summaries of Wesley's mature theology).

171. During this period, Wesley exhibits a tendency to draw a rather sharp contrast between the formula of the *General Rules* with the formula of Romans 14:17. Letter to Henry Stebbing (25 July 1739), §6, *Works*, 25:671; see also 24 November 1739, *Journal* (Curnock), 2:321. See above, at nn. 74, 122.

172. *Homilies*, "Of Salvation," Pt III; and "Of the salvation of mankind," §15, in Wesley's *The Doctrine of Salvation, Faith and Good Works* (1738).

173. ". . . Joy, though not *unfelt*, yet *unspeakable* and full of glory." Letter to Henry Stebbing (25 July 1739), *Works*, 25:671. Wesley is beginning to deal more explicity with the manner of interpreting how one knows and understands the sensible operations of

the Holy Spirit. In 1741, he further develops the relationship between inward and outward religion, pointing out that the "power of godliness" cannot be without the "form": "Outward religion may be where inward is not. But if there is none *without* there can be none *within*." Sermon 150, "Hypocrisy in Oxford," II.2, *Works*, 4:400.

174. Ibid. Wesley here and elsewhere equates "feel" with "know" (and implies that to learn from Holy Writ is to know): "You will know you are under the guidance of God's Spirit the same way, namely, by *feeling it in your soul*; by the present peace and joy and love which you feel within, as well as by its outward and more distant effects." Ibid. See also Charles Wesley on sensible operations of the Holy Spirit (e.g., "feeling the Spirit of Christ") in Sermon 3, "Awake Thou that Sleepest," III.8–9, *Works*, 1:155–56.

175. 13 December 1739, *Journal* (Curnock), 2:326.

176. Or, as John put the question to Charles in 1747, "Is justifying faith a sense of pardon?" His own answer was no on several counts, followed by the summary comment, "It is flatly absurd. For how can a sense of our having received pardon be the condition of our receiving it?" By that time he had been pressed hard in this and other matters on more than one occasion over the past two years by John Smith. Letter (31 July 1747), *Works*, 26:255.

177. He had already used the eye metaphor: Christians are more enlightened, their eye is "more clear and single," they look "beyond the veil of the material world," the eyes of their understanding "being enlightened." Sermon 17 (1733), "Circumcision of the Heart," Sermon 147 (1734), "Wiser than Children of Light," *Works*, 1:405; 4:364. John's sermon on "A Single Eye," Charles transcribed as "A Single Intention," an easy change given the comment in the sermon, "The intention is to the soul what the eye is to the body." He would soon begin referring to having "new eyes to see and new ears to hear." Sermon 148 (1736), *Works*, 4:373; cf. 1:306, n. 34.

178. A concept that first appears in the sermon Charles Wesley preached in 1742, "Awake Thou that Sleepest" (I.11). In 1744, Wesley uses the same phrase in "Scriptural Christianity" (I.1–2); that same year he also refers to faith as "the eye of the newborn soul" as well as the ear, the palate, and the feeling of the soul, each image supported by a passage of Scripture. *Appeals*, §§6–7, *Works*, 11:46–47.

179. By 1741, the Wesleys could say, "Neither dare we affirm, as some have done, that all this salvation is given at once. There is indeed an instantaneous, as well as a gradual, work of God in his children; and there wants not, we know, a cloud of witnesses who have received in one moment either a clear sense of the forgiveness of their sins or the abiding witness of the Holy Spirit. But we do not know a single instance, in any place, of a person's receiving, in one and the same moment, remission of sins, the abiding witness of the Spirit, and a new, a clean heart." Preface to *Hymns and Sacred Poems* (1740), *Works* (Jackson), 14:326. Cf. above, at n. 83. By 1747, Wesley also felt that the biblical term "sanctified" did not mean "saved from all sin," and that such use was not proper without adding a modifier such as "wholly" or " entirely." He goes on to say, "Consequently, it behooves us to speak almost continually of the state of justification; but more rarely, at least in full and explicit terms, concerning entire sanctification." *Minutes* (17 June 1747), *Works* (Jackson), 8:294.

180. At the conference of 1746, Wesley answered the question, "Wherein does our doctrine now differ from that we preached when at Oxford?" with only two main points: "(1) We then knew nothing of that righteousness of faith in justification; nor (2) of the nature of faith itself as implying consciousness of pardon." *Minutes* (13 May 1746), *Works* (Jackson), 11:290. John Deschner points out that Aldersgate was not a "theological conversion": "Rather the old theology was reborn that night, reconciled to God, and a lifelong process of theological sanctification, so to speak, began. The theology of his student days . . . was cut off its old tree and grafted onto a new one." *Wesley's Christology* (Dallas: Southern Methodist University Press, 1985), p. 197.

181. Sermon 2 (1741), "The Almost Christian," *Works*, 1:131–41.

182. *Minutes* (2 August 1745), Q. 20, *Works* (Jackson), 8:284.

183. Ibid., Q. 15, 8:283–84. Wesley was occasionally quite candid about the changes in his thinking over the years, even admitting in 1768 that he had not only "relinquished several of my former sentiments," but also "during these last thirty years I may have varied in some of my sentiments or expressions without observing it." *Letter to Dr. Rutherforth*, I.3, *Works*, 9:375. James W. Fowler, looking at Wesley's growth through stages of faith-development, sees these changes as part of his transition to a more "Conjunctive" faith in middle life after the rather prolonged transition to the "Individuative-Reflective" stage was completed with his experiential appropriation of the doctrine of justification by grace through faith. "John Wesley's Development in Faith," in M. Douglas Meeks, ed., *The Future of the Methodist Theological Traditions* (Nashville: Abingdon, 1985), pp. 183–92.

184. Although the sharp theological distinction is not yet attached to the distinction between justification and sanctification, this terminology appears as early as Sermon 1 (1738), "Salvation by Faith," and Sermon 5 (1746), "Justification by Faith," *Works*, 1:122–23, 191.

185. "Thou shalt be saved; first from the guilt of sin, having redemption through his blood; then from the power, which shall have no more dominion over thee; and then from the root of it, into the whole image of God." Sermon 116 (1788), "What is Man?" *Works*, 4:26.

186. 2 Tim. 3:5.

187. Acts 10:35.

188. §2, in *Works*, 9:69.

189. *A Plain Account of the People Called Methodists*, IV.2, in *Works*, 9:265.

190. *A Letter to the Rev. Dr. Rutherforth*, I.4, in *Works*, 9:376.

191. Sermon 67, "On Divine Providence," §18, *Works*, 2:543. He also associates this phrase with the definition of true saving faith: "such a divine conviction of God and of the things of God as even in its infant state enables everyone that possesses it to 'fear God and work righteousness.'" Sermon 106, "On Faith," I.10, *Works*, 3:497.

192. Sermon 89, "The More Excellent Way," §5, *Works*, 3:255–56.

193. *Minutes* (13 May 1746), *Works*, 11:287–88. See also an early use of this distinction in Sermon 9 (1746), "The Spirit of Bondage and of Adoption," §2, *Works*, 1:250.

194. Sermon 117, "On the Discoveries of Faith," §13, *Works*, 4:35; cf. n. 26 above. This changing perspective led Wesley in 1774 to alter his earlier *Journal* accounts of 1738, adding qualifications to his earlier claims that before Aldersgate he had not been converted, did not have faith, was not in a state of salvation, was a child of wrath, and was building on the sand. *Works*, 18:215n, 235n, 242n, 245n, 248n.

195. Sermon 106, "On Faith," I.11, *Works*, 3:497. Bernard G. Holland refers to this "faith of a servant" as "suppliant faith" and points out that John Wesley distinguishes between that and the "faith of a son" as well as another level of "saving" faith. Holland, however, does not follow Wesley's own development but rather confuses faith with assurance and fails to distinguish adequately between justification and sanctification in his description of the Wesleyan typology of faith. "The Conversions of John and Charles Wesley," *Proceedings WHS* 38 (1971):46–53.

196. See Wesley's comment to Thomas Rutherforth (28 March 1768): "Therefore I have not for many years thought a consciousness of acceptance to be essential to justifying faith." *A Letter to the Rev. Dr. Rutherforth*, I.4, *Works*, 9:376. Wesley even went so far at one point to say to Samuel Walker (19 September 1757), "Assurance is a word I do not use because it is not scriptural." *Letters* (Telford), 3:222; and to Dr. Rutherforth (1763), "Some are fond of the *expression*; I am not—I hardly ever use it" (although "a consciousness of being in the favour of God . . . is the common privilege of Christians fearing God and working righteousness"). *Works*, 9:375. See Yates, *Doctrine of Assurance*, pp. 133–34 for an attempted explanation for Wesley's tendencies toward overstatement in the matter of terminology.

197. Robert Southey, *The Life of Wesley* (New York: W. B. Gilley, 1820), 1:258. Cf. Sermon 3, "Awake, Thou that Sleepest," III.6, *Works*, 1:154.

198. First seen in Charles Wesley's sermon, Sermon 3, "Awake, Thou that Sleepest," I.11, *Works*, 1:146. Charles here used the Greek phrase for "evidence of the Spirit"; John frequently translates the text "evidence and conviction."

199. This was the text of his two sermons on "The Witness of the Spirit," written twenty years apart. Sermons 10 and 11 (1746, 1767), *Works*, 1:267–98. See also his other main treatment of the subject in Sermon 12 (1746), "The Witness of Our Own Spirit," *Works*, 1:299–313.

200. This point is developed most fully in Sermon 130, "On Living Without God," especially §§9–11, *Works*, 4:172–73. See also Rex D. Matthews, "Religious Epistemology," pp. 4–9.

201. See especially *An Earnest Appeal* (1743), §32, *Works*, 11:56–57; and Sermon 119, "Walking by Sight and Walking by Faith," *Works*, 4:48–59. Richard Brantley parallels what he calls "Wesley's spiritual sense" with Jonathan Edwards's "religious sense" and sees it as analogous with Locke's finite sensate means of knowing the religious unknown (as well as being "the major English antecedent of the Romantic imagination"); *Locke, Wesley, and the Method of English Romanticism*, p. 100. Frederick Dreyer has pointed out that Wesley's concept of the "spiritual senses" is "a peculiarly eighteenth-century solution to an epistemological problem," drawing a parallel with Francis Hutcheson's "moral sense." "Faith and Experience in the Thought of John Wesley," p. 26. Nagler sees "religious empiricism" as the most important contribution of both Wesley and Pietism; *Pietism and Methodism*, p. 176. Matthews points out, however, that there is no real precedent for Wesley's "transcendental empiricism," the wedding of the notion of "spiritual senses" to a rigorously empiricistic epistemology. "Religious Epistemology," p. 55–56.

202. See his comment in *A Plain Account of Christian Perfection* (1763), §8, which recognizes that Aldersgate itself was not an experience of full assurance for him. *Works* (Jackson), 11:370; see above, at n. 120.

Chapter 7: Early Sermons of John and Charles Wesley

1. The main portion of this essay was the author's first publication, "John Wesley's Early Sermons," appearing in the *Proceedings WHS* 37 (February 1970):110–28; the material on Charles Wesley's early sermons has been added for this edition.

2. *Methodist Recorder* (Winter 1904):46–47.

3. *Journal* (Curnock), 1:60.

4. Ibid., 1:59.

5. Quite frequently Wesley turned the volume round and began writing from the back page forward, resulting in a *dos à dos* book which can be read starting from either end. Consequently the volume with the diary for 1 October 1733 to 22 April 1734 was later numbered twice in the listing of the Colman Collection X as a diary and XIV as "Books read during the year 1733" (the monthly summaries beginning from the back); see *Proceedings WHS* 21 (1937):93–97. Appreciation is extended to the Methodist Archives, Rylands, for access to the early Methodist manuscripts in the collection.

6. These include notes relative to class lists, Holy Club finances, reading lists, poetry, study schedules, and subscription lists for his father's forthcoming book on Job.

7. *Journal* (Curnock), 1:47. This list is hereafter referred to as diary "list B."

8. This is the "exquisitely neat little MS" on Matthew 6:33 to which Curnock referred (note 3); see also *Wesley's First Sermon* (London, 1903).

9. South Leigh is listed between two other entries for 1727. The first daily diary entry for preaching at South Leigh is 12 February 1727.

10. At Wesley College, Bristol. Appreciation is extended to Dr. Frank Baker for calling this manuscript to my attention as an important confirmation of the diary listing.

11. The same correlated evidence is present on the manuscript of sermon 17. A date is quite often noted immediately at the end of the body of the sermon on the manuscript copy, and comparison with the daily diary entries indicates that it is usually the date Wesley finished writing or transcribing the sermon and should not be mistaken for a preaching date.

12. *Sermons by the Late Rev. Charles Wesley, A.M.* (London: Baldwin, 1816). Manuscripts are extant for eleven of the twelve published sermons, as well as for two unpublished ones.

13. Diary entries (28 January–4 February 1735), *Works*, 18:346–49; see Sermon 148, *Works*, 1:371–77. As it turned out, Charles preached this sermon at both Frederica and Savannah; see below, pp. 154–55.

14. The editor of Charles Wesley's sermons apparently was unfamiliar with Byrom's shorthand (John Byrom, *The Universal English Shorthand* [Manchester: Joseph Harrop, 1767]), as is indicated by some of the notes appended to the published sermons. The note on Sermon IX says, "Preached on board the *London Galley*, between Charles Town and Boston," whereas what the editor read as "preached" was in fact five words in shorthand, "transcribed from my brother's copies," and applies to sermons I, II, and V as well. The date of transcription is noted at the end of the manuscript for Sermon V as 4 September 1736, "off Boston," and coincides with a reference in Charles's' journal of that date to his writing by candle-light. *The Journal of the Rev. Charles Wesley, M.A.* (London: Culley, 1910), 1:75.

15. *MS Sermonbook*, Colman Collection, XIX, Methodist Archives, Rylands. The attitude toward plagiarism and the use of someone else's sermons was not quite the same as it is today (see below, pp. 176–77).

16. *Sermons Preached upon Several Occasions: Never before Printed* (London: M. Flesher, 1687). One of Wesley's abridgments was included in his collected works as Sermon CXXXVII, and the nineteenth-century editor, Thomas Jackson, noted that it was "originally written by Benjamin Calamy." *Works* (Jackson), 7:474n.

17. *Sixteen Sermons . . . preached before the University of Oxford, at St. Mary's, upon Several Occasions* (London: Lintott, 1712). This has been noticed by Dr. Charles Rogers in *Proceedings WHS* 35 (1966):137–41 (but with incorrect preaching dates).

18. See below, n. 42.

19. "The Duty of Receiving the Lord's Supper" is the title given in the essay; Colman Collection, XX, Methodist Archives, Rylands. The further abridgment may have occurred as early as March 1732 (diary entry, "transcribed sermon on Sacrament"), although Wesley's note on the published sermon that he has abridged the essay is dated 1788. See *Works*, 4:526–28.

20. There is no extant diary for 20 February 1727 to 29 April 1729 and 9 February to 16 October 1735. The daily diary for the summer of 1734 is also missing, but monthly summaries at the back of *MS Oxford Diary* 4 fill in the essential data for that period. For a more complete chart of information including the preaching places, see "John Wesley's Early Sermons," pp. 115–28.

21. The manuscript of this sermon provides only the one date, not a Sunday, which is presumed to be the date of completion. The manuscript has no indication of preaching dates.

22. John Wesley had recently quoted this text in a letter of advice to his Oxford friends (30 September 1735), *Works*, 25:438. Records of John's preaching include fifty-one instances of his preaching from this text.

23. See at n. 13 above.

24. Sermon 148, *Works*, 4:372.

25. Notes on the sermon MS are confirmed by Charles's journal in the case of preaching at Frederica. John Telford, ed., *The Journal of the Rev. Charles Wesley* (London: Culley, 1910), 1:11. John and Charles alternated preaching responsibilities at Frederica and Savannah. If Charles preached this sermon at both places, it is highly unlikely that

John would have ever used it in Georgia. Notes in Charles's hand on the manuscript also indicate that he preached this sermon at least three times in England during 1736–37; *Works*, 18:371. John eventually wrote and published another sermon on this text: Sermon 125 (1789), "On a Single Eye," *Works*, 4:120–30.

26. The sermon caused an uproar when it was "deciphered into a satire" against one of his parishoners, Mrs. Hawkins, whose reputation was suffering from Charles's allegations. Charles quotes the text as "Keep innocency, and take heed to the thing that is right, for this shall bring a man peace at the last"; the translation by William Wake of this passage from Clement of Rome's First Epistle to the Corinthians is, "Keep innocently, and do the thing that is right, for there shall be a remnant to the peaceable man." *Journal of Charles Wesley*, 1:32; cf. William Wake, *The Genuine Epistles of the Apostolical Fathers* (London: R. Sare, 1693).

27. The day after transcribing this sermon, he transcribed another of John's, on John 13:7, "What I do, thou knowest not now." Sermon 141, *Works*, 4:279–89.

28. On 25 July, Charles preached twice, with John there as lector for the service (*Works*, 18:405). Notes on the MS of the sermon indicate that on one of those occasions Charles preached John's sermon on "Children of Light."

29. See the first eight items on the table of "Charles Wesley's Early Sermons," below.

30. *CW Sermonbook* (Methodist Archives, Rylands), containing texts of Sermons 135, 139, 142, 144; see *Works*, 4:224, 267, 306, 330.

31. The sermon on Job 3:17 was probably John's second sermon on that text (Sermon 109, *Works*, 3:533–41). When Charles's transcriptions of John's sermons were published in 1816, the editor included this sermon by John, no doubt because it was in with the batch of manuscript sermon transcripts that Charles had used and saved. The sermon on Job was easily recognized by the editor as John's, having been previously published (perhaps Charles had even used and saved it in printed form; no manuscript has survived).

32. The preaching dates on this manuscript include two occasions after his evangelical experience of 21 May 1738.

33. This may very well be John's sermon from 1733 (Sermon 17).

34. 21 and 22 June, 9 July 1738.

35. See Thomas R. Albin and Oliver A. Beckerlegge, eds., *Charles Wesley's Earliest Evangelical Sermons* (Ilford: Robert Odcombe, 1987); this is an "Occasional Publication" of the Wesley Historical Society. The earliest of these sermons was preached first on 16 July 1738.

36. There are two entries numbered 30 on "list A."

37. The next fourteen titles are the remaining entries from Diary "list A," not including those also found on "list B." Some of the latter may indeed have been written and preached during this period, 1727–29, but are included with the entries from "list B" at the end of the table.

38. Mentioned in the monthly diary summary for June 1730 but omitted from the yearly summary.

39. This entry has a line drawn through it in the list, as do six others, perhaps indicating that a sermon had been completed on that text as well as suggesting a possible proximity in time of writing.

40. This may be the text for No. 56 and vice versa. Diary evidence is inconclusive.

41. Wesley notes transcribing "sermon on Sacrament," 24 March 1732, and talking with James Hervey about "sermon on Sacrament," 30 March 1734.

42. Since Wesley collected four more of Tilly's sermons in numerical order, beginning with sermon 8, it is probable that this one was from the first seven.

43. Noted by mistake in the daily diary as number 58. In the monthly summary for February 1733, "58" has been changed to "60." A sermon written in May is also noted as number 60. The September summary notes Sermon 61. To add to the confusion, the yearly summary for 1733 lists only two sermons written during the year, number 59

(actually written in 1732) and number 60. The summary for 1734 begins with Sermon 62.

44. The sixth preaching place noted on the manuscript is Epworth, where Wesley preached his farewell sermon in 1735 on "pursuing the one end of our life in all our words and actions." Letter to John Newton (14 May 1765), *Letters* (Telford), 5:299.

45. The following twenty-nine texts are the remaining entries from diary "list B."

46. See n. 39 above.

47. Charles transcribed this from John's copy on 6 May 1736.

48. This sermon was published separately (London: Rivington, 1735) but not included by Wesley in his collected sermons or works.

49. This date is inscribed in shorthand at the top of the first page in Charles Wesley's handwriting; the day was a Sunday and may indicate the date upon which someone (John Wesley?) preached the sermon.

50. This date, not a Sunday, most likely indicates the day of writing or transcription.

Chapter 8: Spirit and Life: John Wesley's Preaching

1. Part of this essay appeared in Appendix B, *Sermons IV*, in *Works*, 4:515–24.

2. *Proceedings WHS* 17 (1929):2–3.

3. *Impartial and Succinct History of the Rise and Declension and Revival of the Church of Christ*, 2nd Amer. ed. (Baltimore: Abner Neal, 1807), 2:435.

4. *Proceedings WHS* 7 (1910):131.

5. R. L. Gwynne, *Estaines Parva* [Easton Parish]; *A Venture* (London, S. Burch, ca. 1923), 76 pp., quoted in Frederick C. Gill, *In the Steps of John Wesley* (Nashville: Abingdon, 1964), p. 123.

6. John Whitehead, *The Life of the Rev. John Wesley* (London: Stephen Couchman, 1793–96), 2:466.

7. *Wesleyan Methodist Magazine* 68 (1845):120.

8. *Arminian Magazine* 5 (1782):126.

9. John Waddington, *Congregational History* (London: Longmans, Green & Co., 1878), p. 48.

10. Letter to Robert Southey, 4 April 1819; in John Gibson Lockhart, *Life of Sir Walter Scott* (London: Macmillan, 1900), 3:266–46.

11. P. Williams, *Short Vindication of the Church of England* (Oxford, 1803), p. 43.

12. Robert Southey, *The Life of John Wesley*, 2nd Amer. ed. (New York: Harper, 1847), 2:344.

13. The eyewitness in this case was the grandfather of Rev. J. P. Lockwood. *Journal* (Curnock), 8:60n.

14. Quoted from her journal for 3 April 1788. Henry Moore, *Life of Mrs. Fletcher* (London: T. Cordeaux, 1818), p. 251.

15. *Proceedings WHS* 7 (1910):131.

16. Southey, *Life of Wesley*, 1:336.

17. *Methodist Magazine* 31 (1808):489–90.

18. Samuel Bradburn, *A Farther Account of the Rev. John Wesley* (London, 1791), p. 11.

19. Founded in August 1780. *Journal* (Curnock), 7:348.

20. The note at the end of the manuscript also mentions that Wesley "had a small Bible in his hand." The latter reference is probably to a "Field Bible" that he often used, a 1763 edition of the Authorized Version, published by John Field in double-duodecimo (approx. six by eleven centimeters). Wesley gave his Field Bible to Henry Moore in 1788, and it has subsequently passed into the hands of the British Methodist Church, where it is used in the annual installation of the President of Conference.

21. This sermon was later published in Wesley's collected sermons and is Sermon 91 in current edition of his *Works*, 3:290–307.

22. *Proceedings WHS* 2 (1900):138.

23. *Life of Wesley* (1796), 2:466.

24. The anecdote about St. George's Hospital confirms a note in Adam Clarke's work on the Wesley family, which indicates that Samuel Wesley, Jun., was "a careful and active promoter of the first infirmary set up at Westminster, for the relief of the sick and needy, in the year 1719." *Memoirs of the Wesley Family* (London: J. & T. Clarke, 1823), p. 386.

25. *Journal* (Curnock), 3:368; 6:17–18.

26. *A Sermon Preached at the Opening of the New Meeting-House at Wakefield, On the 28th of April, 1774, by the Rev. John Wesley* (Leeds:Printed and sold by all the Booksellers, n.d.).

27. Volume XI of the George Story Papers, Manuscript Department of the William R. Perkins Library at Duke University, Durham, North Carolina. For a later sermon on this same topic, see Sermon 86, "A Call to Backsliders" (Ps. 77:7–8), *Works*, 3:210–26.

28. Sermons 13 and 14 in *Works*, 1:314–52.

29. Charles Wesley, "After Preaching to the Newcastle Colliers," st. 9, lines 3–4, in *Hymns and Sacred Poems* (1749), 1:311; orig., "They listen, and heaven springs up in their heart."

30. Orig., "soul devour"; *Collection of Hymns* (1780), No. 421, lines 5–6; *Works*, 7:596.

31. Bartholomew Gallatin was a Swiss army officer who moved to England and was commissioned in the British army in 1744. See *Works*, 3:584n; 26:432n.

32. Sermon 67, "On Divine Providence," *Works*, 2:534–50.

33. In Sermon No. 67, §6, Wesley says this expression is not a literal but "proverbial expression."

34. See ibid., §§6, 23–24.

35. See ibid., §§9–10.

36. MS reads "Theocrates"; the quotation is found in Virgil, *Eclogues*, iii.60 (see Sermon 23, I.6 and n., and Sermon 118, II.3; *Works*, 1:513; 4:44).

37. See Sermon 67, §12.

38. These themes are found especially in ibid., §§8, 10–11, 16, and 19. The threefold circles of Providence are listed in reverse order. He seems to have quoted some of the same poetic lines in both versions, e.g., "Lord of all / A hero perish, or a sparrow fall" (Alexander Pope, *Essay on Man*, i.87–88; see §19).

Chapter 9: Plain Truth: Sermons as Standards of Doctrine

1. This paper was presented at Drew University in October 1986 as one of the Vosburgh Lectures and was published in *The Drew Gateway* 57 (Fall 1987):16–30.

2. *Works*, 1:104.

3. *Certain Sermons, Appointed by the Queen's Majesty, to be declared and read by all parsons, vicars, and curates . . . for the better understanding of the simple people* (London: 1562); see Canon XLIX (1603), in Edmund Gibson, *Codex iuris ecclesiastici Anglicani*, 2 vol. (London: Baskett, 1713), 1:378.

4. *Daily Christian Advocate*, May 10, 1984, pp. 412, 613–15.

5. The Restrictive Rules form Section III of Division Two of the Constitution; see p. 21 in the 1984 *Book of Discipline*. The Commission's report became Part II of the *Book of Discipline*; see p. 49 in the 1984 edition for the phrase in question.

6. E.g., *Works*, 1:195, 456; 3:505; 4:405–6; 9:228; 11:78, 115, 166; *Journal* (Curnock), 2:275, 326, 4:425.

7. *Articuli . . . ad tollendam opinionum dissentionem, & consensum in vera religione firmandum* (London: J. Day, 1571).

8. Edward Cardwell, ed., *Synodalia; A Collection of Articles of Religion, Canons, and Proceedings of Convocations*, 2 vols. (Oxford: University Press, 1842), 1:30.

9. Edward Cardwell, ed., *Documentary Annals of the Reformed Church of England*, 2 vols. (Oxford: University Press, 1844), 1:32.

10. Canon XLIX (1603), in Cardwell, *Annals*, 1:125; cf. Gibson, *Codex*, 1:386.

11. Canon XLVI (1603), in Cardwell, *Annals*, 1:224; cf. Gibson, *Codex*, 1:378.

12. 13 Eliz. Cap. 12; see Henry Gee and William Hardy, eds. *Documents Illustrative of English Church History* (London: Macmillan, 1914), pp. 478–79. This authoritative role for the Articles is repeated in Canon 51 of 1603, which specifies that anyone who publishes (preaches) "any doctrine, either strange or disagreeing from the Word of God, or from any of the Articles of Religion agreed upon" (1562) is to be censured; see Gibson, *Codex*, 1:380.

13. Gee and Hardy, *Documents*, p. 516; Cardwell, *Annals*, 2:201.

14. See 13 Eliz. Cap.12.

15. Cardwell, *Annals*, 1:319; see also Canon XLIX (1603), in Gibson, *Codex*, 1:386.

16. Thomas Bennet, *Directions for Studying . . . The Thirty-nine Articles* (London: Innys, 1715), p. 150; Edmund Gibson, *An Exposition of the Thirty-nine Articles of the Church of England* (London: Midwinter, 1746), p. 473.

17. Bennet, *Directions*, p. 151.

18. Ibid.

19. Ibid., p. 153.

20. Ibid., p. 152; Gibson, *Exposition*, p. 474. This attempt at historical relativization, illustrated by Gibson in his explicit treatment of the question of the supposed threat of popery, past and present, is reflected more recently in the United Methodist "Resolution of Intent," sent to the Vatican in 1970 to "explain" the historical context of our anti-Roman Articles.

21. Preface to Sermons, *Works*, 1:103.

22. *Minutes of Several Conversations between the Rev. Mr. John and Charles Wesley and Others*, i.e., "Large Minutes," in *Minutes* (London: Nichols, 1862), 1:608–10.

23. *The Doctrine of Salvation, Faith, and Good Works*; see Frank Baker, *A Union Catalogue of the Publications of John and Charles Wesley* (Durham: Duke, 1966), #9.

24. William Grimshaw, *An Answer to a Sermon Lately Preached against the Methodists* (Preston: Stanley & Moon, 1749), p. 54.

25. *Journal* (Curnock), 8:332–33.

26. *Articles of Religion Prepared by Order of the Conference of 1806*, publication No. 2 of The Wesley Historical Society (London: Kelly, 1897), pp. 3, 6.

27. *A Summary of Methodist Law and Discipline* (London: Sharp, 1924), p. 541; see also E. H. Sugden, ed., *The Standard Sermons of John Wesley* (London: Epworth, 1921), 2:335.

28. "More often than not, Wesley's published sermons were from texts infrequently used in his oral preaching." Albert C. Outler, introduction to Sermon 91, "On Charity," in *Works*, 3:290.

29. Ibid., 1:40.

30. Ibid., 1:38–45.

31. Sugden, *Standard Sermons*, 2:335.

32. For an account of the debate over the question of "the first four volumes," see John S. Simon, "The First Four Volumes of Wesley's Sermons," *Proceedings of the Wesley Historical Society* 9 (1913):36–45; and Sugden, "The Conference and the Fifty-three Sermons," in *Standard Sermons*, 2:331–40.

33. *Minutes of the Methodist Conferences, Annually Held in America from 1773 to 1794* (Philadelphia: Tuckniss, 1795), pp. 41, 72.

34. Frank Baker suggests that the earlier proposal of Fletcher and Benson (see note 25 above) "was almost certainly present in Wesley's mind and possibly before his eyes" as

he prepared the material to send to America in 1784. *John Wesley and the Church of England* (Nashville: Abingdon, 1970), p. 212.

35. Emora T. Brannan, "Episcopal Overtures to Coke and Asbury during the Christmas Conference, 1784," *Methodist History* 14 (April 1976): 209.

36. *The Articles of Religion, as received and taught in the Methodist Episcopal Church, throughout the United States of America* (New York: Ross, 1788), p. [3].

37. 13 Eliz. Cap. 12; Canon XLIX, in Gibson, *Codex*, 1:386.

38. The *Sermons* were published in America first in 1783 in an abortive attempt to reprint the collection of Wesley's *Works*, which failed to get beyond the first four of the thirty-two volumes. In 1790, Asbury's Council, which had already recommended publishing Fletcher's Works, suggested that Wesley's *Sermons* might be published "if our finances will admit of it, and a sufficient number of subscribers can be obtained." *Minutes taken at a Council of the Bishop and Delegated Elders* (Baltimore: Goddard and Angell), p. 4. Four years later, John Dickins began publishing the eight volumes of Wesley's sermons, which gradually appeared over a period of twelve years (1794–1806). This set was reprinted three times in the next twenty years. After Wesley's *Works* were published in this country (the "first American edition" in 1826 [Benson], the "first American complete and standard edition" in 1831 [Jackson]), the Sermons began appearing rather regularly in separate editions of two or three volumes. The publishing history of the *Explanatory Notes* follows a similar pattern: published first by Dickins in 1791 (3 v.), reprinted fifteen years later by Cooper (1806), and two more times before it started appearing fairly regularly in 1837. Baker, *Union Catalogue*, Nos.172, 276, 420.

39. Typified by William Phoebus' remark, "No doctrine is more scriptural than that taught by Wesley in his four volumes of Sermons, with his notes on the Testament." *An Essay on the Doctrine and Order of the Evangelical Church* (New York: Abraham Paul, 1817), p. 137.

Chapter 10: At Full Liberty: Doctrinal Standards in Early American Methodism

1. This essay was presented as one of the Merrick Lectures at Ohio Wesleyan University in October 1984 and subsequently published in *Quarterly Review* 5 (Fall 1985):6–27.

2. *Journals of the General Conference of the Methodist Episcopal Church* (New York: Carlton & Lanahan, n.d.), vol. 1 (1796–1836), p. 89, hereafter cited as *Journals*. Curiously, only the first volume has a number; others bear only dates. The 1984 *Book of Discipline* (16) contains only slight revisions: "nor" has been changed to "or"; "articles of religion" has been capitalized; most commas have been omitted.

3. The terms *doctrine* and *doctrinal standards* are used in this paper with the specific connotation that their role is distinctly different from the task of *theology* or *theological reflection*. *Doctrinal standards*, established by and for the church, provide criteria for measuring the doctrinal adequacy of the witness of clergy and laity in the church, whereas *theological reflection*, based on norms such as Scripture, tradition, reason, and experience, necessarily is not subject to such standards and in fact is intentionally and appropriately critical in its task of examining such standards. See Schubert M. Ogden, "Doctrinal Standards in the United Methodist Church," *Perkins Journal*, 28 (Fall 1974): 20–25.

4. Preface to Part II, *The Plan of Union, as Adopted by the General Conferences* (the "Blue Book," copyright 1967 by Donald A. Theuer for the Joint Commissions on Church Union of the Methodist Church and the Evangelical United Brethren Church), p. 22 (subsequently contained in 1968 *Book of Discipline*, p. 35).

5. 1984 *Book of Discipline*, ¶67, p. 49. This section of the *Discipline*, which is not a part of the constitution, was adopted in 1972 from the report of the Theological Study Commission on Doctrine and Doctrinal Standards. The line of interpretation contained

in the statement reflects in large part the opinions of the last generation of Methodist constitutional historians, who were writing at the turn of the twentieth century. See note 38, below.

6. *Minutes of the Methodist Conferences, Annually held in America from 1773 to 1794* (Philadelphia: Henry Tuckniss, 1795), p. 77.

7. Benson's proposal to organize Methodism into a distinct denomination separate from the Church of England was passed on to Wesley by Fletcher with some alterations and additions. Two items are of particular note:

> 4. That a pamphlet be published containing the 39 articles of the Church of England rectified according to the purity of the gospel, together with some needful alterations in the liturgy and homilies. . . .
>
> 10. That the most spiritual part of the Common Prayer shall be extracted and published with the 39 rectified articles, and the minutes of the conferences (or the Methodist canons) which (together with such regulations as may be made at the time of this establishment) shall be, next to the Bible, the *vade mecum* ["constant companion" or "handbook"] of the Methodist preachers. *Journal* (Curnock), 8:332–33).

Frank Baker comments that this proposal "was almost certainly present in Wesley's mind, and possibly before his eyes" in 1784 when he put together his scheme for American Methodism. *John Wesley and the Church of England* (Nashville: Abingdon, 1970), p. 212.

8. This assumption is clearly alluded to in an account of a private interview held during the Christmas Conference, at which Coke, Asbury, William West, and John Andrews (the latter two Protestant Episcopal priests in Baltimore county) discussed the possibility of merging the two emerging episcopal churches in America. Andrews's account of the conversation, in a letter to William Smith, notes that *The Sunday Service of the Methodists* makes plain that "the people called Methodists were hereafter to use the same Liturgy that we make use of, to adhere to the same Articles, and to keep up the same three orders of the Clergy" (interesting that he notes no basic difference between the Wesleyan version of these documents and their English counterparts). Andrews also points out that, "as to Articles of faith and forms of worship, they already agreed with us." Emora T. Brannan, "Episcopal Overtures to Coke and Asbury during the Christmas Conference, 1784," *Methodist History* 14 (April 1976): 209.

9. In fact, the interview mentioned above failed to produce a working agreement in part because West and Andrews perceived that Coke and Asbury considered it "indispensably necessary that Mr Wesley be the first link of the Chain upon which their Church is suspended." The "binding minute" makes it clear that the American preachers at the Christmas Conference were willing to acknowledge themselves as Wesley's "Sons in the Gospel, ready in matters belonging to church government, to obey his Commands," a very polite and precise acknowledgement of Wesley's relationship to them in matters of polity. This approbation of Wesley's personal leadership disappeared from the *Discipline* after 1786, and Wesley's name was omitted from the published minutes of the American annual conferences from 1786 to 1788.

10. James Everett (who was present at Baltimore in 1785), in his autobiographical reflections written to Asbury in 1788, makes a clear reference to "the Christmas conference, when Dr. Coke came from England, and the Methodist church separated from all connection or dependence on the church of England, *or any other body or society of people*" (italics mine). "An Account of the most Remarkable Occurrences of the Life of Joseph Everett," *Arminian Magazine* (Philadelphia), 2 (1790): 607.

11. *Minutes of Several Conversations between the Rev. Thomas Coke, the Rev. Francis Asbury, and others . . . Composing a Form of Discipline* (Philadelphia: Charles Cist, 1785), p. 3.

12. The references to "Minutes" in the 1785 *Discipline* clearly refer to that document itself, as can be seen in the answer to Question 3, cited above. Also in Question 69, "Questions for a New Helper," where the prospective preacher is asked, "Have you read the *Minutes of the Conference*?," the reference is clearly to the American document, and not to the British *Minutes*, because in 1787, when the third edition of the disciplinary *Minutes* changed its title to *A Form of Discipline*, the question was changed to read, "Have you read the Form of Discipline?"

13. *Minutes of Several Conversations between the Rev. Mr. John and Charles Wesley and others* (London: Paramore, 1780), p. 43. This edition of the "Large Minutes" was in effect at the time of the Christmas Conference; the "model deed" had been included in the three previous editions of the "Large Minutes": 1763, 1770, 1772.

14. The first conference in 1773 agreed that the doctrine and discipline of the British Methodist *Minutes* should be "the sole rule of our conduct who labour, in the connection with Mr. Wesley, in America." The conference in 1781 noted that the preachers were determined "to preach the old Methodist doctrine, and strictly enforce the discipline, as contained in the notes, sermons, and minutes, as published by Mr. Wesley." At the conference of 1784, held the spring previous to the specially called Christmas Conference, the preachers agreed to accept among them only those European preachers who would, among other things, "preach the doctrine taught in the four volumes of Sermons, and Notes on the New Testament . . . [and] follow the directions of the London and American minutes." *Minutes of the Methodist Conferences* (1795), pp. 5, 41, 72.

15. Question 64 in the "Large Minutes." Part of the answer to Question 65 was retained (as Question 74 in the *Discipline*): "Let all our chapels be built plain and decent; but not more expensively than is absolutely unavoidable: otherwise the necessity of raising money will make rich men necessary to us. But if so, we must be dependent upon them, yea, and governed by them. And then farewell to the Methodist-Discipline, if not Doctrine too." *Minutes . . . Composing a Form of Discipline* (1785), p. 32. A parallel comparison of the "Large Minutes" with the first American *Discipline* is published in Appendix VII of John M. Tigert's *Constitutional History of American Episcopal Methodism*, 4th ed. (Nashville: Publishing House of the Methodist Episcopal Church, South, 1911), pp. 532–602.

16. The wording in the American deed follows very closely the wording of the British document before and after the omitted section, indicating that the doctrinal stipulation ("preach no other doctrine than is contained in . . .) was consciously dropped from the American form.

17. The "fifth edition" of the *Discipline* (New York: William Ross, 1789), §XXXIII.

18. This wording is on the title page of the *Discipline*; the "useful pieces" have separate title pages but are paged continuously in the volume. In 1790, the Articles of Religion became section XXXV of the *Form of Discipline*; in 1791, section XXXVI.

19. The answer stipulates that the preacher of such "erroneous doctrines" shall confront the same process as is observed "in cases of gross immorality," which had just been spelled out.

20. This wording, not only used in 1808 in the Restrictive Rules but also still in effect today in the section on trials, implies a method of measure quite different from the early British rule that allowed preaching of "*no other doctrine* than is contained in Mr. Wesley's Notes upon the New Testament and four volumes of Sermons," which is strictly delimiting in its intention (my italics). The "contrary to" concept and language was adopted by the British Conference in 1832.

21. The explanatory notes of Asbury and Coke, included in the 1796 *Discipline*, for the section on trial of a minister for erroneous doctrines, point out that "the heretical doctrines are as dangerous, at least to the hearers, as the immoral life of a preacher." The heretics mentioned specifically were "arian, socinian, and universalian." *The Doctrines and Discipline of the Methodist Episcopal Church in America* (Philadelphia: Tuckniss, 1798), p. 113.

22. Wesley's *Works, Notes, Christian Library, Primitive Physick,* Fletcher's tracts, Richard Baxter's *Gildus Salvianus,* Kempis, and the *Instructions for Children*. These were all carried over from the British *Minutes*; the American *Discipline* omitted some, such as the reference to Wesley's fourth volume of *Sermons* in Question 33 (Question 51 in the *Discipline*). The bishops' notes in the 1798 *Discipline* say nothing after the two doctrinal sections, simply referring the reader to "Mr. Wesley's excellent treatise" after the section "Of Christian Perfection" and to "that great writer, Mr. Fletcher" after the section "Against Antinomianism." A footnote in George Roberts' address to the conference at Baltimore in 1807, in a section headed "take heed unto the doctrine," refers the reader to several guides to understanding the Bible, including works by Stackhouse, Doddridge, Bonnett, Watson, Addison and Beattie, Jenny, Wilberforce, Leland, and Ogden, but no mention is made of Wesley's *Notes*.

23. In 1790 when the doctrinal treatises were introduced into the body of the *Discipline* (with section numbers), the title was altered to read, *A Form of Discipline . . . (now comprehending the Principles and Doctrines) of the Methodist Episcopal Church in America*. Two years later, the sacramental services were added, and the title became *The Doctrines and Discipline of the Methodist Episcopal Church in America* as we noted above. The doctrinal treatises were by and large "Wesleyan" tracts, though only half of them were by John Wesley: *Scripture Doctrine of Predestination, Election, and Reprobation*, by Henry Haggar, abridged by Wesley (inserted beginning in 1788); *Serious Thoughts on the Infallible, Unconditional Perseverance of All That Have Once Experienced Faith in Christ* (beginning in 1788); *A Plain Account of Christian Perfection* (beginning in 1789); *An Extract on the Nature and Subjects of Christian Baptism*, by Moses Hemmenway (beginning in 1790). The tracts were omitted from the 1798 *Discipline* (tenth edition) to make room for the bishops' explanatory notes but (with the exception of the treatise on baptism) were restored in the following (eleventh) edition of 1801.

24. These treatises were removed from the *Discipline* by action of the General Conference of 1812 to be published separately. The directions of the Conference were only slowly and inaccurately heeded.

25. One document, by Coke, contained twenty-eight Articles; the other, probably by Clarke and Benson, contained thirty-eight Articles. See *Articles of Religion Prepared by Order of the Conference of 1806*, publication no. 2 of The Wesley Historical Society (London: Kelly, 1897).

26. *Journals*, 1:76, 79.

27. *Journals*, 1:82; compare "A Journal of the Proceedings of the General Conference of the Methodist Episcopal Church, 1800–1828" (MS, Drew University Library), p. 168; referred to hereafter as "*MS Journal*." The last phrase, starting "contrary to," was inadvertently omitted in the printed version.

28. *Journals*, 1:89.

29. *MS Journal*, p. 68; this page also contains the Restrictive Rules.

30. *Journals*, 1:128–29. The committee that had determined the necessity for such a committee of safety, based on the episcopal address, consisted of one member from each conference and included Philip Bruce and Nelson Reed, two members of the 1808 "committee of fourteen" that had drawn up the Restrictive Rules.

31. Horace M. DuBose, *Life of Joshua Soule* (Nashville: Publishing House of the Methodist Episcopal Church, South, 1916), p. 110.

32. *Journals*, 1:155. The Committee of Safety ended its report with eight resolutions that were passed by the Conference, including, "1. That the General Conference do earnestly recommend the superintendents to make the most careful inquiry to all the annual conferences, in order to ascertain whether any doctrines are embraced or preached contrary to our established articles of faith, and to use their influence to prevent the existence and circulation of all such doctrines" (*Journal*, 1:157). It might also be noted that the following day, the conference adopted the report of the Committee on Ways and Means which included a proposal that the section of the *Discipline* on "The Method of

Receiving Preachers" include the stipulation, "It shall be the duty of the bishops, or of a committee which they may appoint at each annual conference, to point out a course of reading and study proper to be pursued by candidates for the ministry . . . ." (*Journals*, 1:160–61).

33. *Journals*, 1:348.

34. *Journals*, 1:350–51.

35. *Guide-Book in the Administration of the Discipline* (New York: Carlton & Phillips, 1855), p. 152.

36. *A Manual of the Discipline of the Methodist Episcopal Church, South* (Nashville: Publishing House of the Methodist Episcopal Church, South, 1870), p. 131.

37. *Discipline* (1880), ¶213; see also *Journal* (1880, no vol. no.), p. 323.

38. *Constitutional and Parliamentary History of the Methodist Episcopal Church* (New York: Methodist Book Concern, 1912), pp. 157–69. See also John M. Tigert, *A Constitutional History of American Episcopal Methodism* (Nashville: Publishing House of the Methodist Episcopal Church, South, 1894), pp. 113, 139–48, and Thomas B. Neely, *Doctrinal Standards of Methodism* (New York: Revell, 1918), pp. 225–37.

39. At about the same time, the southern church received a report by the College of Bishops to the General Conference of 1914, stating that Wesley's *Notes* and *Sermons* "have never been adopted by organized Episcopal Methodism," and therefore "it is not clear that [they] are standards of doctrine." See the eighteenth edition of Bishop McTyeire's *Manual of the Discipline* (1924); edited by Bishop Collins Denny), pp. 147–48.

Chapter 11: John Wesley and the Historian's Task

1. This essay was presented as one of the Wesley Memorial Lectures in the Centre for Research on Christian Culture of Aoyama Gakuin University, Tokyo, Japan, in October 1988. Portions of the text had previously appeared in "Wesley Studies in the Church and the Academy," *Perkins Journal* 37 (Spring 1984):1–6, and "The Present State of Wesley Studies," *Methodist History* 22 (July 1984):221–33.

2. *Gentleman's Magazine* 61 (March 1791):284.

3. See Betty M. Jarboe, *John and Charles Wesley; A Bibliography* (Metuchen, N.J.: Scarecrow, 1987); see esp. items no. 35–1934.

4. John Wesley, *Short History of the People Called Methodists* (1781). This comment echoes an attitude that Wesley had already expressed several times in works that survey or analyze the Wesleyan movement—that he was the most appropriate person (perhaps the only one fully qualified) to give a full and accurate account of his life and his movement (e.g., in *The Character of a Methodist* (1742)—". . . it being generally believed that I was able to give the clearest account of these things," *Works*, 9:32; in the preface to his *Journal* (1740)—". . . it being my only concern herein nakedly to 'declare the thing as it is,'" *Works*, 18:122; in his sermon "On Laying the Foundation of the New Chapel" (1777)—"There is no other person, if I decline the task, who can supply my place—who has a perfect knowledge of the work in question [Methodism], from the beginning of it to this day," *Works*, 3:580. Wesley's accounts, curiously enough, exhibit in their details many inaccuracies and incongruities that one would not expect.

5. E.g.,"Yet, after all, his own Journal and Letters will always remain the best, almost the only needful, authority for the life of Wesley." C. T. Winchester, *The Life of John Wesley* (New York: Macmillan, 1919), p. viii.

6. For recent surveys of the literature and a list of bibliographies, see Frank Baker, "Unfolding John Wesley: A Survey of Twenty Years' Studies in Wesley's Thought," in *Quarterly Review* 1 (1980): 44–58; and Richard Heitzenrater, "Wesley in Retrospect," in *The Elusive Mr. Wesley* (Nashville: Abingdon, 1984), 2:163–214.

7. *The Appeals to Men of Reason and Religion*, ed. by Gerald R. Cragg, in *Works*, 11:117.

8. For details of these problems, see Frank Baker, "The Oxford Edition of Wesley's Works and Its Text," in *The Place of Wesley in the Christian Tradition*, ed. by Kenneth E. Rowe (Metuchen, N. J.: Scarecrow, 1980), pp. 124–26.

9. This project was begun in 1960, the first four volumes published as THE OXFORD EDITION OF THE WORKS OF JOHN WESLEY (Vol. 11, *The Appeals*; Vols. 25 and 26, *Letters*; Vol. 7, *Collection of Hymns*). The last volume to be published by Oxford University Press appeared in February 1984. Subsequent volumes are being published by Abingdon Press under the series title, THE BICENTENNIAL EDITION OF THE WORKS OF JOHN WESLEY. Six volumes have appeared since 1984: four volumes of *Sermons*, ed. by Albert C. Outler, and the first volume of *Journal and Diaries*, ed. by W. Reginald Ward and Richard P. Heitzenrater, and *The Methodist Societies*, ed. by Rupert Davies. Prof. Heitzenrater, of Southern Methodist University, is General Editor of the project, and James E. Kirby, also of Southern Methodist University, is president of its Board of Directors.

10. One exceptionally valuable work that provides a model for work to be done in this area is Frank Baker's *Representative Verse of Charles Wesley* (London: Epworth Press, 1958). Just now appearing is a three-volume work, *The Unpublished Poetry of Charles Wesley*, edited by S T Kimbrough and Oliver A. Beckerlegge (Nashville: Abingdon, 1988).

11. London: Cully [1910]; reprinted by the Methodist Reprint Society, Taylors, S. C., 1977.

12. Richard P. Heitzenrater, "John Wesley's Early Sermons," *Proceedings WHS* 37 (February 1970): 112–13; see p. 153 above.

13. Thomas R. Albin and Oliver A. Beckerlegge, *Charles Wesley's Earliest Evangelical Sermons* (Ilford: WHS Publications, 1987).

14. John Vickers, *John Wesley, Founder of Methodism* (Loughborough, 1977).

15. Ray C. Petry, "The Critical Temper and the Practice of Tradition," in *The Duke Divinity School Review* 30 (Spring 1965): 96.

16. Papers and discussions focused on such areas as biblical authority, feminist theology, salvation and justice, evangelism, liberation theology, spirituality, faith development, black and ethnic religion, ecumenism, social ethics, worship, religious affections, process theology, and the sacraments. See especially Albert C. Outler, "A New Future for Wesley Studies: An Agenda for 'Phase III,'" and the Wesley Studies Working Group report in Douglas M. Meeks, ed., *The Future of Wesleyan Theology* (Nashville: Abingdon, 1986), pp. 34–66; and Theodore Runyon, ed., *Wesleyan Theology Today* (Nashville: Abingdon, 1985).

17. See Confucius, *The Confucian Analects*, bk. 7:19: "I am not one who was born in the possession of knowledge; I am one who is fond of antiquity, and earnest in seeking it there."

18. *The History of the Peloponnesian War*, Bk. I, §22.

Selected Bibliography

Abbey, Charles John, and John H. Overton. The English Church in the Eighteenth Century. London: Longmans, Green and Co., 1878.

Albin, Thomas R., and Oliver A. Beckerlegge, eds. *Charles Wesley's Earliest Evangelical Sermons*. Ilford: Robert Odcombe, 1987.

Allen, W. O. B., and Edmund McClure. *Two Hundred Years: The History of the Society for Promoting Christian Knowledge, 1698–1898*. London: SPCK, 1898.

Allison, C. F. *The Rise of Moralism*. New York: Seabury Press, 1966.

An Account of Several Work-Houses for Employing and Maintaining the Poor. London: Printed by Joseph Downing, 1732.

Articles of Religion Prepared by Order of the Conference of 1806, Publication no. 2 of The Wesley Historical Society. London: Kelly, 1897.

Atterbury, Francis, et al., *A Representation of the Present State of Religion with Regard to the Late Excessive Growth of Infidelity, Heresy, and Profaneness*. London: Printed for Jonah Bowyer, 1711.

Baker, Frank, comp., *A Union Catalogue of the Publications of John and Charles Wesley*. Durham, NC: Duke University, 1966.

Baker, Frank. "Unfolding John Wesley: A Survey of Twenty Years' Studies in Wesley's Thought." *Quarterly Review* 1 (1980).

__________. *John Wesley and the Church of England*. Nashville: Abingdon Press, 1970.

Benham, Daniel. *Memoirs of James Hutton*. London: Hamilton, Adams, & Co., 1856.

Bogue, David, and James Bennett. *History of Dissenters, from the Revolution in 1688 to the Year 1808*. London: Printed for the author, 1808–12.

Böhler, Peter. "Peter Böhler and the Wesleys," tr. by W. N. Schwarze and S. H. Gapp. *World Parish* 2 (November 1949).

Bouyer, Louis. *A History of Christian Spirituality*. London: Burns & Oates, 1969.

Brannan, Emora T. "Episcopal Overtures to Coke and Asbury during the Christmas Conference, 1784." *Methodist History* 14 (April 1976).

Brantley, Richard E. *Locke, Wesley, and the Method of English Romanticism*. Gainesville: University of Florida Press, 1984.

Bretherton, F. F. "The First Apology for Methodism." *Proceedings of the Wesley Historical Society* 20 (June 1935).

Brockwell, Charles. "Methodist Discipline: From Rule of Life to Canon Law." *Drew Gateway* 54 (Winter/Spring, 1984).

Buckley, James M. *Constitutional and Parliamentary History of the Methodist Episcopal Church.* New York: Methodist Book Concern, 1912.

Cardwell, Edward, ed. *Documentary Annals of the Reformed Church of England.* Oxford: University Press, 1844.

____________, ed. *Synodalia; A Collection of Articles of Religion, Canons, and Proceedings of Convocations.* Oxford: University Press, 1842.

Cell, George Croft. *The Rediscovery of John Wesley.* New York: Henry Holt, 1935.

Clarke, Adam. *Memoirs of the Wesley Family.* London: J. & T. Clarke, 1823.

Clarke, W. K. Lowther. *Eighteenth Century Piety.* London: SPCK, 1944.

Coke, Thomas, and Henry Moore. *The Life of the Rev. John Wesley, A.M.* London: G. Paramore, 1792.

Cragg, Gerald R. *The Church and the Age of Reason.* Baltimore: Penguin Books, 1966.

Curnock, Nehemiah, ed. *The Journal of the Rev. John Wesley.* London: Epworth, 1938.

Daillé, John. *Faith Grounded upon the Holy Scriptures; Against the New Methodists. By John Daillé . . . and now Englished by M. M.* London: Benj. Tooke, 1675.

Dallimore, Arnold. *George Whitefield.* London: Banner of Truth Trust, 1970.

Davies, Rupert, and Gordon Rupp, eds. *A History of the Methodist Church in Great Britain.* London: Epworth Press, 1965.

Deschner, John. *Wesley's Christology.* Dallas: Southern Methodist University Press, 1985.

Dimond, Sydney G. *Psychology of the Methodist Revival.* Nashville: Whitmore, 1926.

Dreyer, Frederick. "Faith and Experience in the Thought of John Wesley." *American Historical Review* 88 (February 1983).

DuBose, Horace M. *Life of Joshua Soule.* Nashville: Publishing House of the Methodist Episcopal Church, South, 1916.

Edelstein, Ludwig. *Ancient Medicine; Selected Papers of Ludwig Edelstein,* ed. by Owsei Temkin and C. Lilian Temkin. Baltimore: Johns Hopkins, 1967.

Gale, Theophilus. *The Court of the Gentiles.* London: John Hill, 1678.

Gambold, John. "The Character of Mr. John Wesley." *Methodist Magazine* 21 (1798).

Gee, Henry, and William Hardy, eds. *Documents Illustrative of English Church History.* London: Macmillan, 1914.

George, M. Dorothy. *Hogarth to Cruikshank: Social Change in Graphic Satire.* London: The Penguin Press, 1957.

Gibson, Edmund. *An Exposition of the Thirty-nine Articles of the Church of England.* London: Midwinter, 1746.

____________. *Codex iuris ecclesiastici Anglicani.* London: Baskett, 1713.

Gill, Frederick C. *Charles Wesley, the First Methodist.* Nashville: Abingdon, 1964.

Godley, A. D. *Oxford in the Eighteenth Century.* London: Methuen & Co., 1908.

Godley, John. "Origins of Methodism; the Leitrim Connection." *Leitrim Guardian Magazine* (1978).

Green, Richard. *A Bibliography of Anti-Methodist Publications of the Eighteenth Century.* London: Kelly, 1902.

Green, Vivian H. H. *The Young Mr. Wesley.* London: Edward Arnold Ltd., 1961.

Halévy, Elie. *England in 1815* (2nd ed.). London: Ernest Benn, Ltd., 1949.

Hearne, Thomas. *Remarks and Collections,* ed. by H. E. Salter. Oxford: Clarendon, 1921.

Heitzenrater, Richard P. "John Wesley and Oxford Methodists." Ph.D. dissertation, Duke University, 1972.

____________. *The Elusive Mr. Wesley.* Nashville: Abingdon, 1984.

Holland, Bernard. "The Conversions of John and Charles Wesley." *Proceedings of the Wesley Historical Society* 38 (1971).

Horst, Mark. "Experimenting with Christian Wholeness: Method in Wesley's Theology." *Quarterly Review* 7 (Summer 1987).

Hutton, James. "The Beginning of The Lord's Work in England," tr. by J. N. Libbey. *Proceedings of the Wesley Historical Society* 15 (1926)

Ingham, Benjamin. *Diary of an Oxford Methodist; Benjamin Ingham, 1733–34,* ed. by Richard P. Heitzenrater. Durham, NC: Duke University Press, 1985.

Jarboe, Betty M. *John and Charles Wesley; A Bibliography.* Metuchen, NJ: Scarecrow, 1987.

Journals of the General Conference of the Methodist Episcopal Church. New York: Carlton & Lanahan, n.d.

Källstad, Thorvald. *John Wesley and the Bible; A Psychological Study.* Stockholm: Nya Bokförlags, 1974.

Kidd, B. J. *Documents Illustrative of the Continental Reformation.* Oxford: Clarendon, 1911.

Kimbrough, S T, and Oliver A. Beckerlegge, eds. *The Unpublished Poetry of Charles Wesley.* Nashville: Abingdon, 1988.

Kirkham, Donald. "Pamphlet Opposition to the Rise of Methodism." Ph.D diss., Duke University, 1973.

Legg, Wickham. *English Church Life from the Restoration to the Tractarian Movement Considered in some of its Neglected or Forgotten Features*. London: Longmans, Green and Co., 1914.

A Manual of the Discipline of the Methodist Episcopal Church, South. Nashville: Publishing House of the Methodist Episcopal Church, South, 1870.

Magrath, John Richard. *The Queen's College*. Oxford: Clarendon, 1921.

Martz, Louis. *The Poetry of Meditation*. New Haven: Yale University Press, 1954.

Matthews, Rex D. "'Religion and Reason Joined': A Study in the Theology of John Wesley." Th.D. diss., Harvard University, 1986.

___________. "'We Walk by Faith, not by Sight': Religious Epistemology in the Later Sermons of John Wesley." Paper privately circulated.

McAdoo, Harry R. *The Spirit of Anglicanism*. New York: Charles Scribner's Sons, 1965.

Meeks, M. Douglas, ed. *The Future of the Methodist Theological Traditions*. Nashville: Abingdon, 1985.

Minutes of Several Conversations between the Rev. Mr. John and Charles Wesley and others. London: Paramore, 1780.

Minutes of Several Conversations between the Rev. Thomas Coke, the Rev. Francis Asbury, and others . . . Composing a Form of Discipline. Philadelphia: Charles Cist, 1785.

Minutes of the Methodist Conferences, Annually Held in America from 1773 to 1794. Philadelphia: Tuckniss, 1795.

Mosheim, John Lawrence. *An Ecclesiastical History, Ancient and Modern*. London: Tegg, 1826.

Nagler, Arthur Wilfred. *Pietism and Methodism; The Significance of German Pietism in the Origin and Early Development of Methodism*. Nashville: Smith & Lamar, 1918.

Neely, Thomas B. *Doctrinal Standards of Methodism*. New York: Revell, 1918.

Oberman, H. A. *The Harvest of Medieval Theology*. Cambridge: Harvard University Press, 1963.

Ogden, Schubert M. "Doctrinal Standards in the United Methodist Church." *Perkins Journal* 28 (Fall 1974).

Olin, John C., ed. *A Reformation Debate*. New York: Harper, 1966.

Ong, Walter J. "Peter Ramus and the Naming of Methodist; Medieval Science through Ramist Homiletic." *Journal of the History of Ideas* 14 (1953).

Orcibal, Jean. "The Theological Originality of John Wesley," in *A History of the Methodist Church in Great Britain*. London: Epworth Press, 1965.

Orders Belonging to a Religious Society. London: [n.p.] 1724.

Outler, Albert C. "A Focus on the Holy Spirit: Spirit and Spirituality in John Wesley." *Quarterly Review* 8 (Summer 1988).

___________. "Methodism's Theological Heritage," in Paul M. Minus, Jr., ed., *Methodism's Destiny in an Ecumenical Age*. Nashville: Abingdon, 1969.

___________. *John Wesley*. New York: Oxford University Press, 1964.

The Oxford Methodists: Being some Account of a Society of Young Gentlemen in that City, so Denominated. London: Roberts, 1733.

Pattison, Mark. "Tendencies of Religious Thought in England, 1688–1750," in *Essays and Reviews*. London: J. W. Parker, 1860.

Petry, Ray C. "The Critical Temper and the Practice of Tradition." *The Duke Divinity School Review* 30 (Spring 1965).

Portus, Garnet Vere. *Caritas Anglicana; or, An Historical Inquiry into those Religious and Philanthropical Societies that Flourished in England between the Years 1678 and 1740*. London: A. R. Mowbray & Co. Ltd., 1912.

Rowe, Kenneth E., ed. *The Place of Wesley in the Christian Tradition*. Metuchen, N.J.: Scarecrow, 1976.

Runyon, Theodore, ed. *Wesleyan Theology Today*. Nashville: Abingdon, 1985.

Salmon, T. *The Present State of the Universities and of the Five Adjacent Counties, of Cambridge, Huntingdon, Bedford, Buckingham and Oxford*. London: J. Roberts, 1744.

Schmidt, Martin. *John Wesley: A Theological Biography* (2 vols. in 3). Nashville: Abingdon, 1962–73.

Simon, John S. "The First Four Volumes of Wesley's Sermons." *Proceedings of the Wesley Historical Society* 9 (1913).

___________. *John Wesley and the Religious Societies*. London: The Epworth Press, 1921.

Squires, Thomas W. *In West Oxford*. London: A. R. Mowbray, 1928.

The Standing Rules and Orders of the Society for Promoting Christian Knowledge. London: Joseph Downing, 1732.

Starkey, Lycurgus M., Jr. *The Work of the Holy Spirit*. New York: Abingdon, 1962.

Stephen, Leslie (Sir). *History of English Thought in the Eighteenth Century* (3rd ed.). New York: Peter Smith, 1949.

Stoeffler, F. Ernest. *The Rise of Evangelical Pietism*. Leiden: E. J. Brill, 1965.

Sugden, E. H., ed. *The Standard Sermons of John Wesley*. London: Epworth, 1921.

Telford, John, ed. *Sayings and Portraits of John Wesley*. London: Epworth, 1924.

___________, ed.. *The Letters of the Rev. John Wesley*. London: Epworth, 1936.

Thornton, Catherine, and Frances McLaughlin. *The Fothergills of Ravenstonedale*. London: William Heinemann, 1906.

Tigert, John M. *Constitutional History of American Episcopal Methodism* (4th ed.). Nashville: Publishing House of the Methodist Episcopal Church, South, 1911.

Towlson, Clifford W. *Moravian and Methodist*. London: Epworth, 1957.

Turberville, A. S. *English Men and Manners in the Eighteenth Century*. New York: Oxford University Press, 1964.

Tyerman, Luke. *The Oxford Methodists*. London: Hodder and Stoughton, 1873.

Vickers, John. *John Wesley, Founder of Methodism*. Loughborough: Ladybird, 1977.

Vlak, Johannes. *Dissertationes Trias: de Dei operum & pacis foederibus, atque de justificatione*. Amsterdam: Blankard, 1689.

Wake, William. *A Defence of the Exposition of the Doctrine of the Church of England against the Exceptions of Monsieur de Meaux, Late Bishop of Condom, and his Vindicator*. London: Richard Chiswell, 1686.

Wakefield, Gordon. *Puritan Devotion*. London: Epworth Press, 1957.

A War Among the Angels of the Churches; wherein is shewed the Principles of the New Methodists in the great Point of Justification, by a Country Professor of Jesus Christ. London: Jaye and Baldwin, 1693.

Ware, Thomas. *Sketches of the Life and Travels of Rev. Thomas Ware*. New York: Mason and Lane, 1839.

Watson, Richard. *Life of Wesley*. New York: Phillips & Hunt, 1831.

Wesley, Charles. *The Journal of the Rev. Charles Wesley*. London: Culley, 1910.

[Wesley, Charles?] *Sermons by the Late Rev. Charles Wesley, A.M.* London: Baldwin, 1816.

Wesley, John. *The Works of John Wesley*. Nashville: Abingdon, 1976– .

Whitefield, George. *A Short Account of God's Dealings with the Reverend Mr. Whitefield*. London: W. Strahan, 1740.

____________. *Journals*. London: Banner of Truth Trust, 1960.

Whitehead, John. *The Life of the Rev. John Wesley*. London: Shephen Couchman, 1793–96.

Willey, Basil. *The Eighteenth Century Background*. Boston: Beacon Press, 1964.

____________. *The Seventeenth Century Background*. New York: Columbia, 1934.

Williams, Colin W. *John Wesley's Theology Today*. Nashville: Abingdon, 1960.

Woodward, Josiah. *An Account of the Rise and Progress of the Religious Societies in the City of London* (3rd ed.). London: Sympson, 1701.

Workman, Herbert B. *The Place of Methodism in the Catholic Church*. New York: Methodist Book Concern, 1921.

Wright, Fred C. "On the Origin of the Name Methodist." *Proceedings of the Wesley Historical Society* 3 (1900).

Wright, Joseph G. "Some Portraits of John Wesley." *Proceedings of the Wesley Historical Society* 3 (1902).

Yates, Arthur S. *The Doctrine of Assurance*. London: Epworth Press, 1952.

General Index

Printed in the United States
77924LV00004B/96

9 780687 270699